WELCOME TO THE BALLROOM

no.3 | TOMO TAKEUCHI

Contents

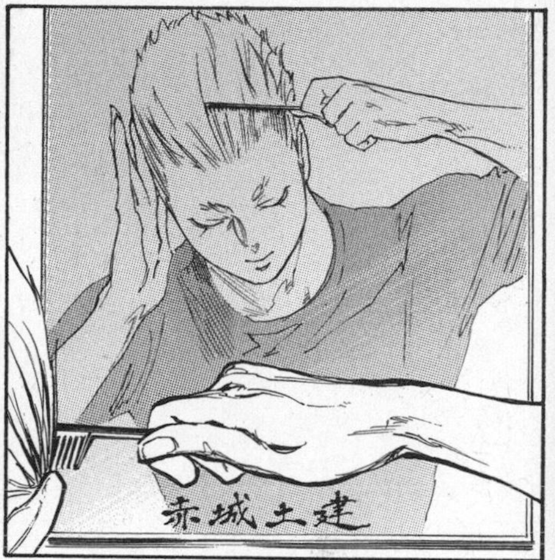
赤城土建

MIRROR: AKAGI CONSTRUCTION

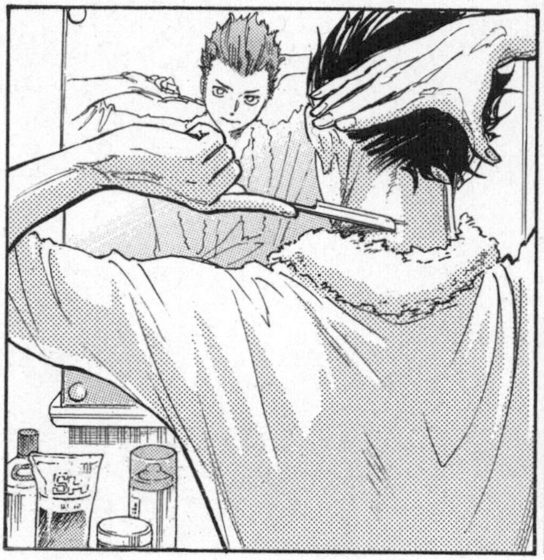

Heat 8: The Tenpei Cup

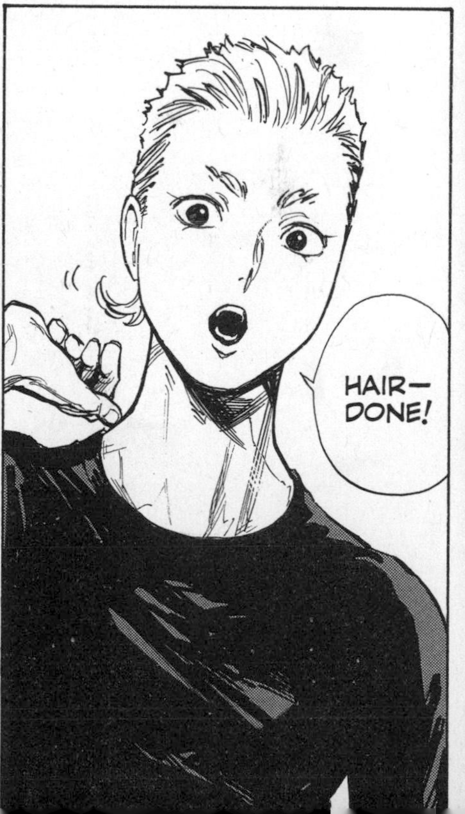
HAIR—DONE!

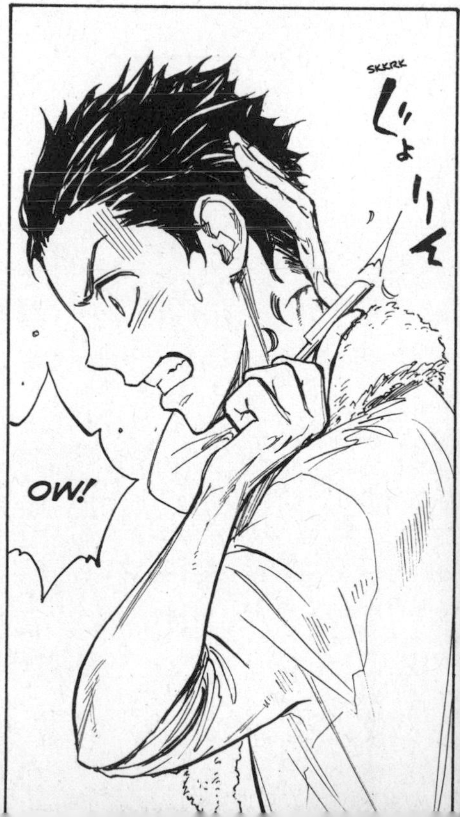
SKKRK
じょりん
OW!

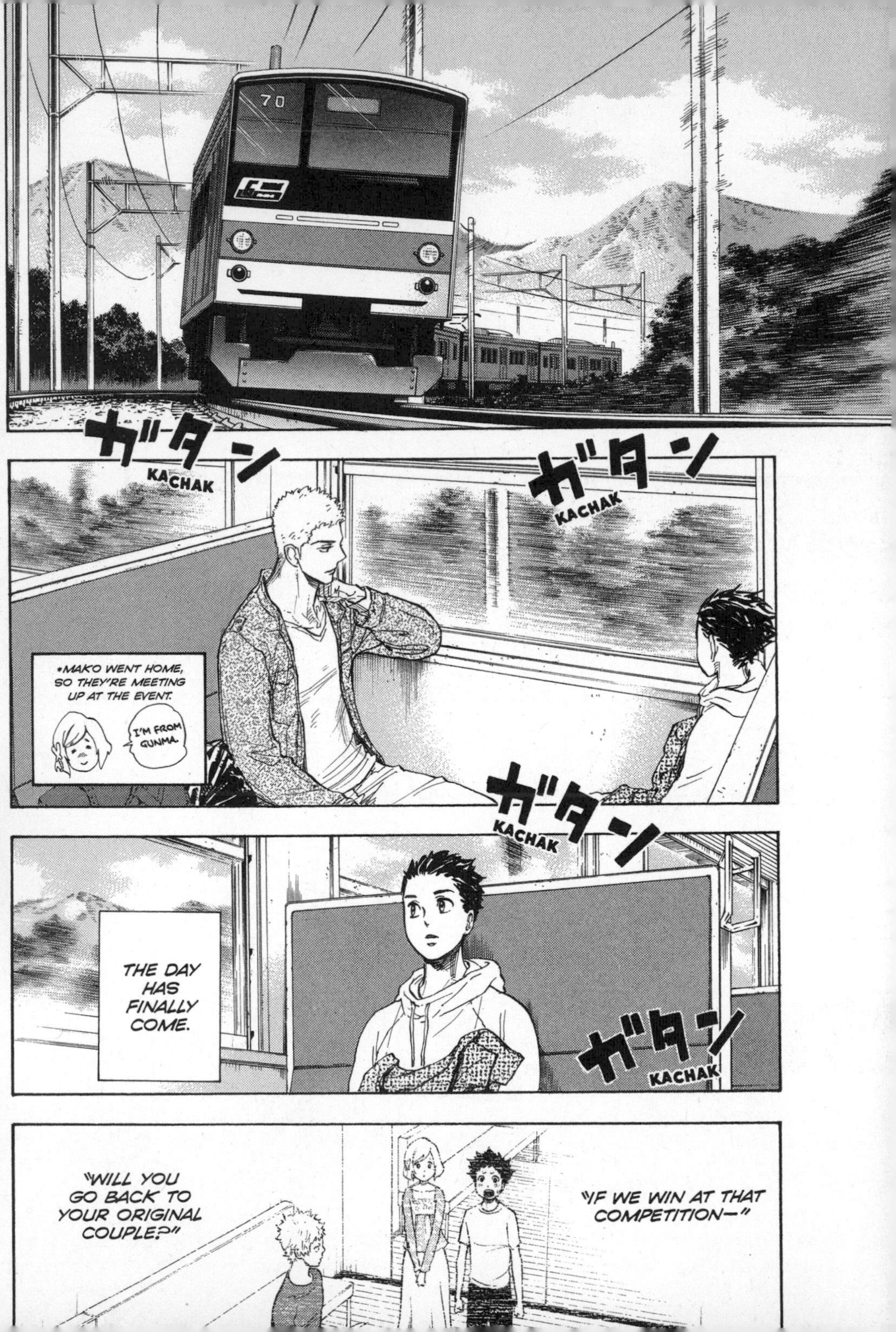
ガタン
KACHAK
ガタン
KACHAK
*MAKO WENT HOME, SO THEY'RE MEETING UP AT THE EVENT.
I'M FROM GUNMA.
ガタン
KACHAK
THE DAY HAS FINALLY COME.
ガタン
KACHAK
"IF WE WIN AT THAT COMPETITION—"
"WILL YOU GO BACK TO YOUR ORIGINAL COUPLE?"

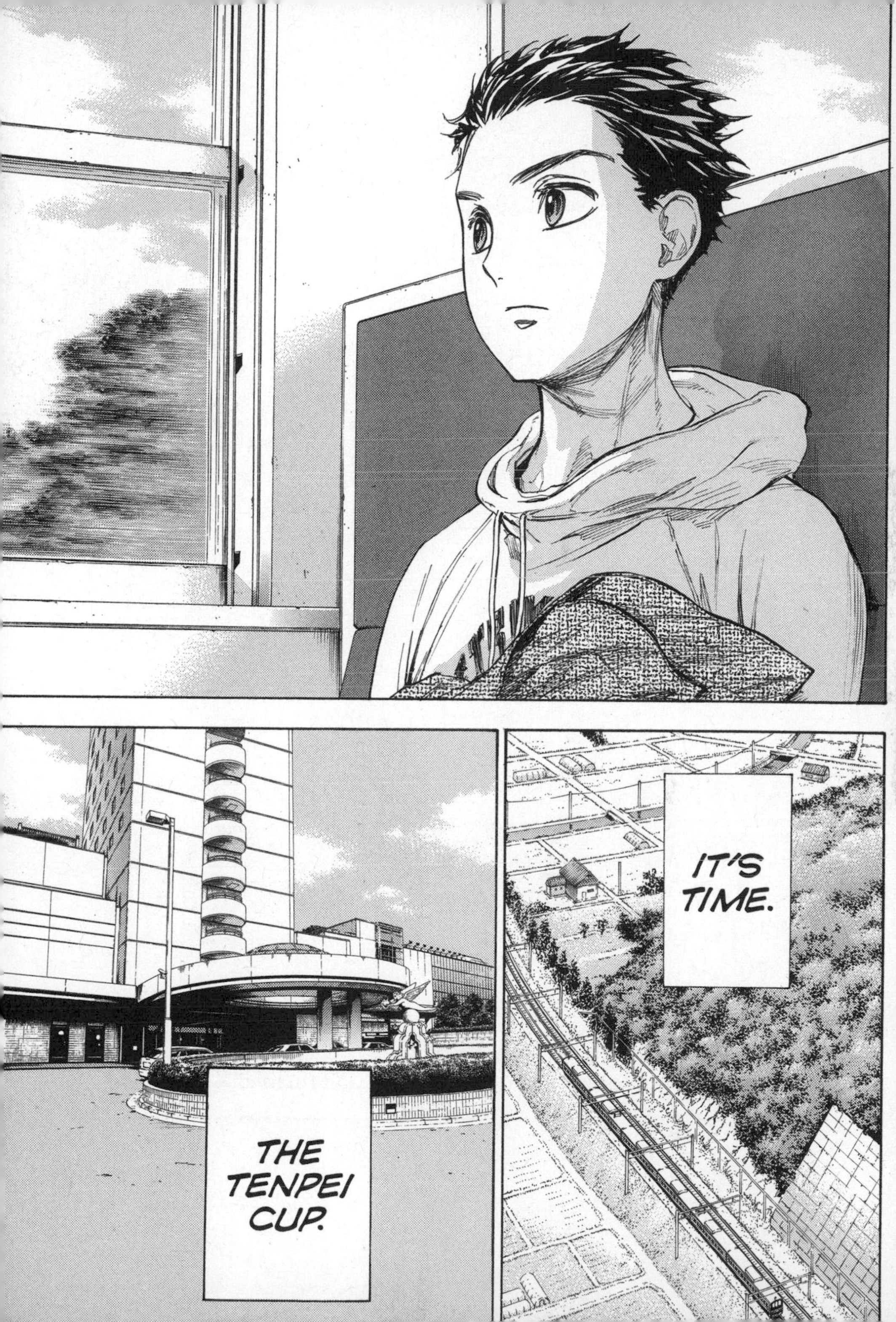
IT'S TIME.
THE TENPEI CUP.

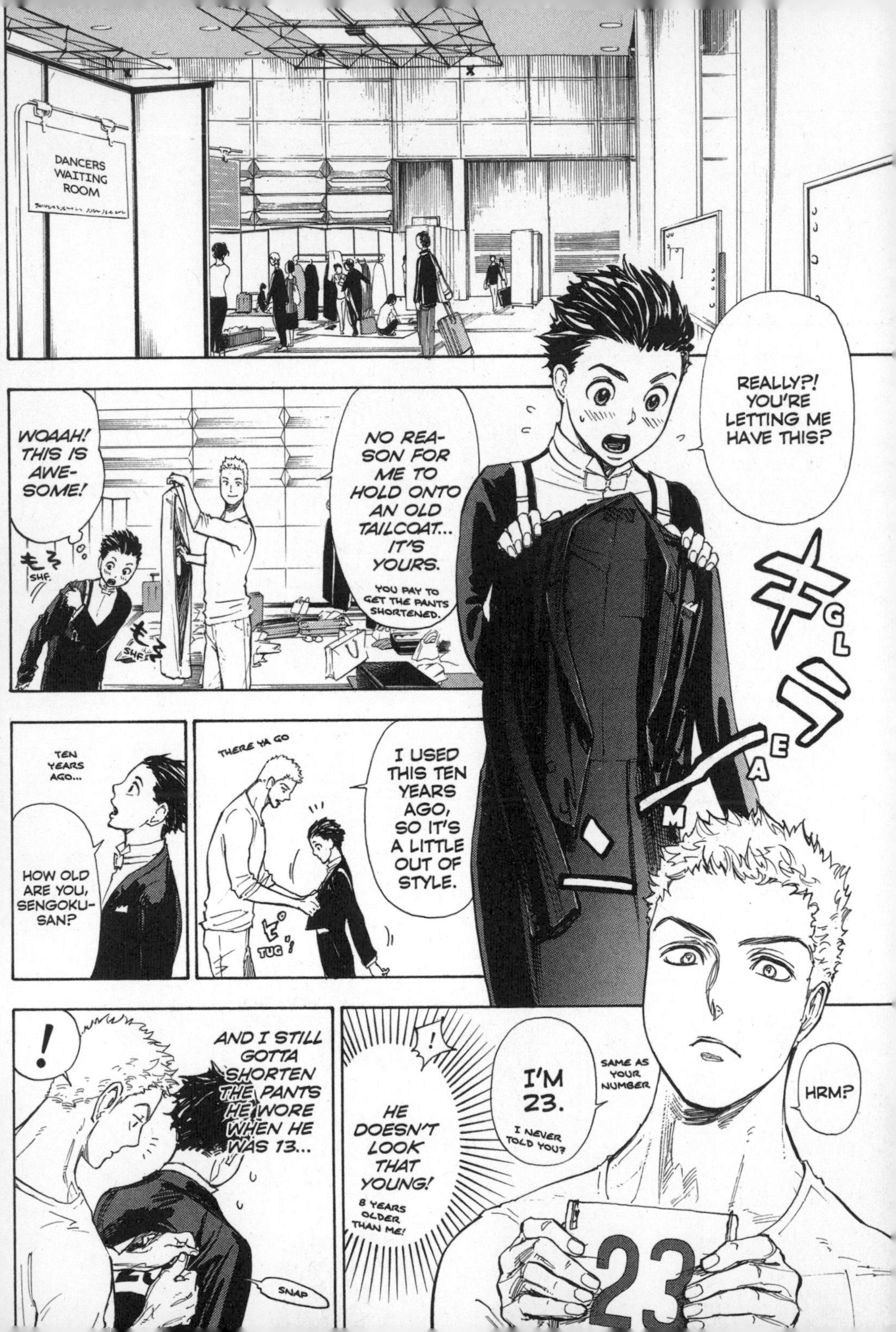
DANCERS
WAITING
ROOM
REALLY?! YOU'RE LETTING ME HAVE THIS?
GLEAM
NO REASON FOR ME TO HOLD ONTO AN OLD TAILCOAT... IT'S YOURS.
YOU PAY TO GET THE PANTS SHORTENED.
WOAAH! THIS IS AWESOME!
SHF
SHF
THERE YA GO
I USED THIS TEN YEARS AGO, SO IT'S A LITTLE OUT OF STYLE.
TUG
TEN YEARS AGO...
HOW OLD ARE YOU, SENGOKU-SAN?
HRM?
I'M 23.
SAME AS YOUR NUMBER
I NEVER TOLD YOU?
!
HE DOESN'T LOOK THAT YOUNG!
8 YEARS OLDER THAN ME!
23
!
AND I STILL GOTTA SHORTEN THE PANTS HE WORE WHEN HE WAS 13...
SNAP

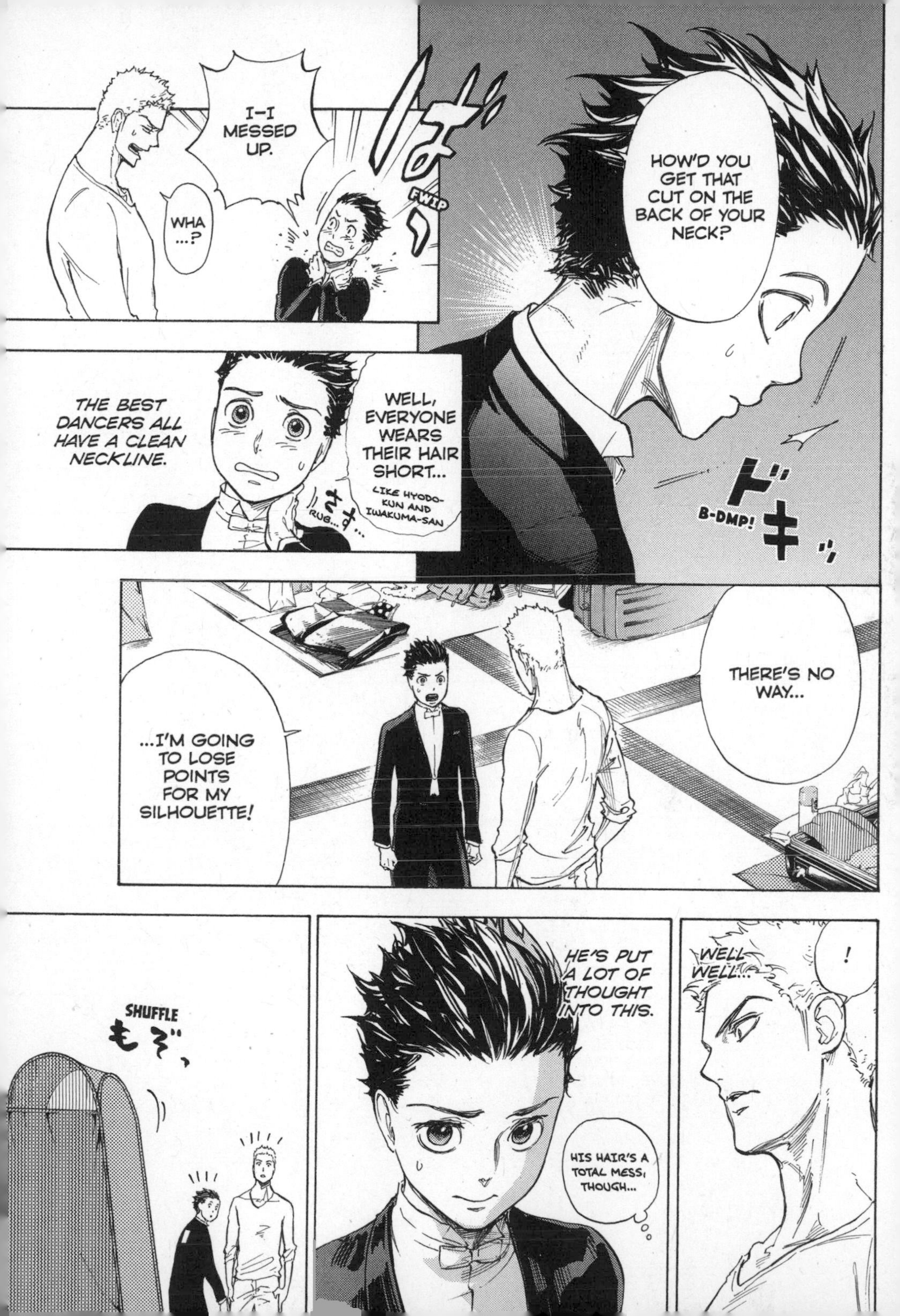
HOW'D YOU GET THAT CUT ON THE BACK OF YOUR NECK?
B-DMP!
FWIP
I-I MESSED UP.
WHA ...?
WELL, EVERYONE WEARS THEIR HAIR SHORT...
LIKE HYODO-KUN AND IWAKUMA-SAN
RUB...
THE BEST DANCERS ALL HAVE A CLEAN NECKLINE.
THERE'S NO WAY...
...I'M GOING TO LOSE POINTS FOR MY SILHOUETTE!
WELL WELL...
!
HE'S PUT A LOT OF THOUGHT INTO THIS.
HIS HAIR'S A TOTAL MESS, THOUGH...
SHUFFLE

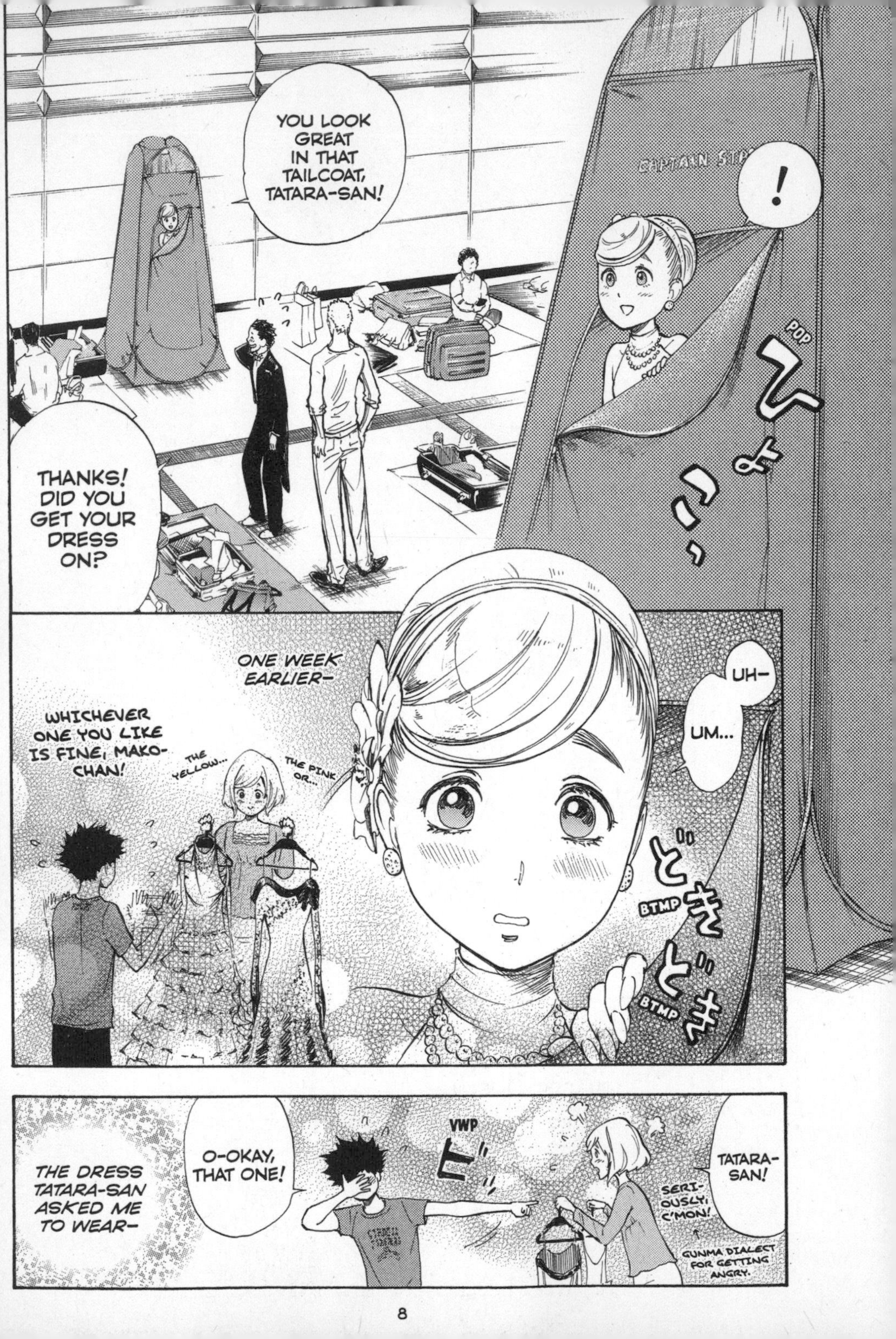
!
POP
YOU LOOK GREAT IN THAT TAILCOAT, TATARA-SAN!
THANKS! DID YOU GET YOUR DRESS ON?
UH-
UM...
BTMP
BTMP
ONE WEEK EARLIER—
WHICHEVER ONE YOU LIKE IS FINE, MAKO-CHAN!
THE PINK OR...
THE YELLOW...
TATARA-SAN!
SERI-OUSLY, C'MON!
GUNMA DIALECT FOR GETTING ANGRY.
VWP
O-OKAY, THAT ONE!
THE DRESS TATARA-SAN ASKED ME TO WEAR—

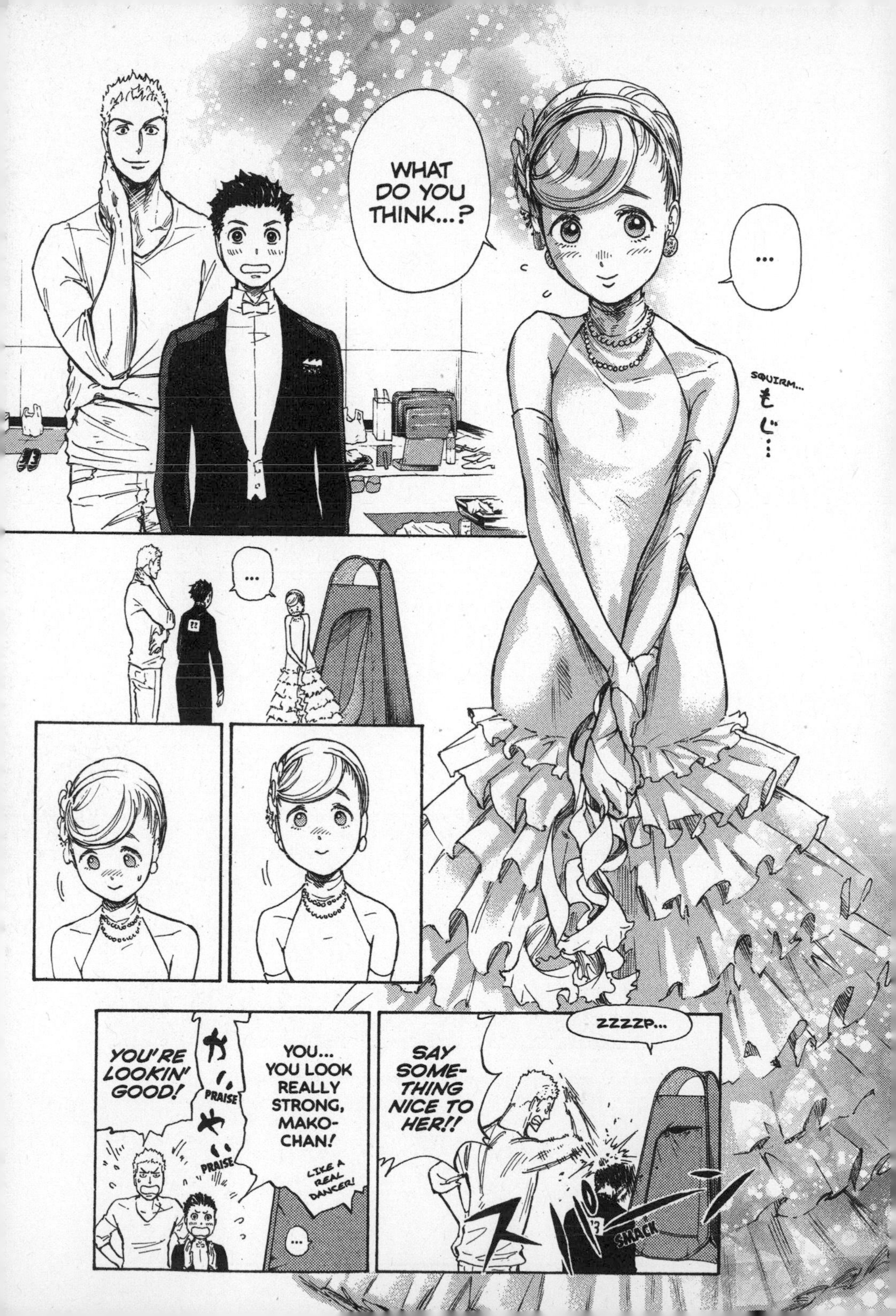
WHAT DO YOU THINK...?
...
SQUIRM...
もじ…
...
ZZZZP...
SAY SOME-THING NICE TO HER!!
SMACK
YOU... YOU LOOK REALLY STRONG, MAKO-CHAN!
LIKE A REAL DANCER!
PRAISE
PRAISE
YOU'RE LOOKIN' GOOD!
...

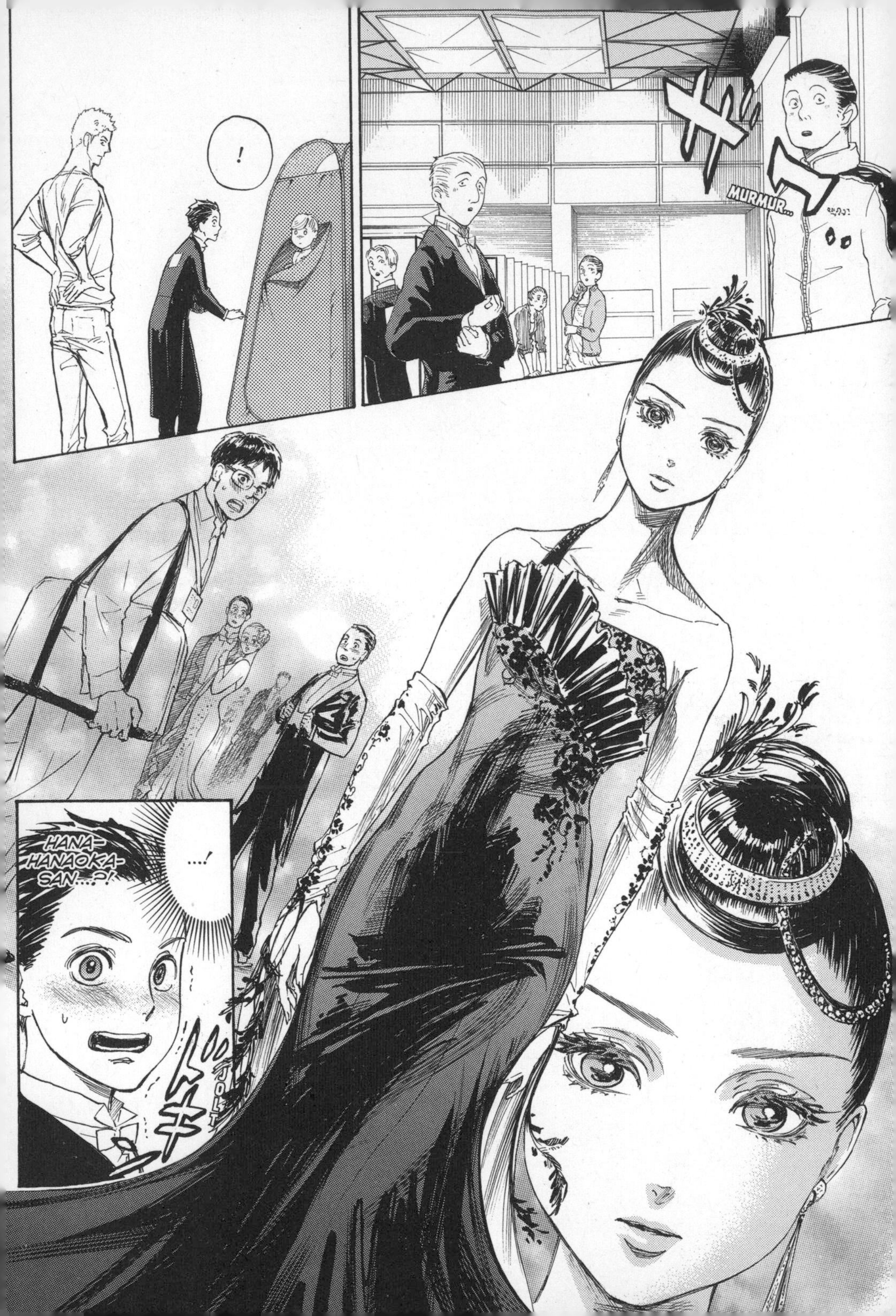
MURMUR...
!
...!
HANA-HANAOKA-SAN...?!
JOLT

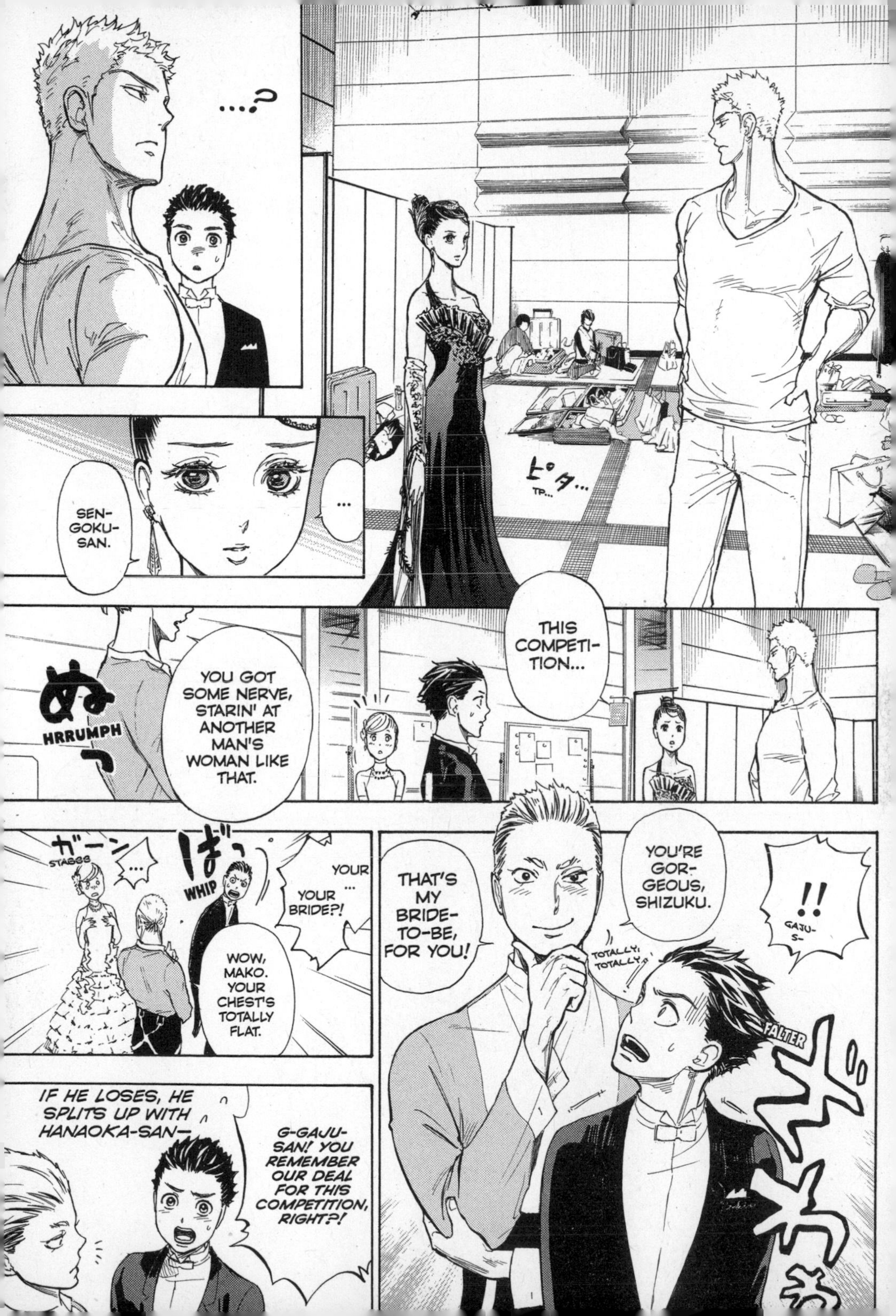
ピタ…
TP...
…?
…
SEN-GOKU-SAN.
THIS COMPETI-TION...
YOU GOT SOME NERVE, STARIN' AT ANOTHER MAN'S WOMAN LIKE THAT.
ぬっ
HRRUMPH
!!
GAJU-S-
YOU'RE GOR-GEOUS, SHIZUKU.
THAT'S MY BRIDE-TO-BE, FOR YOU!
TOTALLY, TOTALLY
FALTER
YOUR ... YOUR BRIDE?!
WOW, MAKO. YOUR CHEST'S TOTALLY FLAT.
ばっ
WHIP
…
ガーン
STAGGG
G-GAJU-SAN! YOU REMEMBER OUR DEAL FOR THIS COMPETITION, RIGHT?!
IF HE LOSES, HE SPLITS UP WITH HANAOKA-SAN—

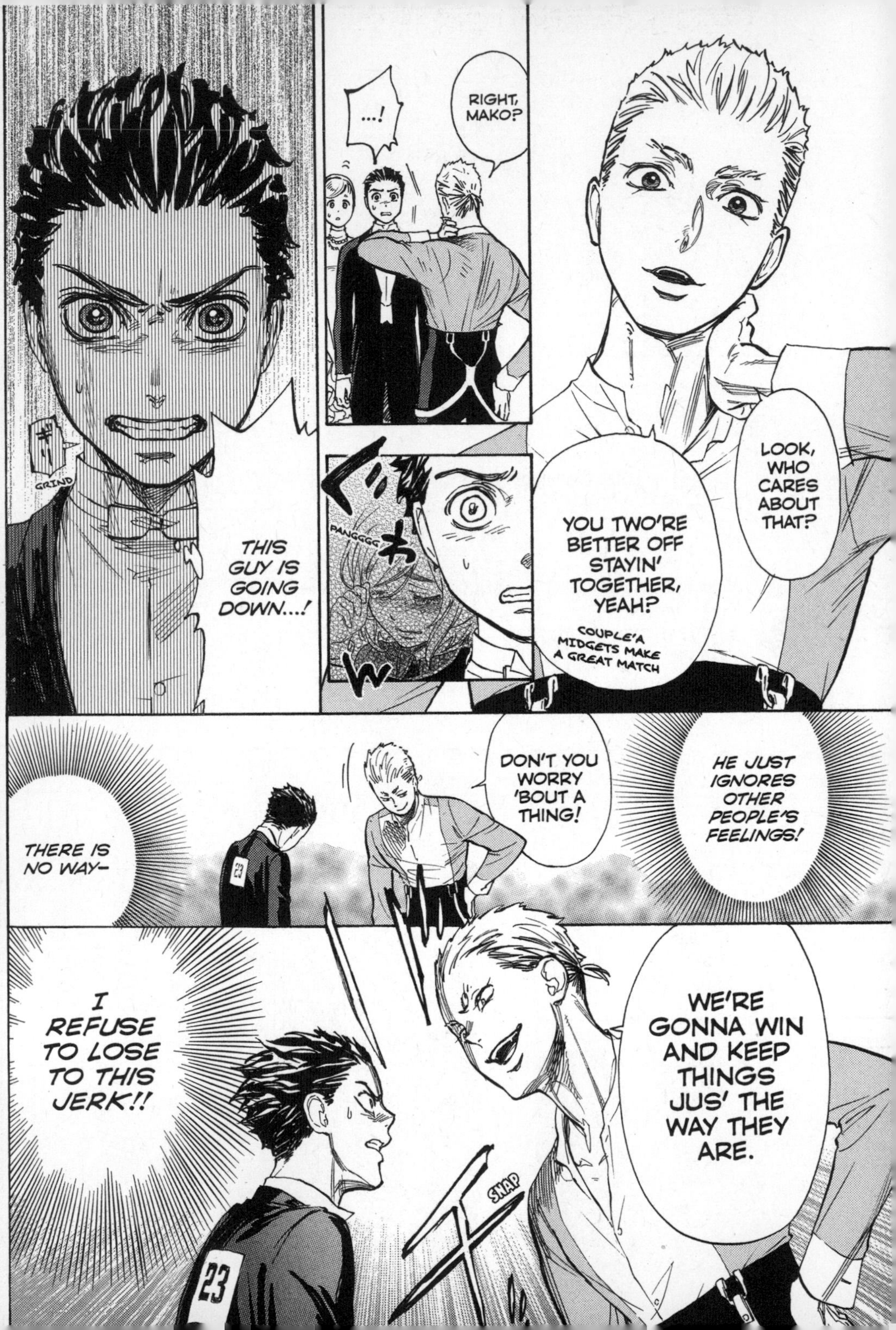
LOOK, WHO CARES ABOUT THAT?
YOU TWO'RE BETTER OFF STAYIN' TOGETHER, YEAH?
COUPLE'A MIDGETS MAKE A GREAT MATCH
RIGHT, MAKO?
...!
PANGGGG
THIS GUY IS GOING DOWN...!
GRIND
HE JUST IGNORES OTHER PEOPLE'S FEELINGS!
DON'T YOU WORRY 'BOUT A THING!
THERE IS NO WAY-
WE'RE GONNA WIN AND KEEP THINGS JUS' THE WAY THEY ARE.
SNAP
I REFUSE TO LOSE TO THIS JERK!!

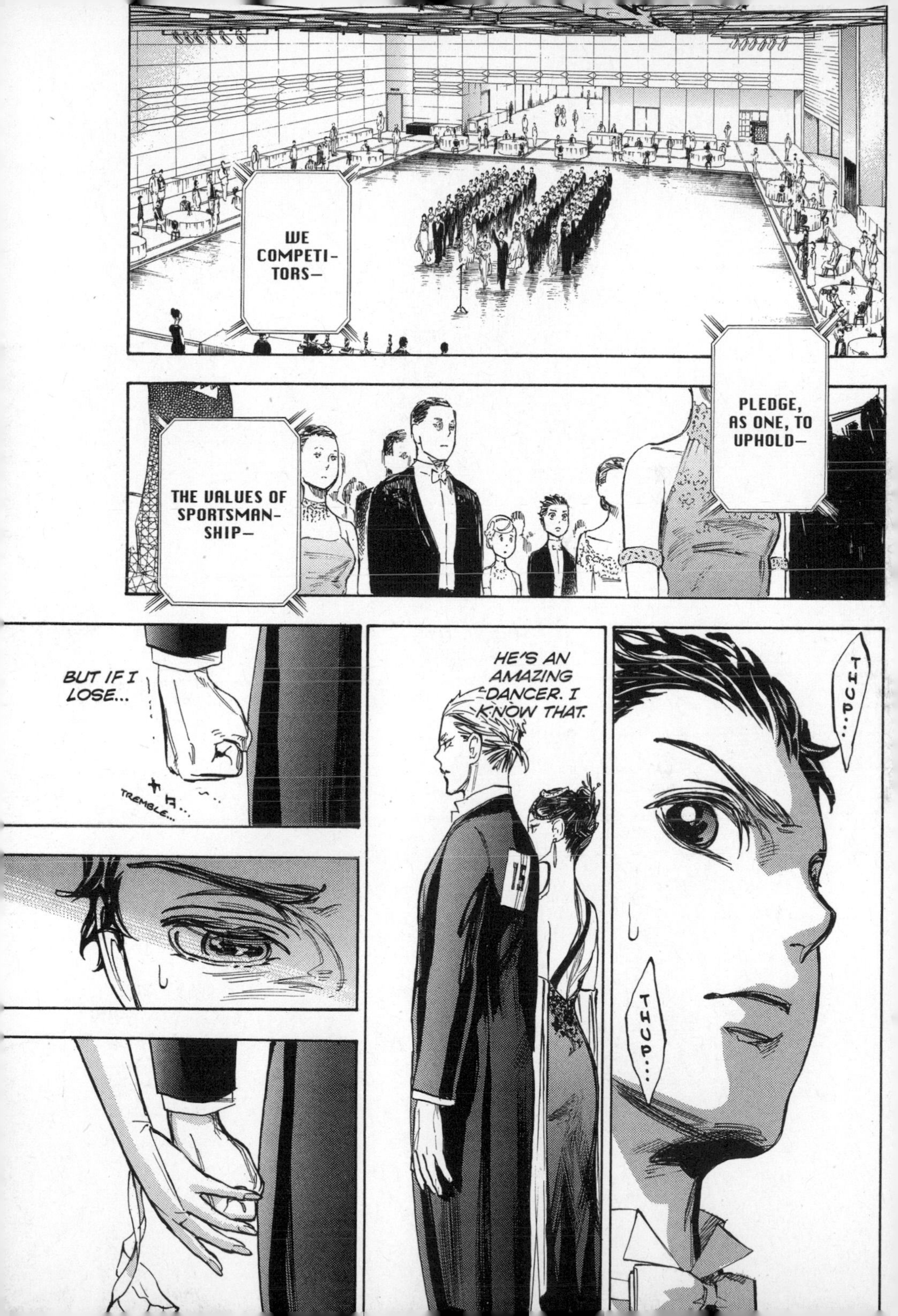
WE COMPETITORS—
PLEDGE, AS ONE, TO UPHOLD—
THE VALUES OF SPORTSMANSHIP—
THUP...
THUP...
HE'S AN AMAZING DANCER. I KNOW THAT.
BUT IF I LOSE...
TREMBLE...

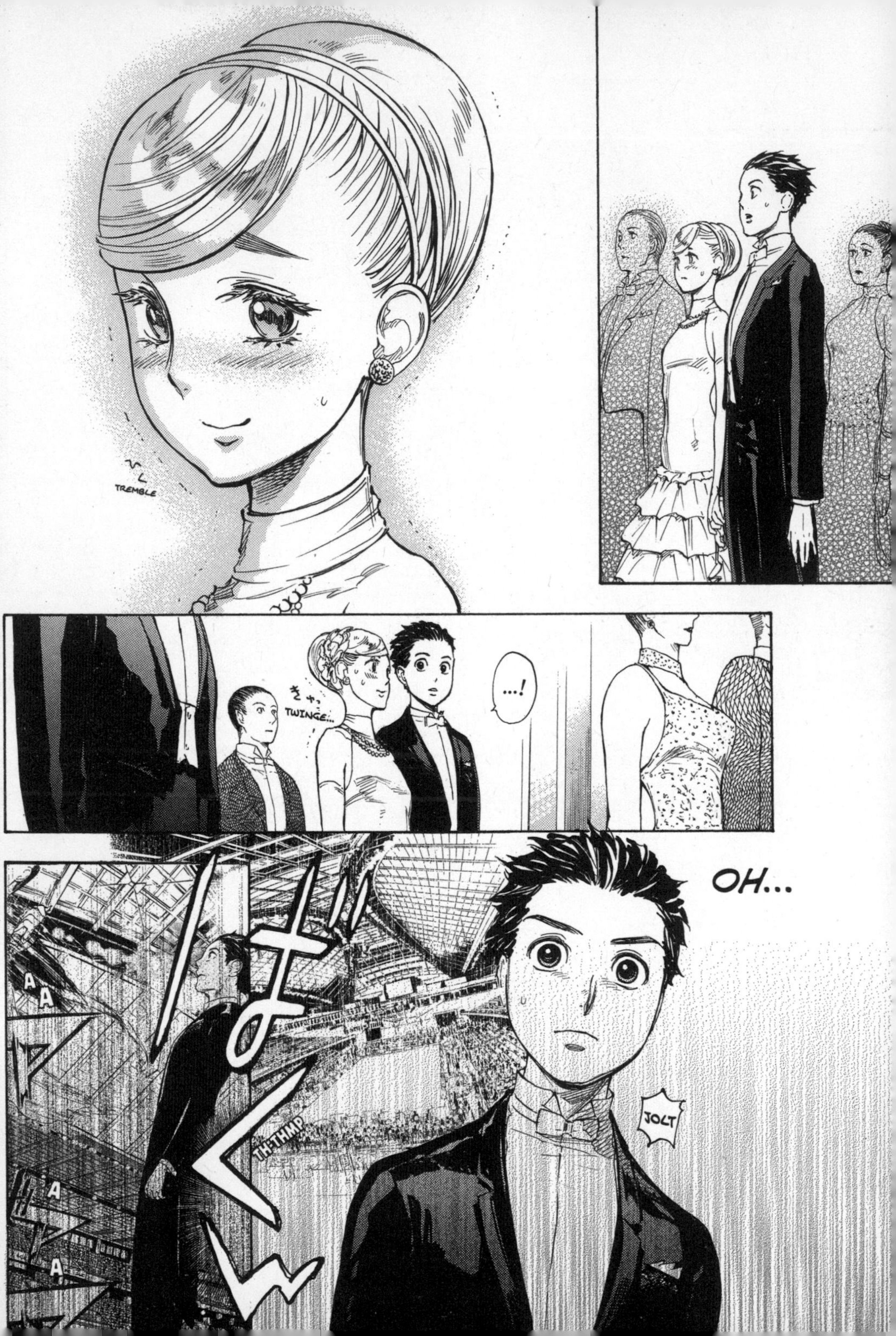
TREMBLE
...!
TWINGE...
OH...
JOLT
TH-THMP
A
A
A
A

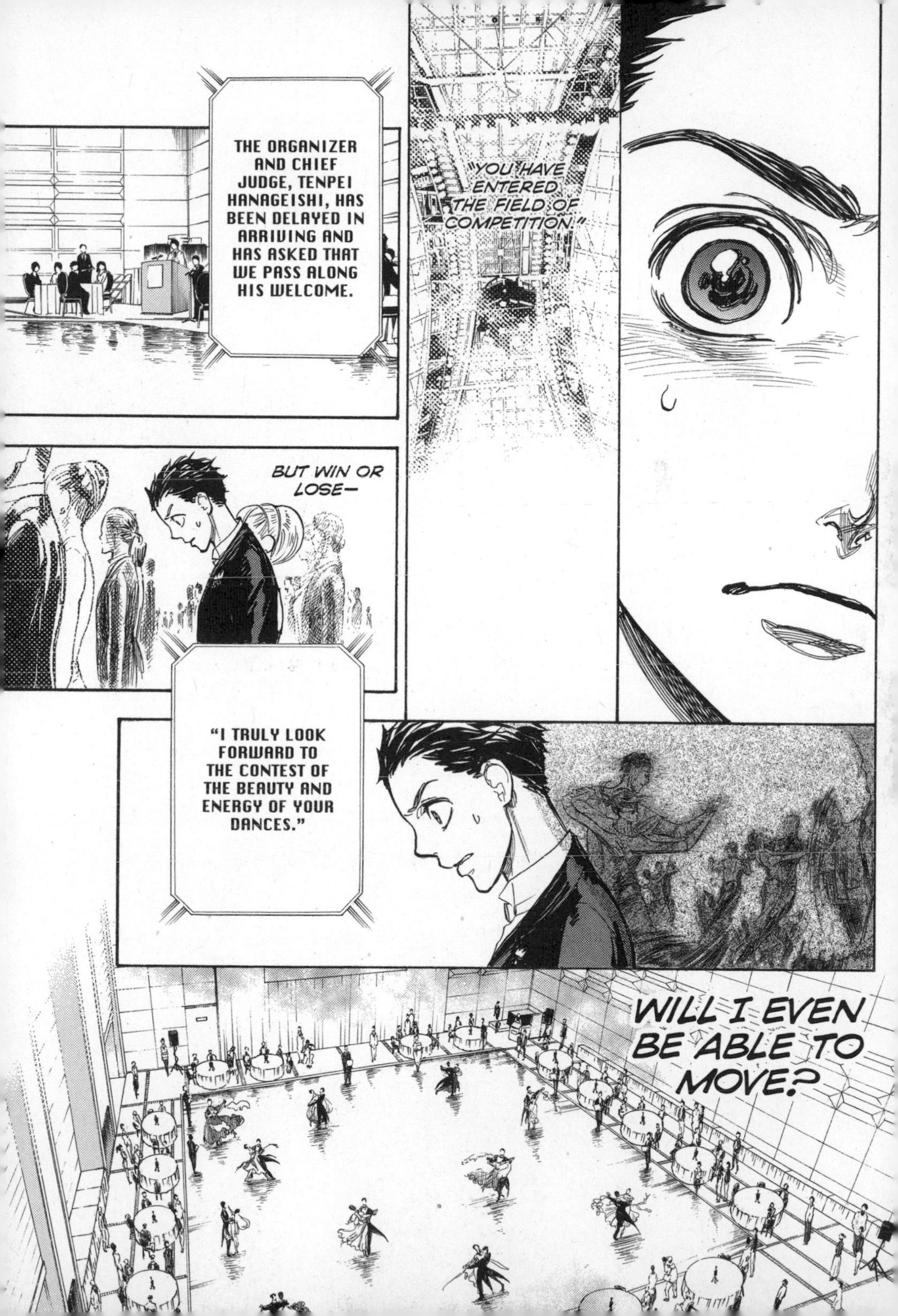
"YOU HAVE ENTERED THE FIELD OF COMPETITION."
THE ORGANIZER AND CHIEF JUDGE, TENPEI HANAGEISHI, HAS BEEN DELAYED IN ARRIVING AND HAS ASKED THAT WE PASS ALONG HIS WELCOME.
BUT WIN OR LOSE—
"I TRULY LOOK FORWARD TO THE CONTEST OF THE BEAUTY AND ENERGY OF YOUR DANCES."
WILL I EVEN BE ABLE TO MOVE?

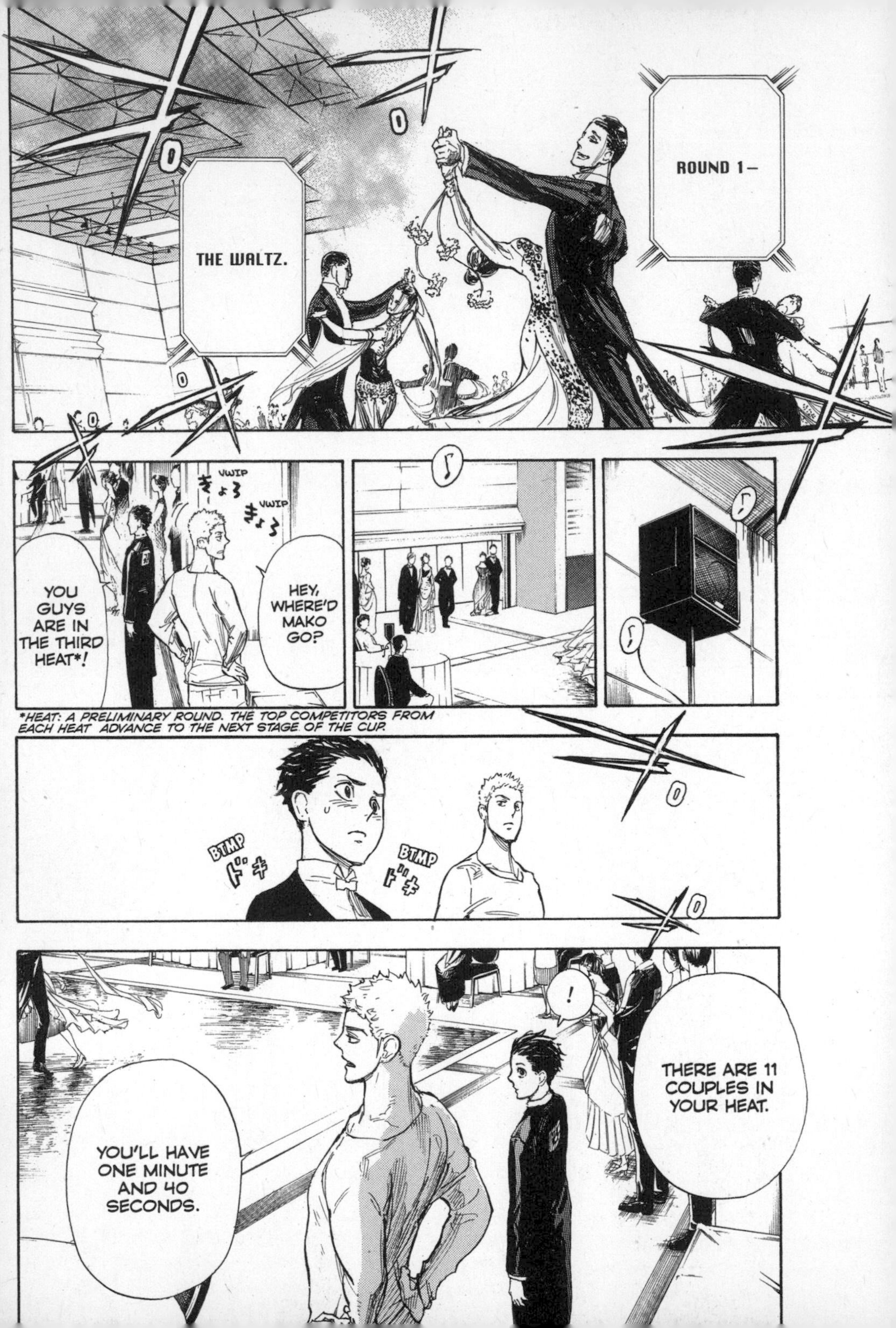
ROUND 1—
THE WALTZ.
VWIP きょろ
VWIP きょろ
HEY, WHERE'D MAKO GO?
YOU GUYS ARE IN THE THIRD HEAT*!
*HEAT: A PRELIMINARY ROUND. THE TOP COMPETITORS FROM EACH HEAT ADVANCE TO THE NEXT STAGE OF THE CUP.
BTMP ドキ
BTMP ドキ
!
THERE ARE 11 COUPLES IN YOUR HEAT.
YOU'LL HAVE ONE MINUTE AND 40 SECONDS.

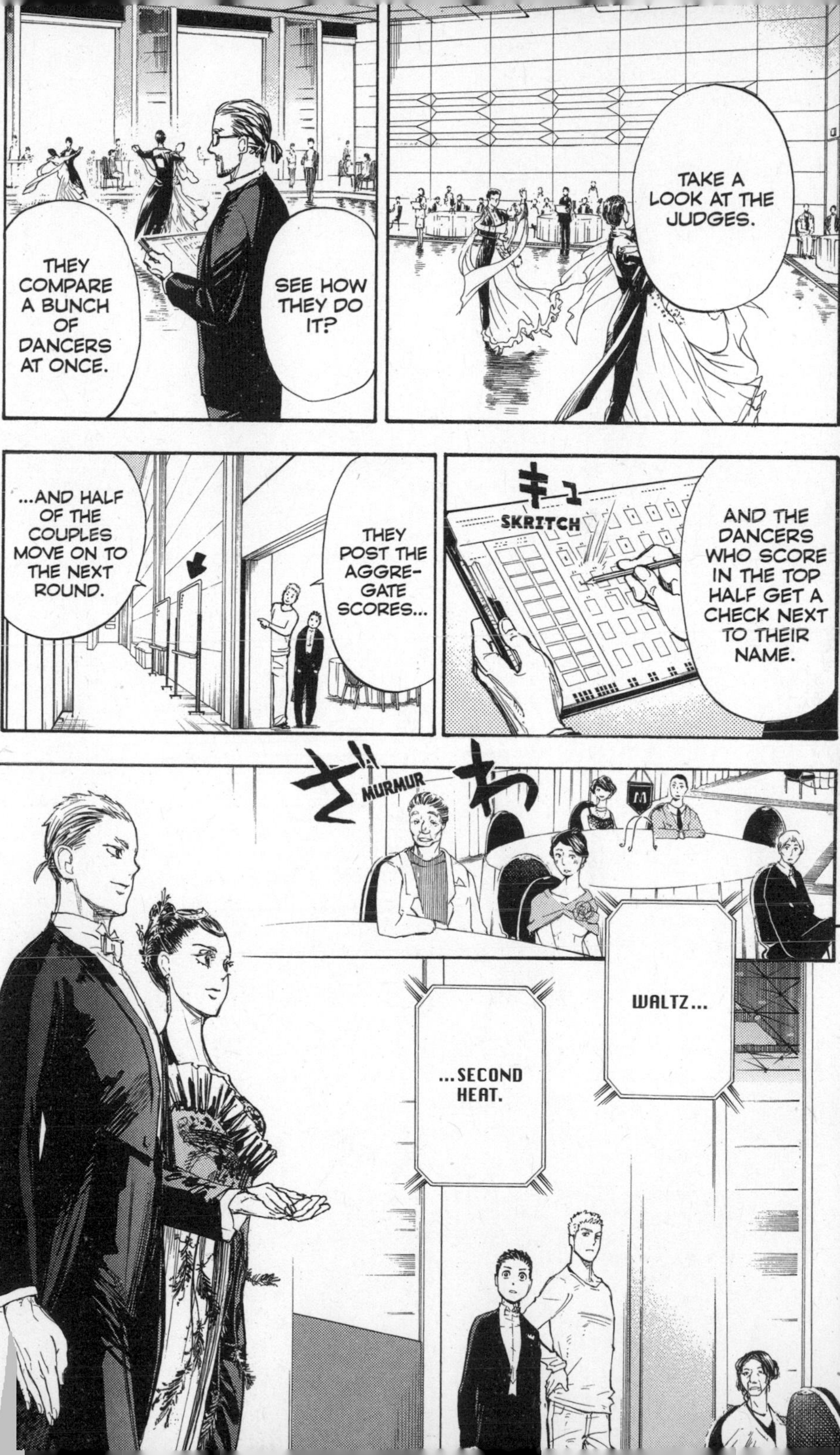
TAKE A LOOK AT THE JUDGES.
SEE HOW THEY DO IT?
THEY COMPARE A BUNCH OF DANCERS AT ONCE.
キュ
SKRITCH
AND THE DANCERS WHO SCORE IN THE TOP HALF GET A CHECK NEXT TO THEIR NAME.
THEY POST THE AGGREGATE SCORES...
...AND HALF OF THE COUPLES MOVE ON TO THE NEXT ROUND.
ざわ
MURMUR
WALTZ...
...SECOND HEAT.

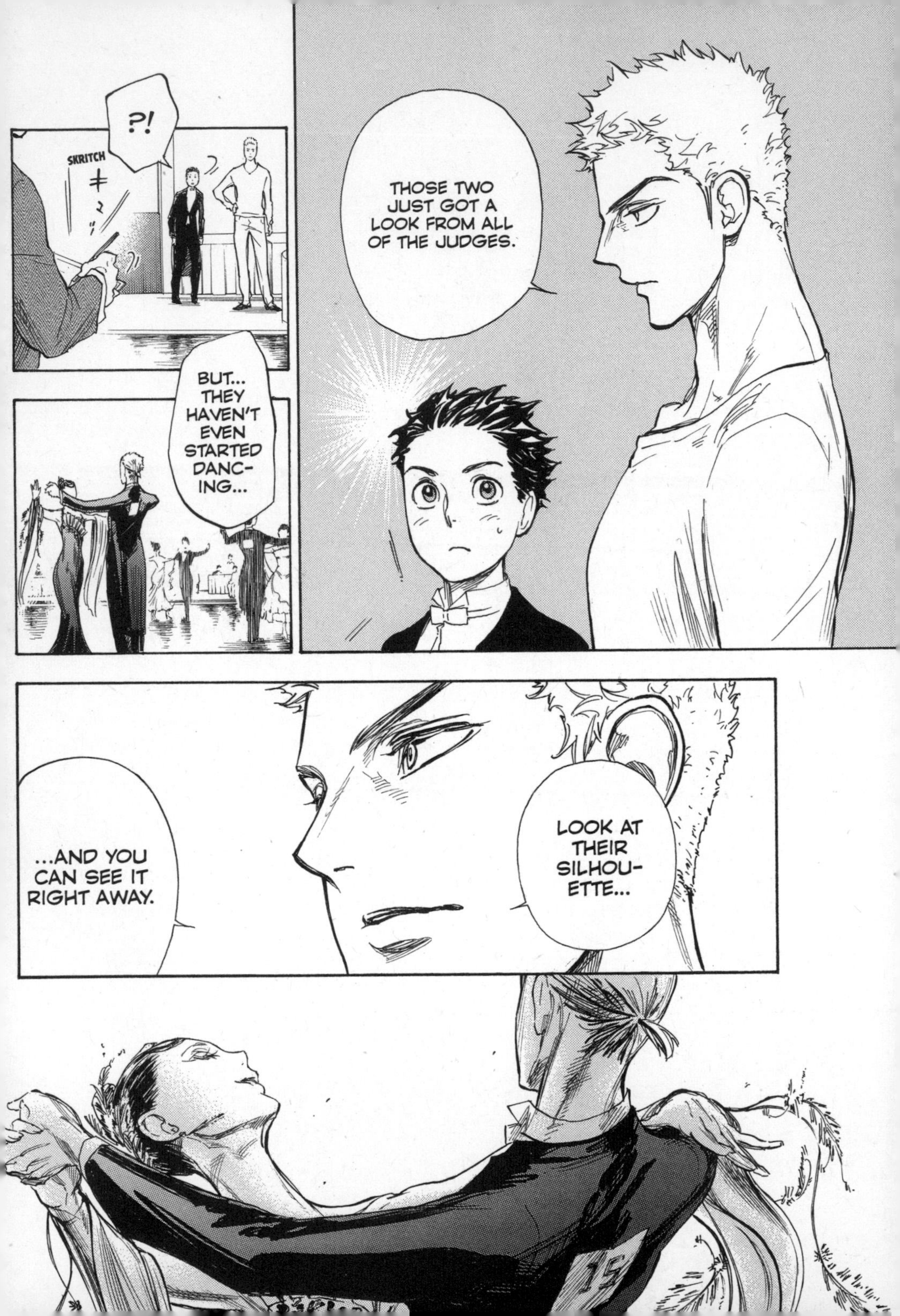
THOSE TWO JUST GOT A LOOK FROM ALL OF THE JUDGES.
?!
SKRITCH
BUT... THEY HAVEN'T EVEN STARTED DANCING...
LOOK AT THEIR SILHOUETTE...
...AND YOU CAN SEE IT RIGHT AWAY.

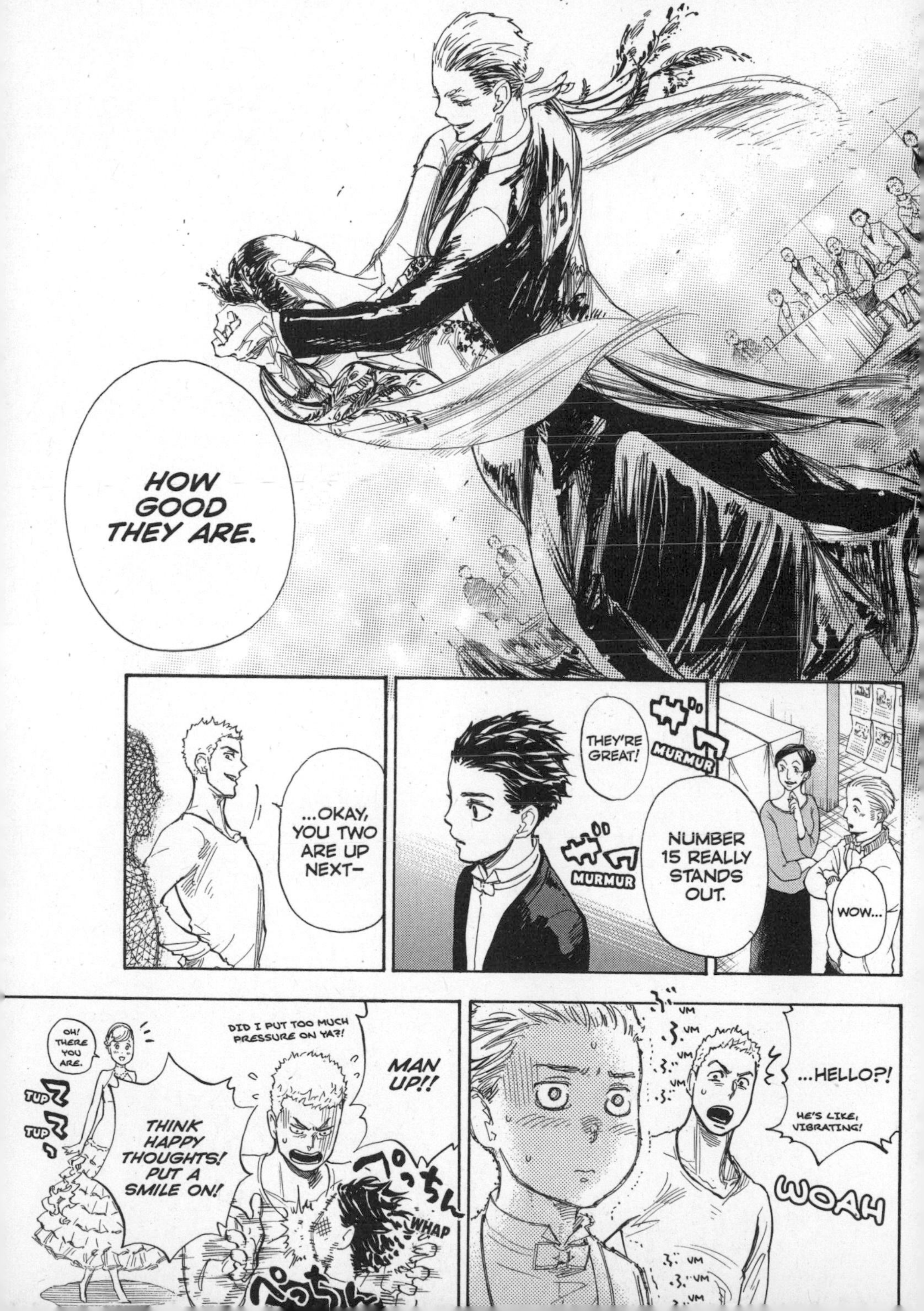
HOW GOOD THEY ARE.
WOW...
THEY'RE GREAT!
MURMUR
NUMBER 15 REALLY STANDS OUT.
MURMUR
...OKAY, YOU TWO ARE UP NEXT—
VM VM VM VM
...HELLO?!
HE'S LIKE, VIBRATING!
WOAH
VM VM VM
DID I PUT TOO MUCH PRESSURE ON YA?!
MAN UP!!
OH! THERE YOU ARE.
TUP TUP
THINK HAPPY THOUGHTS! PUT A SMILE ON!
WHAP

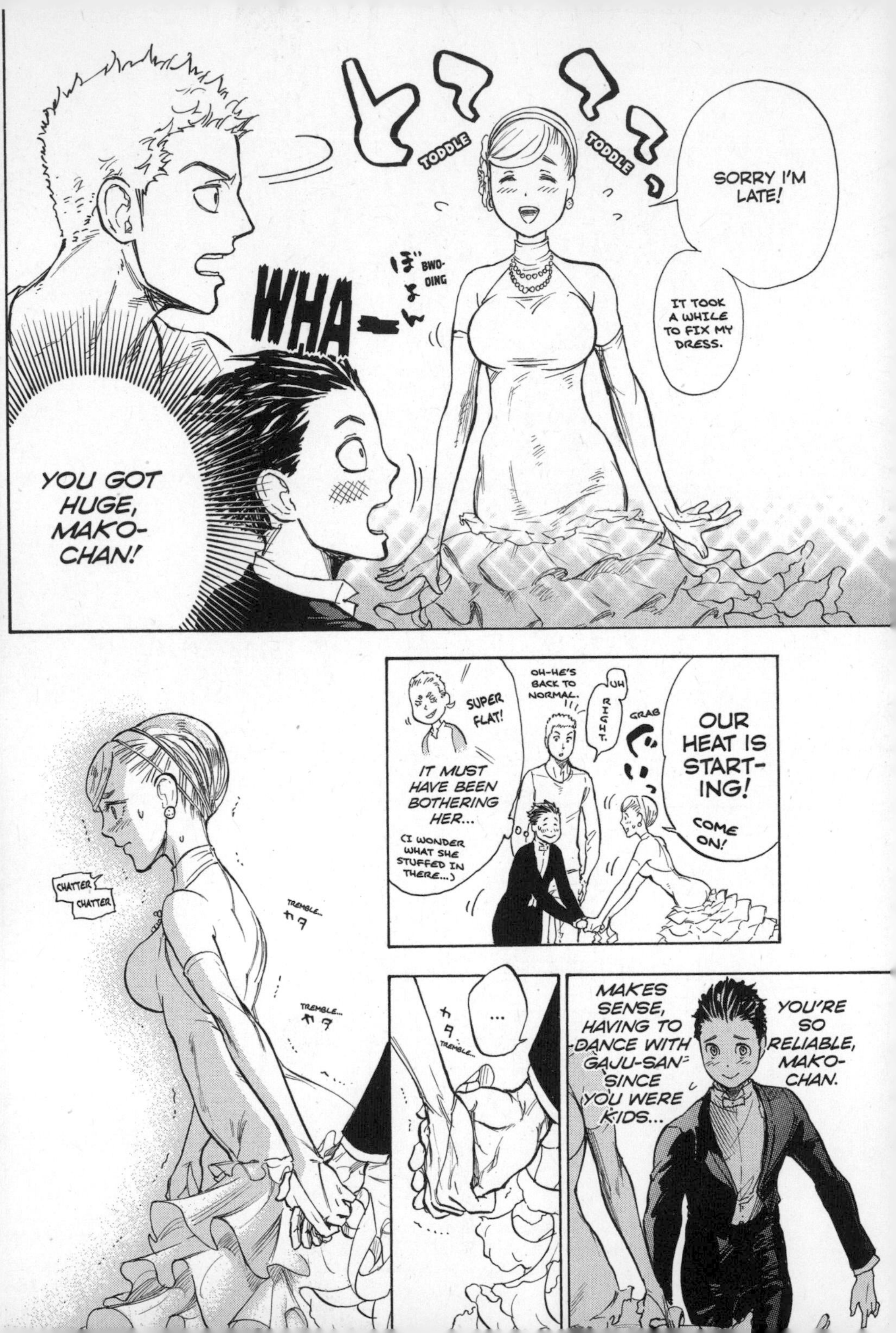
SORRY I'M LATE!
IT TOOK A WHILE TO FIX MY DRESS.
TODDLE
TODDLE
ぼよん
BWO-OING
WHA—
YOU GOT HUGE, MAKO-CHAN!
OUR HEAT IS STARTING!
COME ON!
GRAB
UH RIGHT.
OH-HE'S BACK TO NORMAL.
SUPER FLAT!
IT MUST HAVE BEEN BOTHERING HER...
(I WONDER WHAT SHE STUFFED IN THERE...)
YOU'RE SO RELIABLE, MAKO-CHAN.
MAKES SENSE, HAVING TO DANCE WITH GAJU-SAN SINCE YOU WERE KIDS...
...
カタ
TREMBLE...
TREMBLE...
カタ
TREMBLE...
カタ
CHATTER
CHATTER

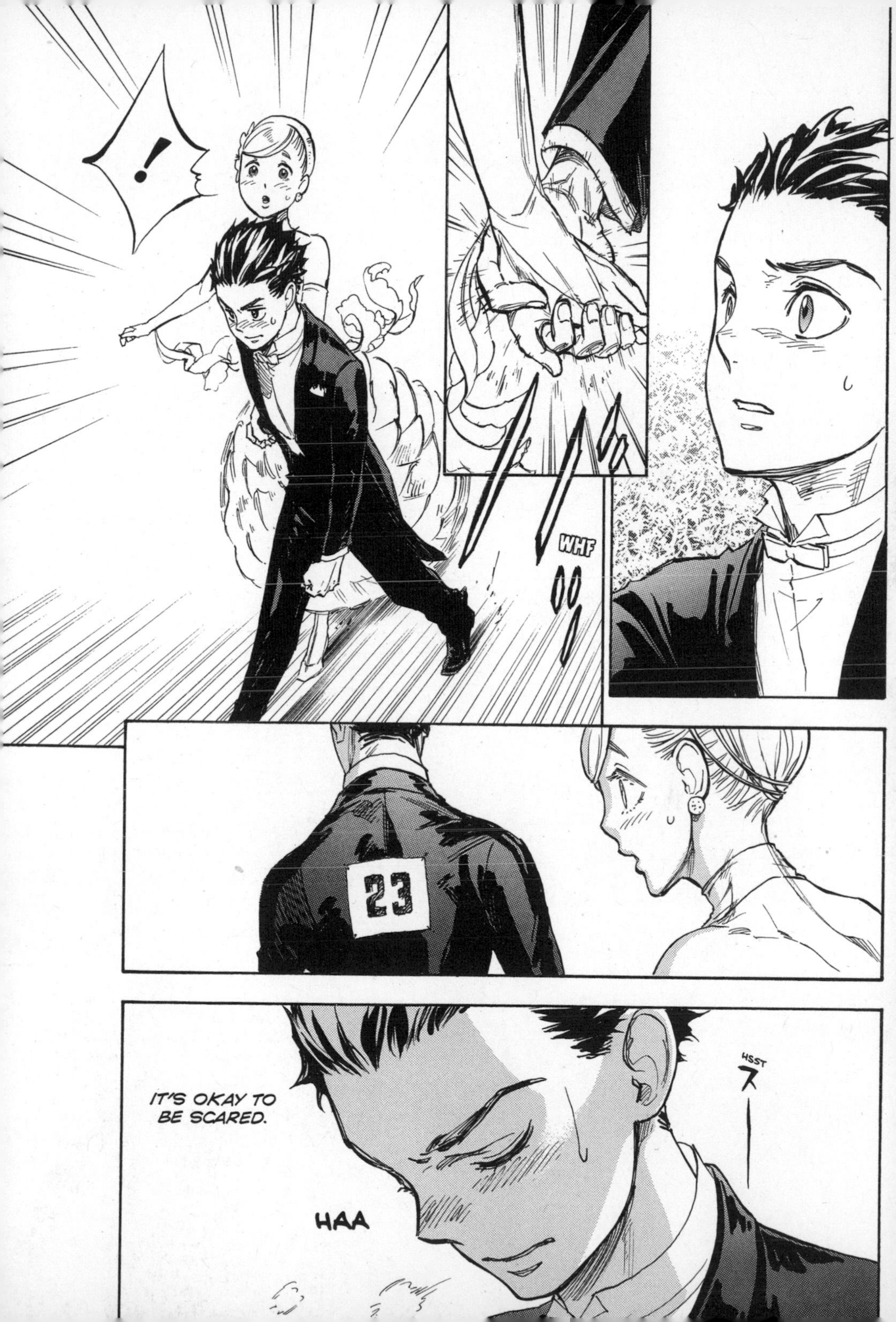
WHF
!
HSST
IT'S OKAY TO BE SCARED.
HAA

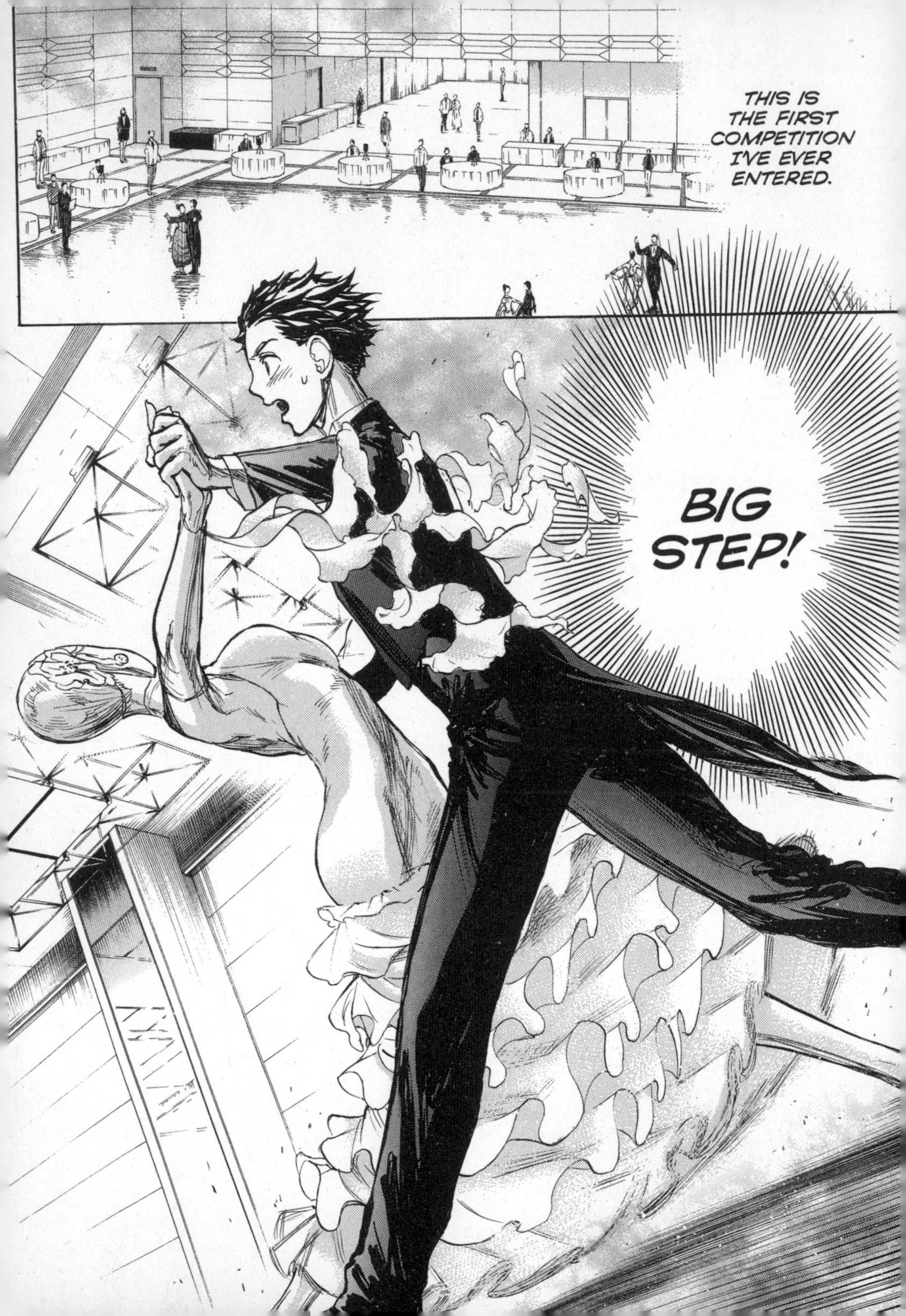
THIS IS THE FIRST COMPETITION I'VE EVER ENTERED.
BIG STEP!

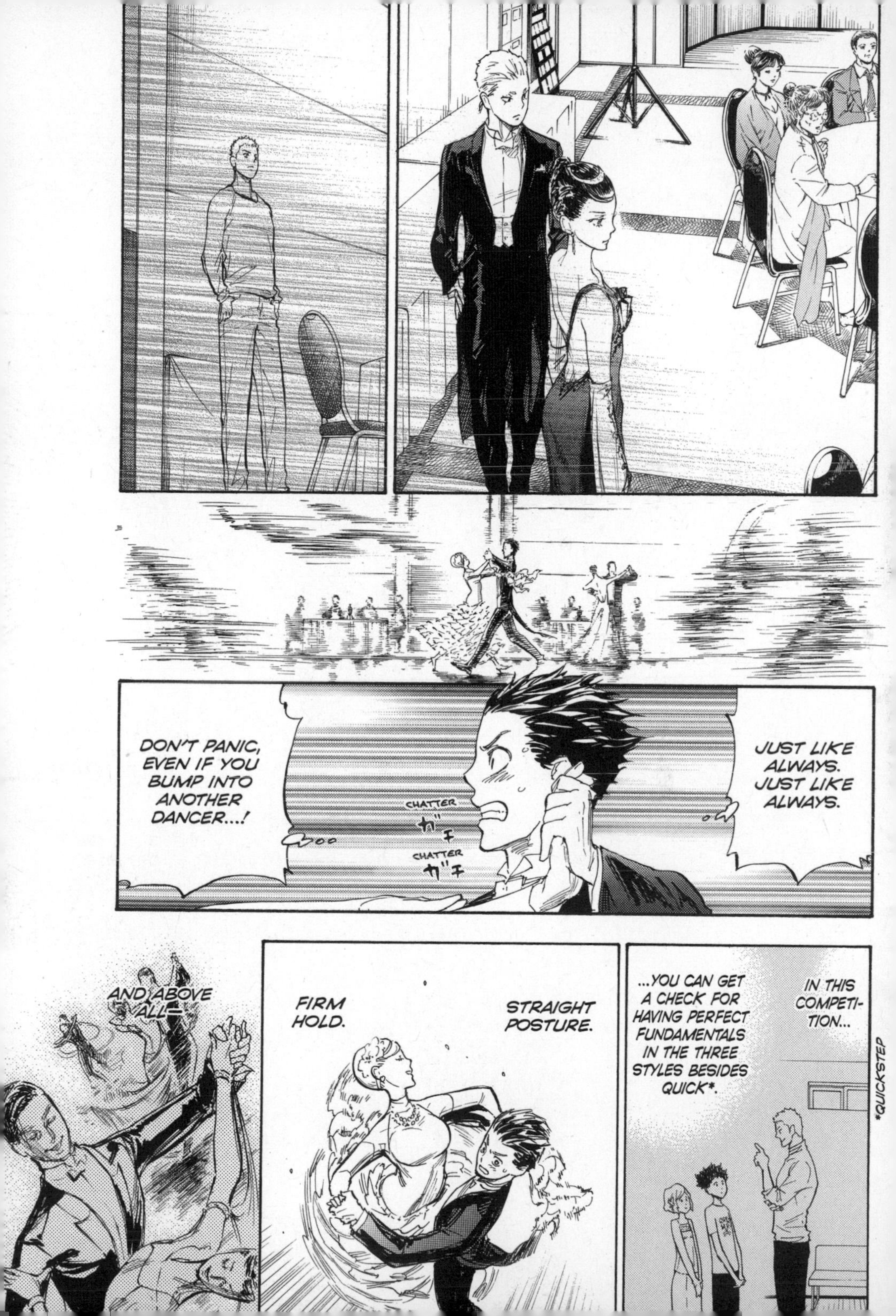
JUST LIKE ALWAYS. JUST LIKE ALWAYS.
DON'T PANIC, EVEN IF YOU BUMP INTO ANOTHER DANCER...!
CHATTER
ガチ
CHATTER
ガチ
IN THIS COMPETI-TION...
...YOU CAN GET A CHECK FOR HAVING PERFECT FUNDAMENTALS IN THE THREE STYLES BESIDES QUICK*.
*QUICKSTEP
STRAIGHT POSTURE.
FIRM HOLD.
AND ABOVE ALL—

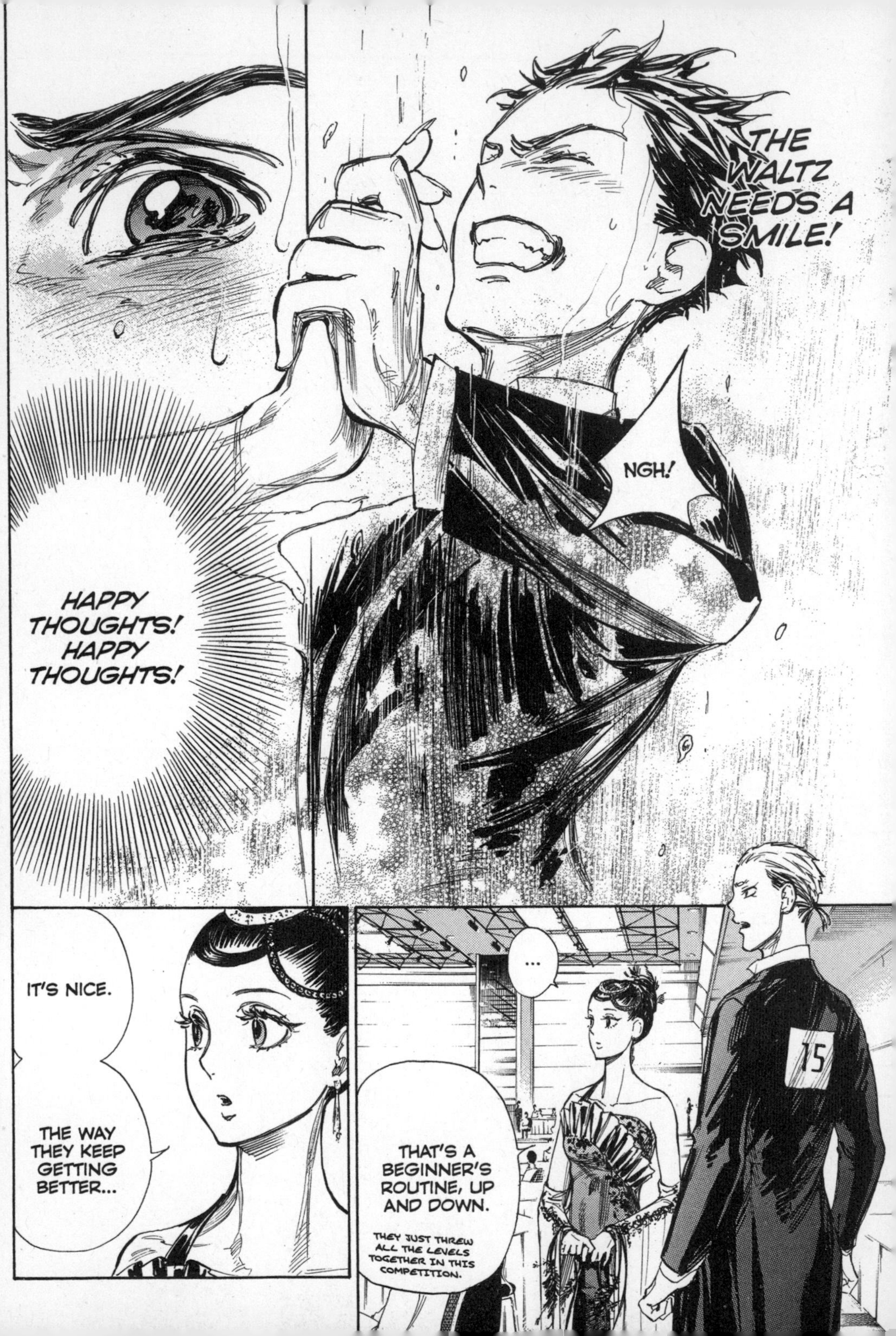
THE WALTZ NEEDS A SMILE!
NGH!
HAPPY THOUGHTS! HAPPY THOUGHTS!
...
15
THAT'S A BEGINNER'S ROUTINE, UP AND DOWN.
THEY JUST THREW ALL THE LEVELS TOGETHER IN THIS COMPETITION.
IT'S NICE.
THE WAY THEY KEEP GETTING BETTER...

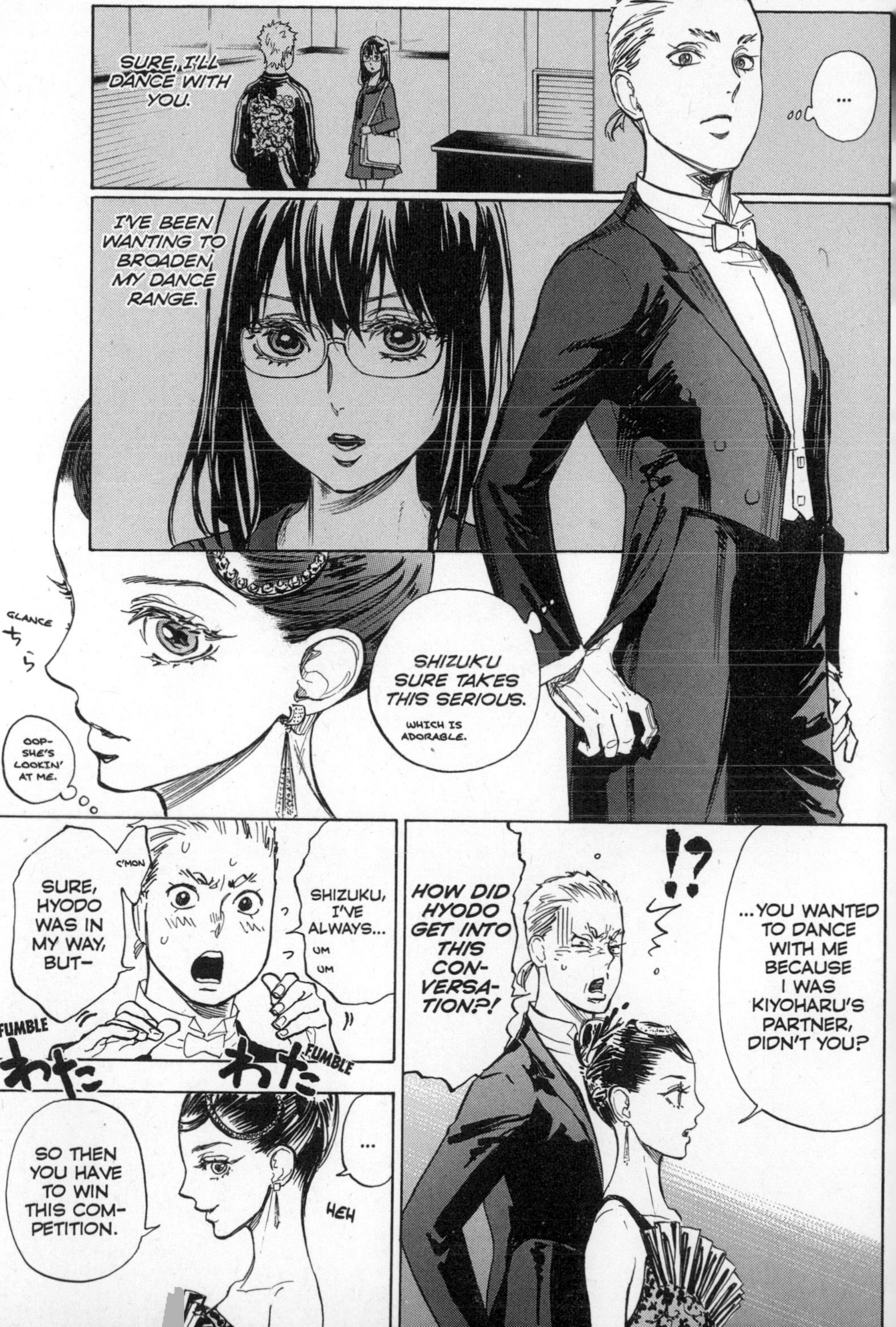
...
SURE, I'LL DANCE WITH YOU.
I'VE BEEN WANTING TO BROADEN MY DANCE RANGE.
SHIZUKU SURE TAKES THIS SERIOUS.
WHICH IS ADORABLE.
GLANCE
ちら
OOP- SHE'S LOOKIN' AT ME.
...YOU WANTED TO DANCE WITH ME BECAUSE I WAS KIYOHARU'S PARTNER, DIDN'T YOU?
!?
HOW DID HYODO GET INTO THIS CONVERSATION?!
SHIZUKU, I'VE ALWAYS...
UM
UM
C'MON
SURE, HYODO WAS IN MY WAY, BUT–
FUMBLE
わた
FUMBLE
わた
...
HEH
SO THEN YOU HAVE TO WIN THIS COMPETITION.

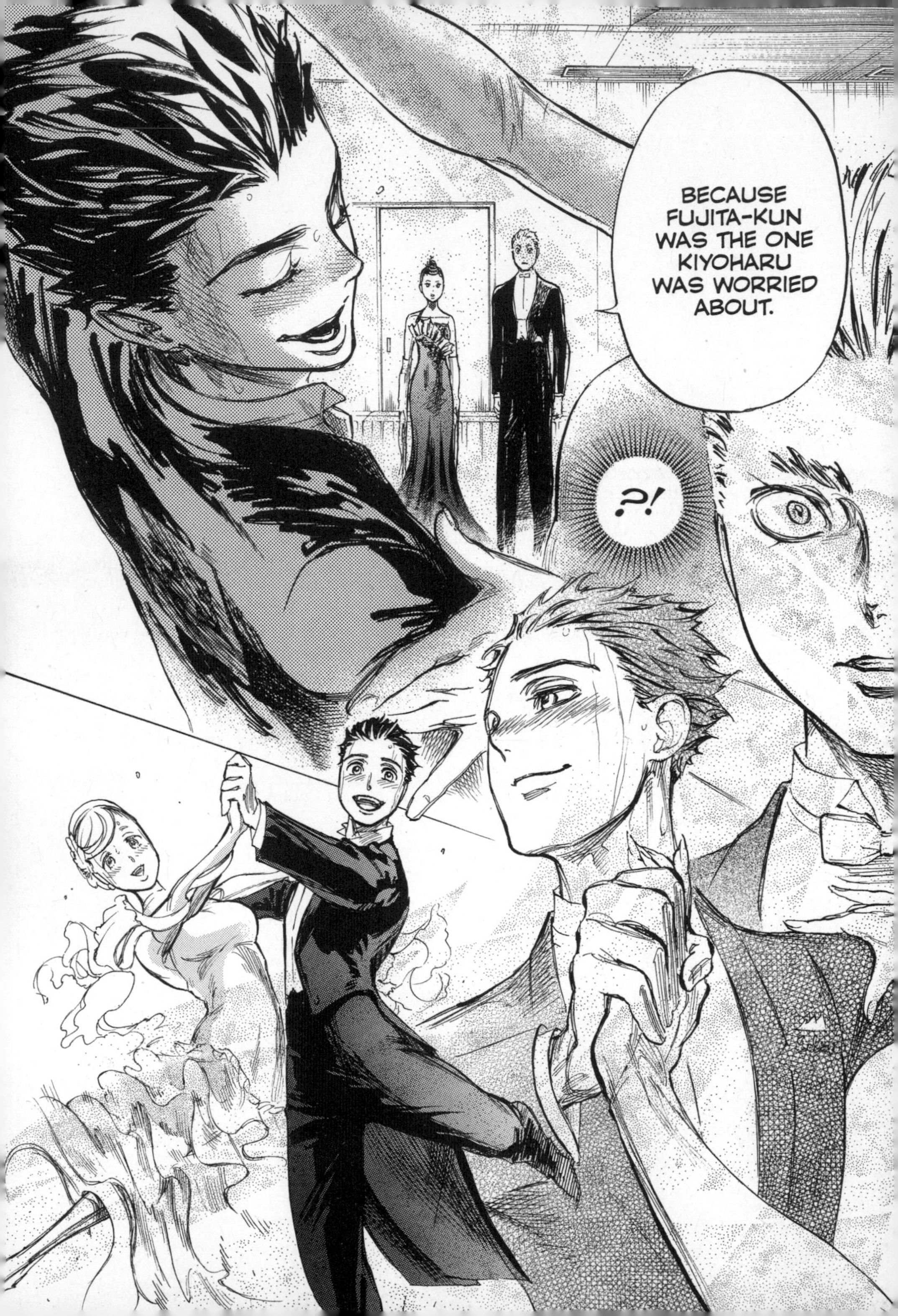
BECAUSE FUJITA-KUN WAS THE ONE KIYOHARU WAS WORRIED ABOUT.
?!

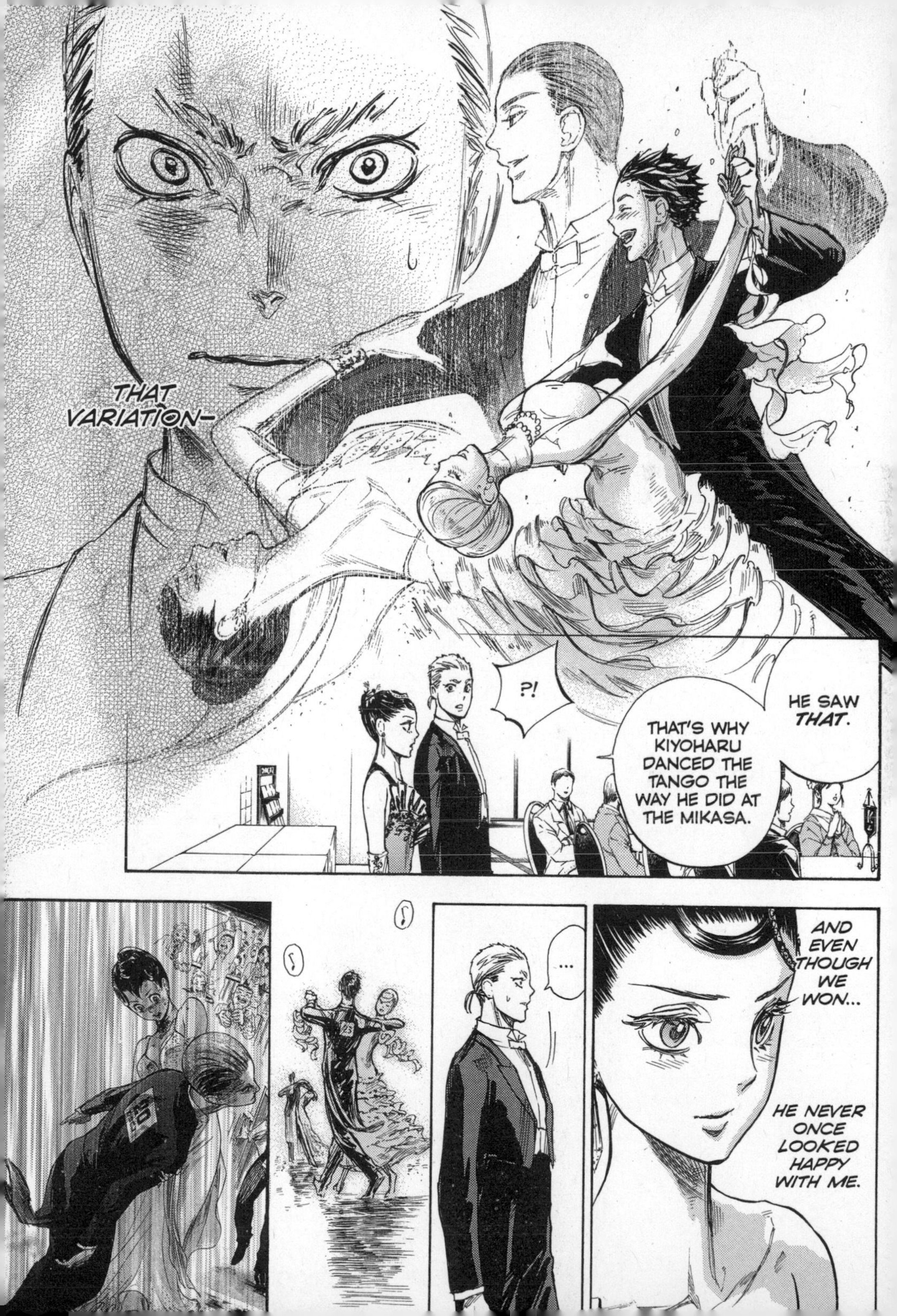
THAT VARIATION–
HE SAW *THAT*.
THAT'S WHY KIYOHARU DANCED THE TANGO THE WAY HE DID AT THE MIKASA.
?!
AND EVEN THOUGH WE WON...
HE NEVER ONCE LOOKED HAPPY WITH ME.
...

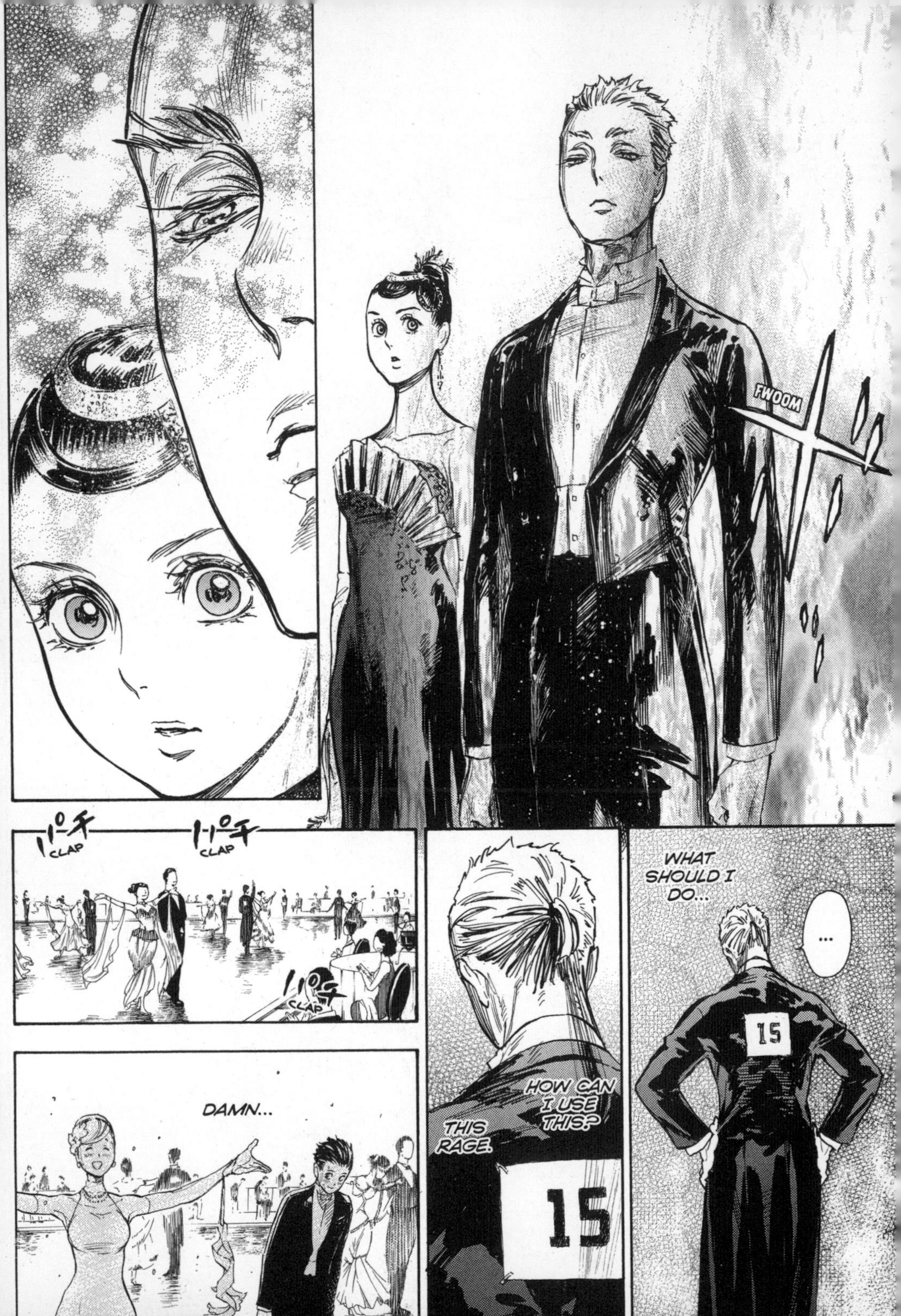
FWOOM
WHAT SHOULD I DO...
...
HOW CAN I USE THIS?
THIS RAGE.
CLAP
CLAP
CLAP
DAMN...

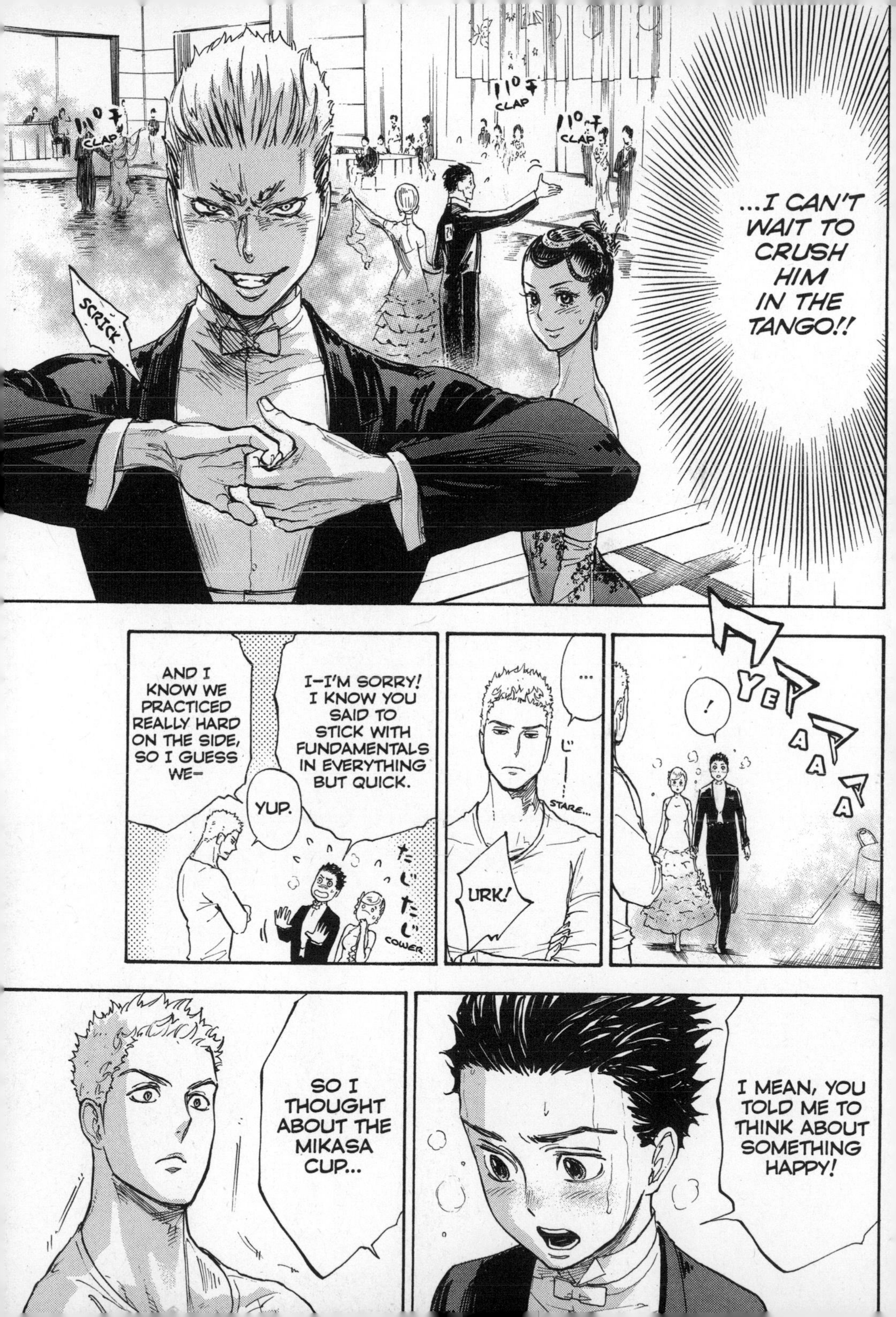
CLAP
CLAP
CLAP
SCRICK
...I CAN'T WAIT TO CRUSH HIM IN THE TANGO!!
YEAAA
!
...
STARE...
URK!
I-I'M SORRY! I KNOW YOU SAID TO STICK WITH FUNDAMENTALS IN EVERYTHING BUT QUICK.
AND I KNOW WE PRACTICED REALLY HARD ON THE SIDE, SO I GUESS WE–
YUP.
COWER
I MEAN, YOU TOLD ME TO THINK ABOUT SOMETHING HAPPY!
SO I THOUGHT ABOUT THE MIKASA CUP...

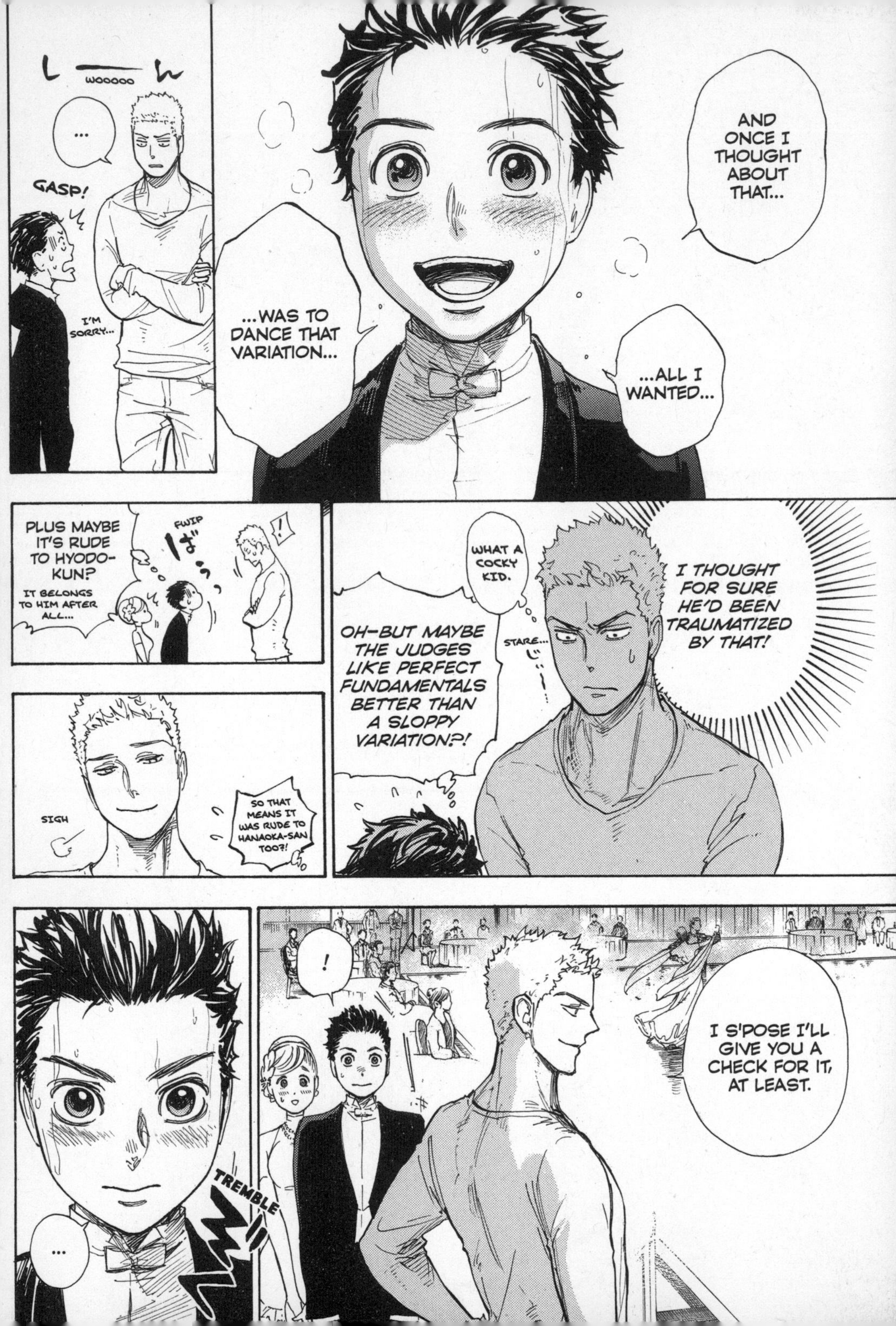
AND ONCE I THOUGHT ABOUT THAT...
...ALL I WANTED...
...WAS TO DANCE THAT VARIATION...
しーーん
WOOOOO
...
GASP!
I'M SORRY...
I THOUGHT FOR SURE HE'D BEEN TRAUMATIZED BY THAT!
WHAT A COCKY KID.
STARE...
じー
OH—BUT MAYBE THE JUDGES LIKE PERFECT FUNDAMENTALS BETTER THAN A SLOPPY VARIATION?!
!
FWIP
ばっ
PLUS MAYBE IT'S RUDE TO HYODO-KUN?
IT BELONGS TO HIM AFTER ALL...
SO THAT MEANS IT WAS RUDE TO HANAOKA-SAN TOO?!
SIGH
I S'POSE I'LL GIVE YOU A CHECK FOR IT, AT LEAST.
!
TREMBLE
...

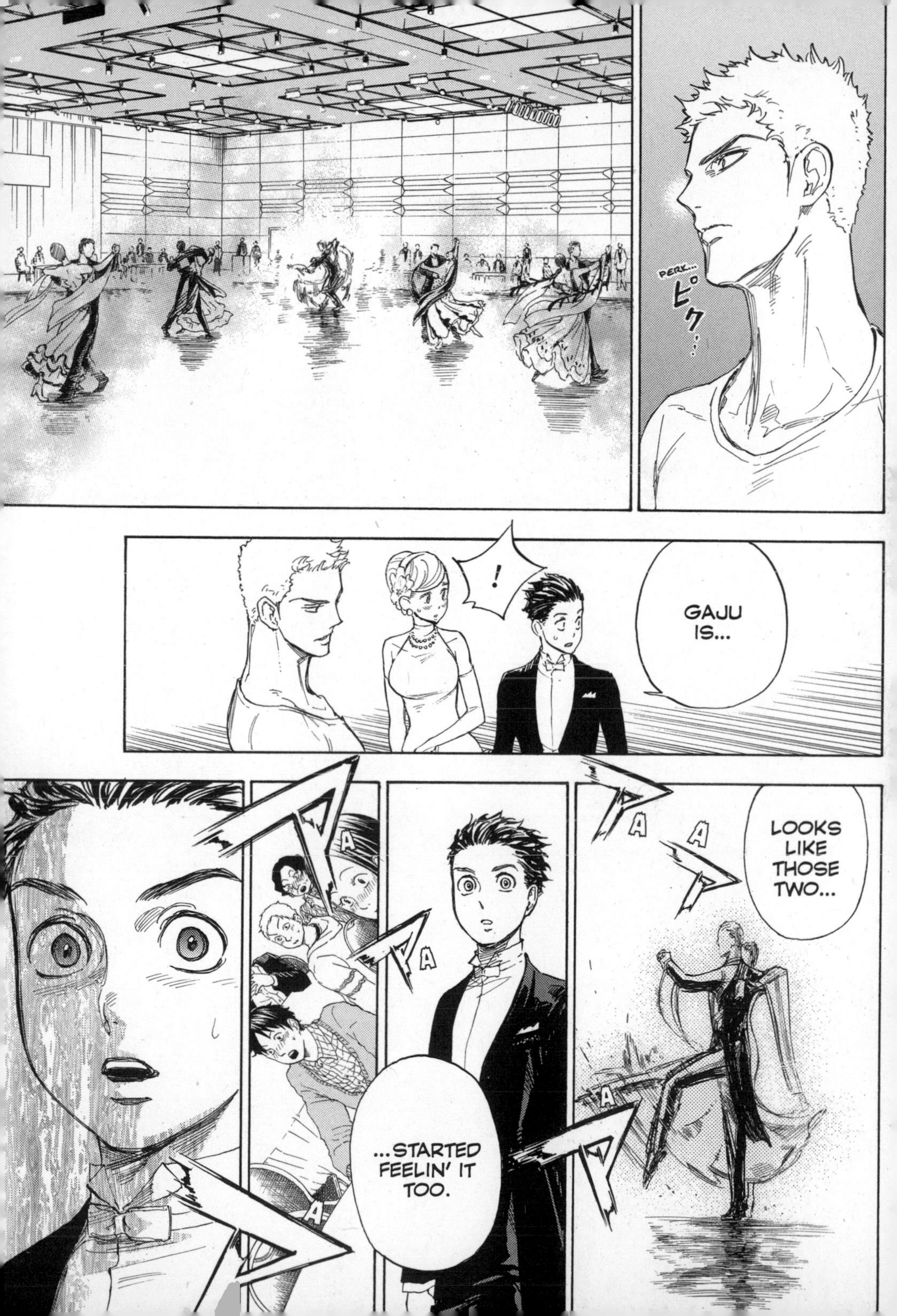
PERK...
ピク...
GAJU IS...
!
LOOKS LIKE THOSE TWO...
A
A
A
A
...STARTED FEELIN' IT TOO.
A
A

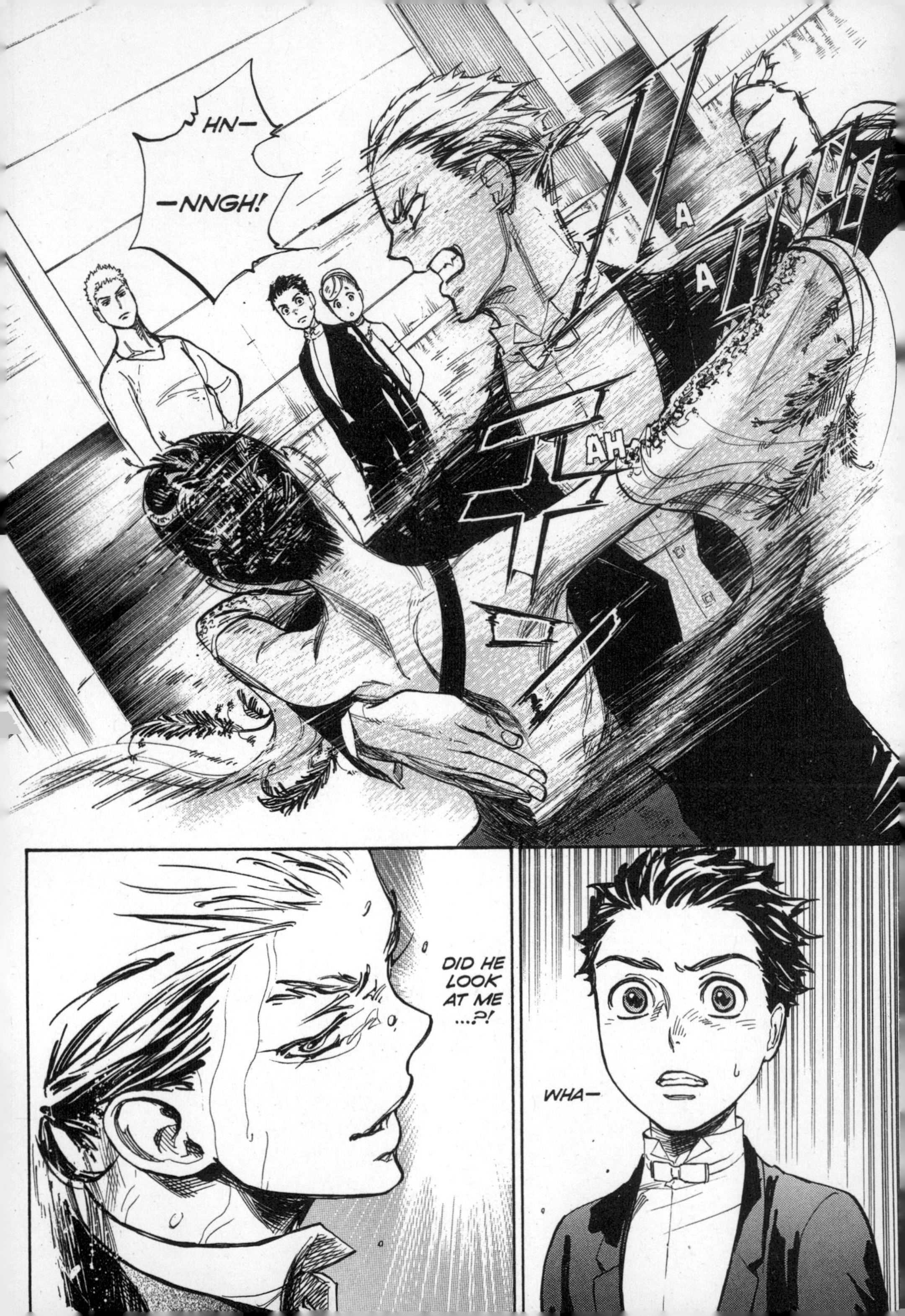
HN—
—NNGH!
A
A
AH
WHA—
DID HE LOOK AT ME ...?!

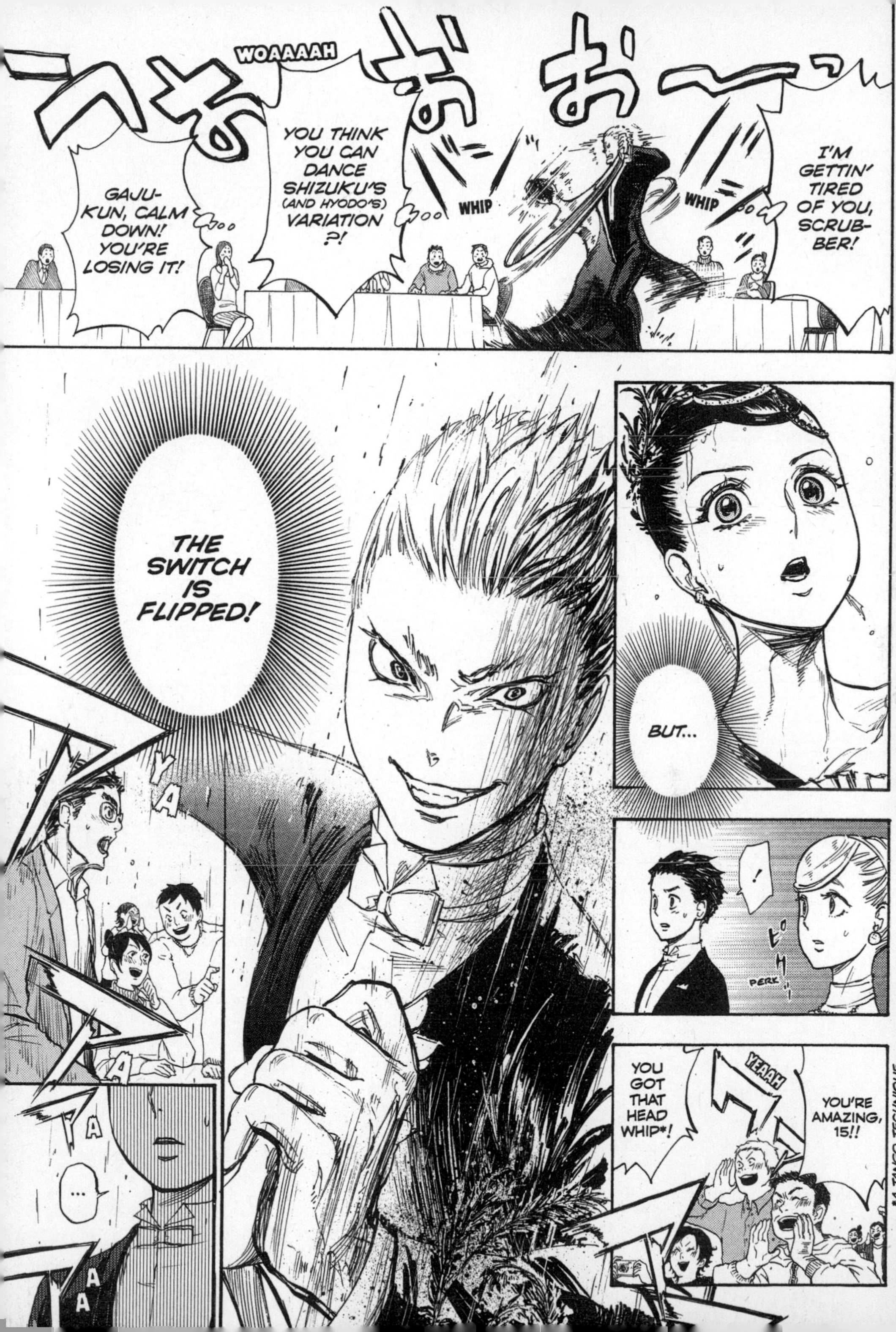
I'M GETTIN' TIRED OF YOU, SCRUBBER!
WHIP
WHIP
YOU THINK YOU CAN DANCE SHIZUKU'S (AND HYODO'S) VARIATION ?!
WOAAAAH
GAJU-KUN, CALM DOWN! YOU'RE LOSING IT!
BUT...
THE SWITCH IS FLIPPED!
YA
A
A
A
A
A
!
PERK
YEAAH
YOU'RE AMAZING, 15!!
YOU GOT THAT HEAD WHIP*!
...

*A TANGO TECHNIQUE

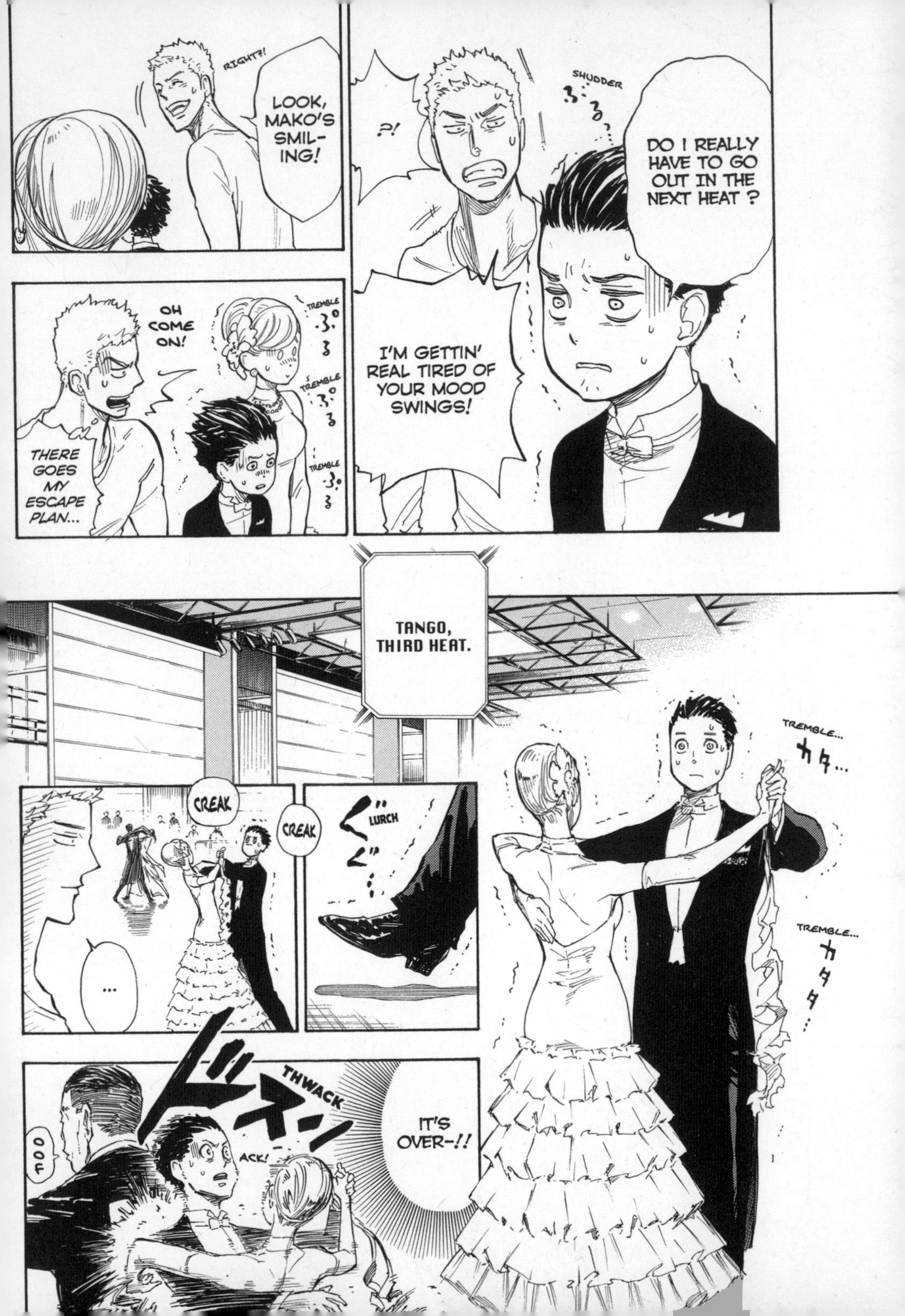
SHUDDER
DO I REALLY HAVE TO GO OUT IN THE NEXT HEAT ?
?!
I'M GETTIN' REAL TIRED OF YOUR MOOD SWINGS!
RIGHT?!
LOOK, MAKO'S SMIL-ING!
TREMBLE
TREMBLE
TREMBLE
OH COME ON!
THERE GOES MY ESCAPE PLAN...
TANGO, THIRD HEAT.
TREMBLE...
TREMBLE...
LURCH
CREAK
CREAK
...
IT'S OVER-!!
THWACK
ACK!
OOF

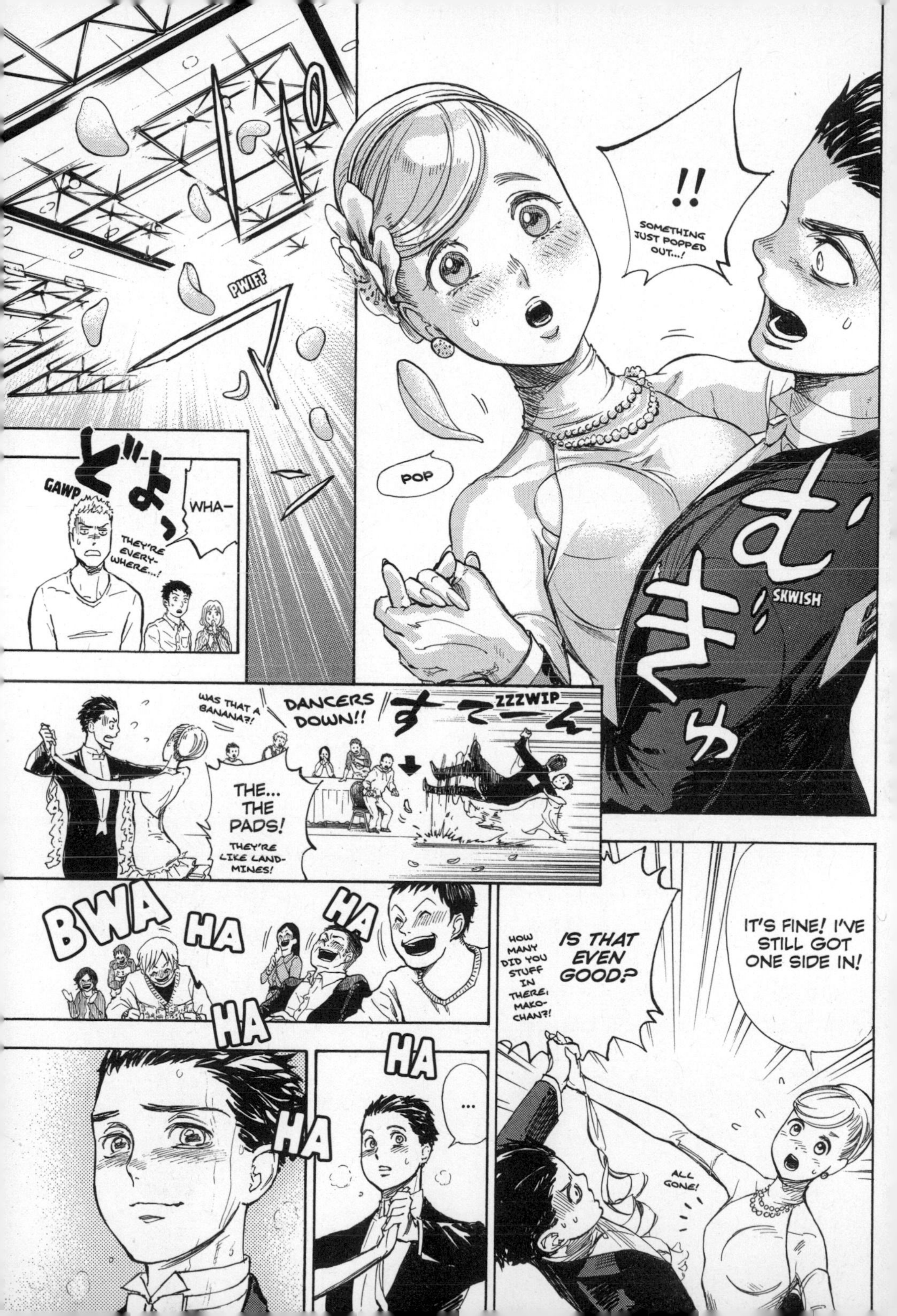
!!
SOMETHING JUST POPPED OUT...!
POP
むぎゅ
SKWISH
PWIFF
どよっ
GAWP
WHA-
THEY'RE EVERYWHERE...!
すてーん
ZZZWIP
DANCERS DOWN!!
WAS THAT A BANANA?!
THE... THE PADS!
THEY'RE LIKE LANDMINES!
IT'S FINE! I'VE STILL GOT ONE SIDE IN!
IS THAT EVEN GOOD?
HOW MANY DID YOU STUFF IN THERE, MAKO-CHAN?!
ALL GONE!
BWA HA HA HA
HA
HA
...
HA

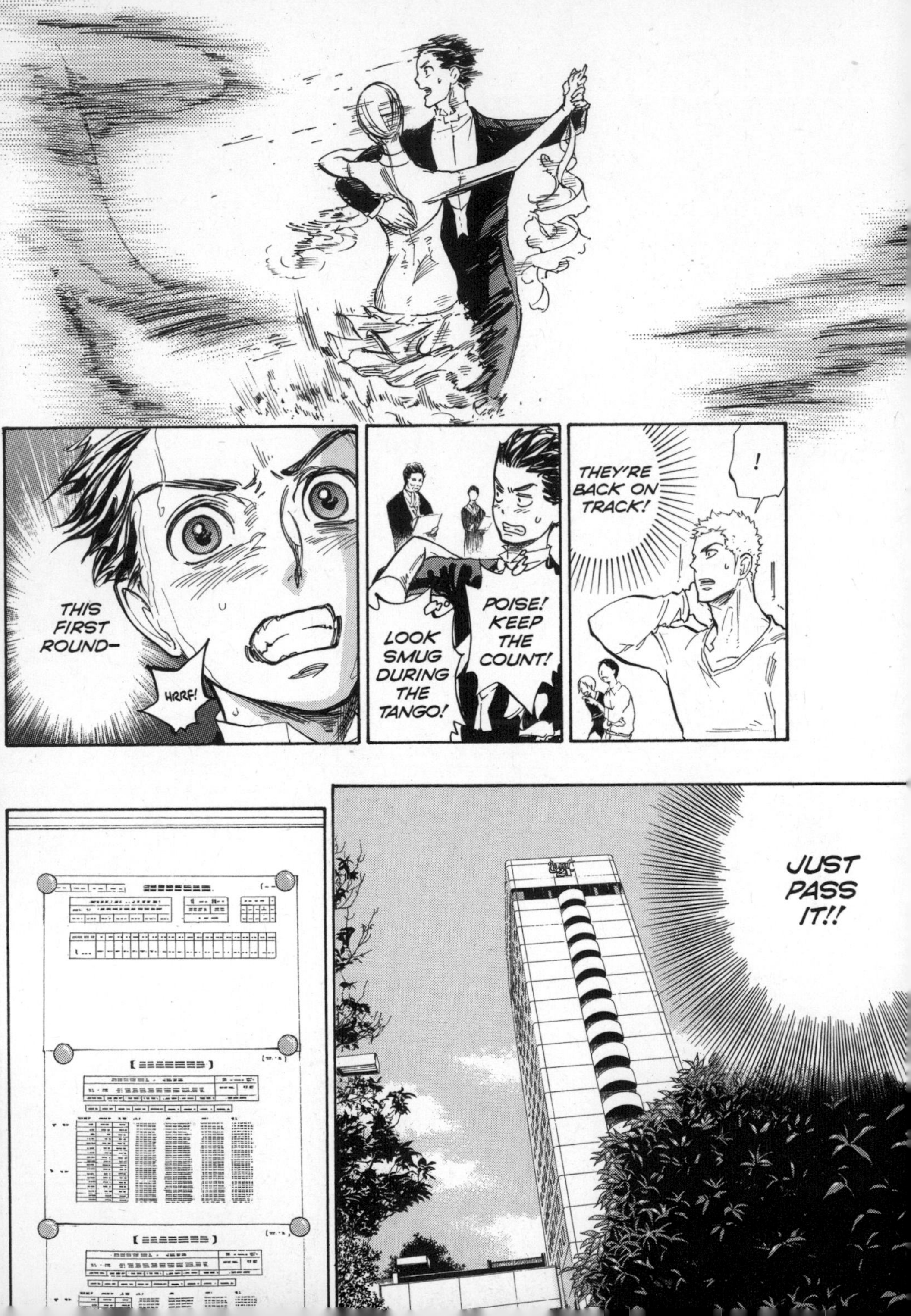
!
THEY'RE BACK ON TRACK!
POISE! KEEP THE COUNT!
LOOK SMUG DURING THE TANGO!
THIS FIRST ROUND—
HRRF!
JUST PASS IT!!

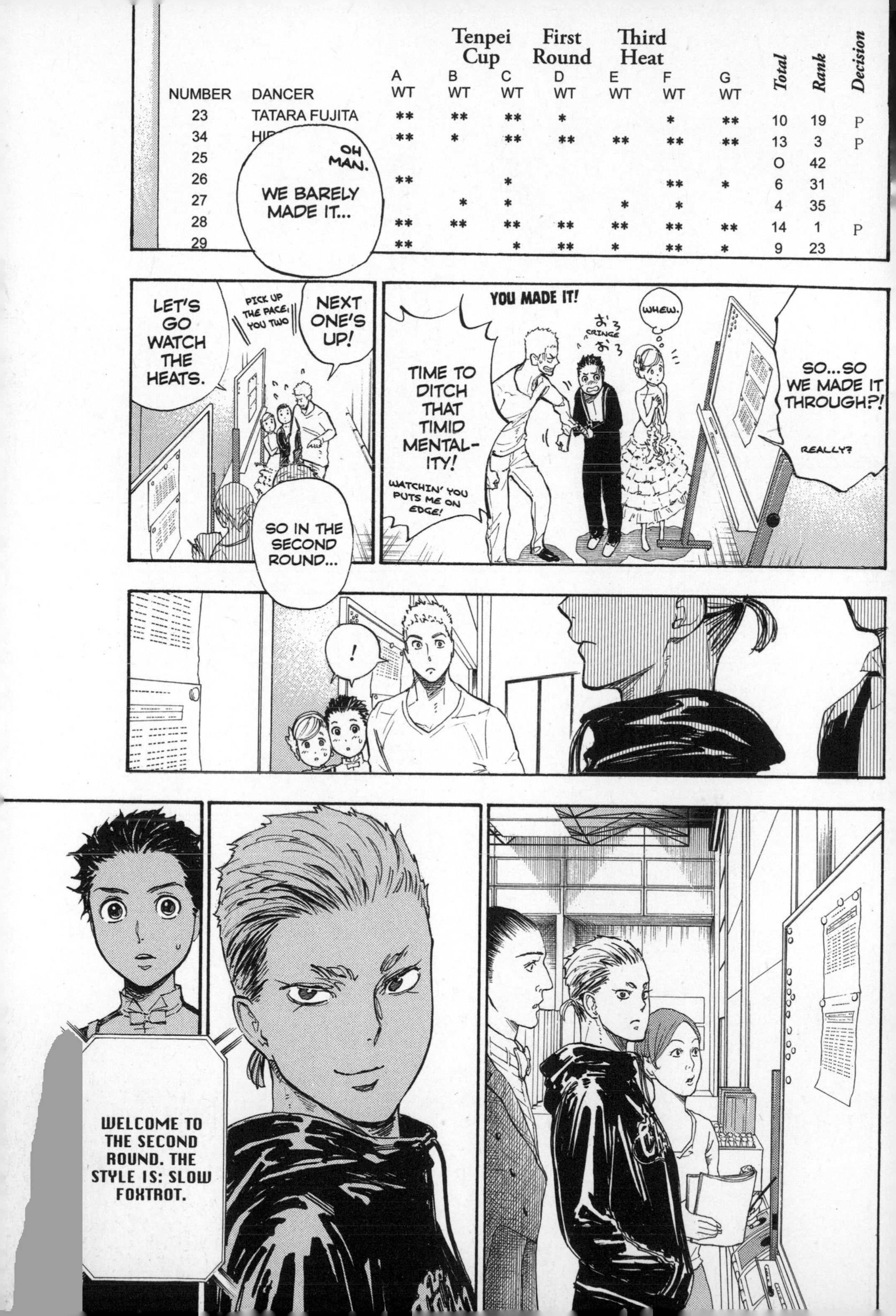

Tenpei Cup First Round Third Heat

NUMBER	DANCER	A WT	B WT	C WT	D WT	E WT	F WT	G WT	Total	Rank	Decision
23	TATARA FUJITA	**	**	**	*		*	**	10	19	P
34	HIR	**	*	**	**	**	**	**	13	3	P
25									O	42	
26		**		*			**	*	6	31	
27			*	*		*	*		4	35	
28		**	**	**	**	**	**	**	14	1	P
29		**		*	**	*	**	*	9	23	

OH MAN.
WE BARELY MADE IT...
SO...SO WE MADE IT THROUGH?!
REALLY?
WHEW.
YOU MADE IT!
おろ CRINGE おろ
TIME TO DITCH THAT TIMID MENTALITY!
WATCHIN' YOU PUTS ME ON EDGE!
NEXT ONE'S UP!
PICK UP THE PACE, YOU TWO
LET'S GO WATCH THE HEATS.
SO IN THE SECOND ROUND...
!
WELCOME TO THE SECOND ROUND. THE STYLE IS: SLOW FOXTROT.

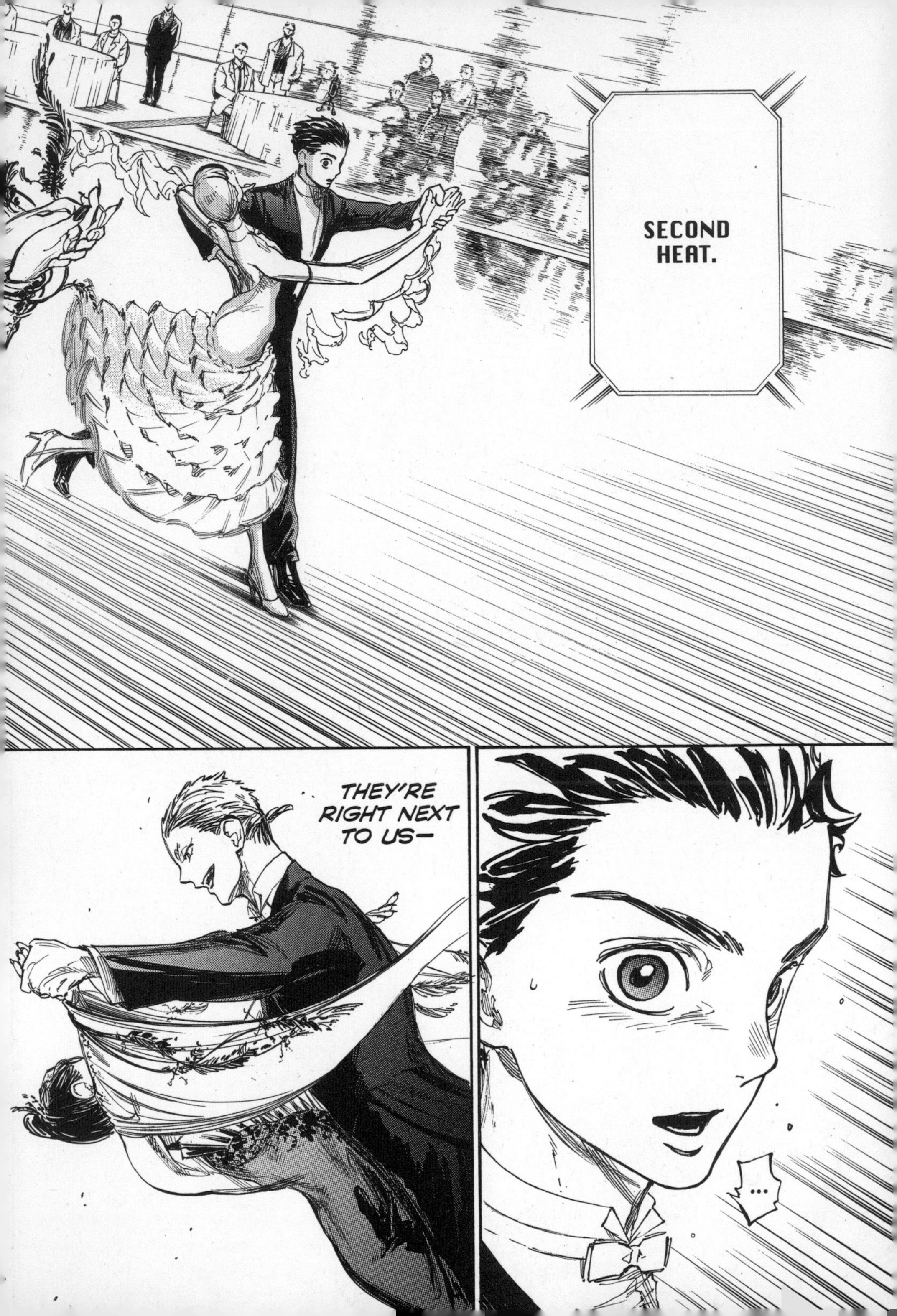
SECOND HEAT.
...
THEY'RE RIGHT NEXT TO US—

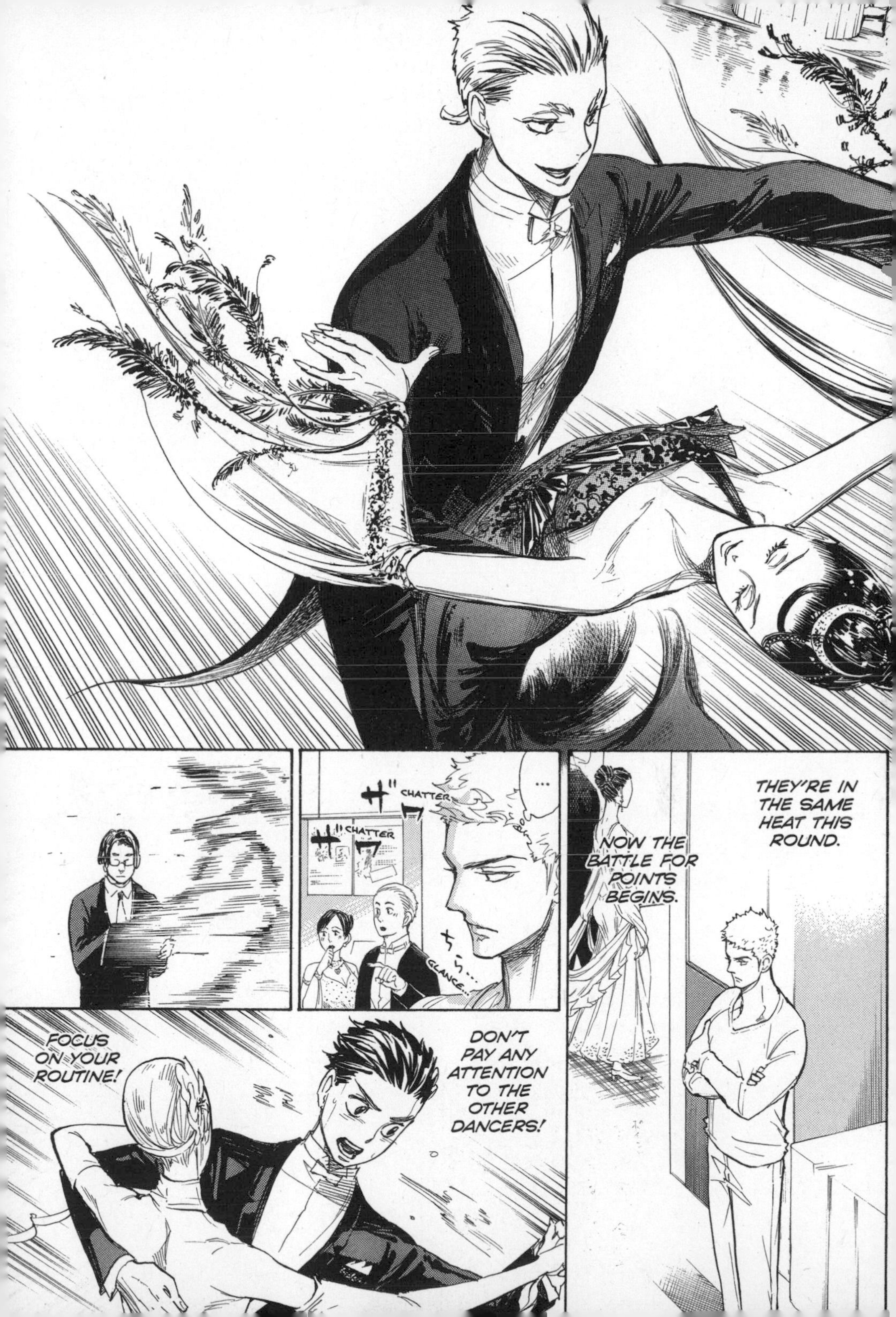
THEY'RE IN THE SAME HEAT THIS ROUND.
NOW THE BATTLE FOR POINTS BEGINS.
...
CHATTER
CHATTER
GLANCE...
DON'T PAY ANY ATTENTION TO THE OTHER DANCERS!
FOCUS ON YOUR ROUTINE!

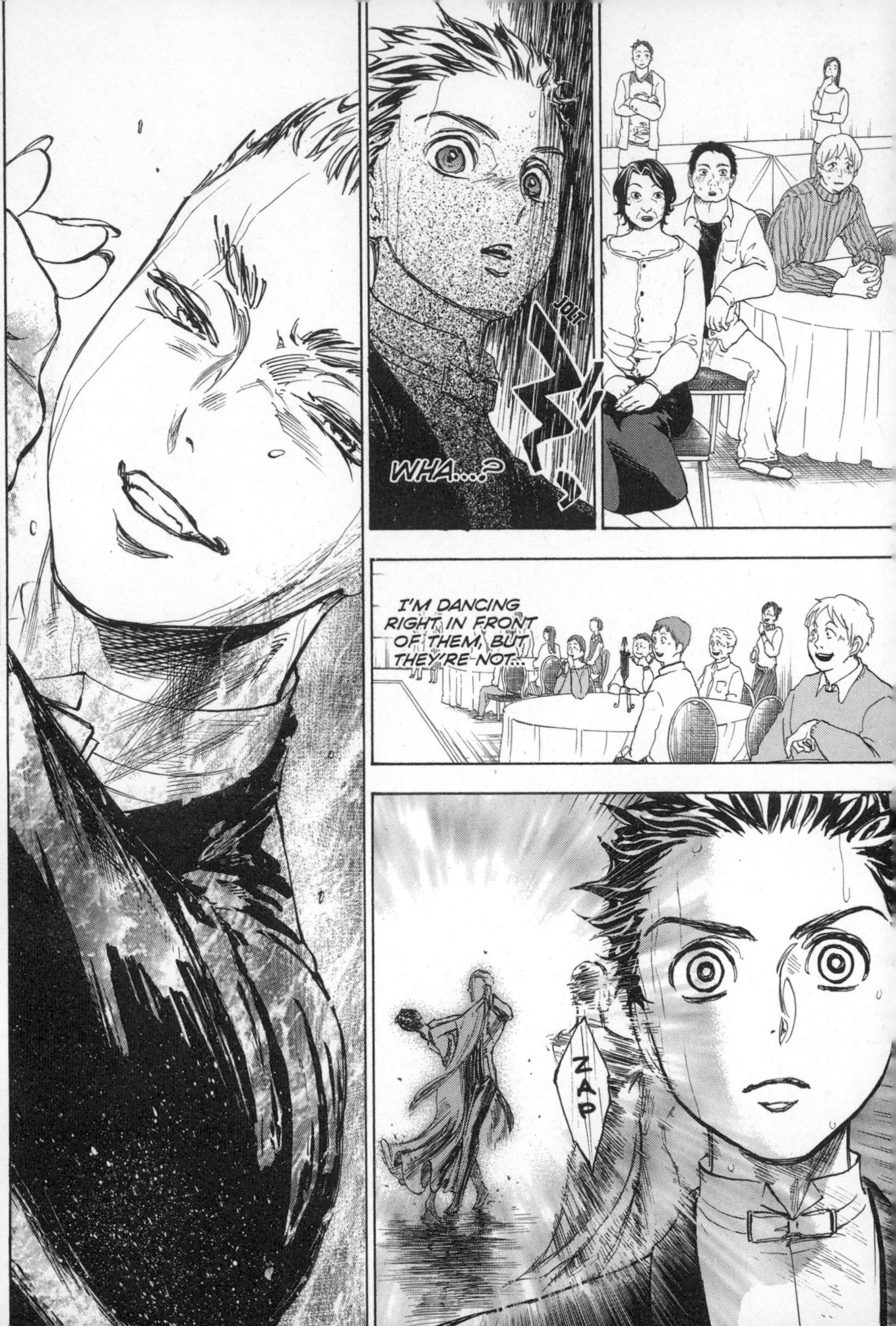
JOLT
WHA...?
I'M DANCING RIGHT IN FRONT OF THEM, BUT THEY'RE NOT...
ZAP

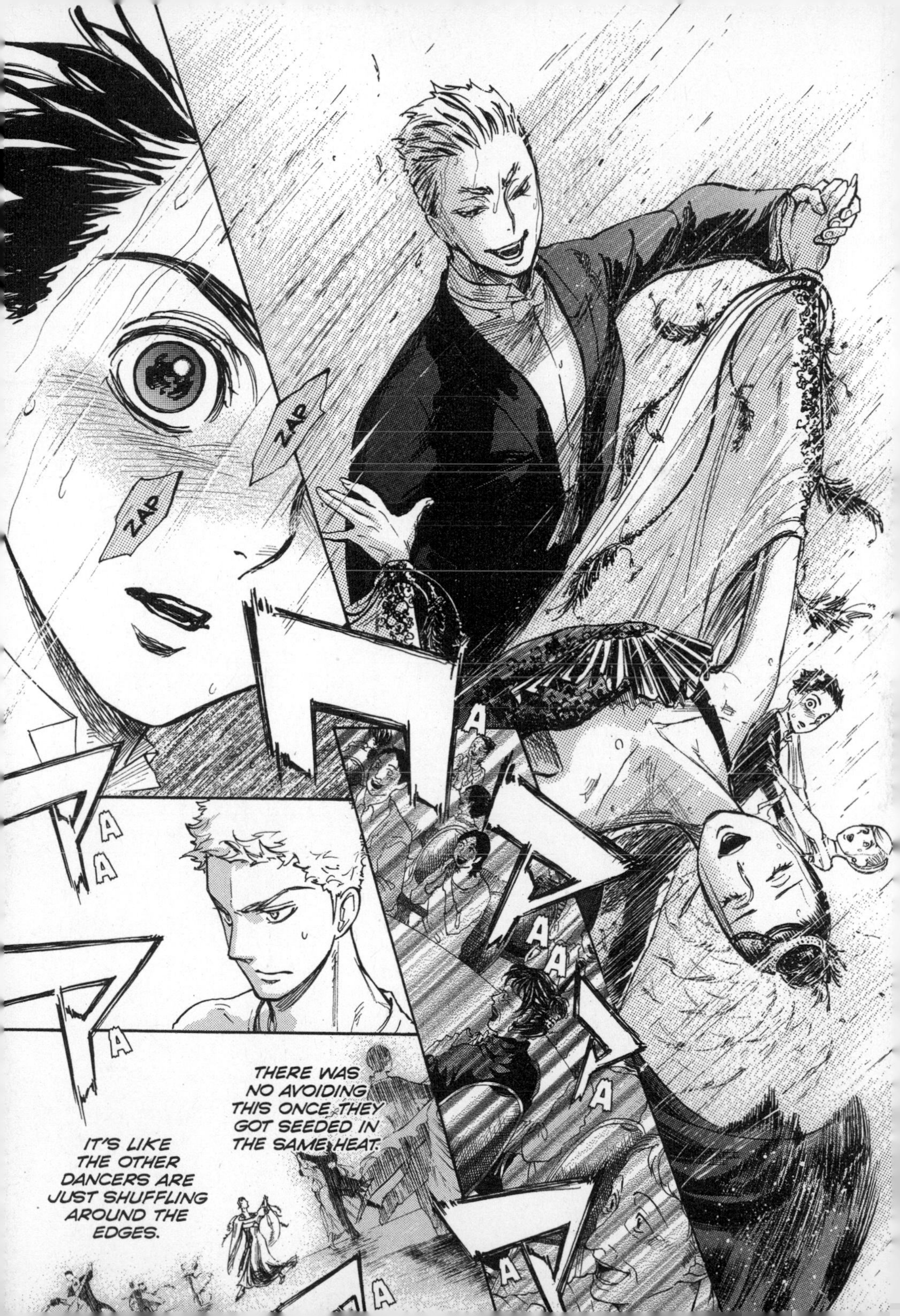
ZAP
ZAP
A
A
A
A
A
A
A
A
A
A
THERE WAS NO AVOIDING THIS ONCE THEY GOT SEEDED IN THE SAME HEAT.
IT'S LIKE THE OTHER DANCERS ARE JUST SHUFFLING AROUND THE EDGES.

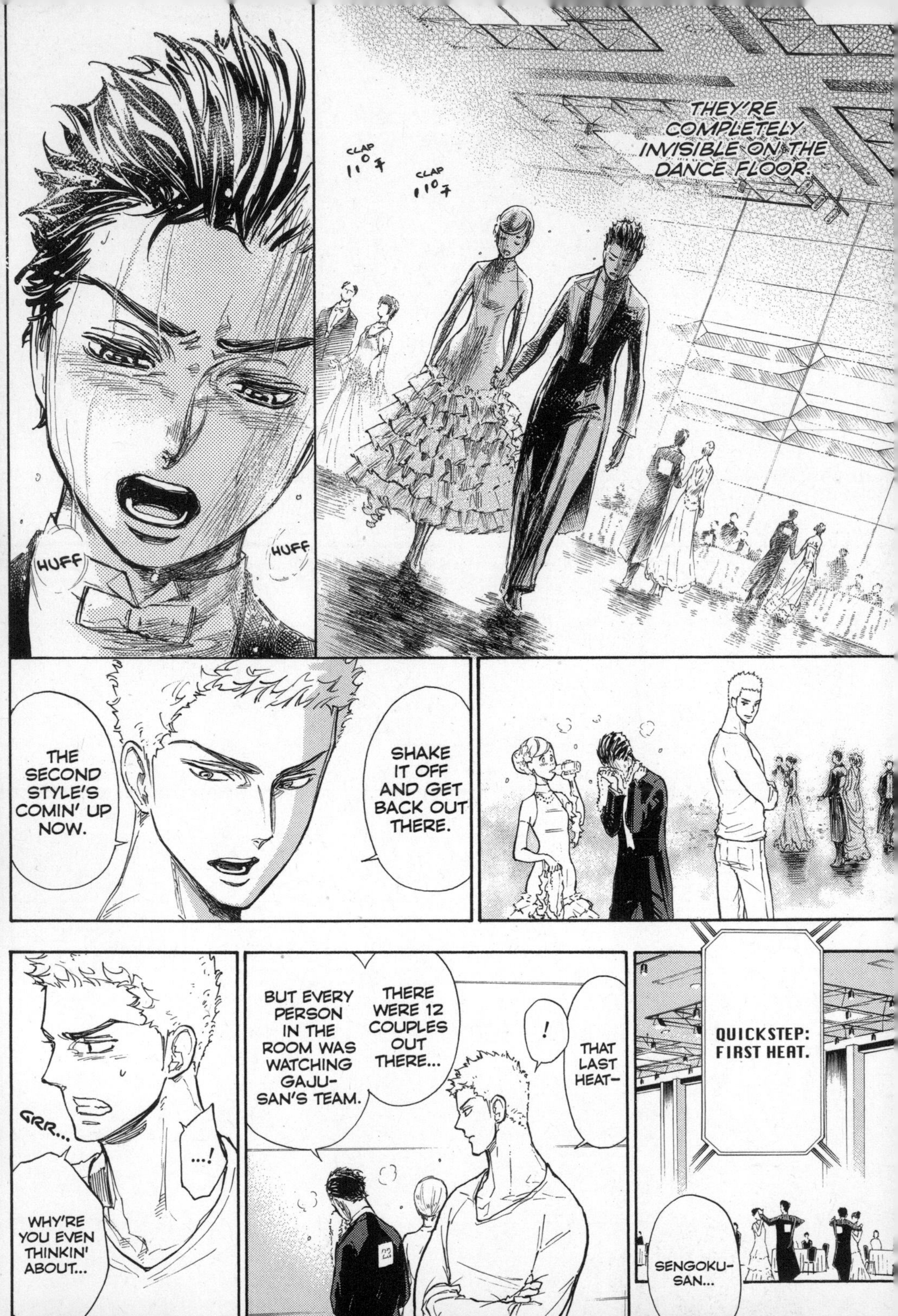
THEY'RE COMPLETELY INVISIBLE ON THE DANCE FLOOR.
CLAP
CLAP
HUFF
HUFF
SHAKE IT OFF AND GET BACK OUT THERE.
THE SECOND STYLE'S COMIN' UP NOW.
QUICKSTEP: FIRST HEAT.
SENGOKU-SAN...
!
THAT LAST HEAT–
THERE WERE 12 COUPLES OUT THERE...
BUT EVERY PERSON IN THE ROOM WAS WATCHING GAJU-SAN'S TEAM.
GRR...
...!
WHY'RE YOU EVEN THINKIN' ABOUT...

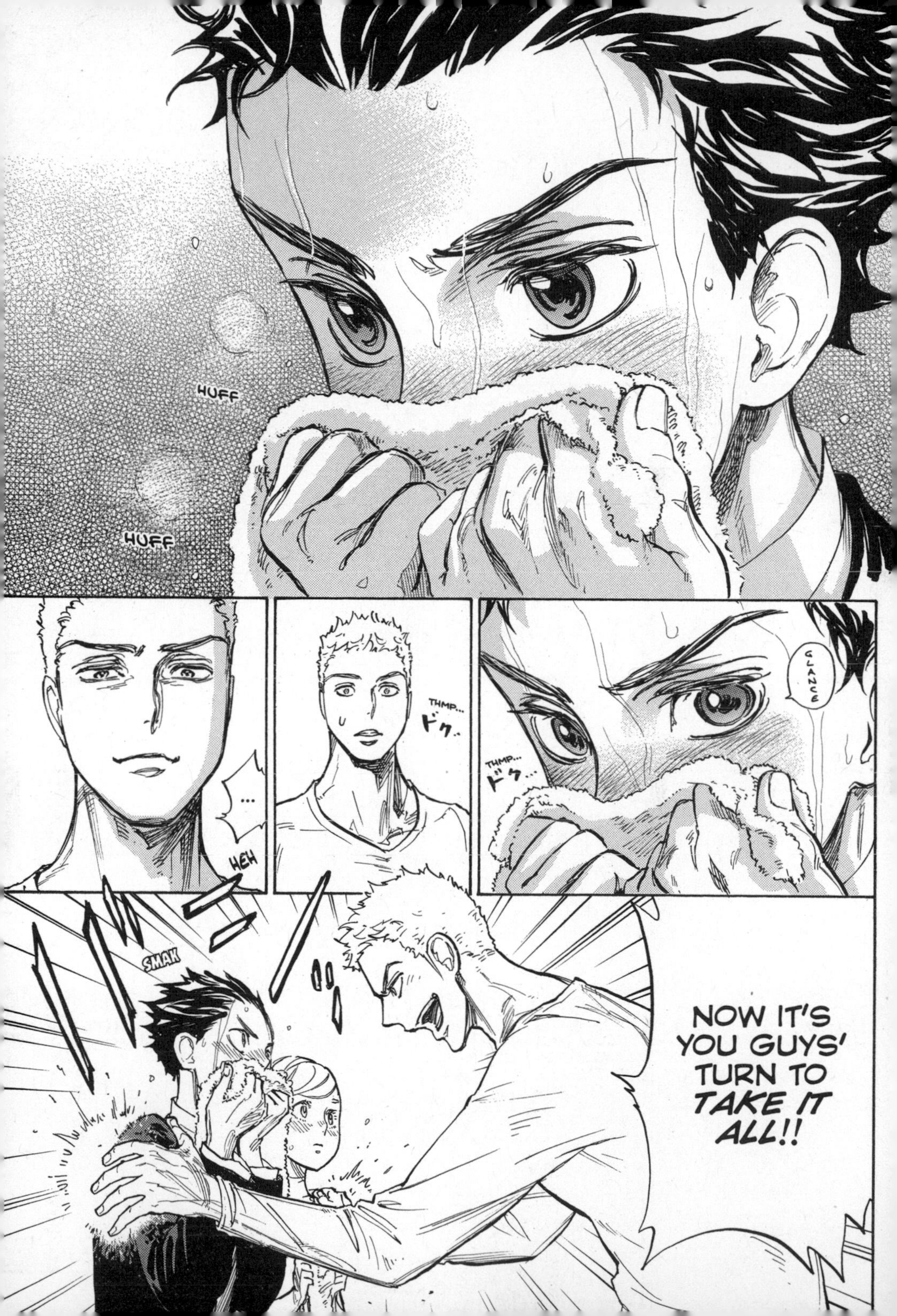
HUFF
HUFF
GLANCE
THMP...
ドク...
THMP...
ドク...
...
HEH
SMAK
NOW IT'S YOU GUYS' TURN TO *TAKE IT ALL!!*

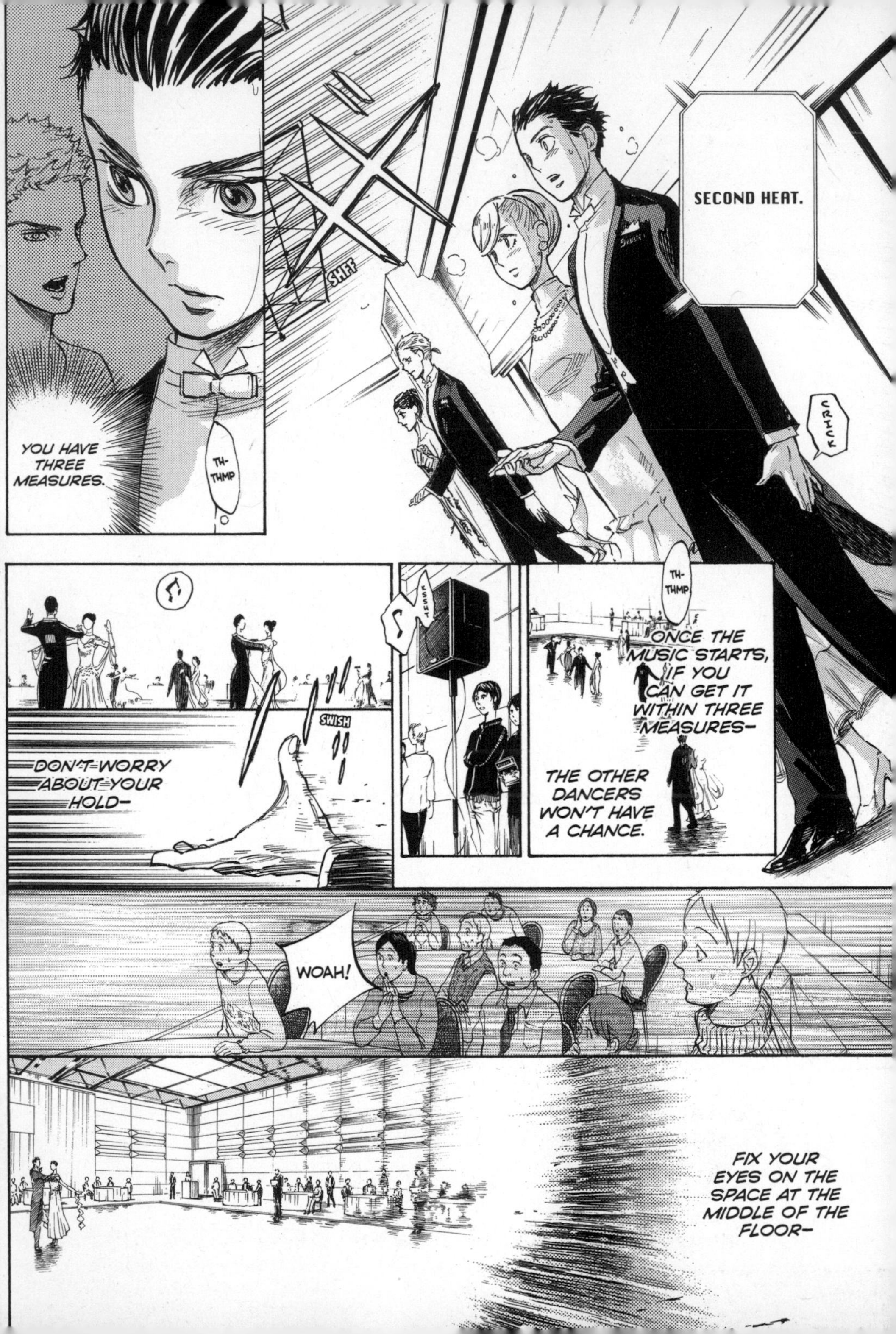
SECOND HEAT.
CRICK
SHFF
YOU HAVE THREE MEASURES.
TH-THMP
TH-THMP
ONCE THE MUSIC STARTS, IF YOU CAN GET IT WITHIN THREE MEASURES—
THE OTHER DANCERS WON'T HAVE A CHANCE.
KSSHT
SWISH
DON'T WORRY ABOUT YOUR HOLD—
WOAH!
FIX YOUR EYES ON THE SPACE AT THE MIDDLE OF THE FLOOR—

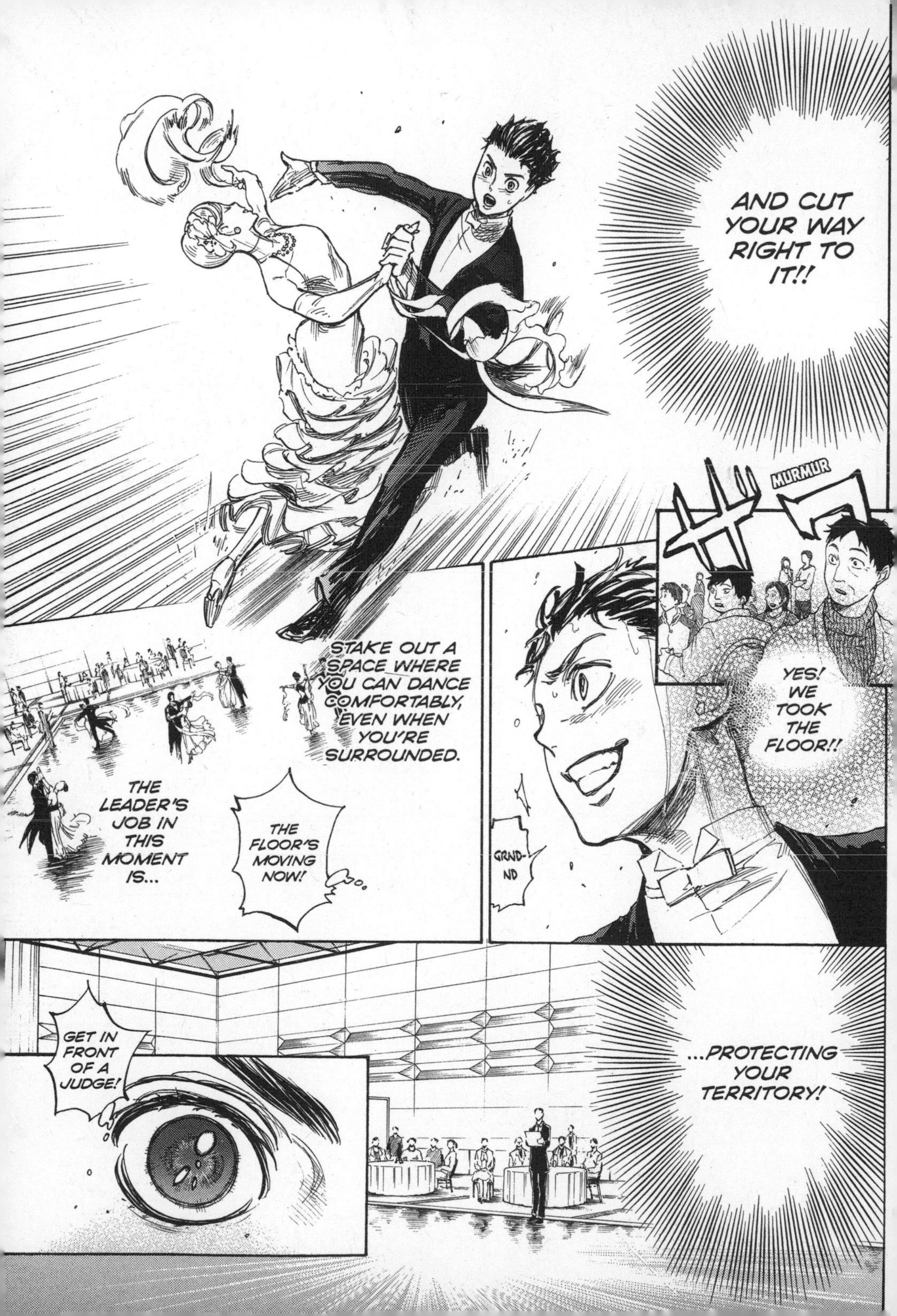
AND CUT YOUR WAY RIGHT TO IT!!
MURMUR
YES! WE TOOK THE FLOOR!!
GRND-ND
STAKE OUT A SPACE WHERE YOU CAN DANCE COMFORTABLY, EVEN WHEN YOU'RE SURROUNDED.
THE FLOOR'S MOVING NOW!
THE LEADER'S JOB IN THIS MOMENT IS...
...PROTECTING YOUR TERRITORY!
GET IN FRONT OF A JUDGE!

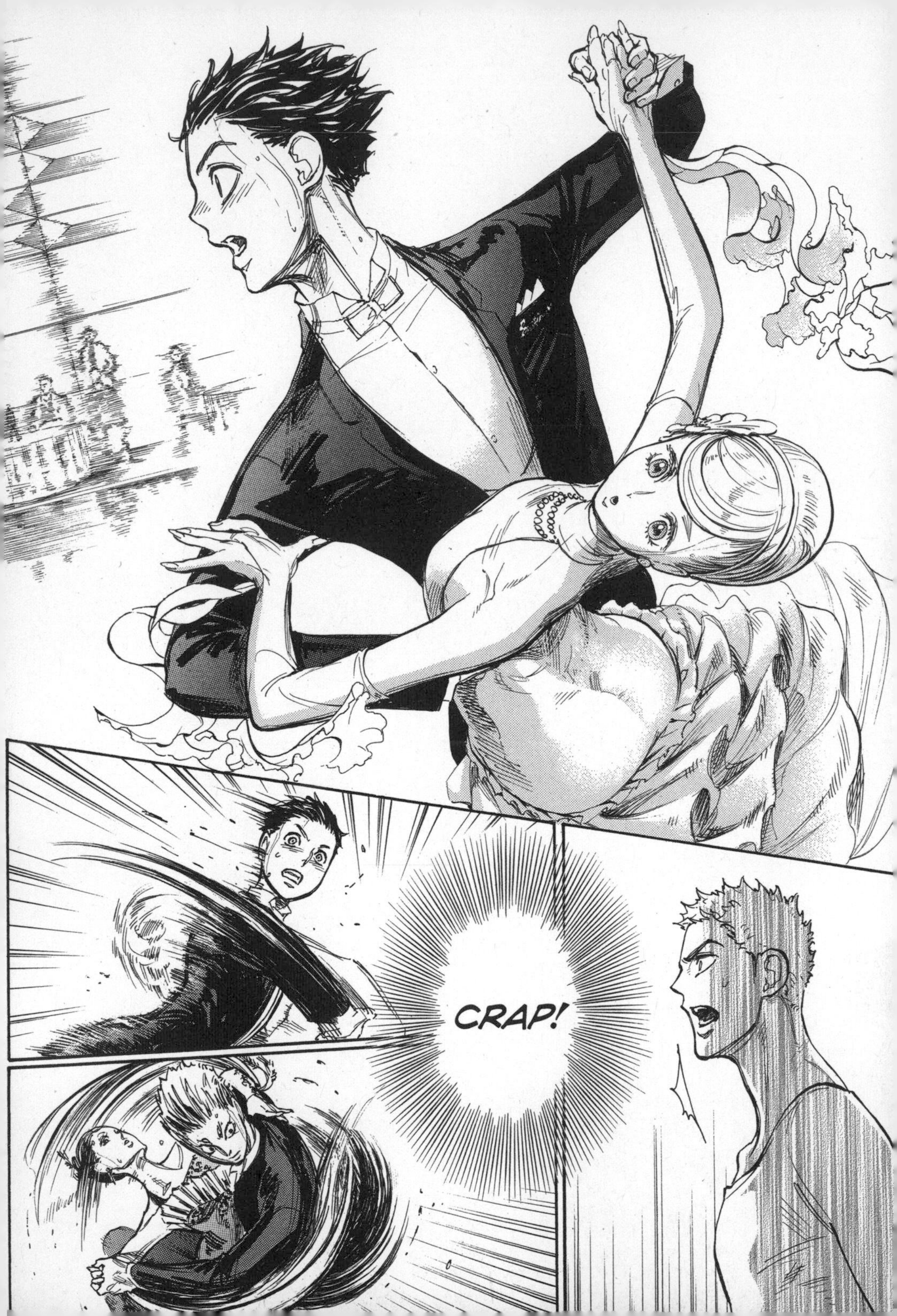
CRAP!

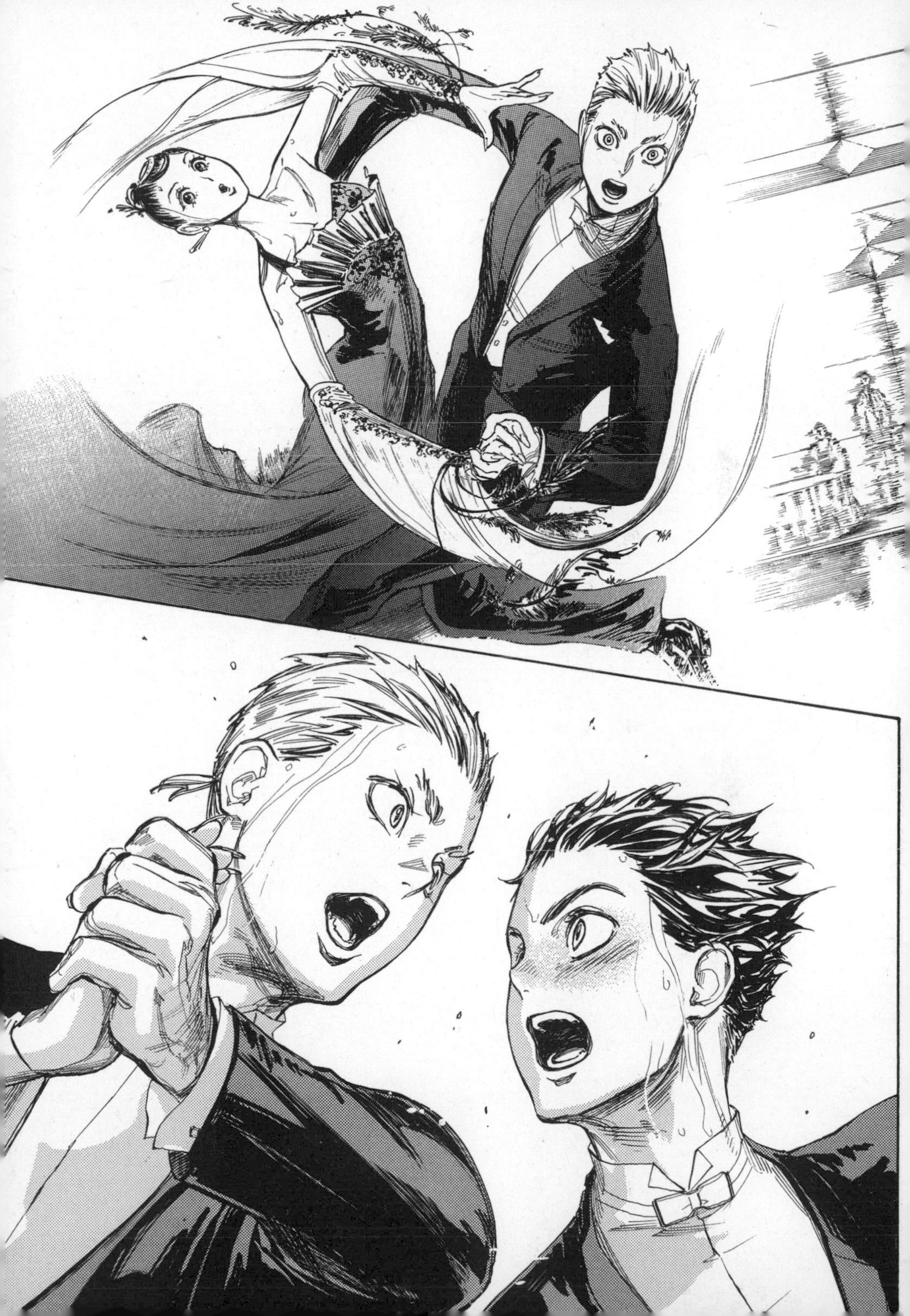

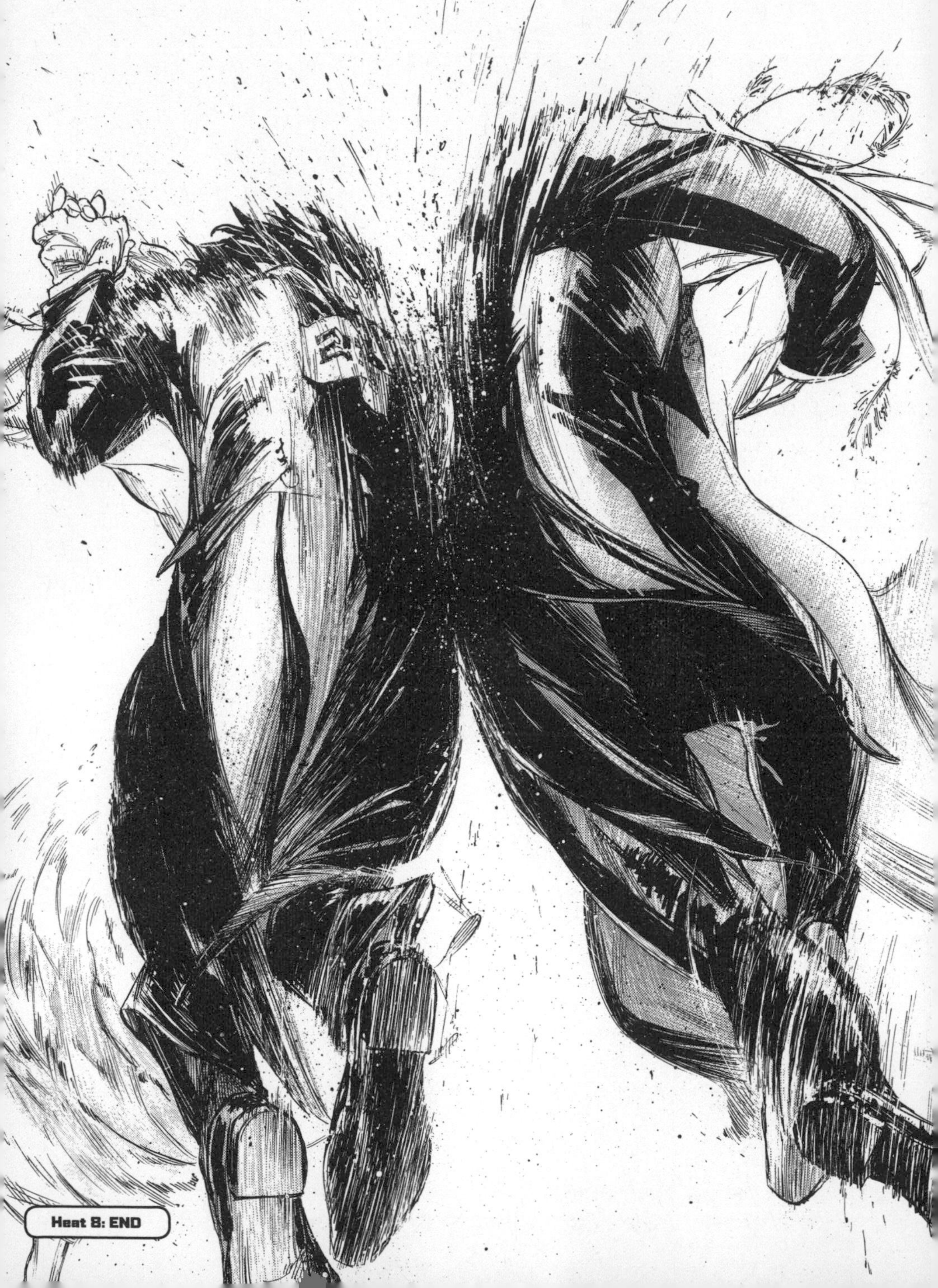
Heat 8: END

WELCOME TO THE BALLROOM

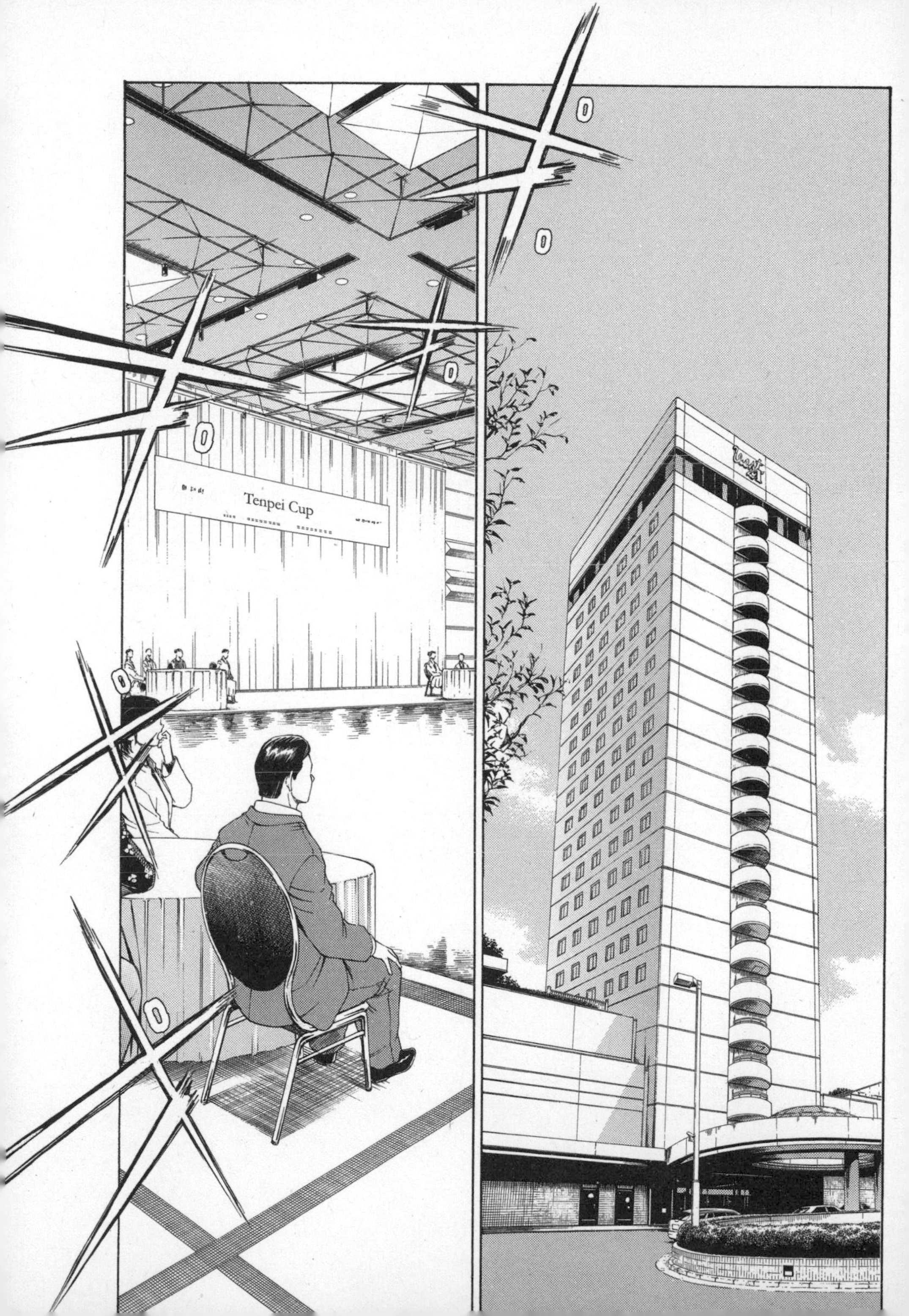
Tenpei Cup

Heat 9: Reality

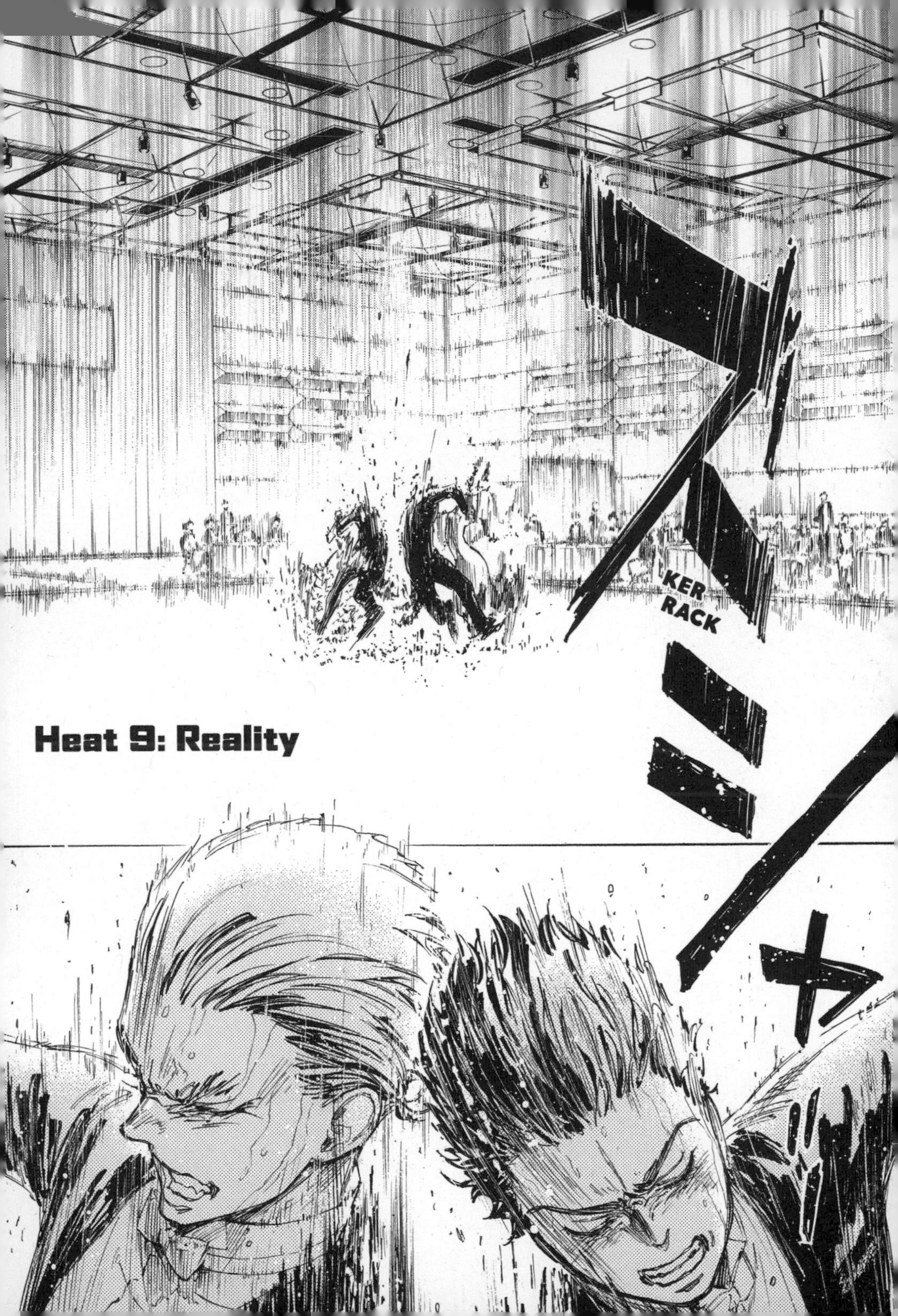
KER
RACK

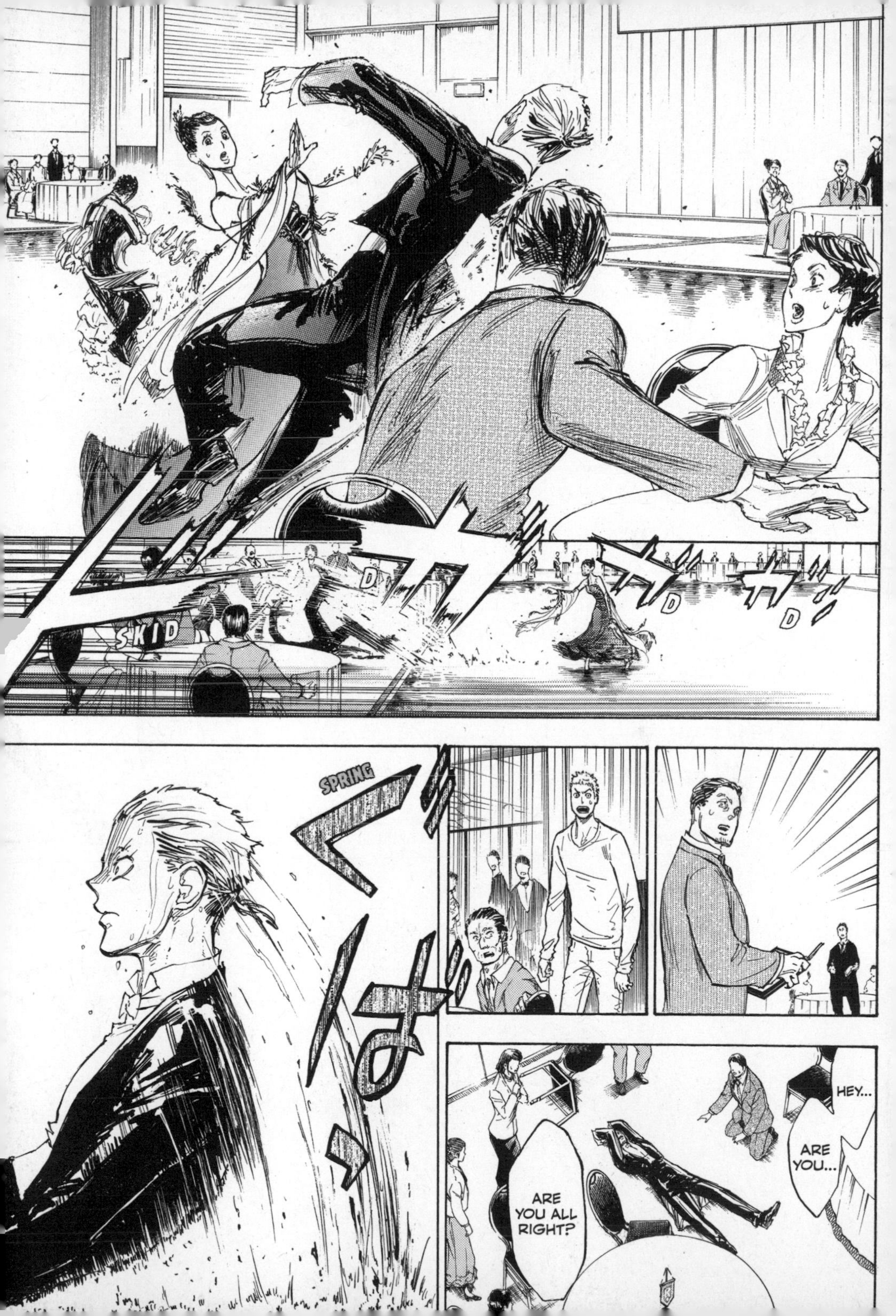
D
D
D
SKID
HEY...
ARE YOU...
ARE YOU ALL RIGHT?
SPRING

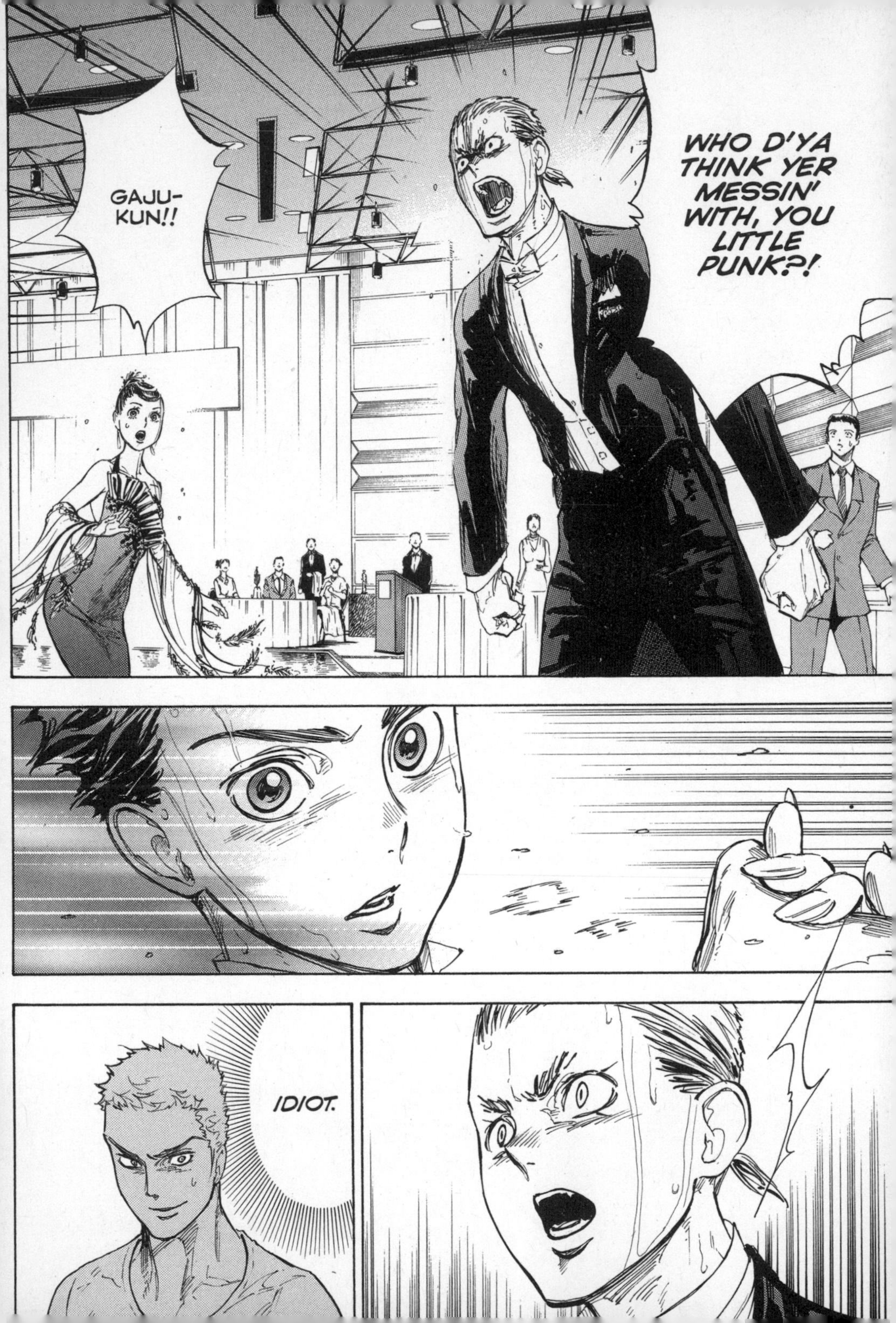
WHO D'YA THINK YER MESSIN' WITH, YOU LITTLE PUNK?!
GAJU-KUN!!
IDIOT.

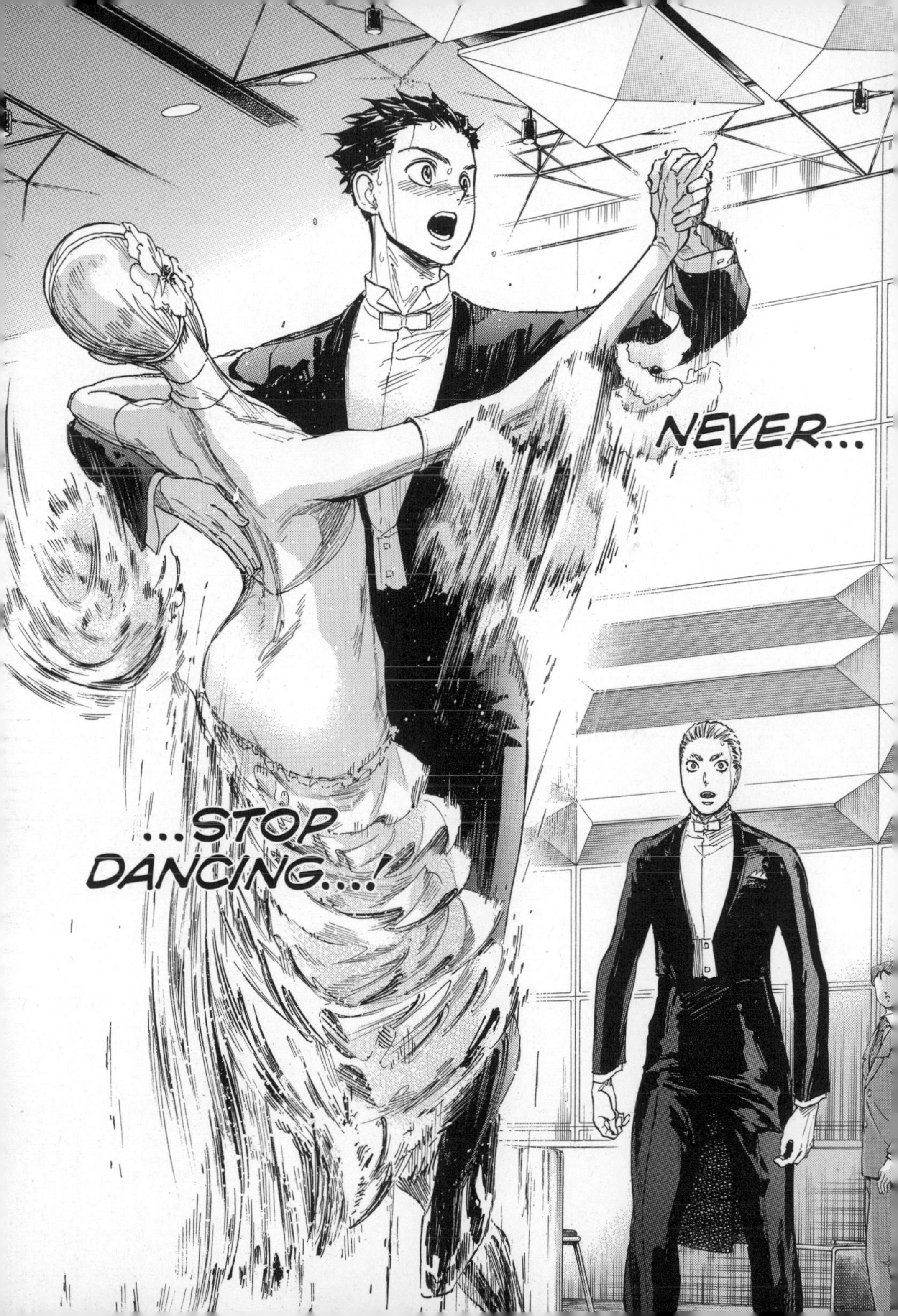
NEVER...
...STOP DANCING...!

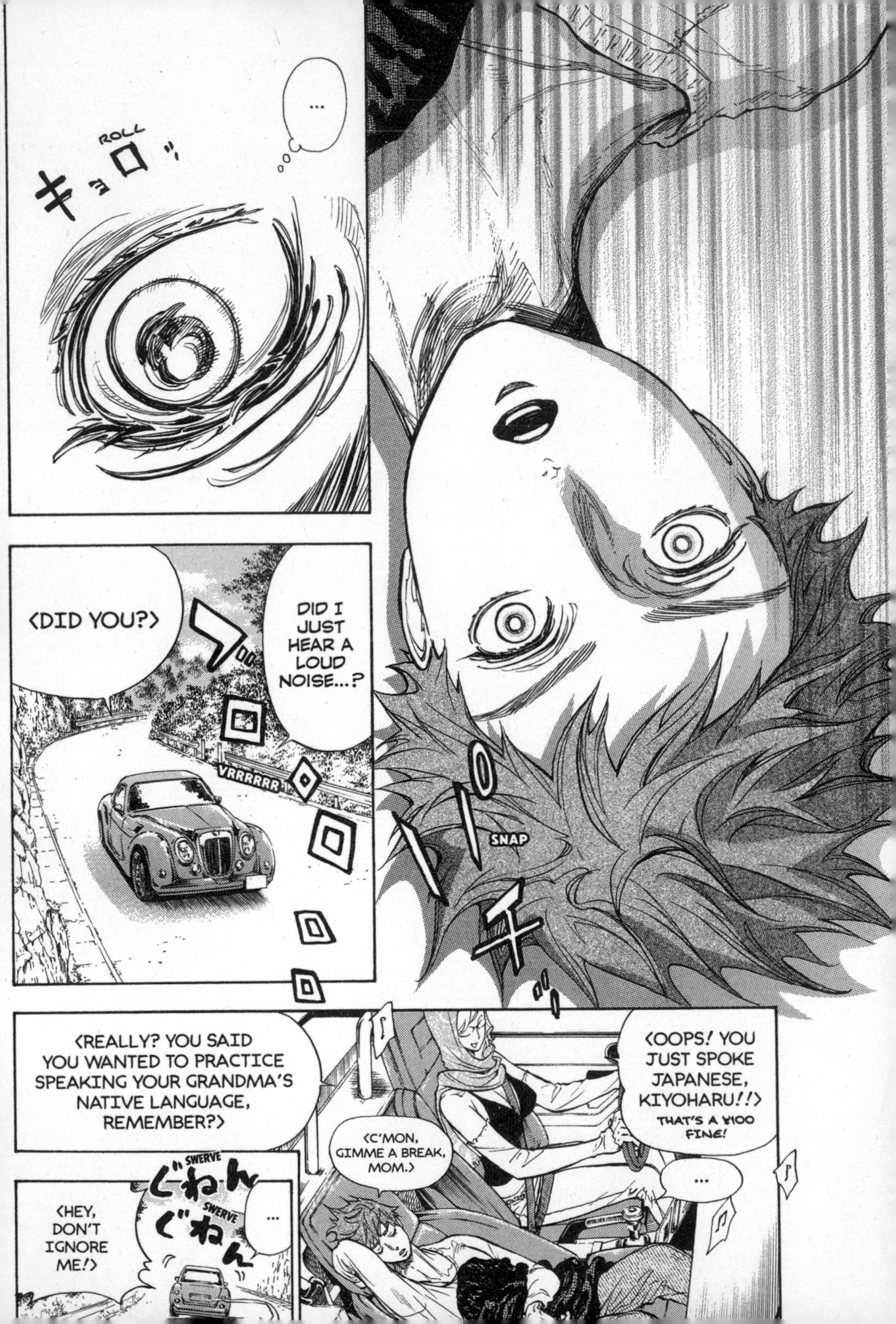
SNAP
ROLL
キョロッ
...
DID I JUST HEAR A LOUD NOISE...?
‹DID YOU?›
VRRRRRR
‹OOPS! YOU JUST SPOKE JAPANESE, KIYOHARU!!›
THAT'S A ¥100 FINE!
‹REALLY? YOU SAID YOU WANTED TO PRACTICE SPEAKING YOUR GRANDMA'S NATIVE LANGUAGE, REMEMBER?›
‹C'MON, GIMME A BREAK, MOM.›
...
...
SWERVE
ぐわん
SWERVE
ぐわん
‹HEY, DON'T IGNORE ME!›

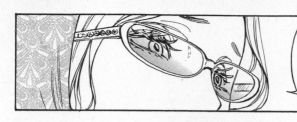

<YOU KNOW...I'M REALLY SORRY I'M ALWAYS SO BUSY WITH WORK AND LEAVING YOU HOME ALONE. ALTHOUGH YOU DO LIKE BEING ALONE.>

<IT'S NICE TO BE ABLE TO TEASE EACH OTHER WHEN WE DO SPEND TIME TOGETHER.>

...

<AND TENPEI-SENSEI DID INVITE US OUT TODAY. THE HOT SPRING WILL BE GOOD FOR YOUR LEG, TOO...>

HE FELL ASLEEP...

OH...

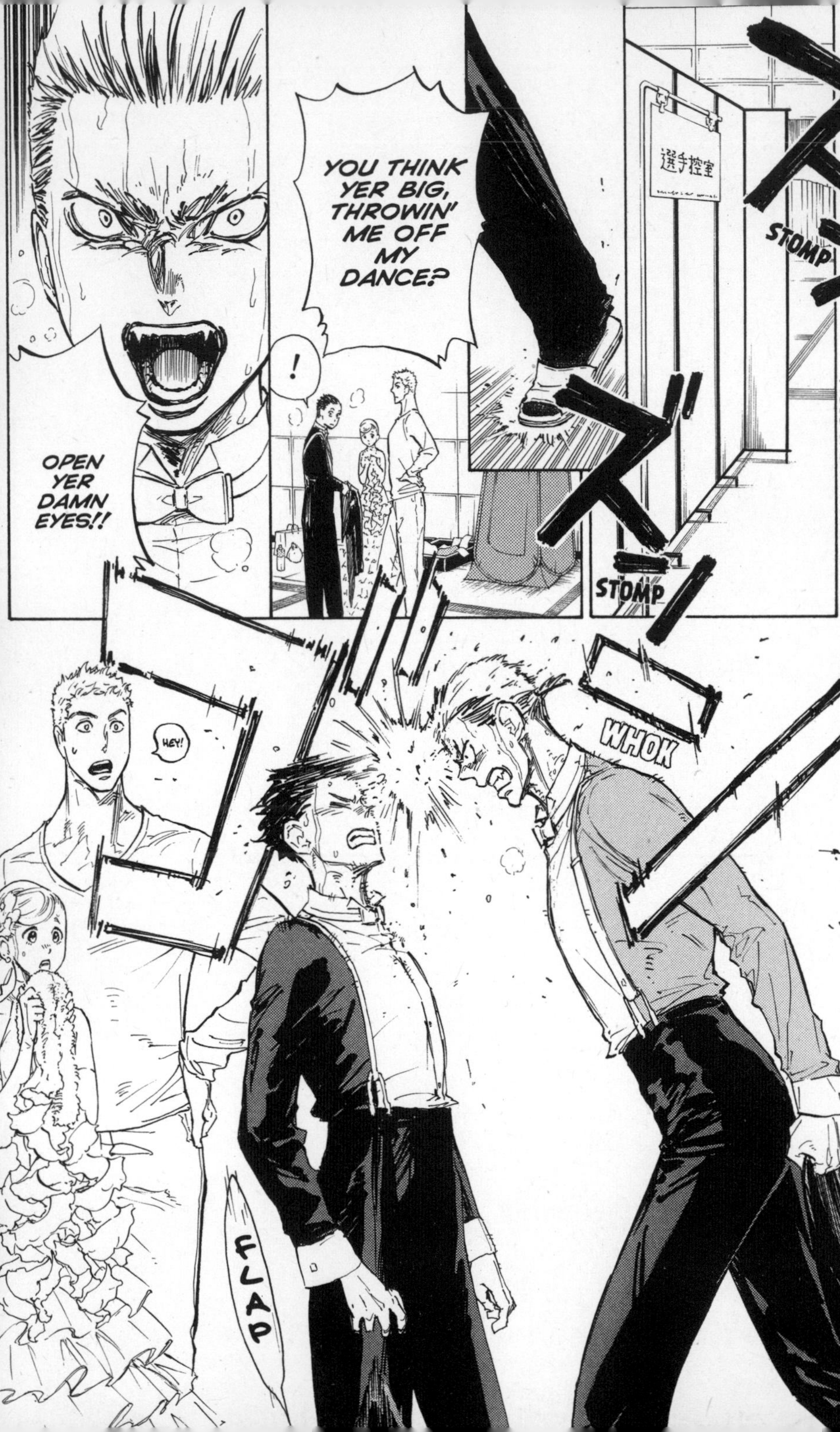
選手控室
STOMP
STOMP
YOU THINK YER BIG, THROWIN' ME OFF MY DANCE?
!
OPEN YER DAMN EYES!!
WHOK
HEY!
FLAP
SIGN: DANCERS WAITING ROOM

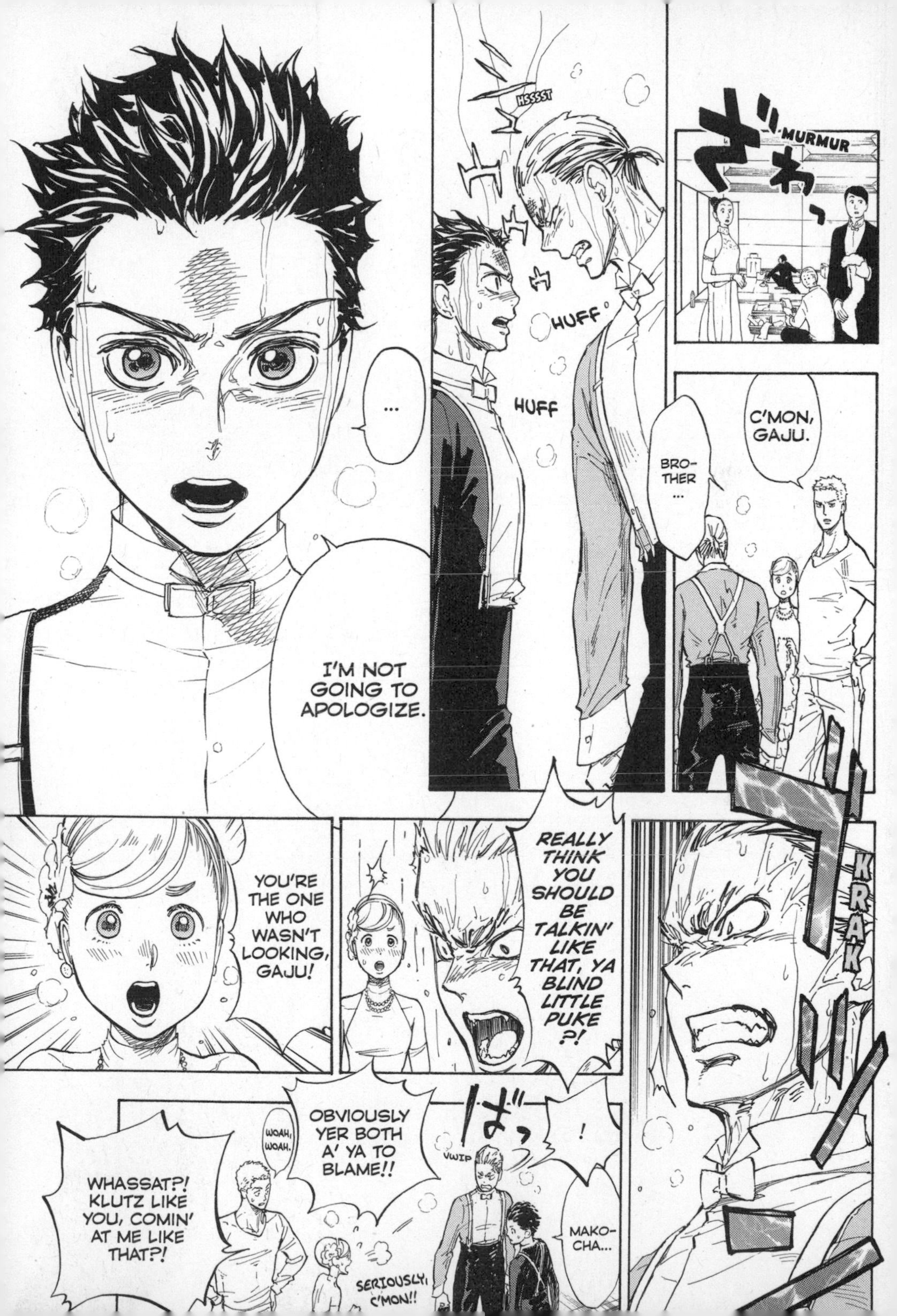
ざわっ
MURMUR
C'MON, GAJU.
BRO-THER ...
HSSSST
HUFF
HUFF
...
I'M NOT GOING TO APOLOGIZE.
KRAK
REALLY THINK YOU SHOULD BE TALKIN' LIKE THAT, YA BLIND LITTLE PUKE ?!
YOU'RE THE ONE WHO WASN'T LOOKING, GAJU!
!
ばっ
VWIP
MAKO-CHA...
OBVIOUSLY YER BOTH A' YA TO BLAME!!
WOAH, WOAH.
WHASSAT?! KLUTZ LIKE YOU, COMIN' AT ME LIKE THAT?!
SERIOUSLY, C'MON!!

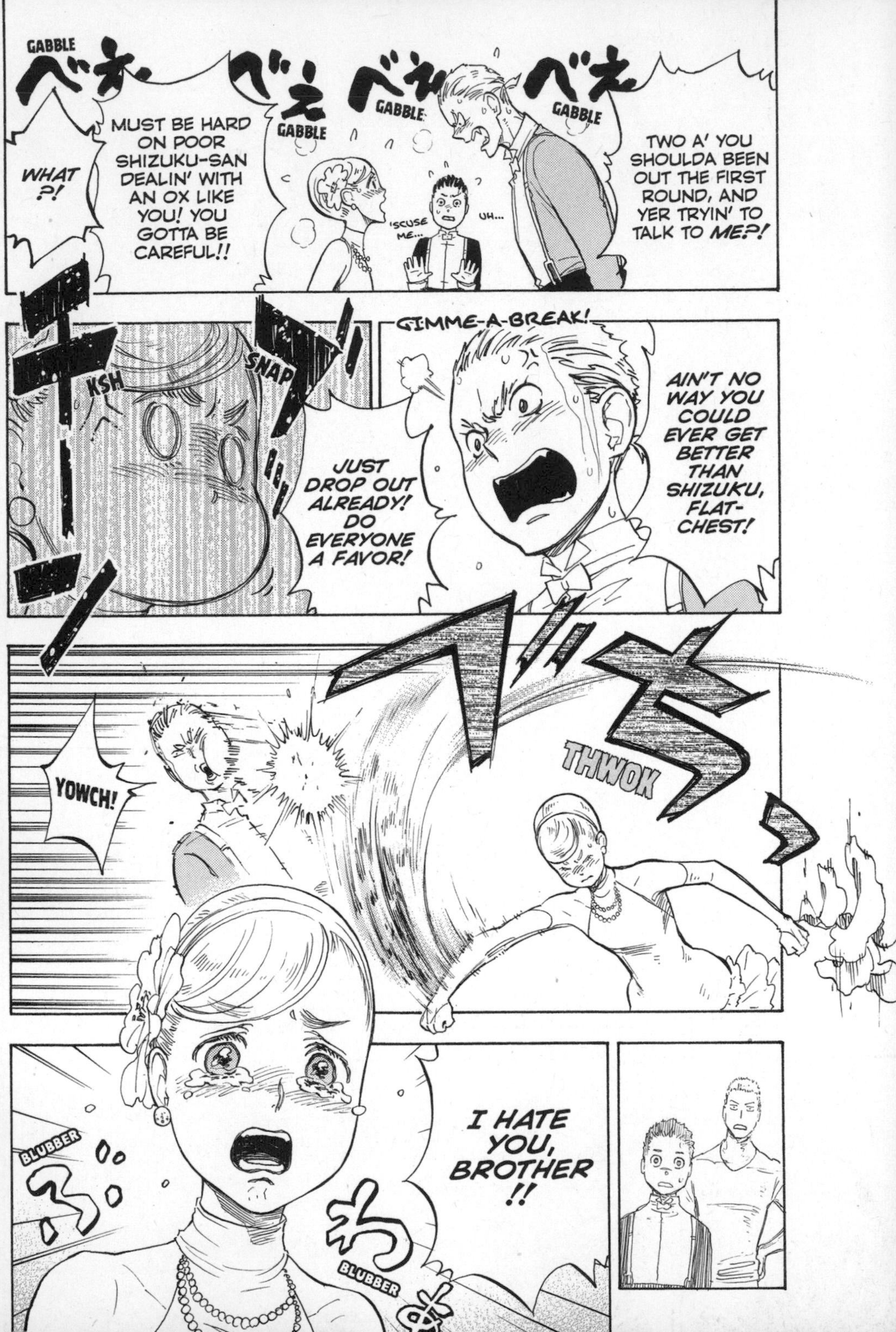
GABBLE
GABBLE
GABBLE
GABBLE
TWO A' YOU SHOULDA BEEN OUT THE FIRST ROUND, AND YER TRYIN' TO TALK TO ME?!
UH...
'SCUSE ME...
MUST BE HARD ON POOR SHIZUKU-SAN DEALIN' WITH AN OX LIKE YOU! YOU GOTTA BE CAREFUL!!
WHAT?!
GIMME-A-BREAK!
AIN'T NO WAY YOU COULD EVER GET BETTER THAN SHIZUKU, FLAT-CHEST!
JUST DROP OUT ALREADY! DO EVERYONE A FAVOR!
SNAP
KSH
THWOK
YOWCH!
I HATE YOU, BROTHER!!
BLUBBER
BLUBBER

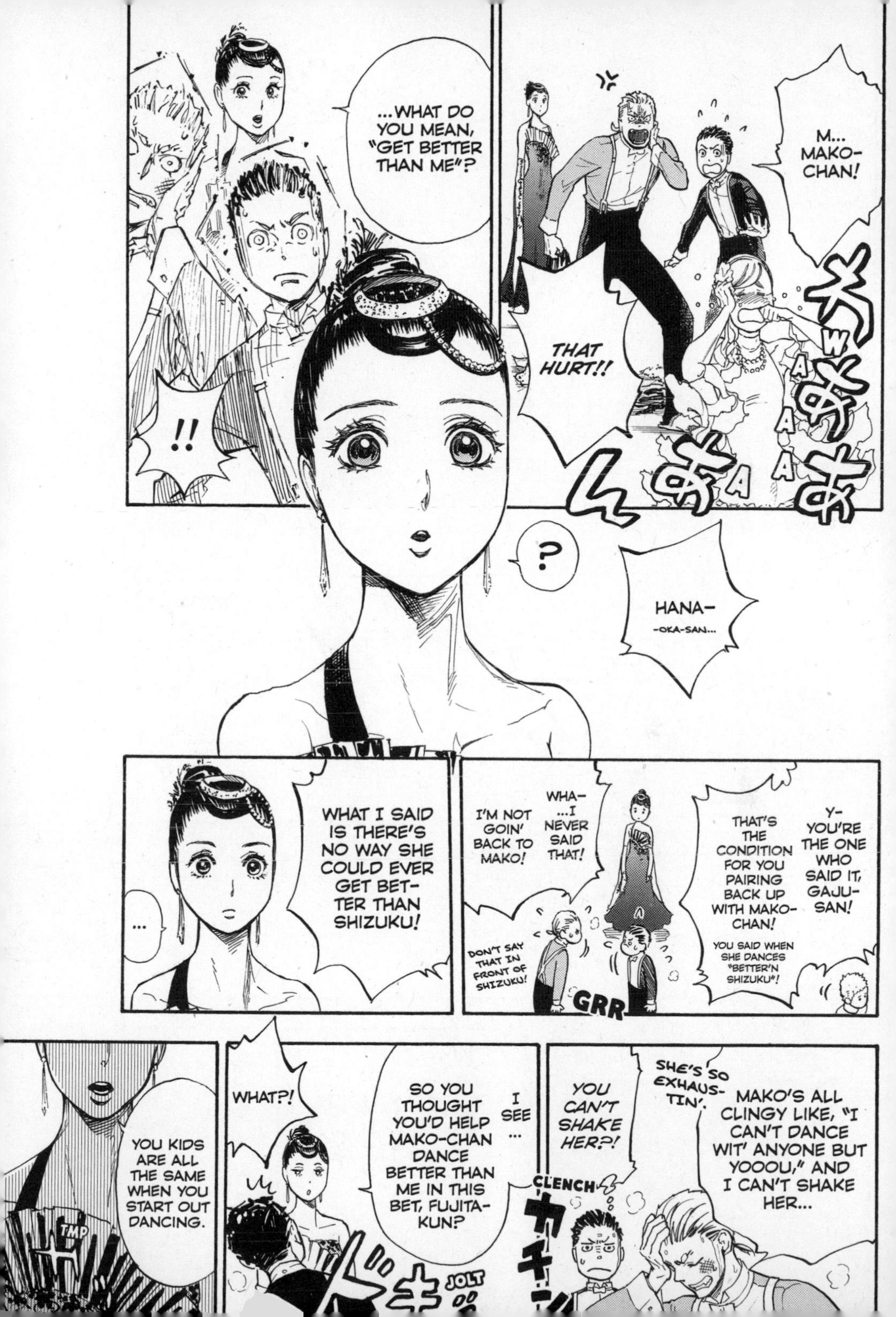
M... MAKO-CHAN!
THAT HURT!!
WAAAA
...WHAT DO YOU MEAN, "GET BETTER THAN ME"?
!!
?
HANA- -OKA-SAN...
Y-YOU'RE THE ONE WHO SAID IT, GAJU-SAN!
THAT'S THE CONDITION FOR YOU PAIRING BACK UP WITH MAKO-CHAN!
YOU SAID WHEN SHE DANCES "BETTER'N SHIZUKU"!
WHA- ...I NEVER SAID THAT!
I'M NOT GOIN' BACK TO MAKO!
DON'T SAY THAT IN FRONT OF SHIZUKU!
GRR
WHAT I SAID IS THERE'S NO WAY SHE COULD EVER GET BET-TER THAN SHIZUKU!
...
SHE'S SO EXHAUS-TIN'.
MAKO'S ALL CLINGY LIKE, "I CAN'T DANCE WIT' ANYONE BUT YOOOU," AND I CAN'T SHAKE HER...
YOU CAN'T SHAKE HER?!
CLENCH
I SEE...
SO YOU THOUGHT YOU'D HELP MAKO-CHAN DANCE BETTER THAN ME IN THIS BET, FUJITA-KUN?
WHAT?!
JOLT
YOU KIDS ARE ALL THE SAME WHEN YOU START OUT DANCING.
TMP

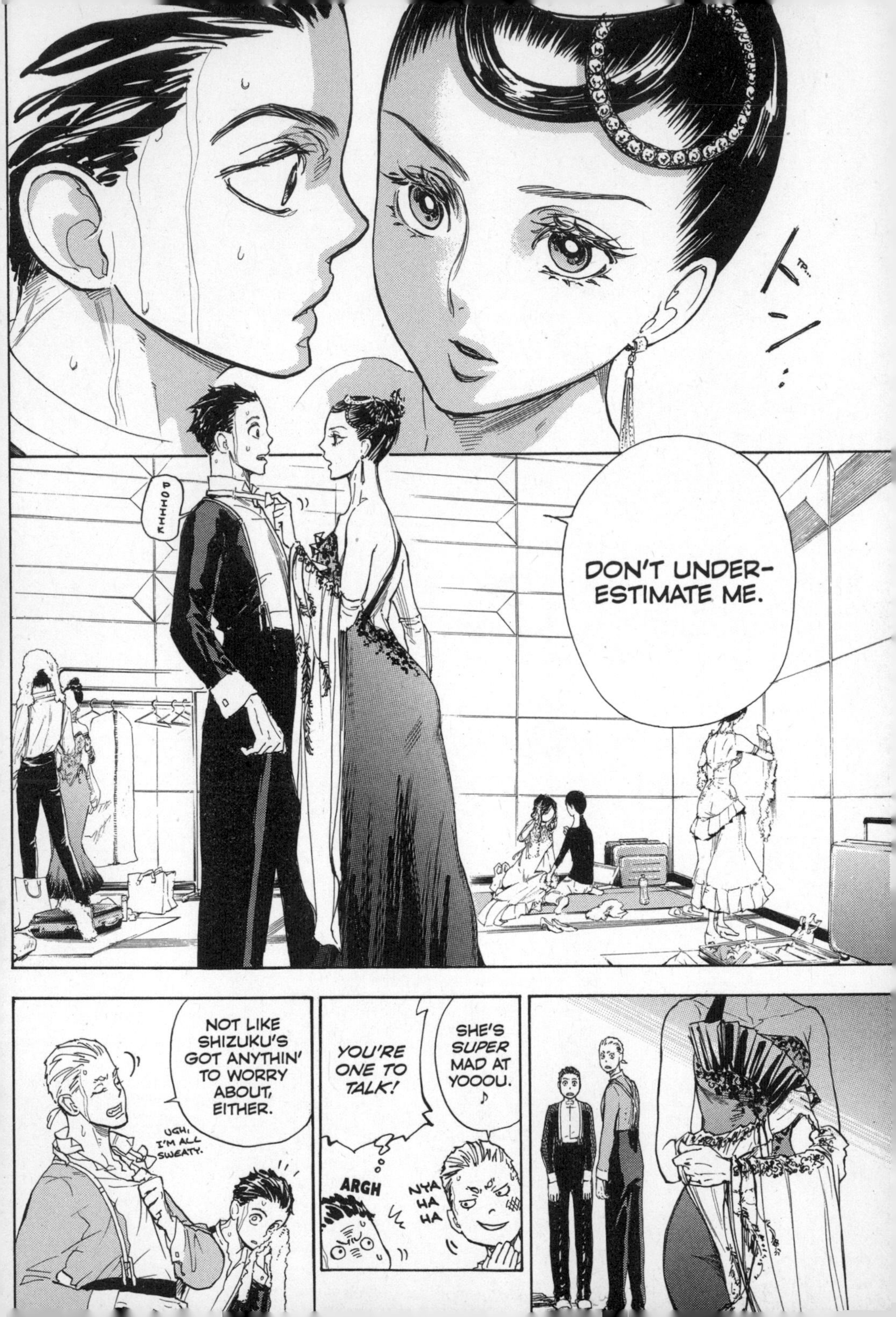
TP...
DON'T UNDER-ESTIMATE ME.
POIIIK
SHE'S SUPER MAD AT YOOOU. ♪
YOU'RE ONE TO TALK!
NYA HA HA
ARGH
NOT LIKE SHIZUKU'S GOT ANYTHIN' TO WORRY ABOUT, EITHER.
UGH, I'M ALL SWEATY.

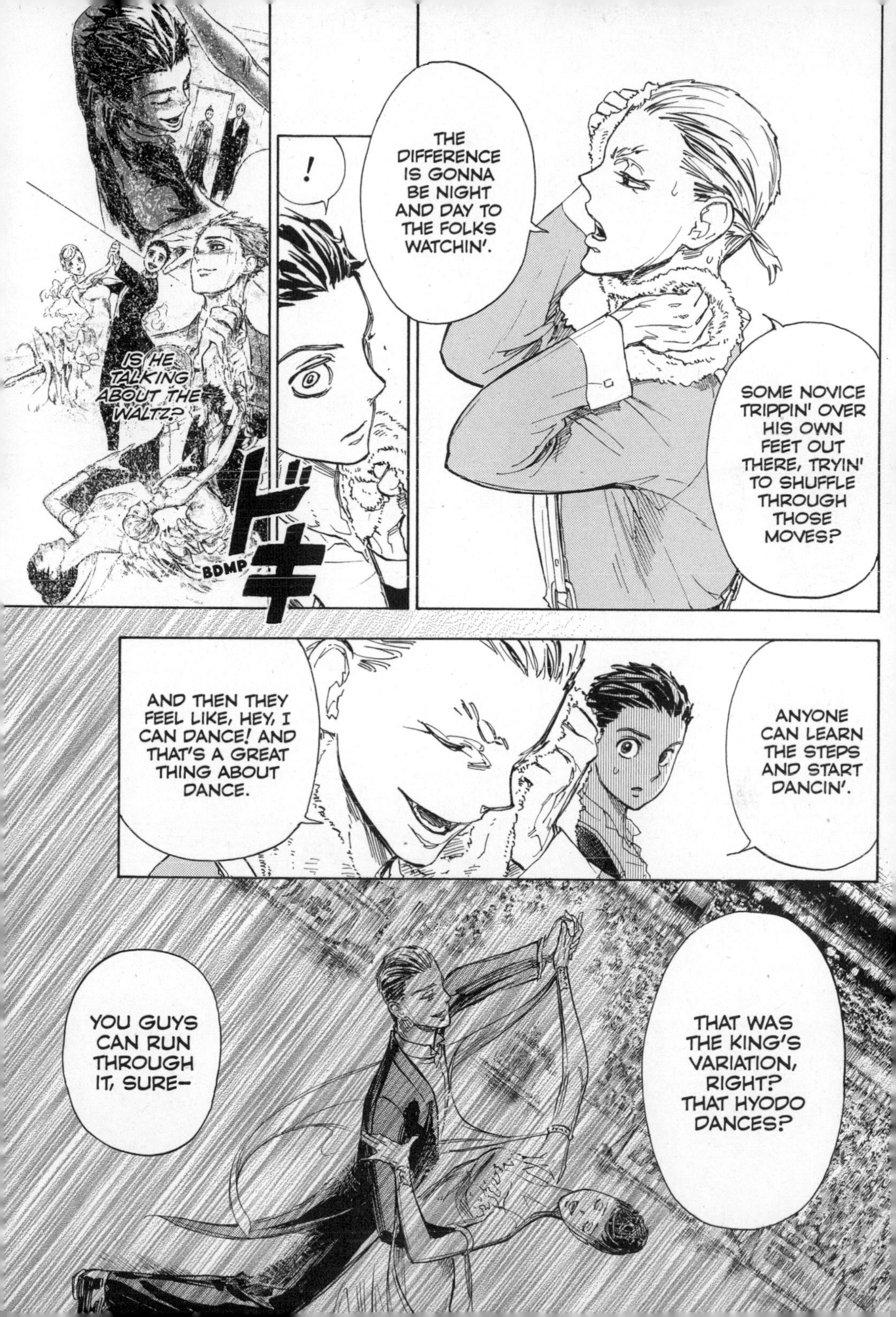
SOME NOVICE TRIPPIN' OVER HIS OWN FEET OUT THERE, TRYIN' TO SHUFFLE THROUGH THOSE MOVES?
THE DIFFERENCE IS GONNA BE NIGHT AND DAY TO THE FOLKS WATCHIN'.
!
IS HE TALKING ABOUT THE WALTZ?
BDMP
ANYONE CAN LEARN THE STEPS AND START DANCIN'.
AND THEN THEY FEEL LIKE, HEY, I CAN DANCE! AND THAT'S A GREAT THING ABOUT DANCE.
THAT WAS THE KING'S VARIATION, RIGHT? THAT HYODO DANCES?
YOU GUYS CAN RUN THROUGH IT, SURE–

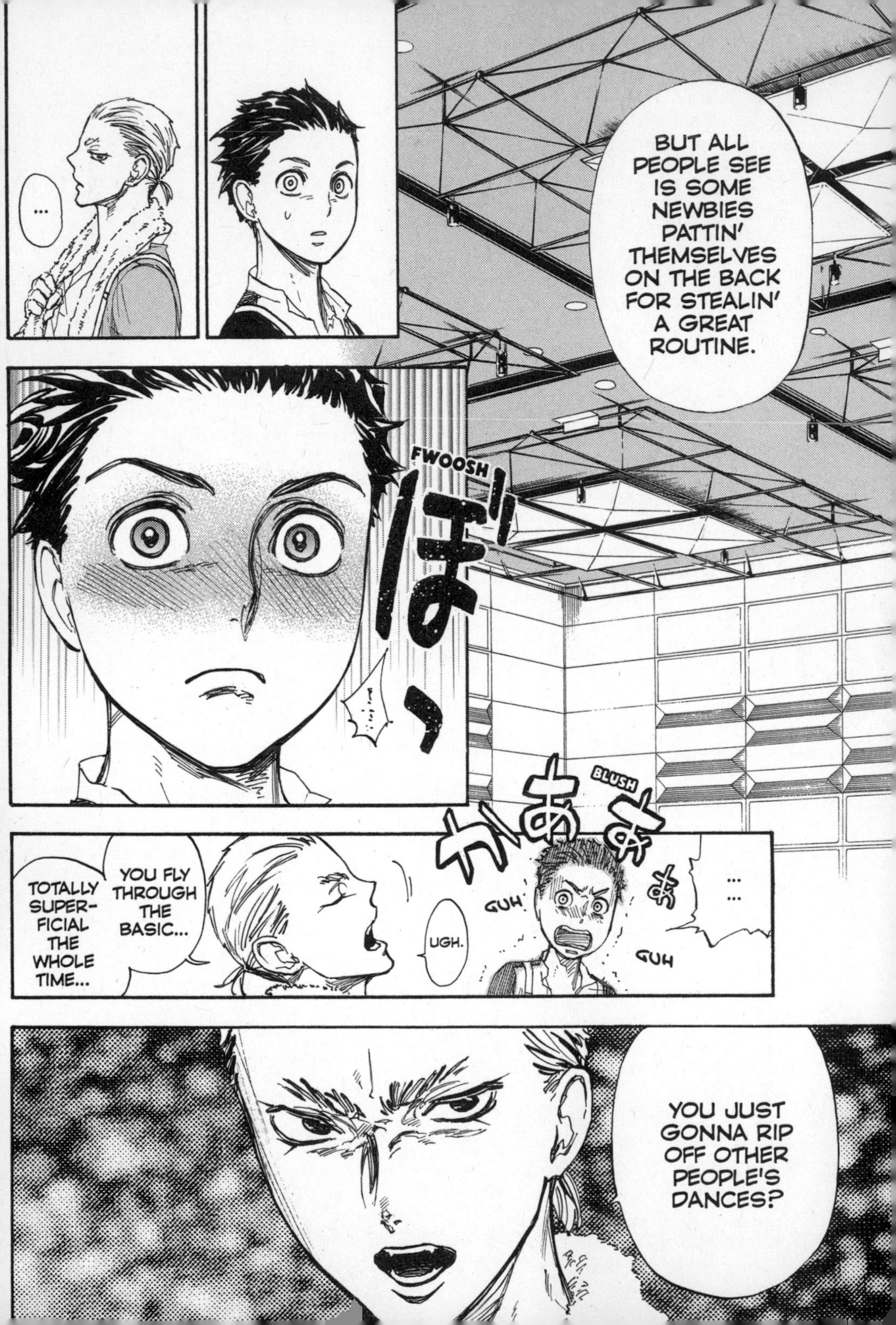
BUT ALL PEOPLE SEE IS SOME NEWBIES PATTIN' THEMSELVES ON THE BACK FOR STEALIN' A GREAT ROUTINE.
...
FWOOSH
ぼ
BLUSH
わあぁぁ
...
...
GUH
GUH
UGH.
YOU FLY THROUGH THE BASIC...
TOTALLY SUPER-FICIAL THE WHOLE TIME...
YOU JUST GONNA RIP OFF OTHER PEOPLE'S DANCES?

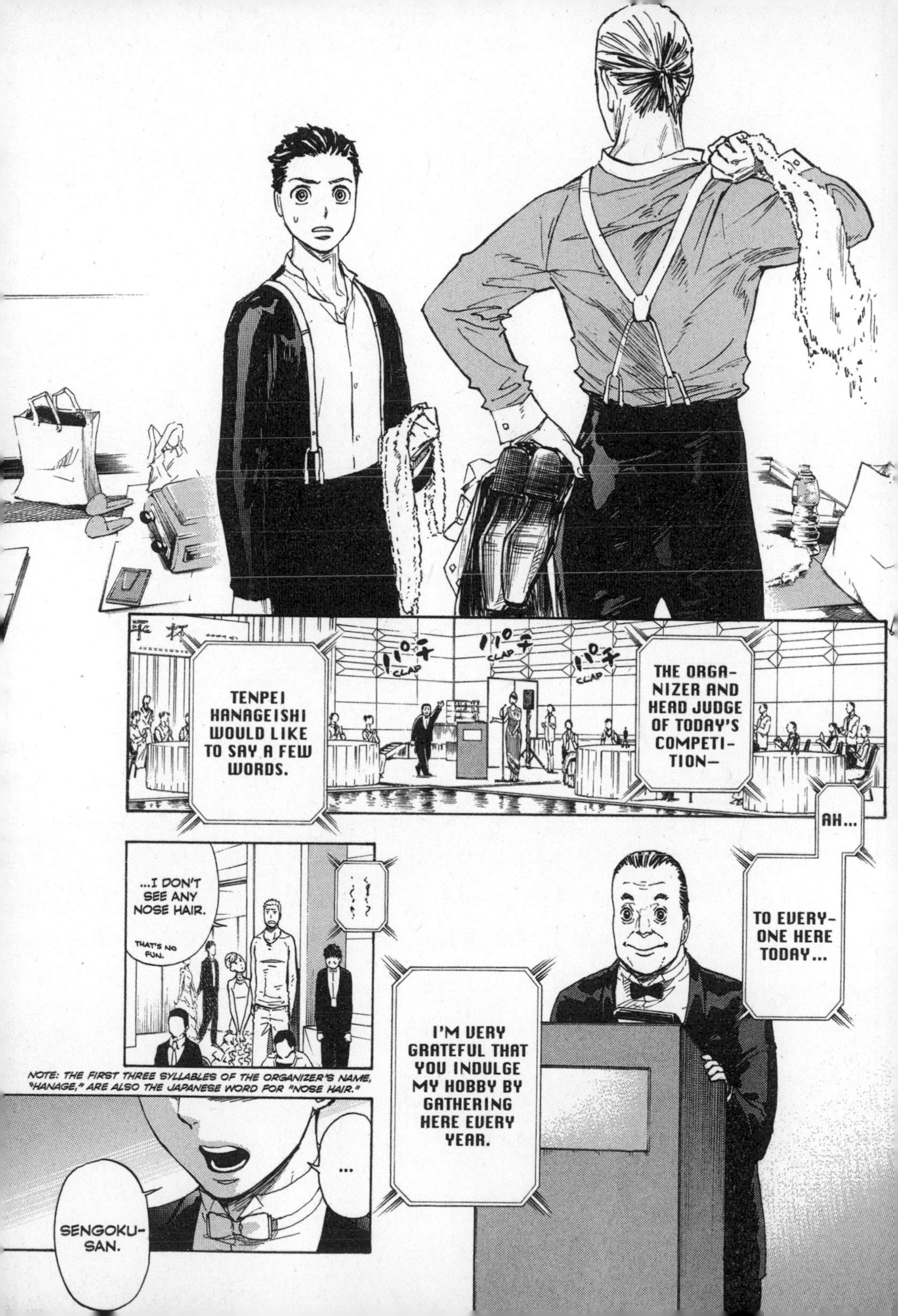

THE ORGA-NIZER AND HEAD JUDGE OF TODAY'S COMPETI-TION—
パチ CLAP
パチ CLAP
パチ CLAP
TENPEI HANAGEISHI WOULD LIKE TO SAY A FEW WORDS.
AH...
TO EVERY-ONE HERE TODAY...
I'M VERY GRATEFUL THAT YOU INDULGE MY HOBBY BY GATHERING HERE EVERY YEAR.
...I DON'T SEE ANY NOSE HAIR.
THAT'S NO FUN.
...
SENGOKU-SAN.

NOTE: THE FIRST THREE SYLLABLES OF THE ORGANIZER'S NAME, "HANAGE," ARE ALSO THE JAPANESE WORD FOR "NOSE HAIR."

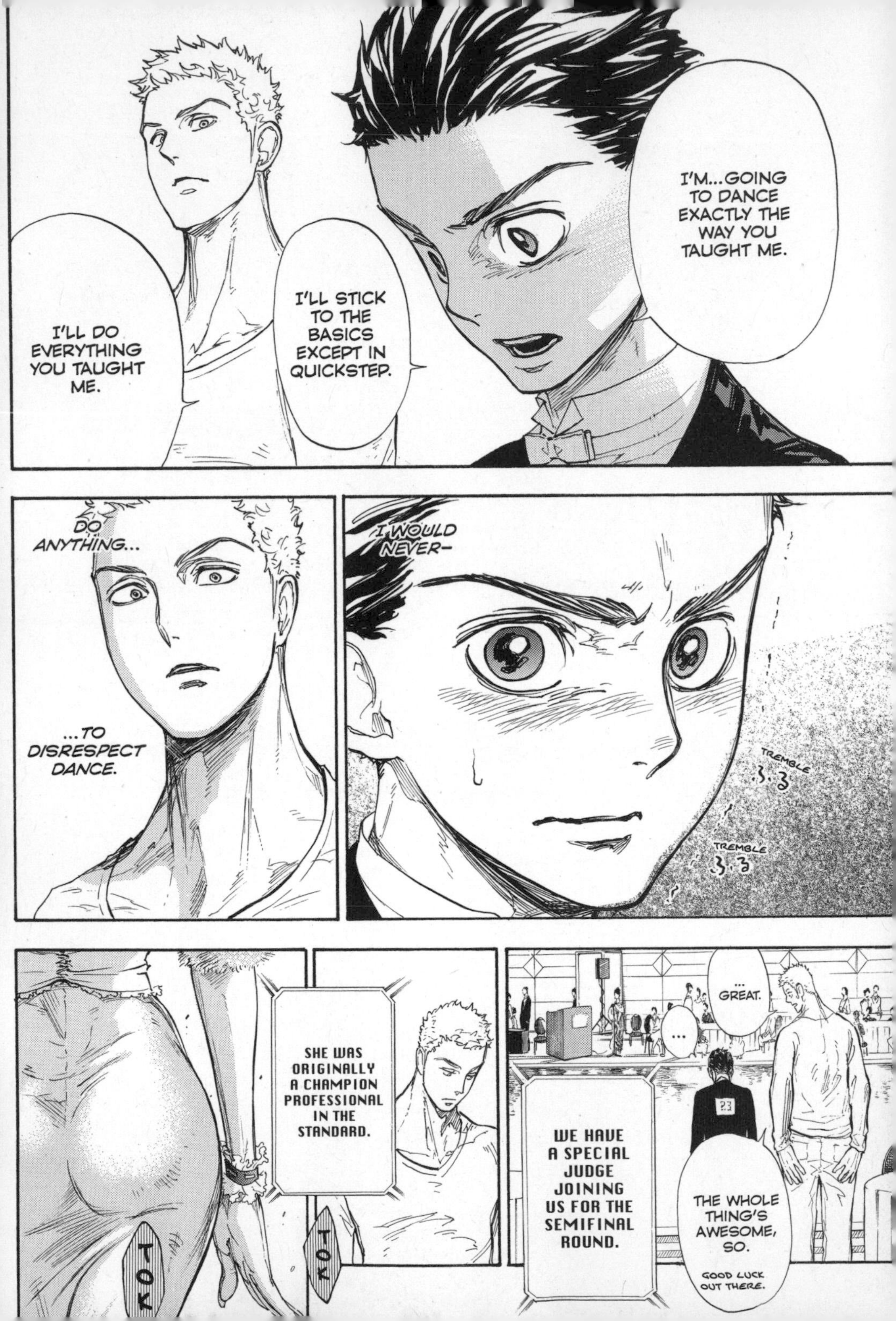
I'M...GOING TO DANCE EXACTLY THE WAY YOU TAUGHT ME.
I'LL STICK TO THE BASICS EXCEPT IN QUICKSTEP.
I'LL DO EVERYTHING YOU TAUGHT ME.
I WOULD NEVER—
TREMBLE
TREMBLE
DO ANYTHING...
...TO DISRESPECT DANCE.
...GREAT.
...
THE WHOLE THING'S AWESOME, SO.
GOOD LUCK OUT THERE.
WE HAVE A SPECIAL JUDGE JOINING US FOR THE SEMIFINAL ROUND.
SHE WAS ORIGINALLY A CHAMPION PROFESSIONAL IN THE STANDARD.
TOK
TOK

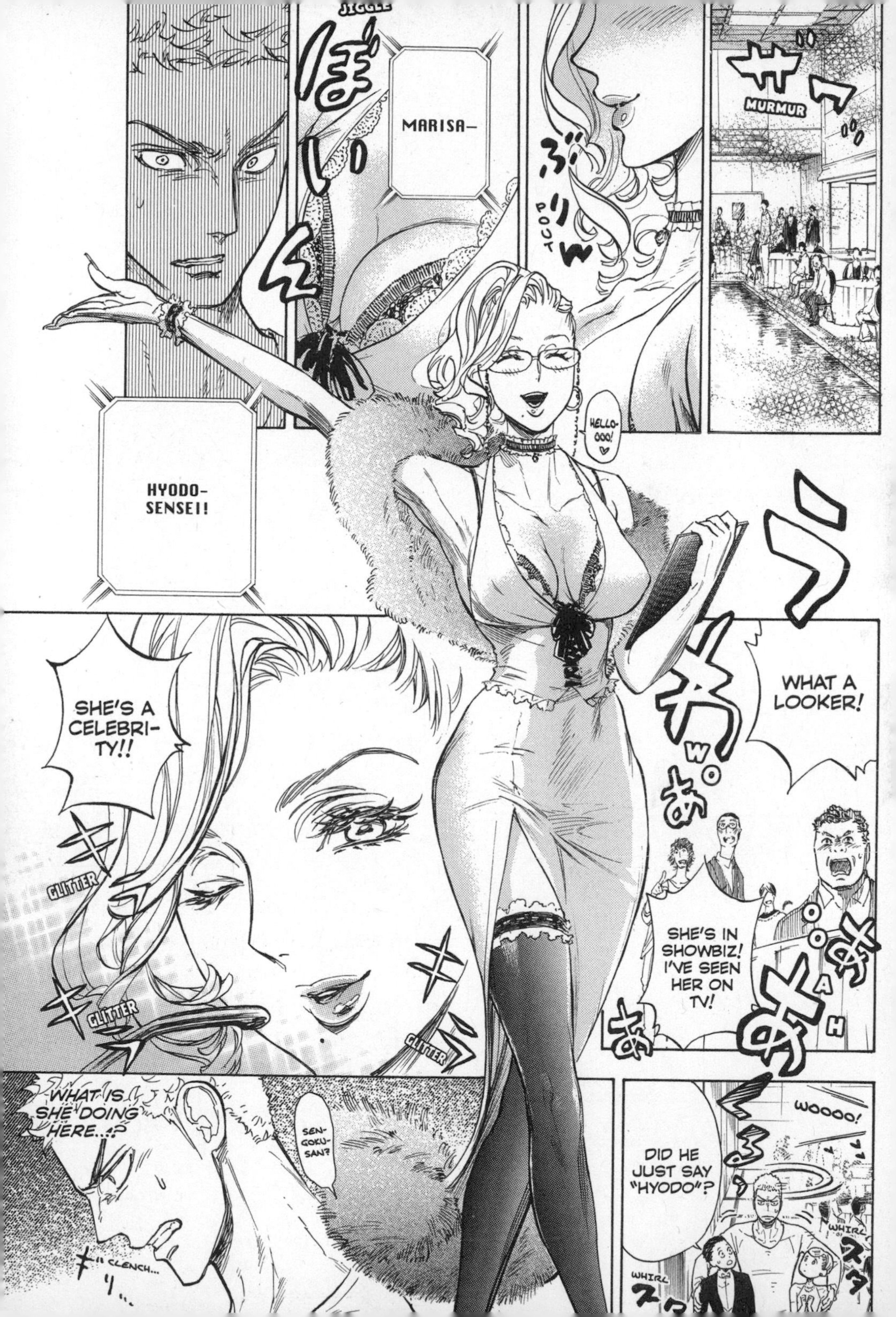
MURMUR
POUT
JIGGLE
MARISA—
HYODO-SENSEI!
HELLO-OOO! ♥
WHAT A LOOKER!
WO
AH
SHE'S IN SHOWBIZ! I'VE SEEN HER ON TV!
SHE'S A CELEBRITY!!
GLITTER
GLITTER
GLITTER
WOOOO!
DID HE JUST SAY "HYODO"?
WHIRL
WHIRL
SENGOKU-SAN?
WHAT IS SHE DOING HERE...!?
CLENCH...

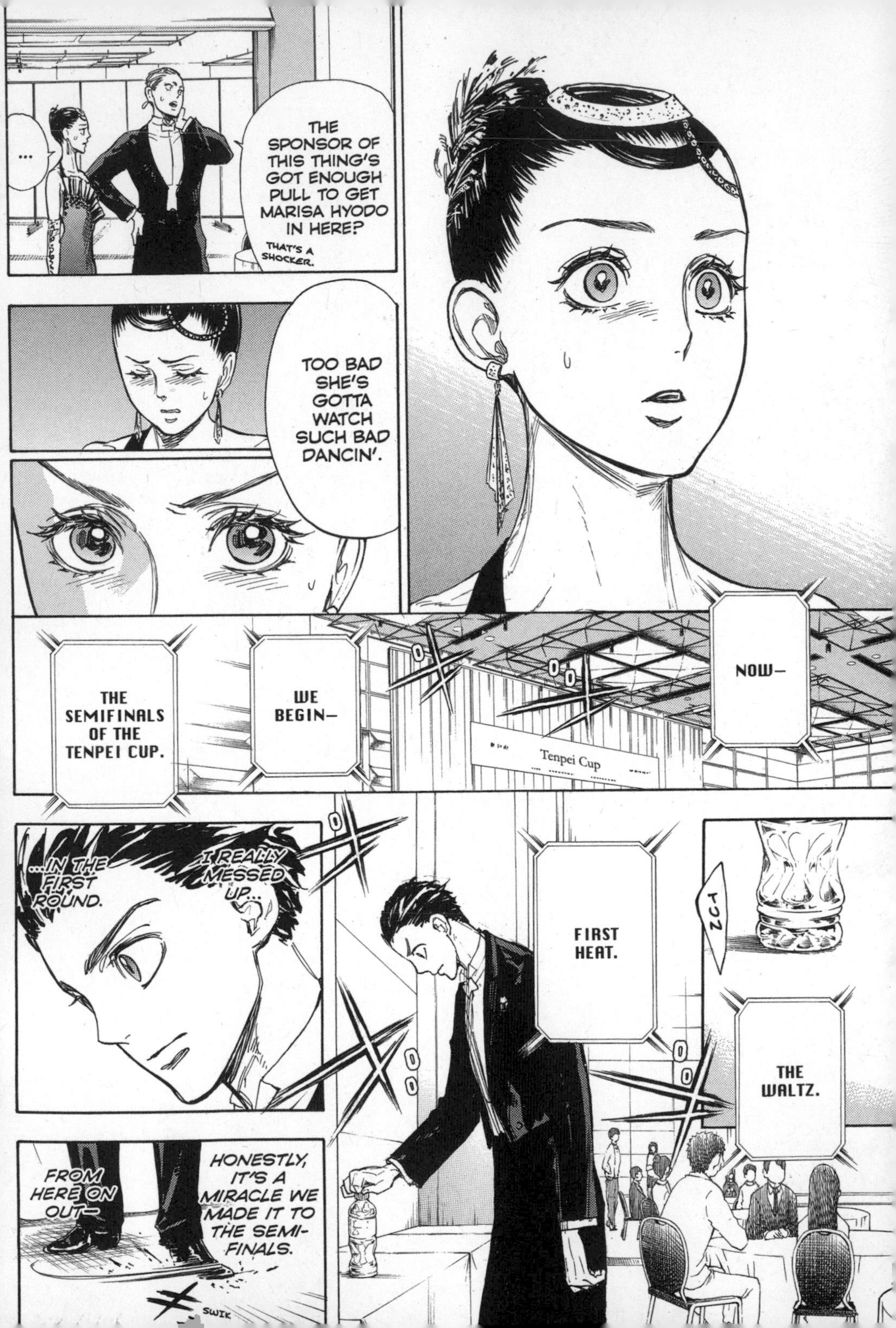
THE SPONSOR OF THIS THING'S GOT ENOUGH PULL TO GET MARISA HYODO IN HERE?
THAT'S A SHOCKER.
...
TOO BAD SHE'S GOTTA WATCH SUCH BAD DANCIN'.
NOW—
WE BEGIN—
THE SEMIFINALS OF THE TENPEI CUP.
Tenpei Cup
TUN
FIRST HEAT.
THE WALTZ.
I REALLY MESSED UP...
...IN THE FIRST ROUND.
HONESTLY, IT'S A MIRACLE WE MADE IT TO THE SEMI-FINALS.
FROM HERE ON OUT—
SWIK

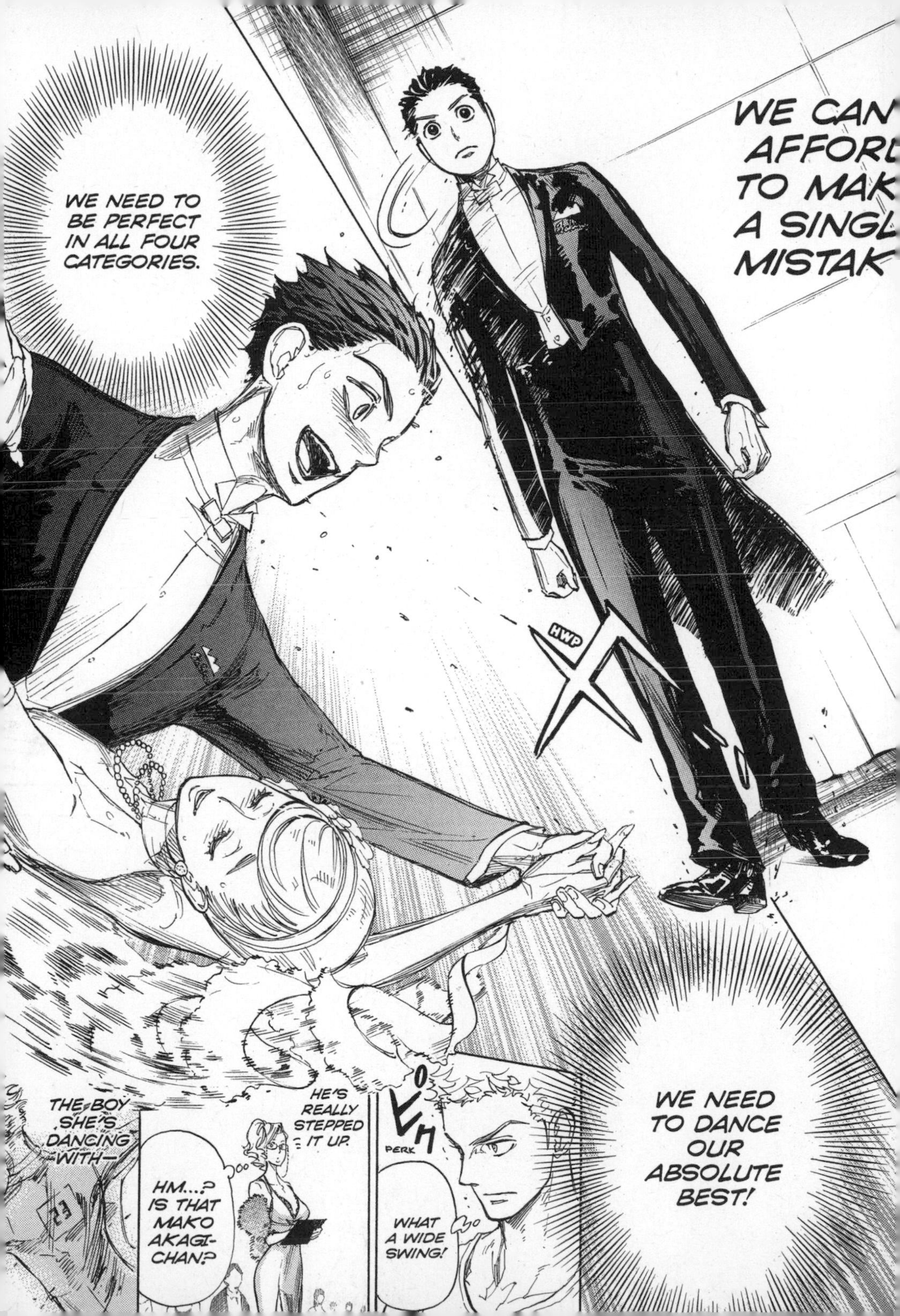
WE CAN'
AFFORD
TO MAK
A SINGL
MISTAK
WE NEED TO BE PERFECT IN ALL FOUR CATEGORIES.
HWP
WE NEED TO DANCE OUR ABSOLUTE BEST!
PERK
WHAT A WIDE SWING!
HE'S REALLY STEPPED IT UP.
HM...? IS THAT MAKO AKAGI-CHAN?
THE BOY SHE'S DANCING WITH—

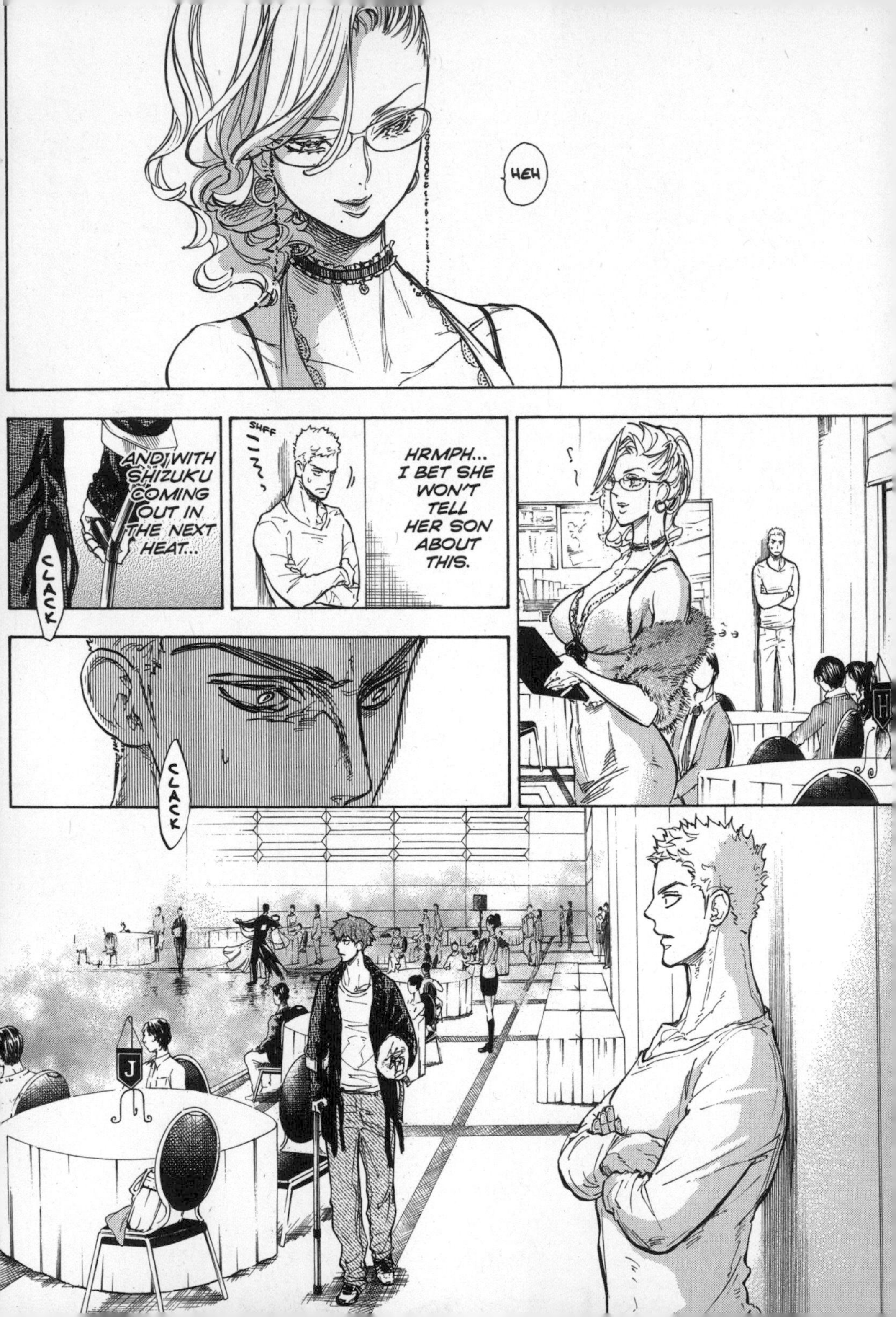
HEH
HRMPH... I BET SHE WON'T TELL HER SON ABOUT THIS.
SHFF
AND WITH SHIZUKU COMING OUT IN THE NEXT HEAT...
CLACK
CLACK

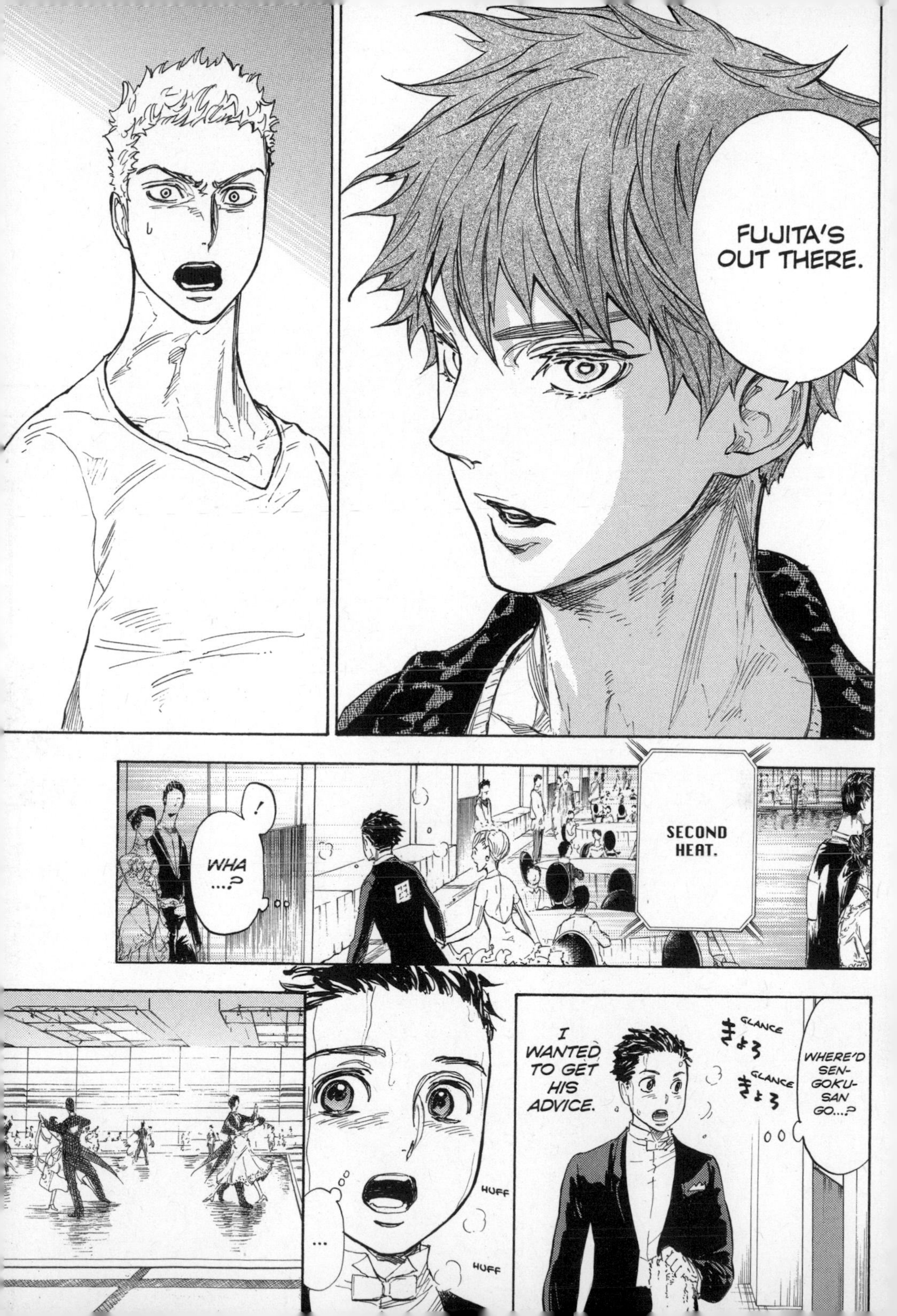
FUJITA'S OUT THERE.
SECOND HEAT.
!
WHA ...?
WHERE'D SEN-GOKU-SAN GO...?
きょろ GLANCE
きょろ GLANCE
I WANTED TO GET HIS ADVICE.
HUFF
...
HUFF

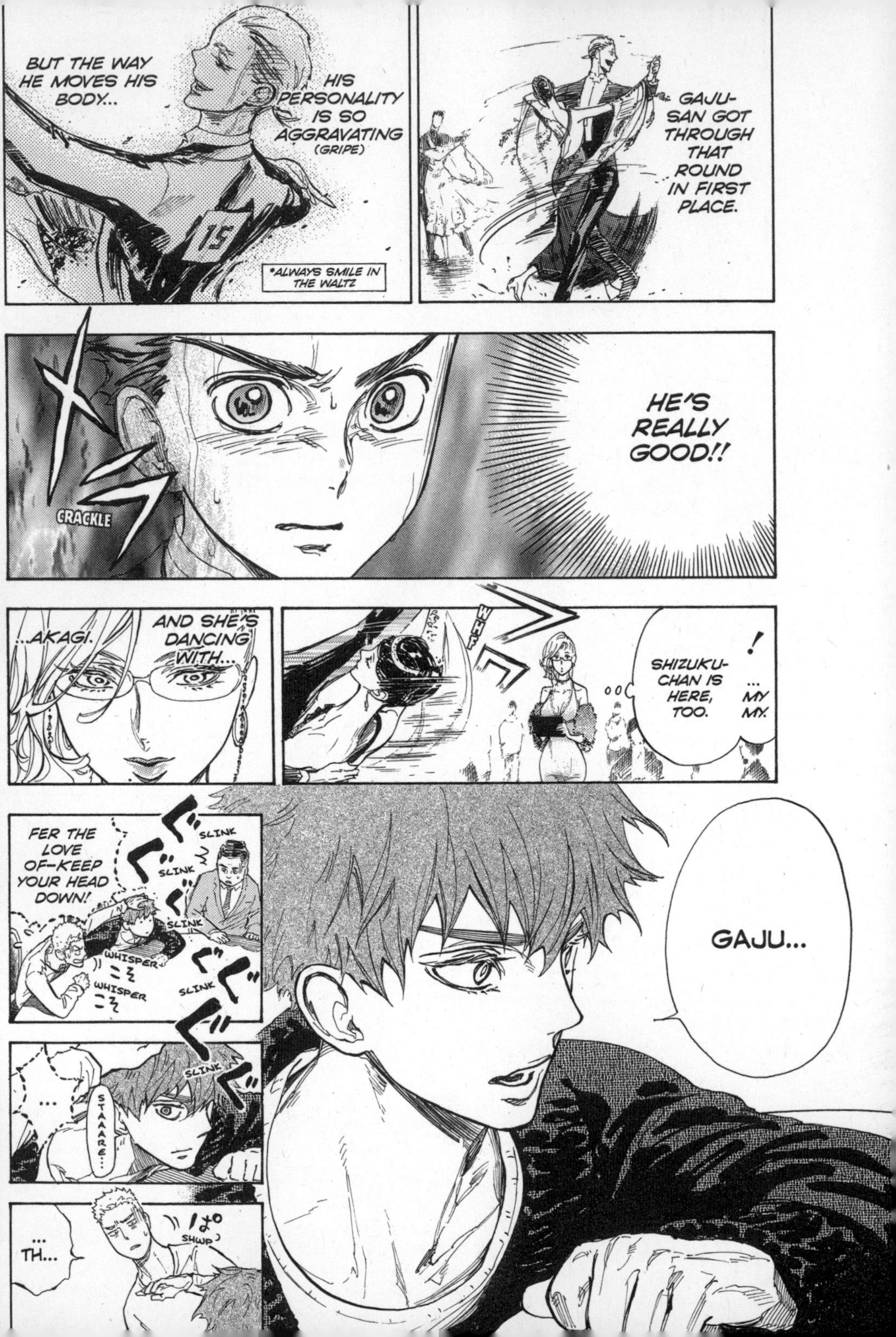
GAJU-SAN GOT THROUGH THAT ROUND IN FIRST PLACE.
HIS PERSONALITY IS SO AGGRAVATING (GRIPE)
BUT THE WAY HE MOVES HIS BODY...
15
*ALWAYS SMILE IN THE WALTZ
HE'S REALLY GOOD!!
CRACKLE
WHF
! ... MY MY.
SHIZUKU-CHAN IS HERE, TOO.
AND SHE'S DANCING WITH...
...AKAGI.
GAJU...
FER THE LOVE OF-KEEP YOUR HEAD DOWN!
SLINK
SLINK
SLINK
WHISPER
WHISPER
SLINK
SLINK
...
STAAARE...
SHWUP
... TH...

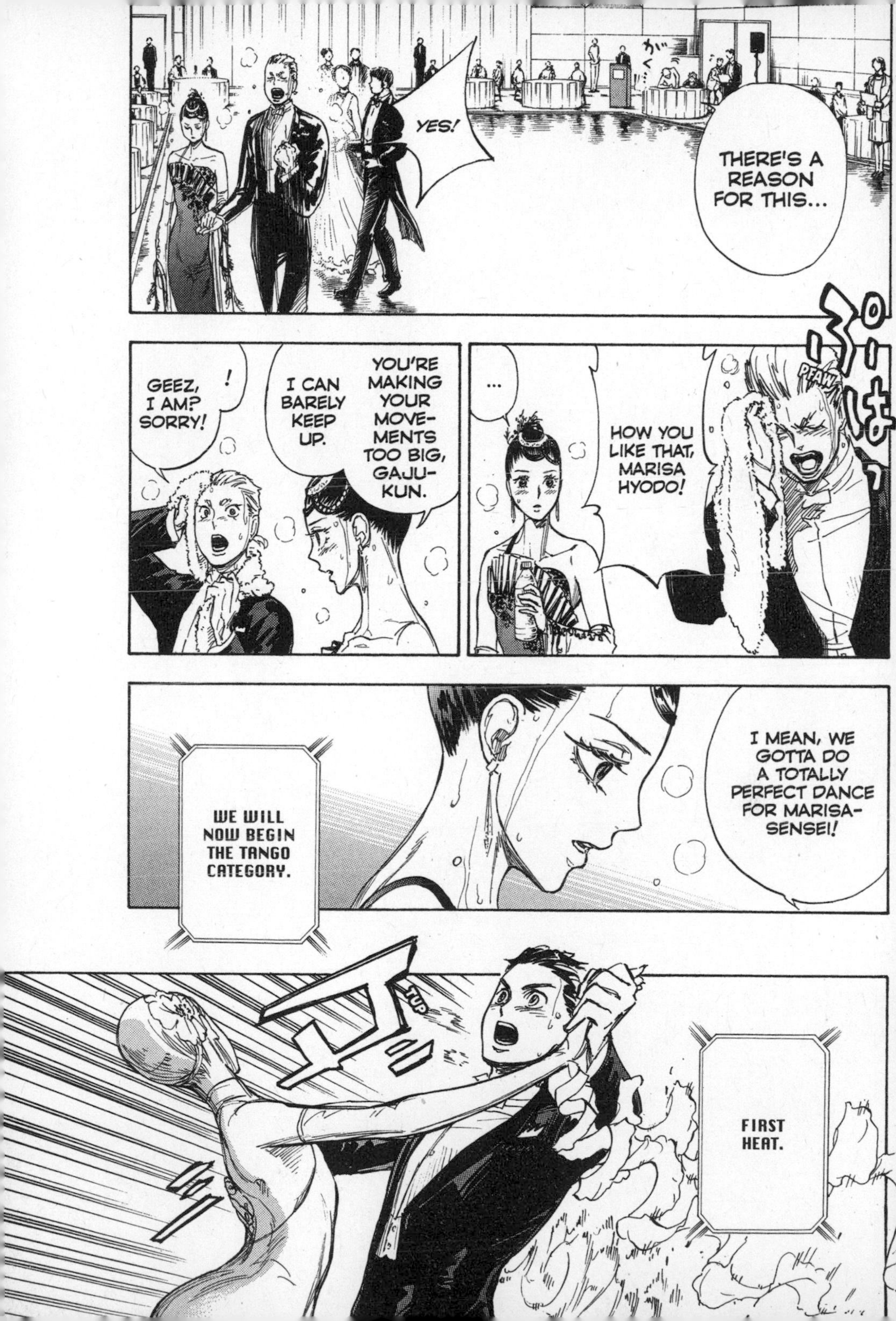
THERE'S A REASON FOR THIS...
YES!
ぷはっ
PFAW
HOW YOU LIKE THAT, MARISA HYODO!
...
YOU'RE MAKING YOUR MOVEMENTS TOO BIG, GAJU-KUN.
I CAN BARELY KEEP UP.
!
GEEZ, I AM? SORRY!
I MEAN, WE GOTTA DO A TOTALLY PERFECT DANCE FOR MARISA-SENSEI!
WE WILL NOW BEGIN THE TANGO CATEGORY.
FIRST HEAT.
TUP

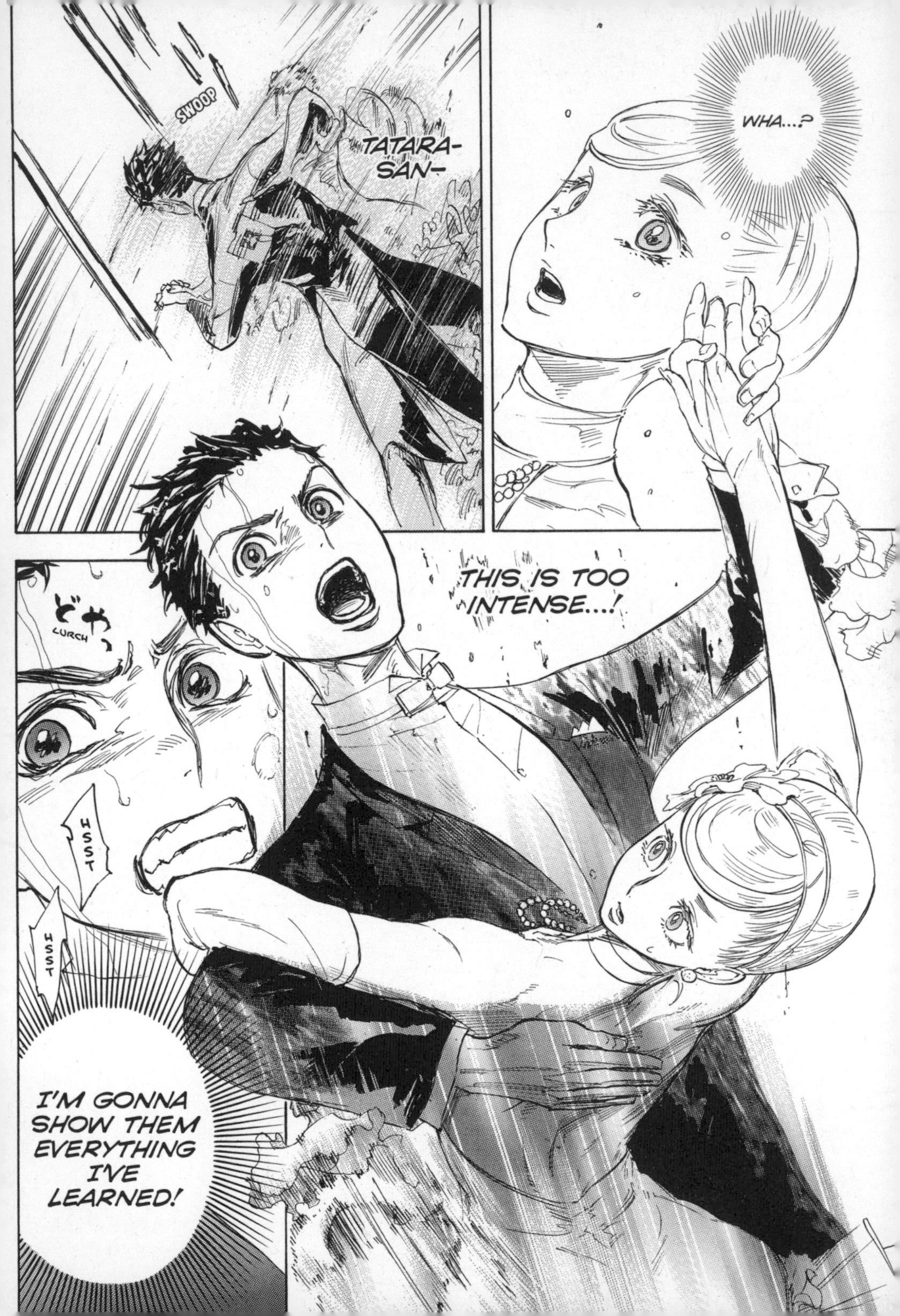
WHA...?
SWOOP
TATARA-SAN-
THIS IS TOO INTENSE...!
どやっ
LURCH
HSST
HSST
I'M GONNA SHOW THEM EVERYTHING I'VE LEARNED!

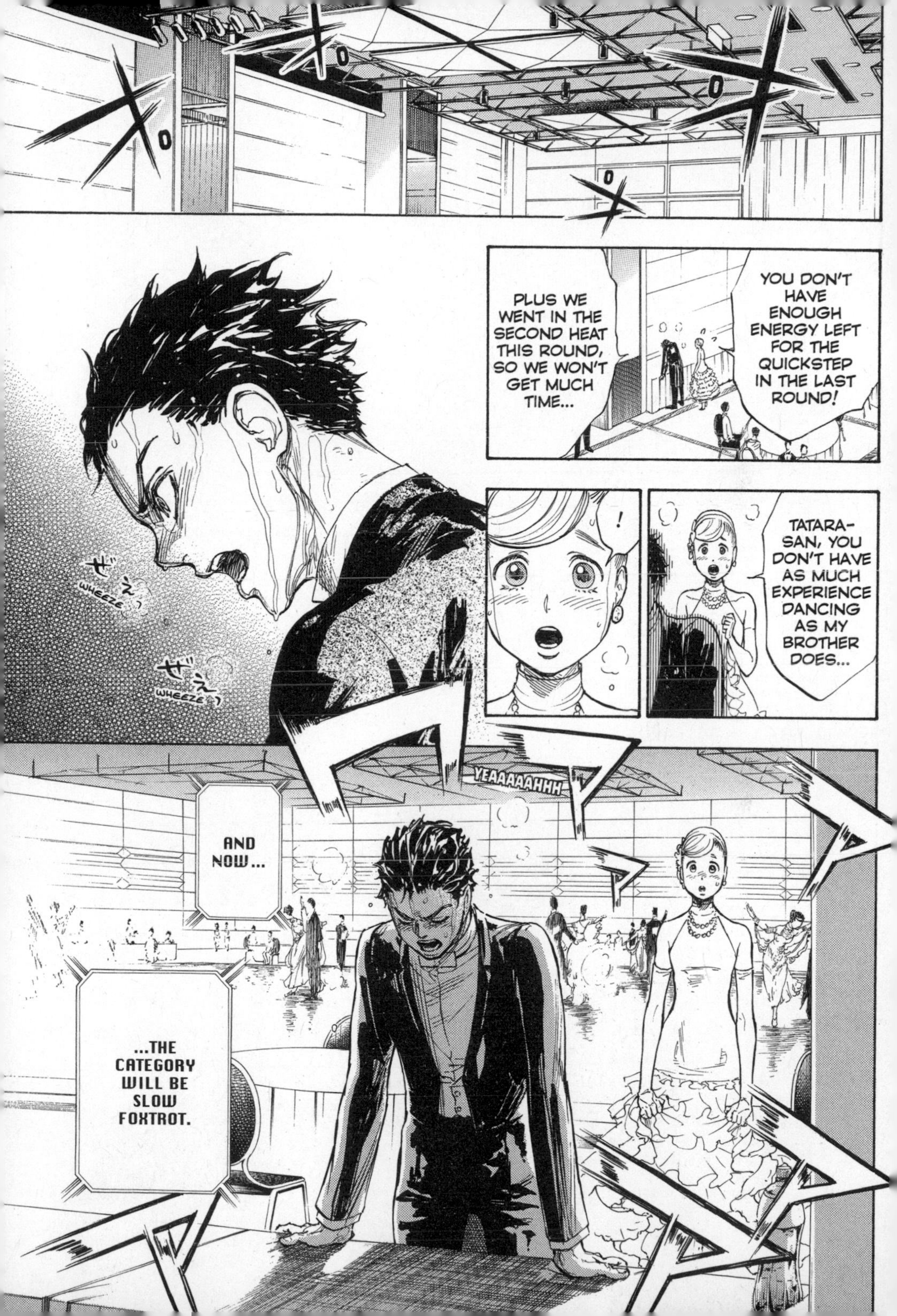

YOU DON'T HAVE ENOUGH ENERGY LEFT FOR THE QUICKSTEP IN THE LAST ROUND!
PLUS WE WENT IN THE SECOND HEAT THIS ROUND, SO WE WON'T GET MUCH TIME...
TATARA-SAN, YOU DON'T HAVE AS MUCH EXPERIENCE DANCING AS MY BROTHER DOES...
!
WHEEZE
WHEEZE
YEAAAAAHHH
AND NOW...
...THE CATEGORY WILL BE SLOW FOXTROT.

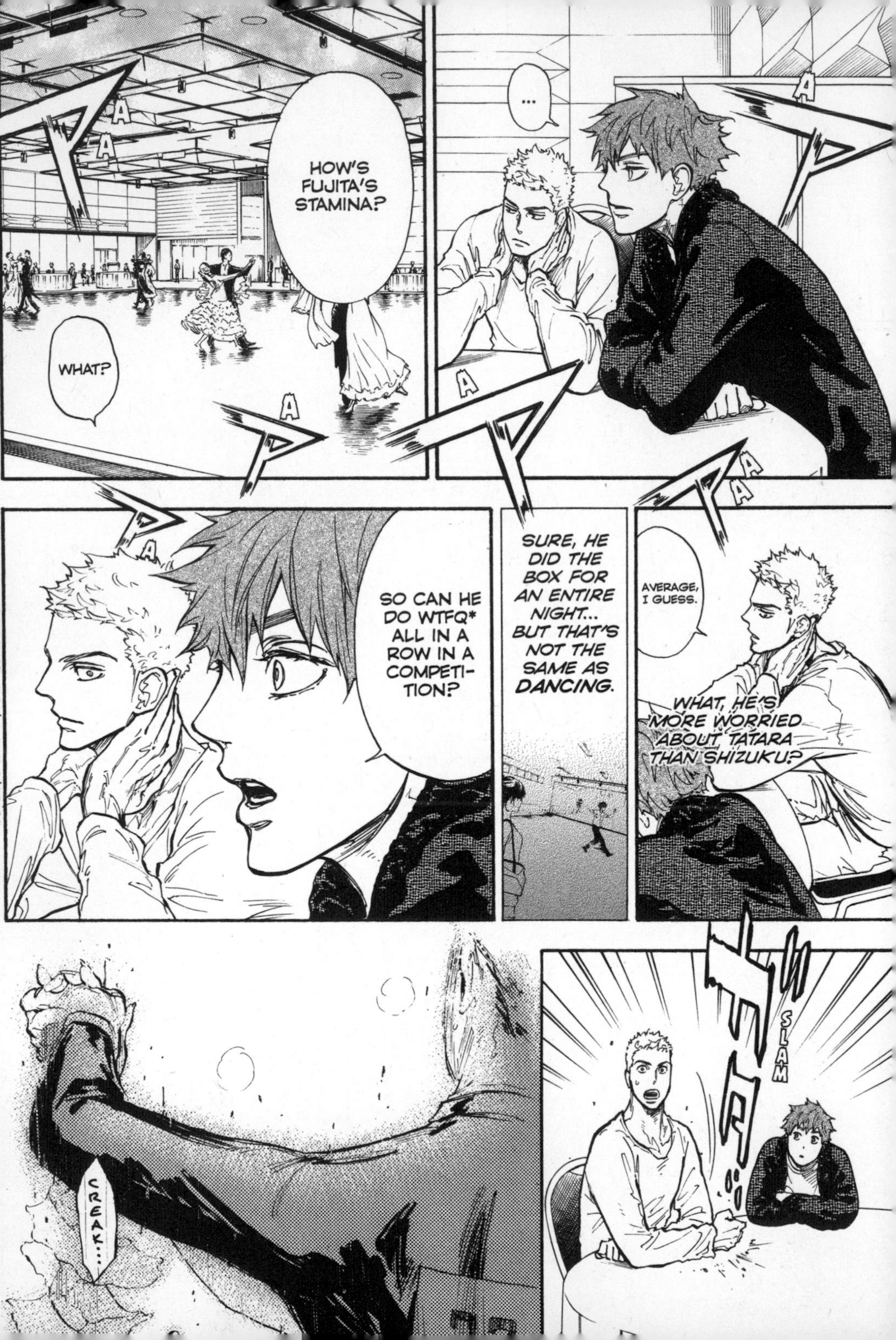
...
HOW'S FUJITA'S STAMINA?
WHAT?
AVERAGE, I GUESS.
WHAT, HE'S MORE WORRIED ABOUT TATARA THAN SHIZUKU?
SURE, HE DID THE BOX FOR AN ENTIRE NIGHT... BUT THAT'S NOT THE SAME AS *DANCING*.
SO CAN HE DO WTFQ* ALL IN A ROW IN A COMPETITION?
SLAM
CREAK...

TANGO, FOXTROT, AND QUICKSTEP.

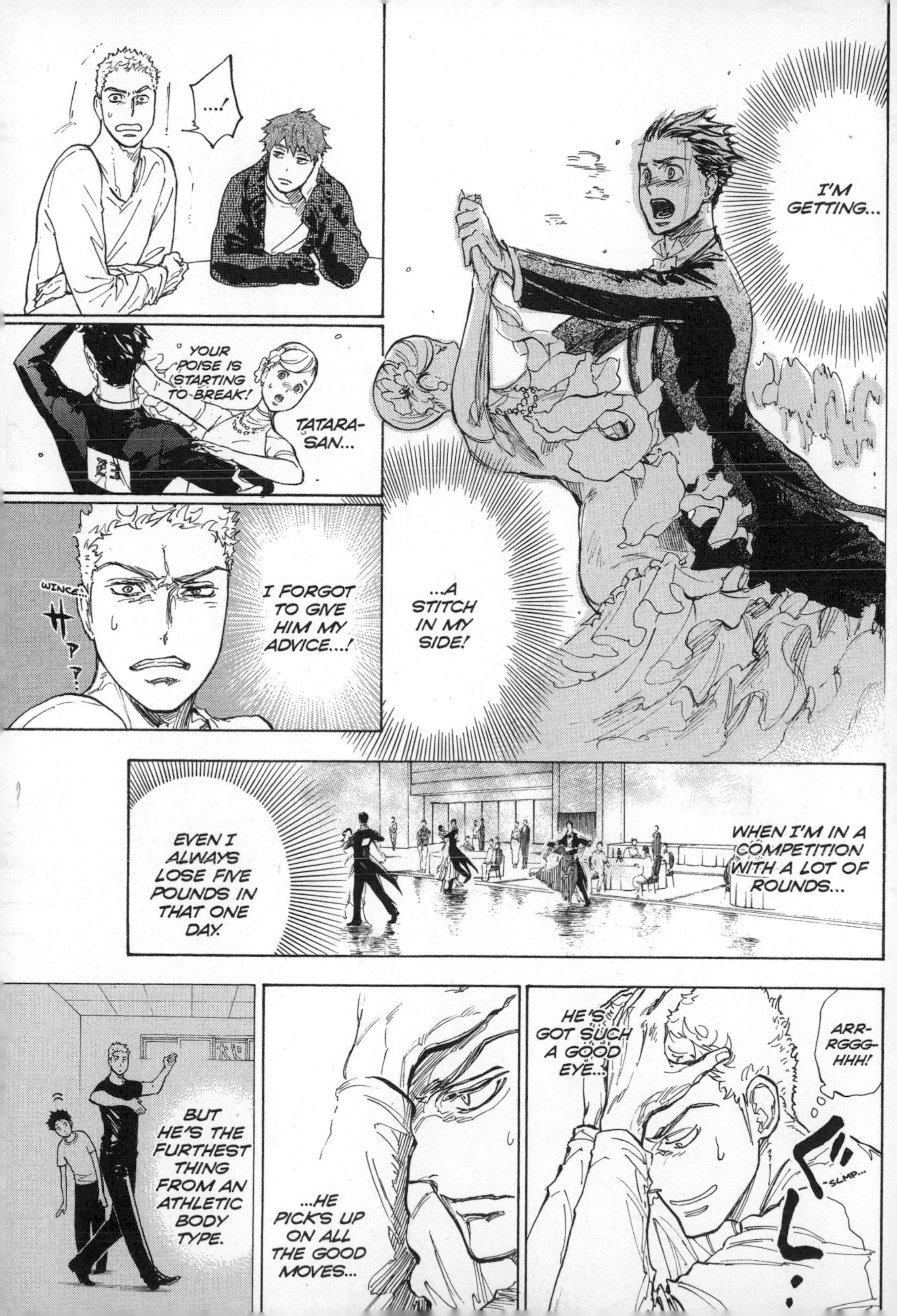
I'M GETTING...
...A STITCH IN MY SIDE!
....!
YOUR POISE IS STARTING TO BREAK!
TATARA-SAN...
WINCE...
I FORGOT TO GIVE HIM MY ADVICE...!
WHEN I'M IN A COMPETITION WITH A LOT OF ROUNDS...
EVEN I ALWAYS LOSE FIVE POUNDS IN THAT ONE DAY.
ARR-RGGG-HHH!
HE'S GOT SUCH A GOOD EYE...
SLMP...
...HE PICKS UP ON ALL THE GOOD MOVES...
BUT HE'S THE FURTHEST THING FROM AN ATHLETIC BODY TYPE.

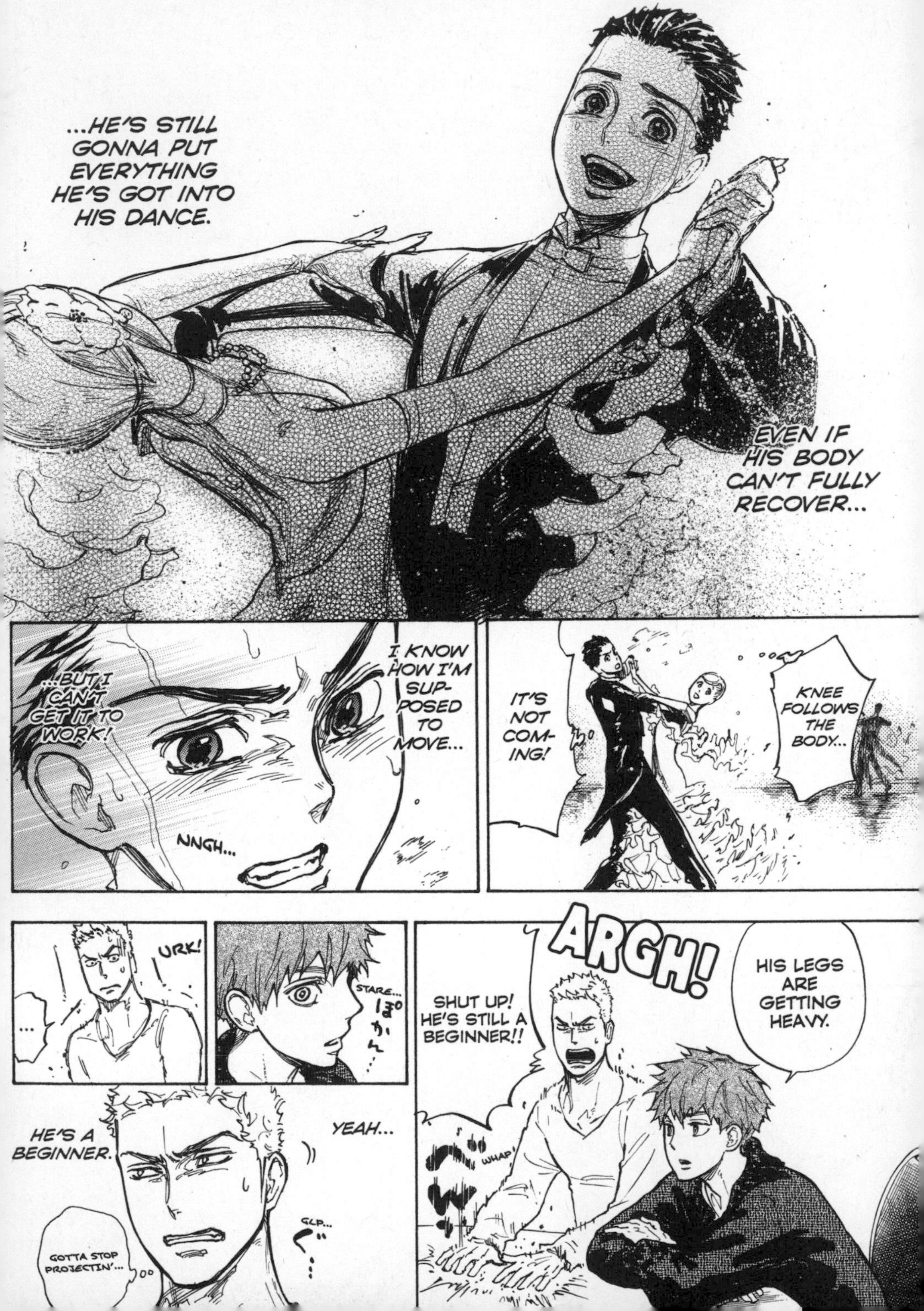
EVEN IF HIS BODY CAN'T FULLY RECOVER...
...HE'S STILL GONNA PUT EVERYTHING HE'S GOT INTO HIS DANCE.
KNEE FOLLOWS THE BODY...
IT'S NOT COMING!
I KNOW HOW I'M SUP-POSED TO MOVE...
...BUT I CAN'T GET IT TO WORK!
NNGH...
HIS LEGS ARE GETTING HEAVY.
ARGH!
SHUT UP! HE'S STILL A BEGINNER!!
WHAP!
STARE... ぽかん...
URK!
...
YEAH...
HE'S A BEGINNER.
GLP... ぐ...
GOTTA STOP PROJECTIN'...

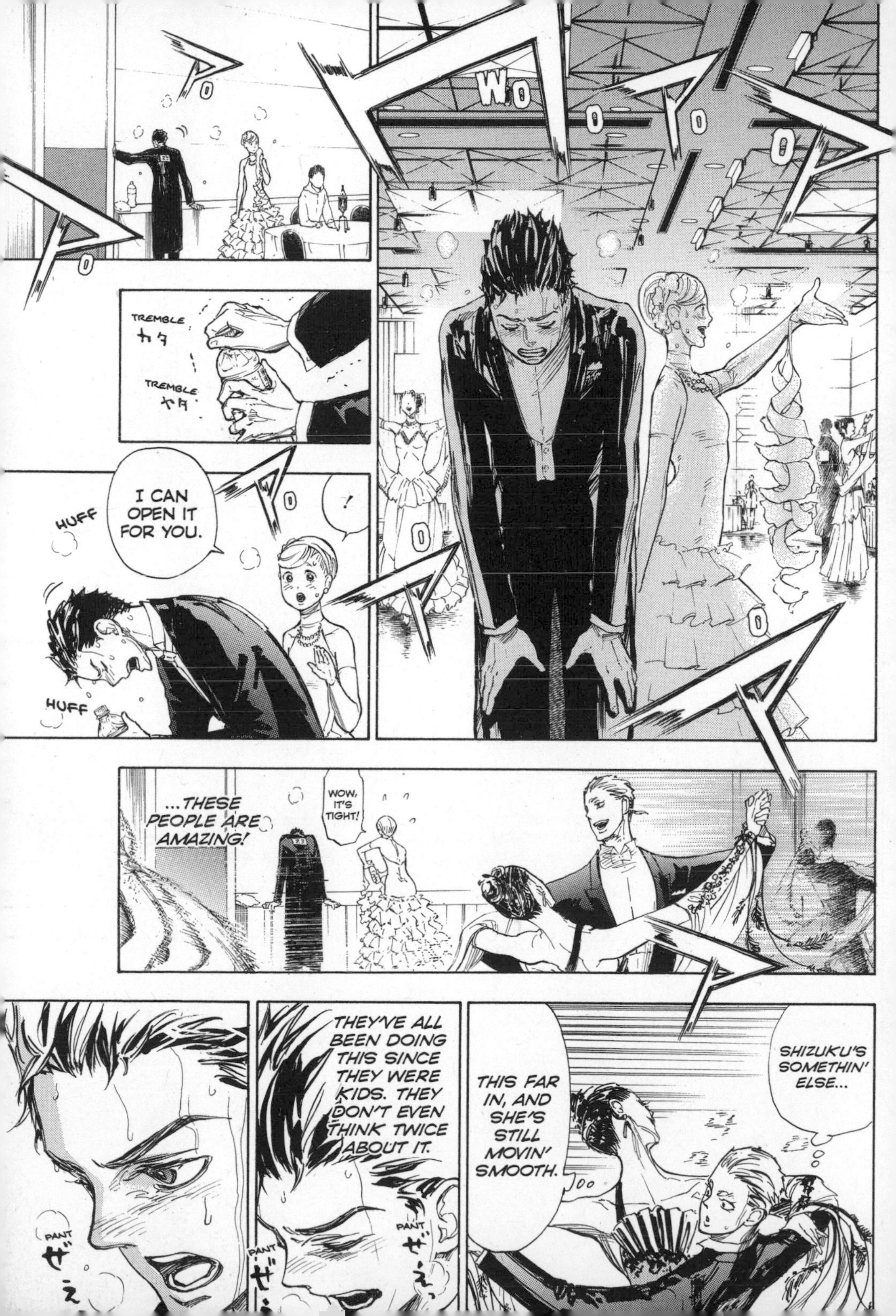
WOOOOOO
TREMBLE
カタ
TREMBLE
カタ
!
I CAN OPEN IT FOR YOU.
HUFF
HUFF
WOW, IT'S TIGHT!
...THESE PEOPLE ARE AMAZING!
SHIZUKU'S SOMETHIN' ELSE...
THIS FAR IN, AND SHE'S STILL MOVIN' SMOOTH.
THEY'VE ALL BEEN DOING THIS SINCE THEY WERE KIDS. THEY DON'T EVEN THINK TWICE ABOUT IT.
PANT
ぜぇっ
PANT
ぜぇ

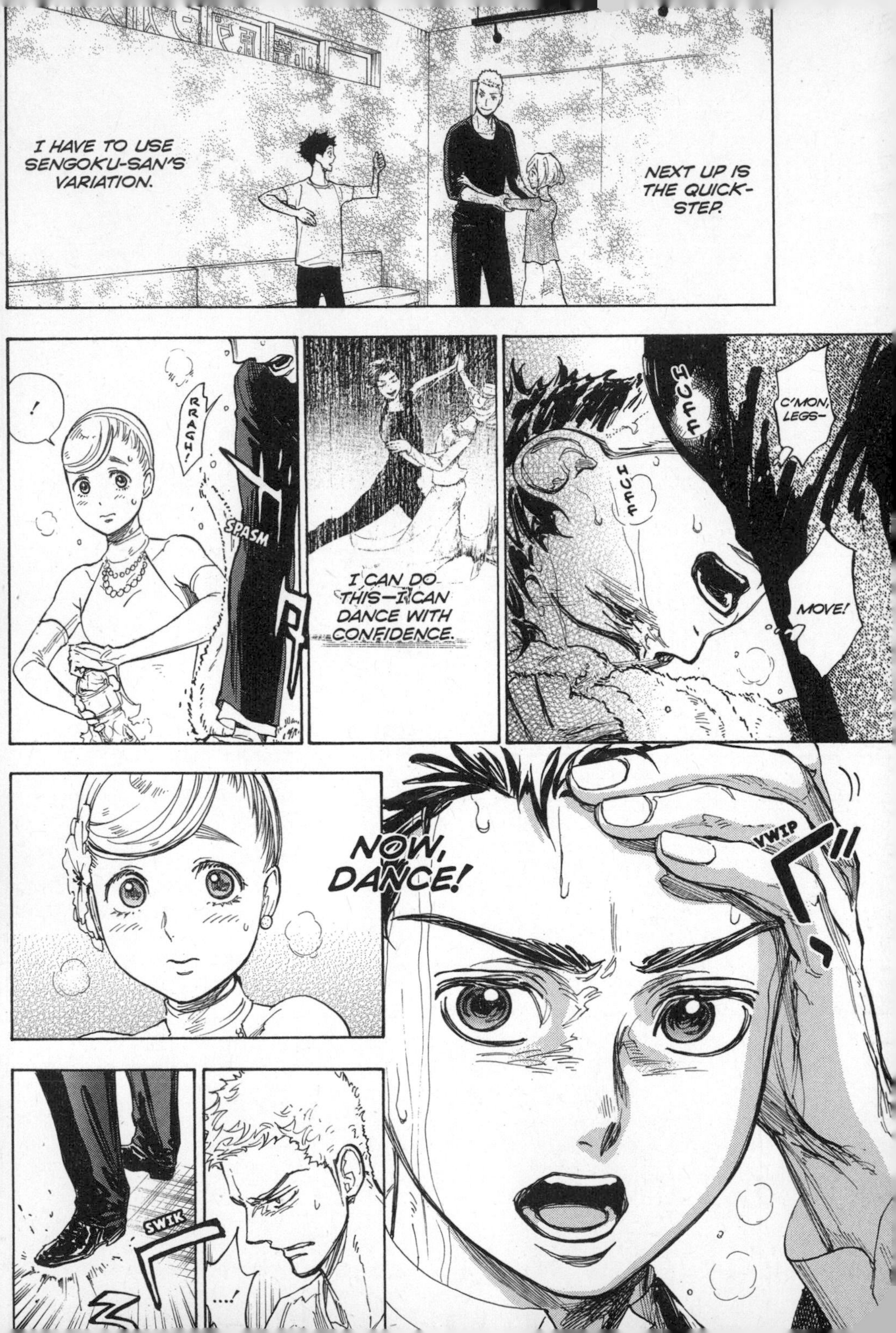
NEXT UP IS THE QUICK-STEP.
I HAVE TO USE SENGOKU-SAN'S VARIATION.
HUFF
C'MON, LEGS—
HUFF
MOVE!
I CAN DO THIS—I CAN DANCE WITH CONFIDENCE.
RRAGH!
SPASM
!
VWIP
NOW, DANCE!
SWIK
....!

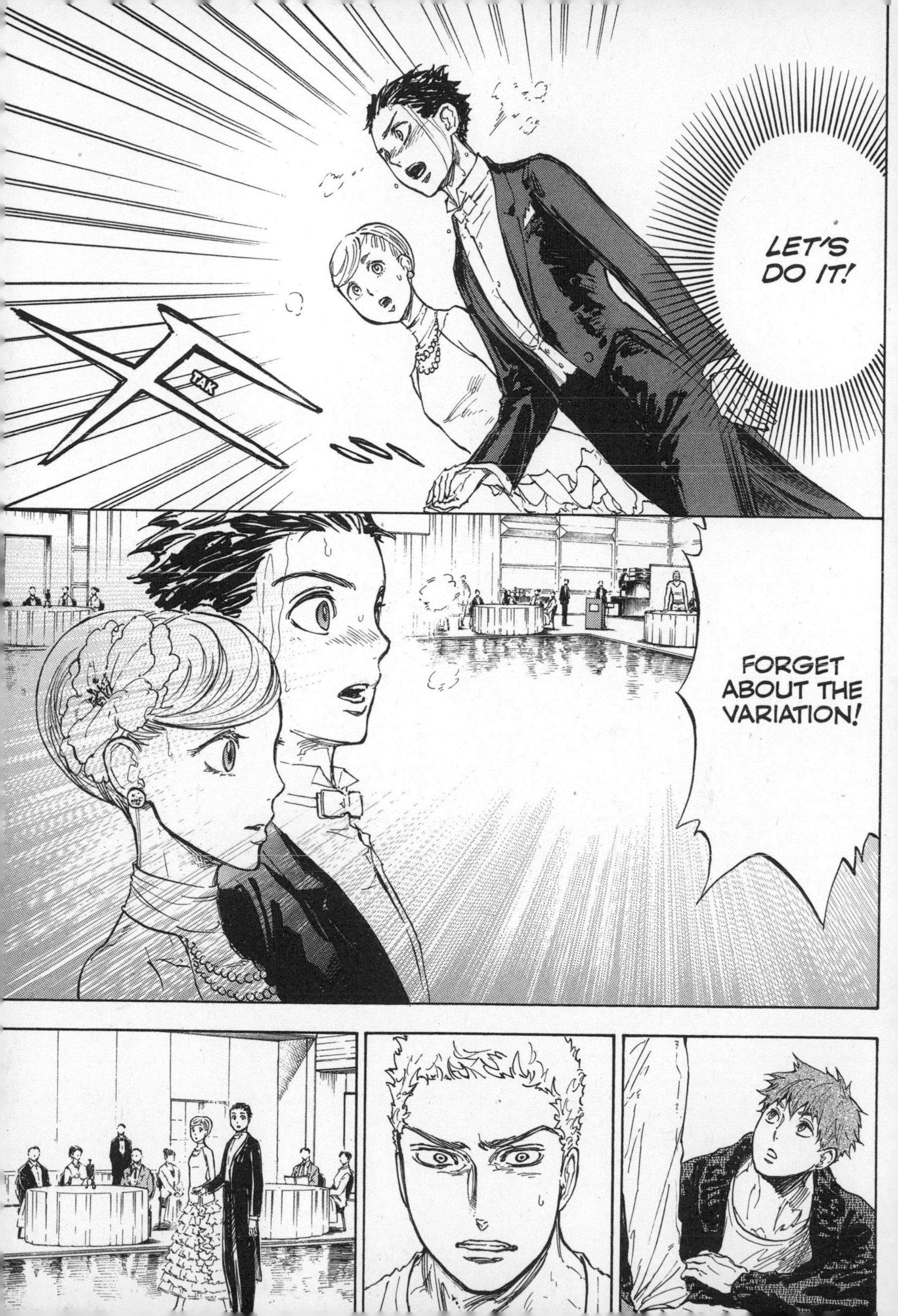
LET'S DO IT!
TAK
FORGET ABOUT THE VARIATION!

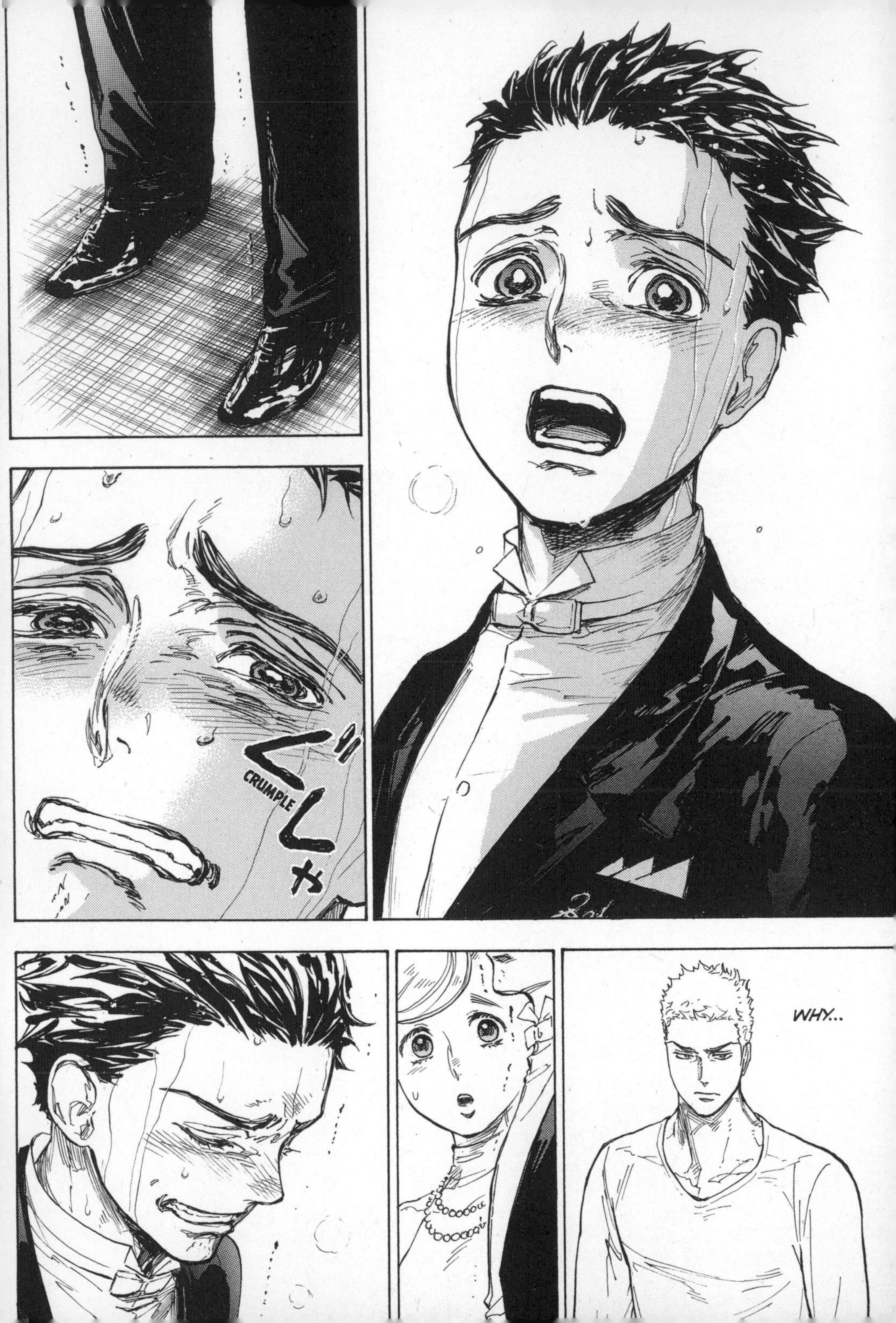
ぐしゃ
CRUMPLE
WHY...

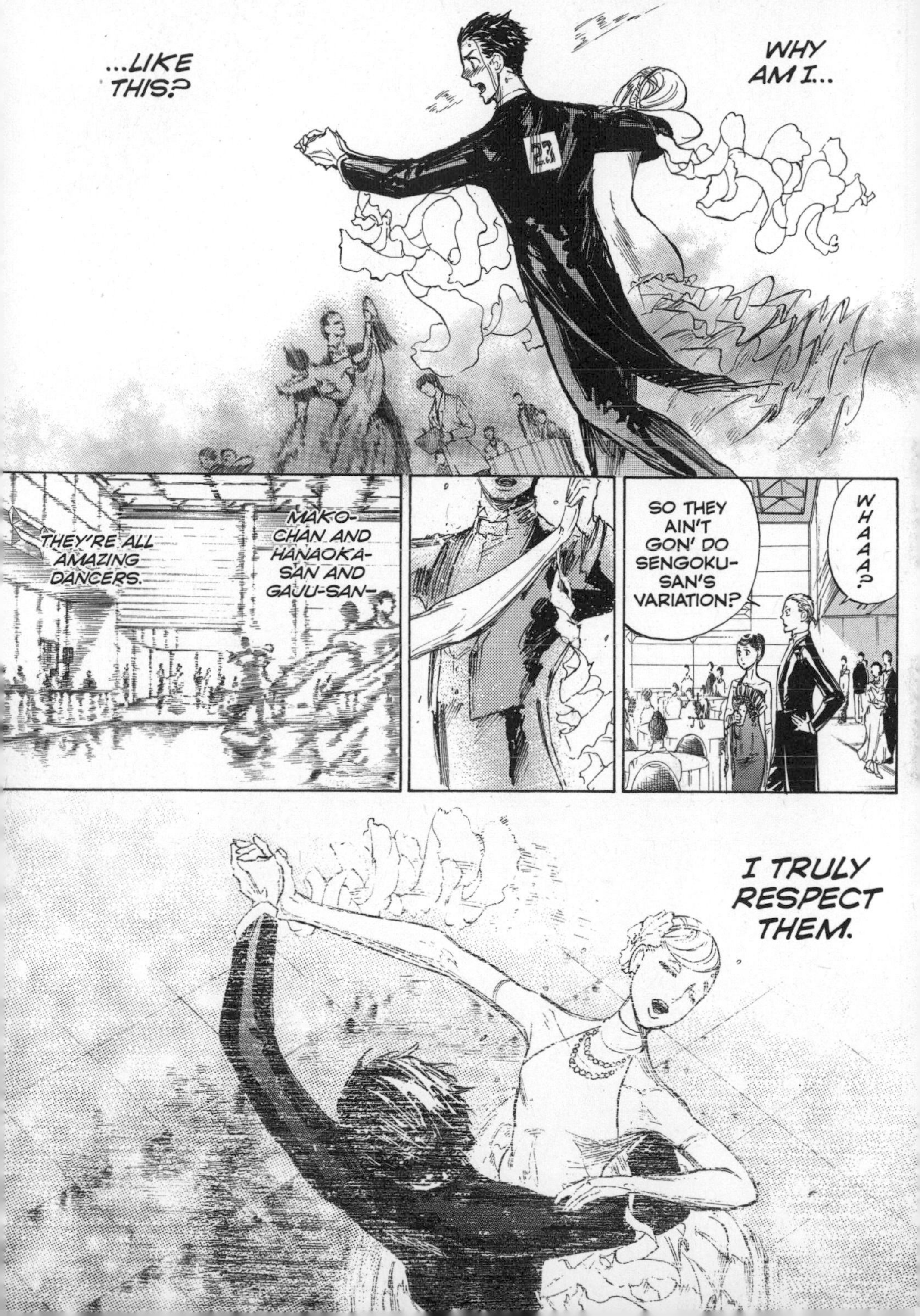
WHY AM I...
...LIKE THIS?
WHAAAA?
SO THEY AIN'T GON' DO SENGOKU-SAN'S VARIATION?
MAKO-CHAN AND HANAOKA-SAN AND GAJU-SAN—
THEY'RE ALL AMAZING DANCERS.
I TRULY RESPECT THEM.

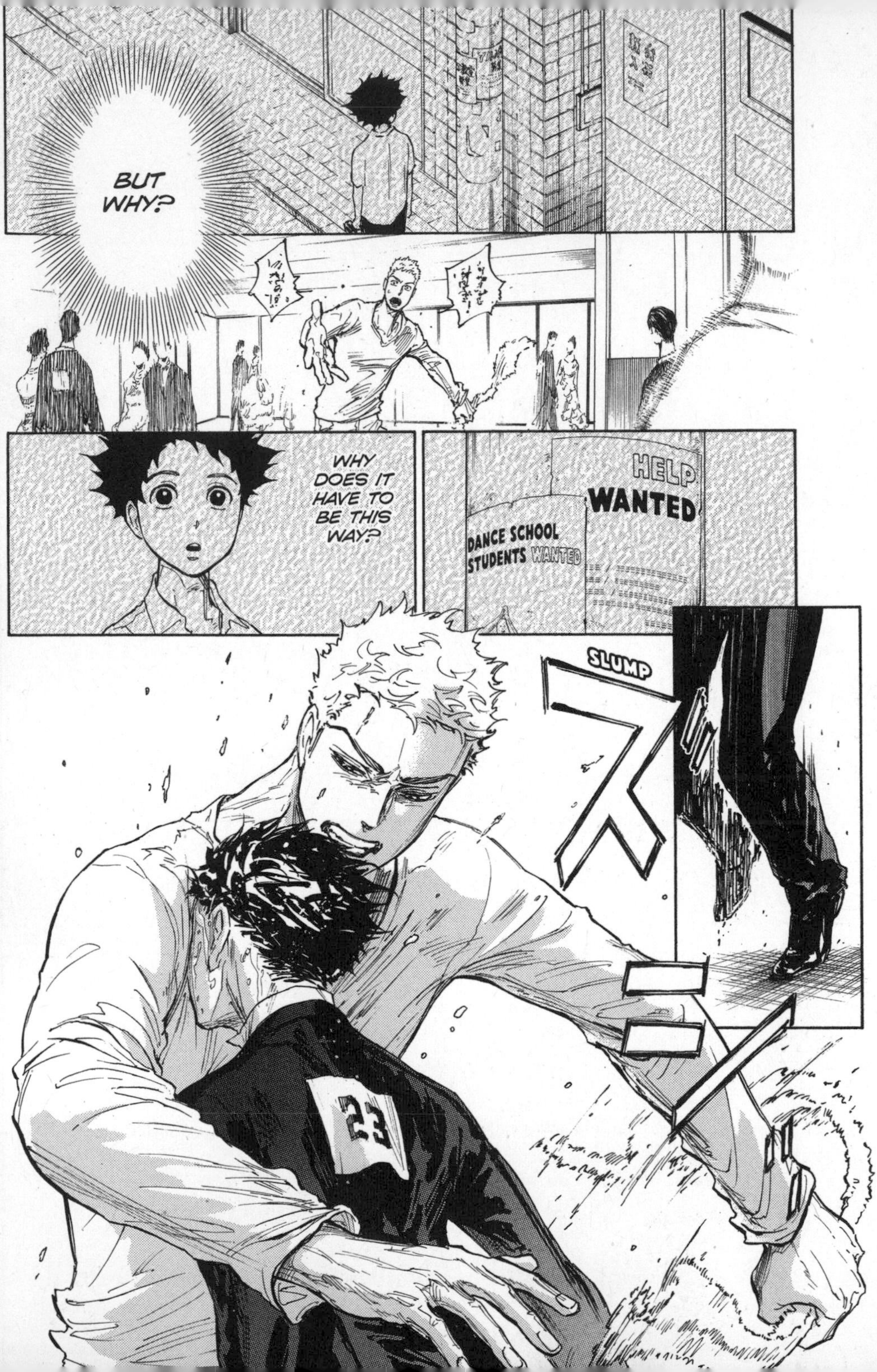
BUT WHY?
HELP WANTED
DANCE SCHOOL STUDENTS WANTED
WHY DOES IT HAVE TO BE THIS WAY?
SLUMP

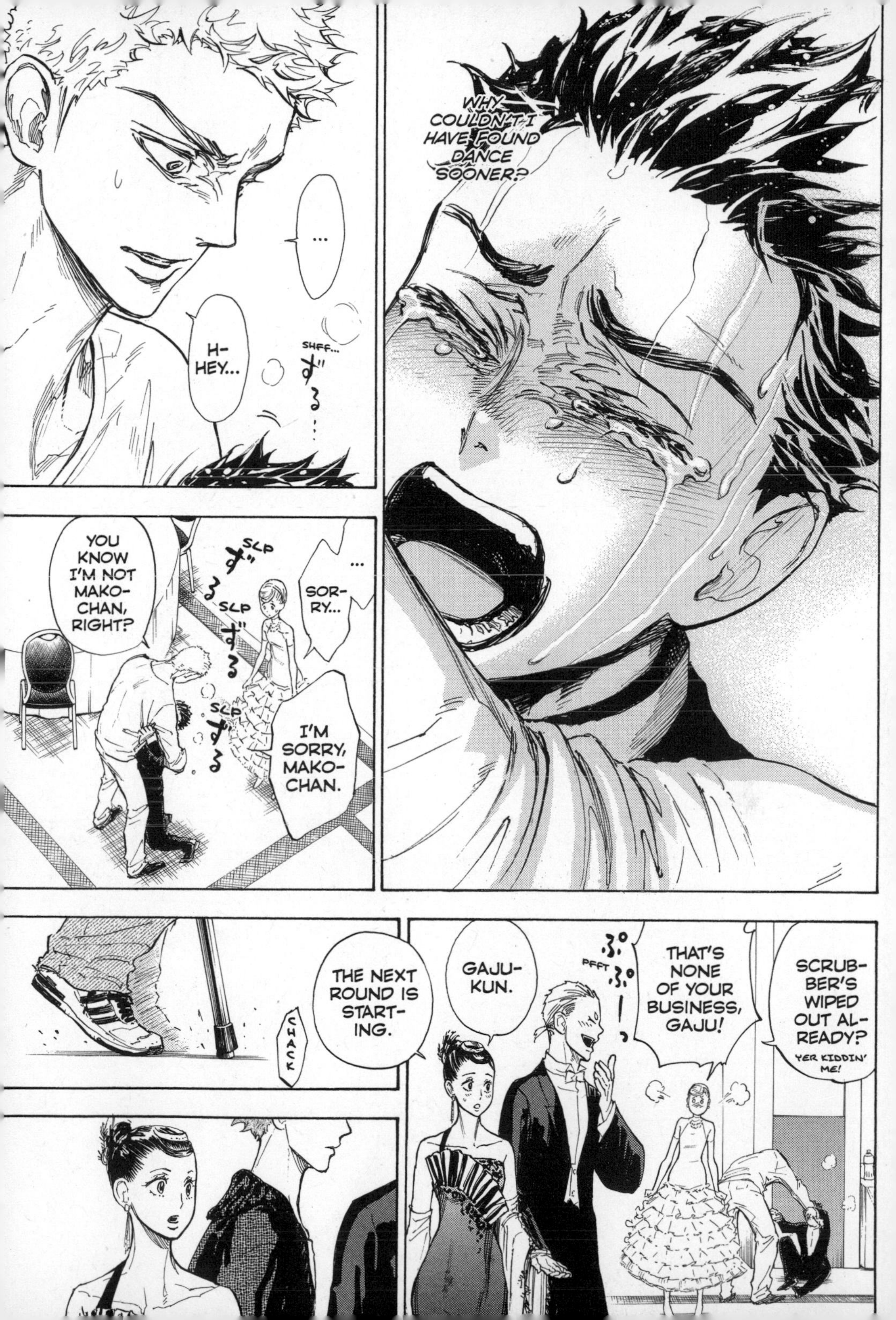
WHY COULDN'T I HAVE FOUND DANCE SOONER?
...
H-HEY...
SHFF... ずる
...
SORRY...
I'M SORRY, MAKO-CHAN.
SLP ずる SLP ずる SLP ずる
YOU KNOW I'M NOT MAKO-CHAN, RIGHT?
SCRUBBER'S WIPED OUT ALREADY?
YER KIDDIN' ME!
THAT'S NONE OF YOUR BUSINESS, GAJU!
PFFT ぷぷ
GAJU-KUN.
THE NEXT ROUND IS STARTING.
CHACK

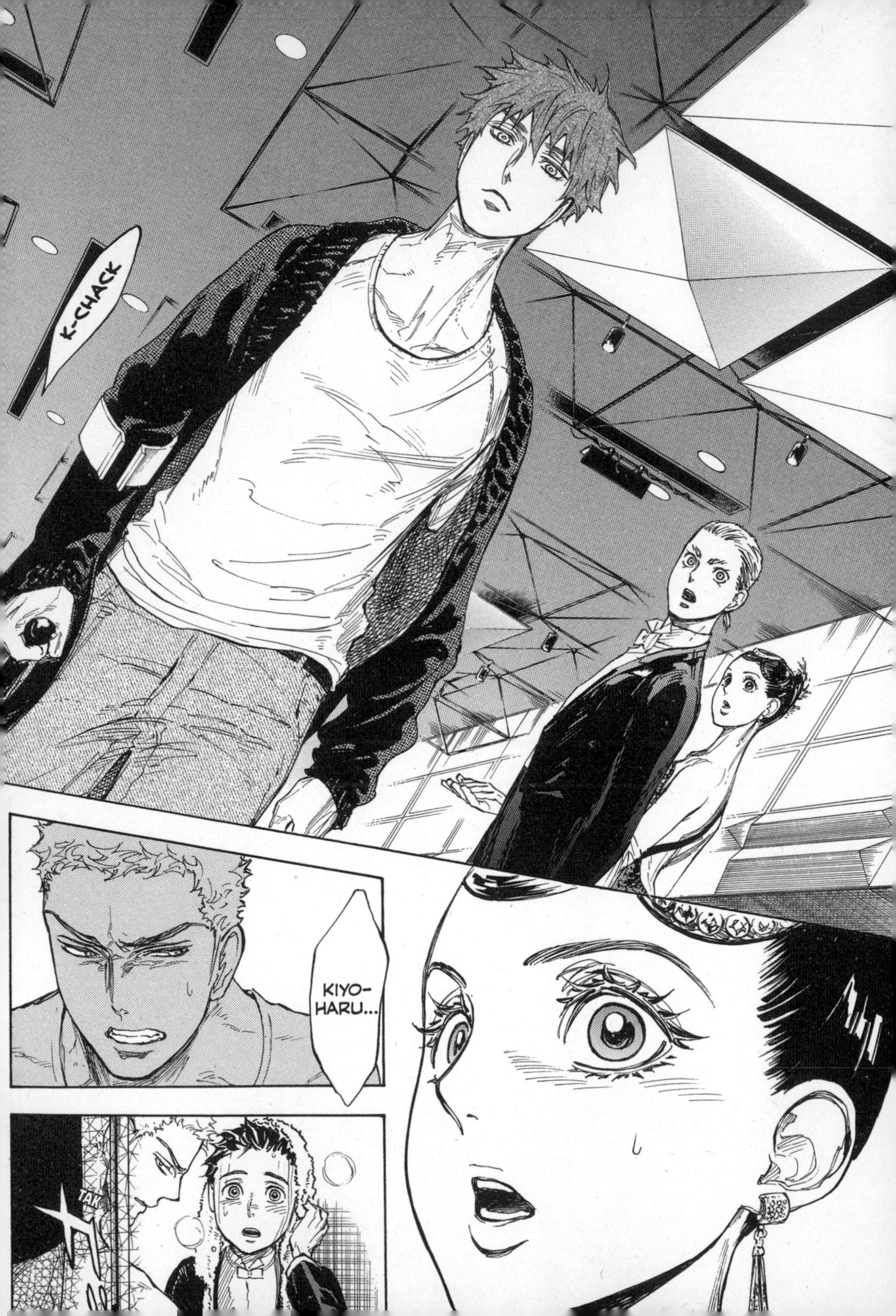
K-CHACK
KIYO-HARU...
TAK

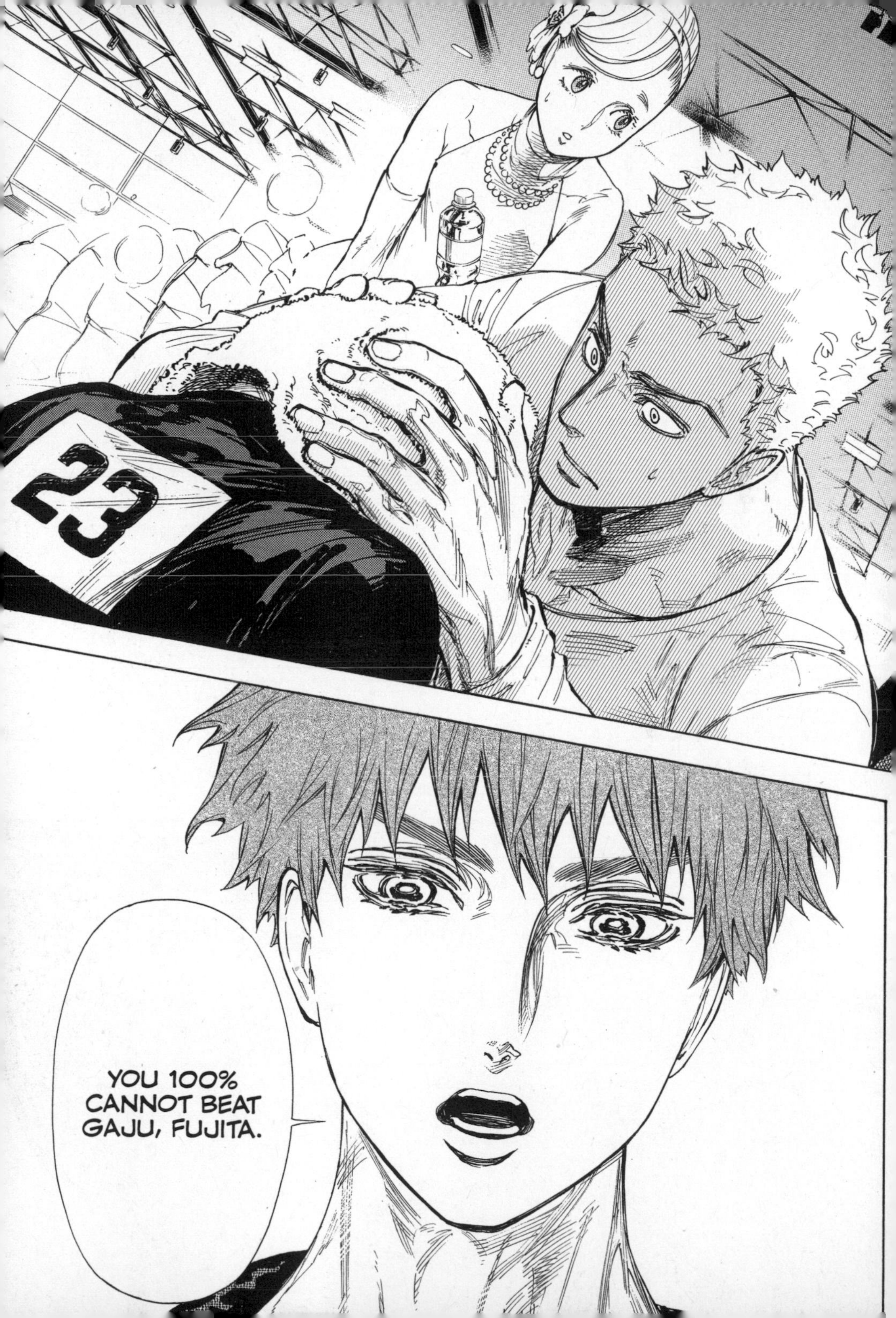
23
YOU 100% CANNOT BEAT GAJU, FUJITA.

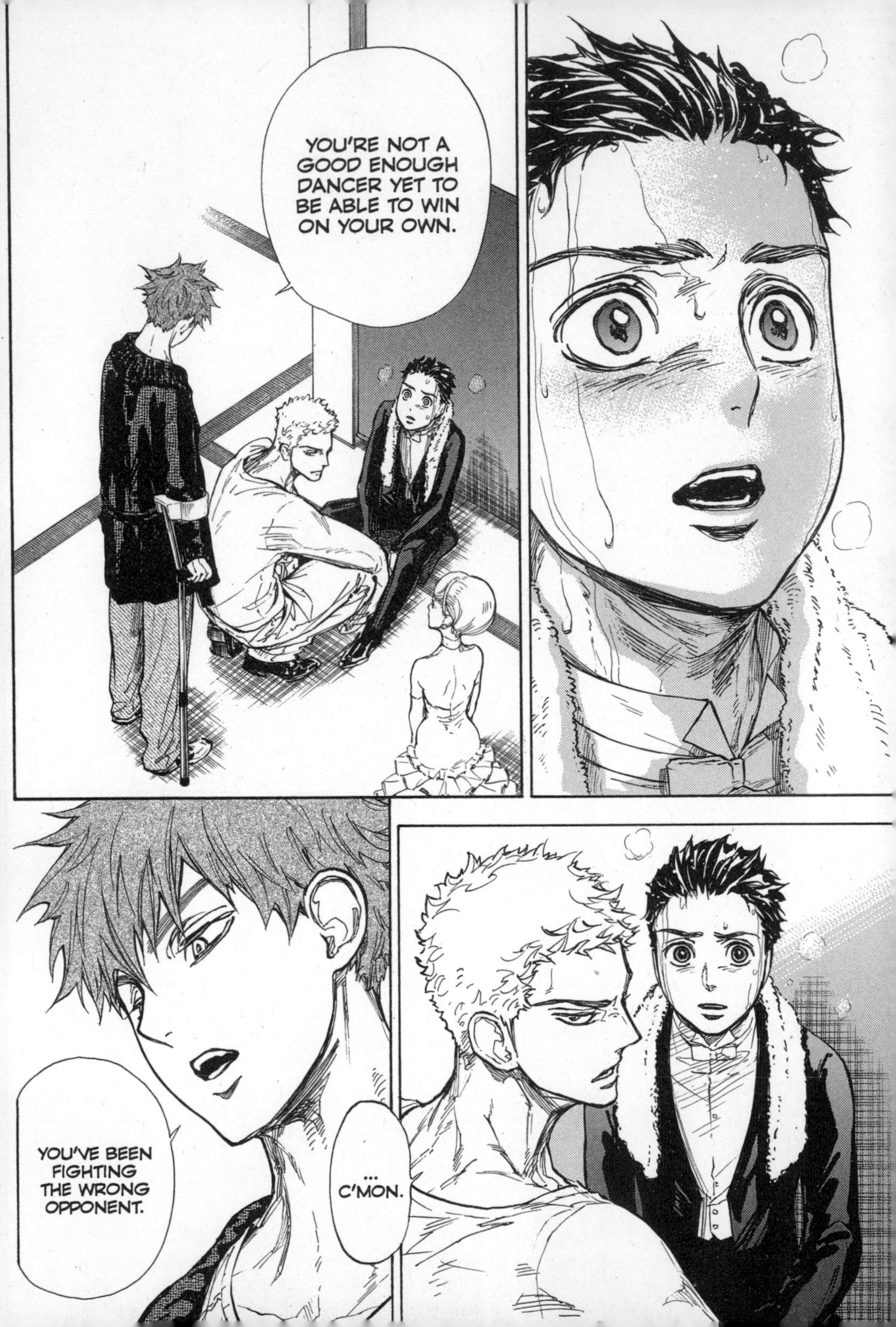
YOU'RE NOT A GOOD ENOUGH DANCER YET TO BE ABLE TO WIN ON YOUR OWN.
... C'MON.
YOU'VE BEEN FIGHTING THE WRONG OPPONENT.

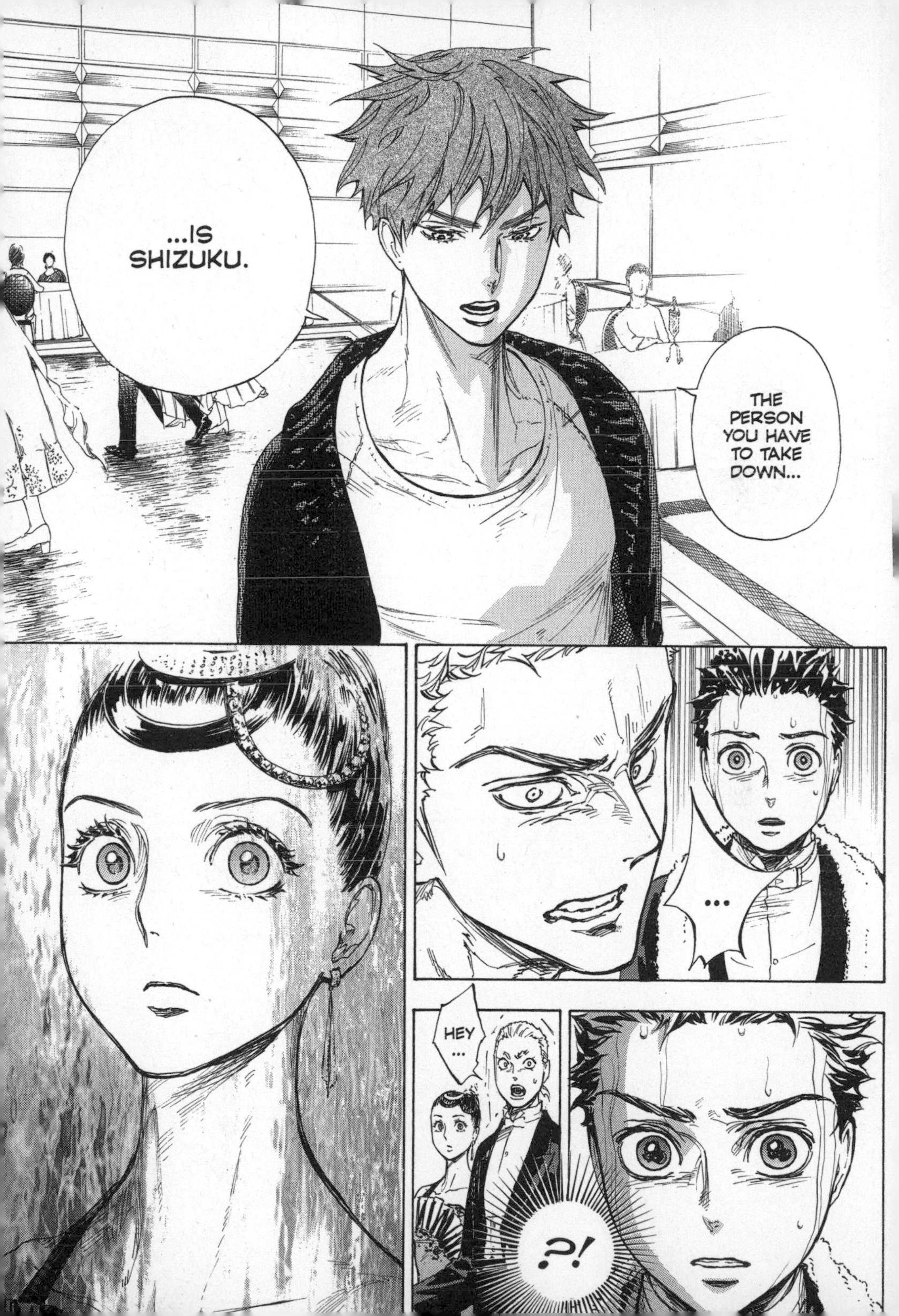
THE PERSON YOU HAVE TO TAKE DOWN...
...IS SHIZUKU.
...
?!
HEY ...

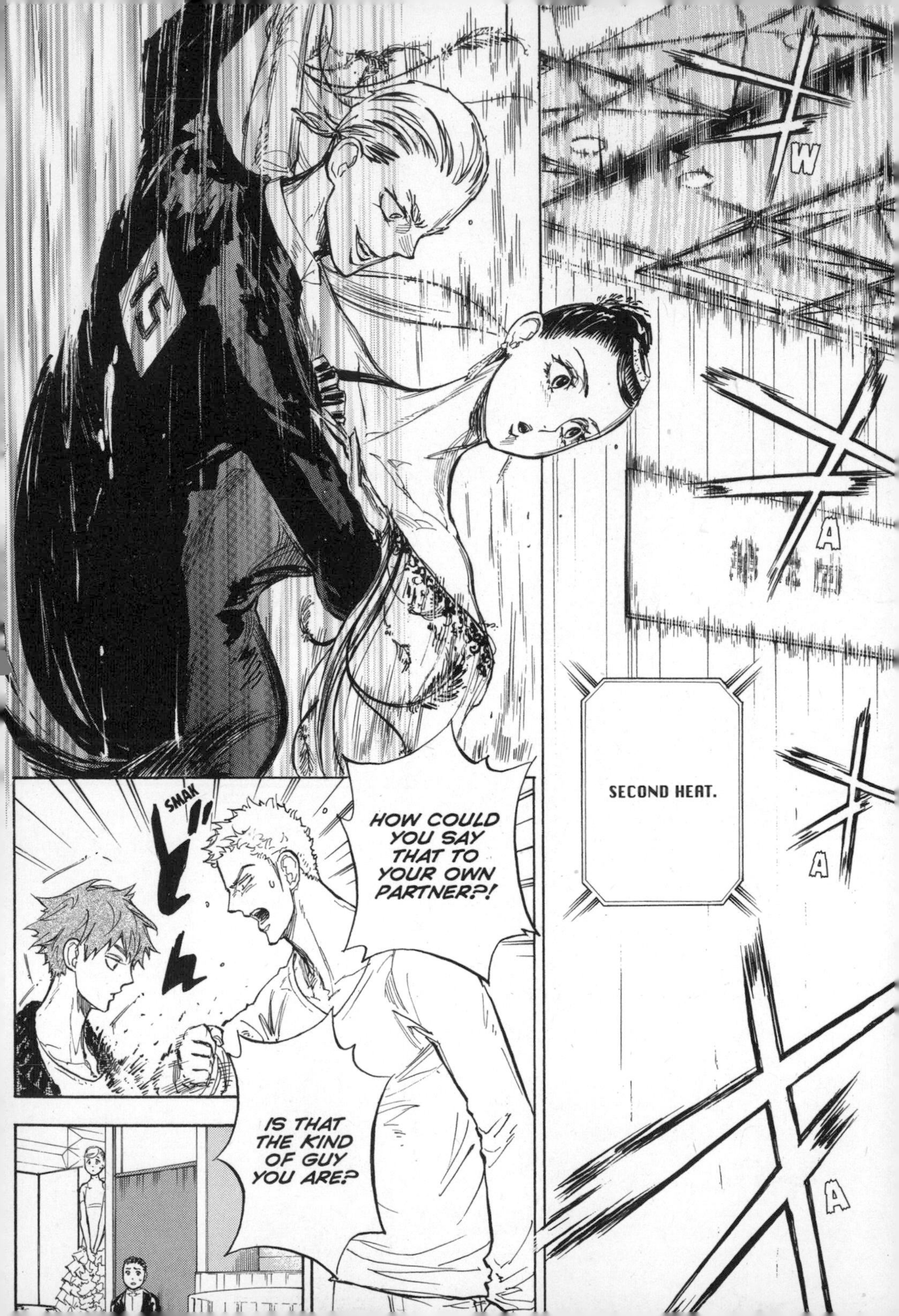
W
A
A
A
SECOND HEAT.
HOW COULD YOU SAY THAT TO YOUR OWN PARTNER?!
SMAK
IS THAT THE KIND OF GUY YOU ARE?

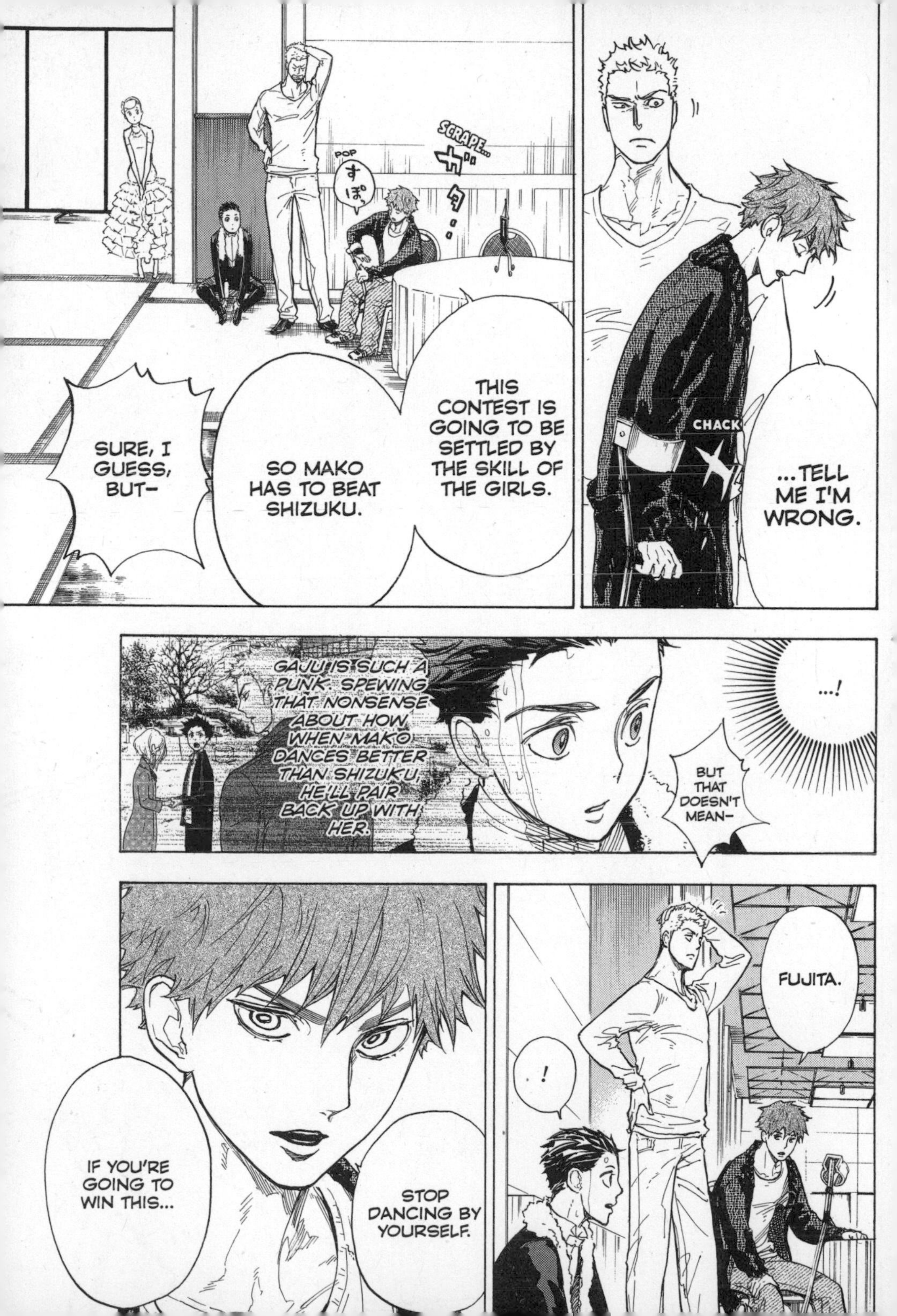
CHACK
...TELL ME I'M WRONG.
SCRAPE...
ガタ
POP
すぽっ
THIS CONTEST IS GOING TO BE SETTLED BY THE SKILL OF THE GIRLS.
SO MAKO HAS TO BEAT SHIZUKU.
SURE, I GUESS, BUT—
...!
BUT THAT DOESN'T MEAN—
GAJU IS SUCH A PUNK. SPEWING THAT NONSENSE ABOUT HOW WHEN MAKO DANCES BETTER THAN SHIZUKU, HE'LL PAIR BACK UP WITH HER.
FUJITA.
!
IF YOU'RE GOING TO WIN THIS...
STOP DANCING BY YOURSELF.

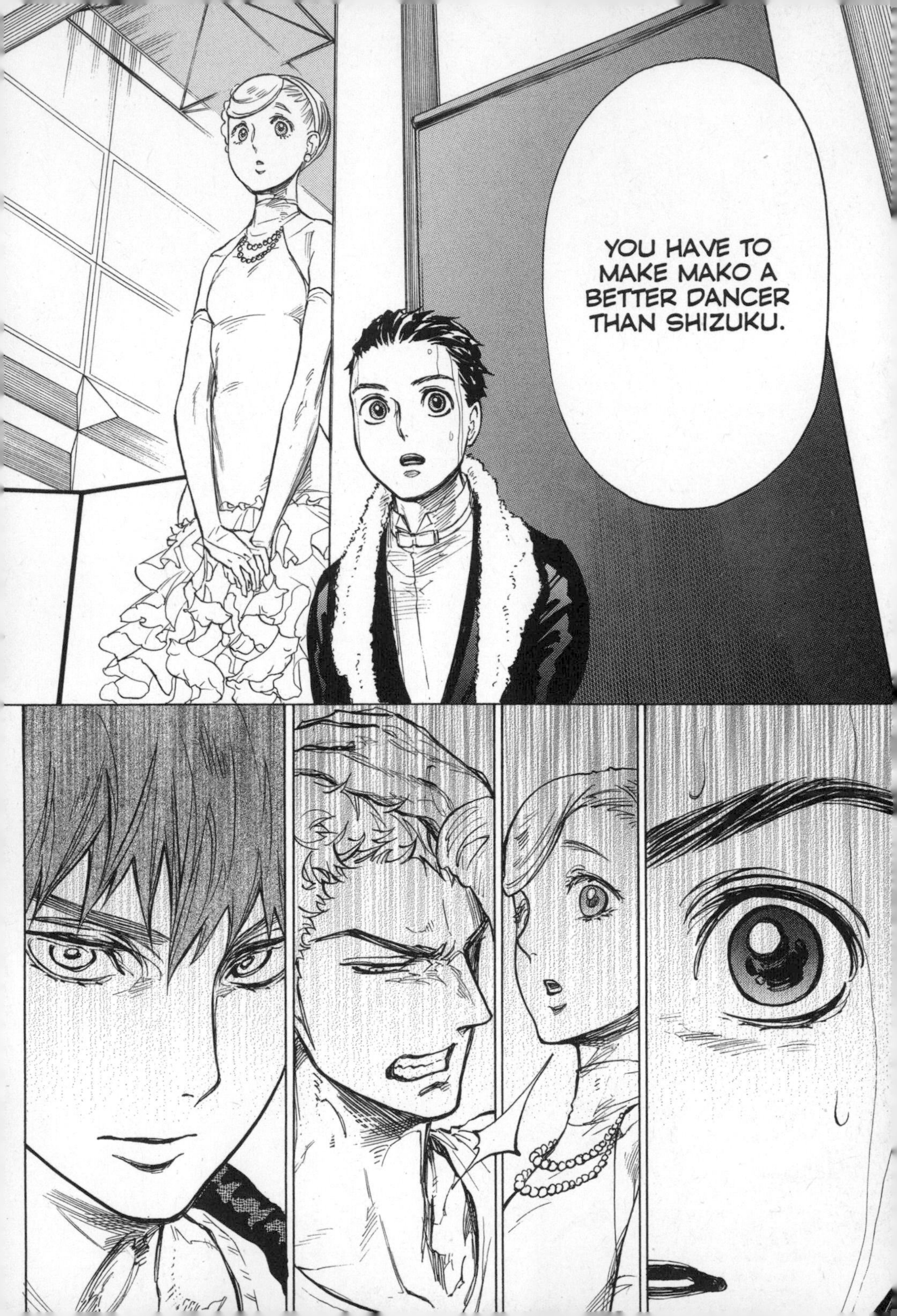
YOU HAVE TO MAKE MAKO A BETTER DANCER THAN SHIZUKU.

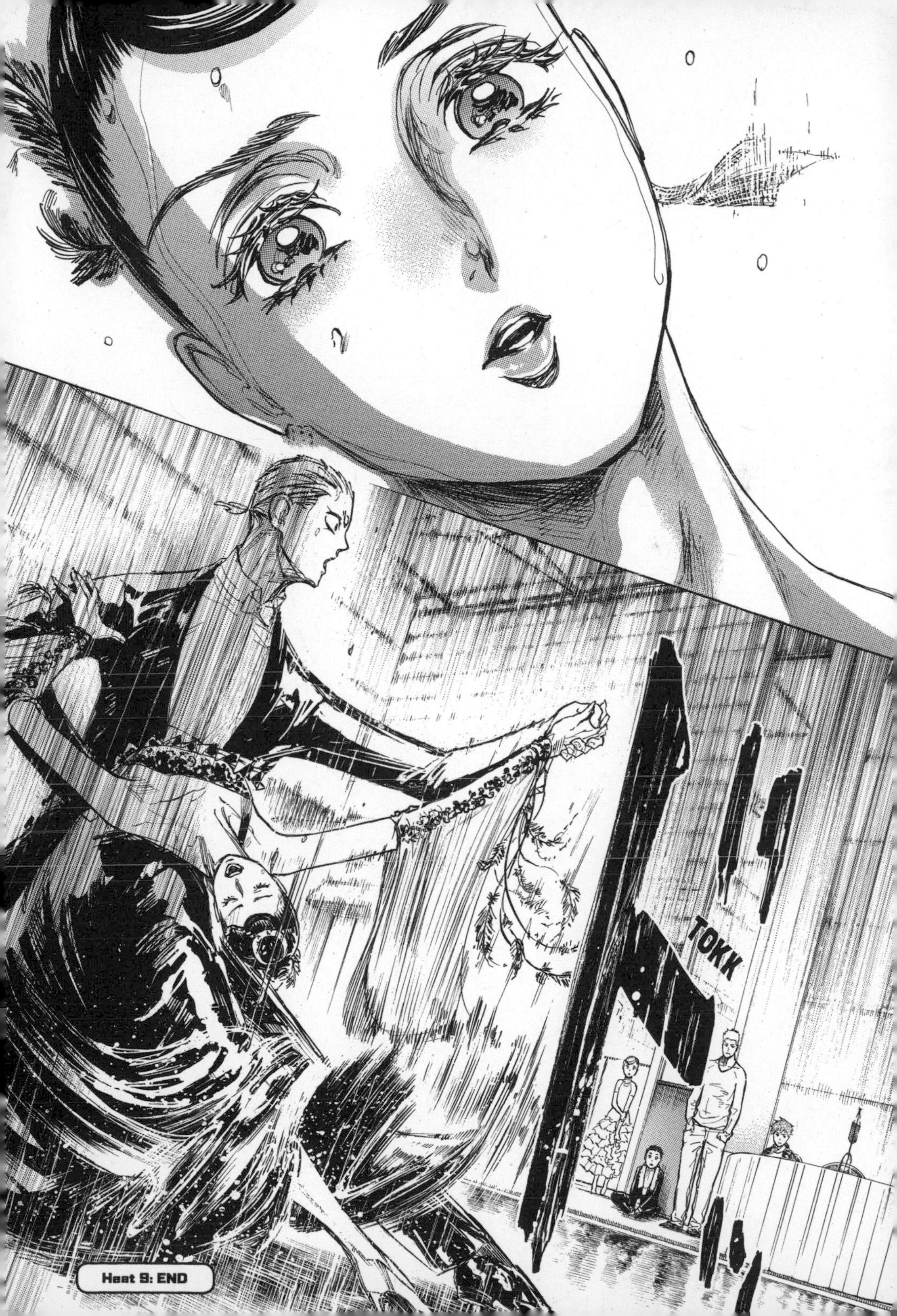
TOKK
Heat 9: END

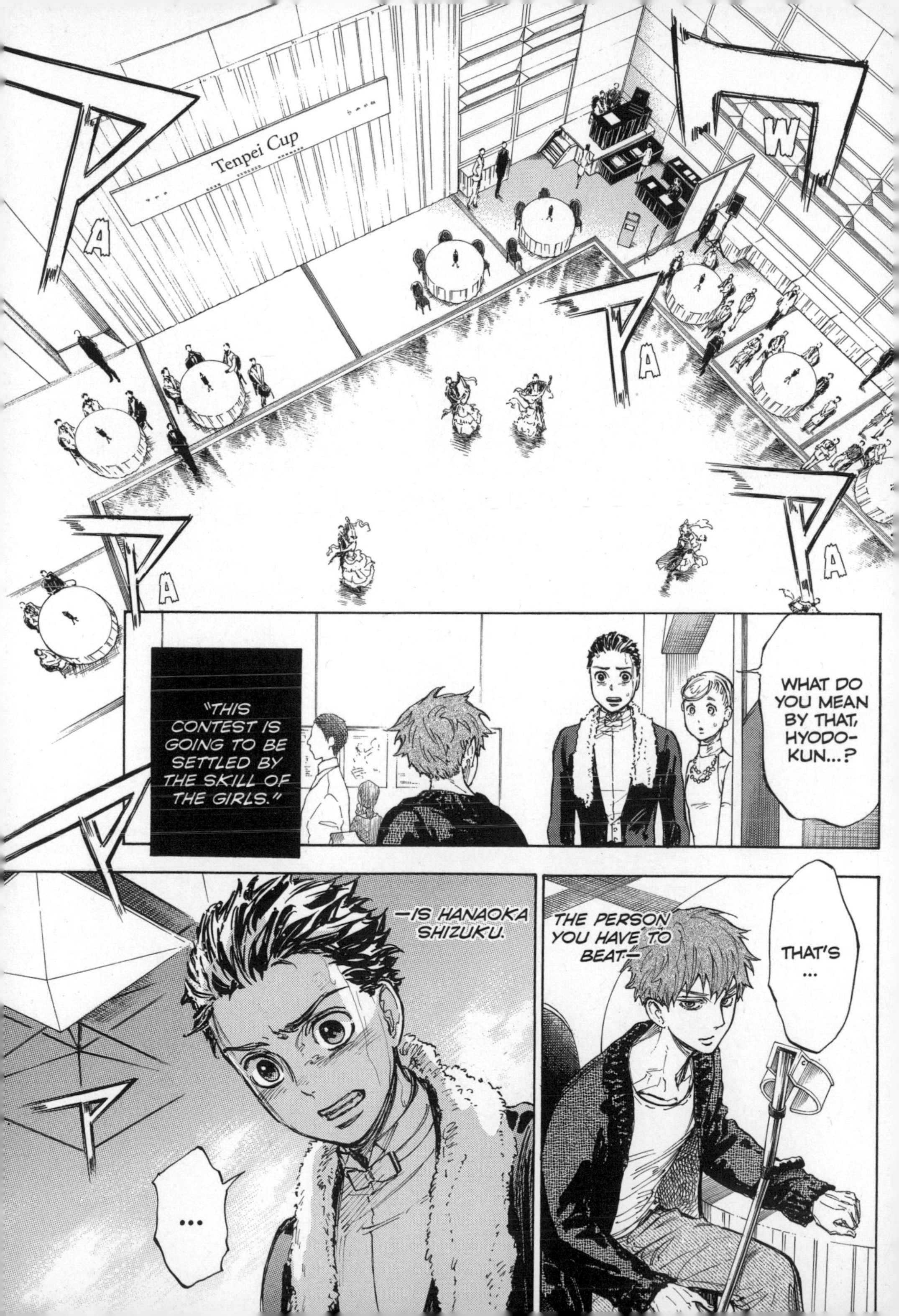

Tenpei Cup
WHAT DO YOU MEAN BY THAT, HYODO-KUN...?
"THIS CONTEST IS GOING TO BE SETTLED BY THE SKILL OF THE GIRLS."
THAT'S ...
THE PERSON YOU HAVE TO BEAT—
—IS HANAOKA SHIZUKU.
...

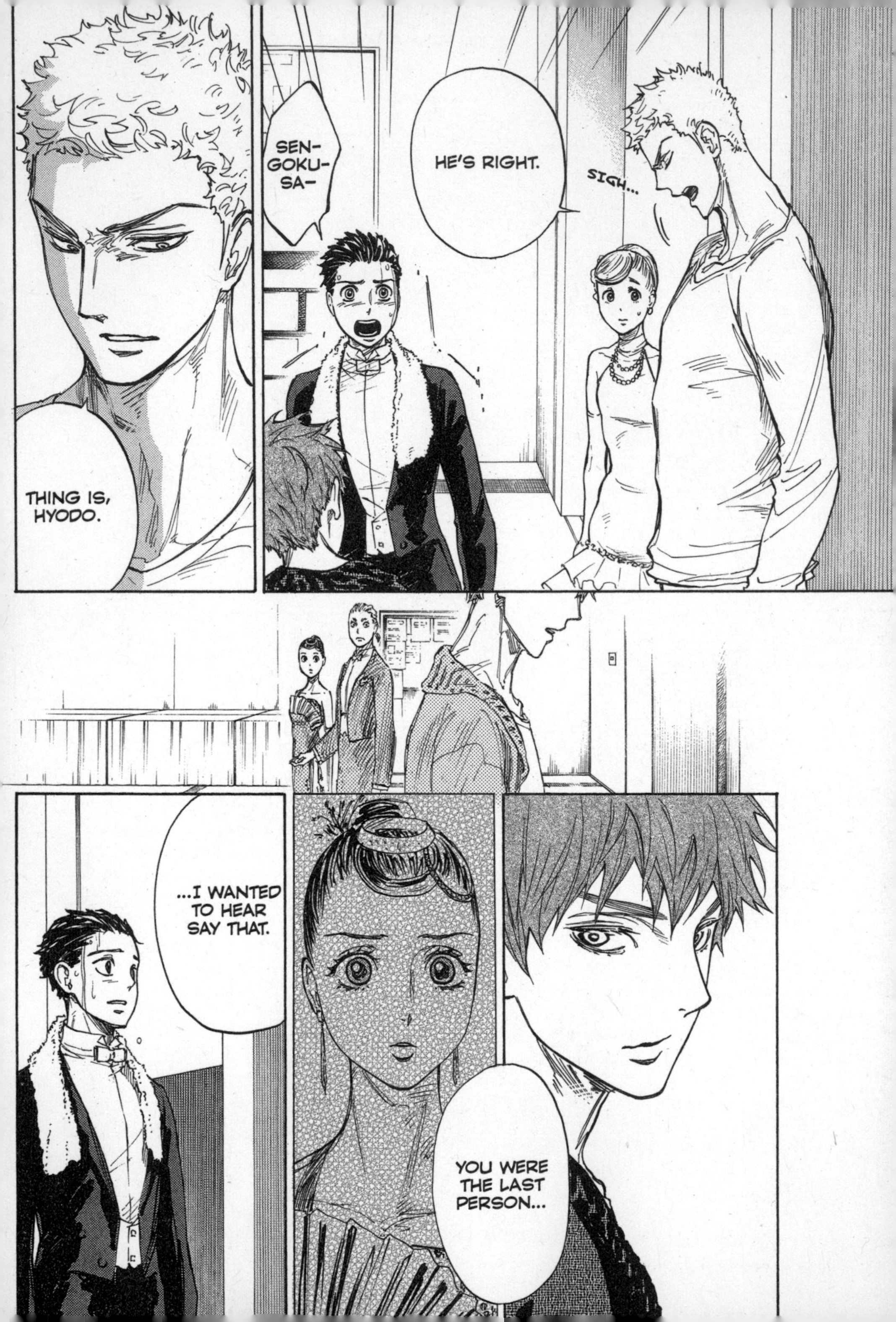
SIGH...
HE'S RIGHT.
SEN-GOKU-SA-
THING IS, HYODO.
YOU WERE THE LAST PERSON...
...I WANTED TO HEAR SAY THAT.

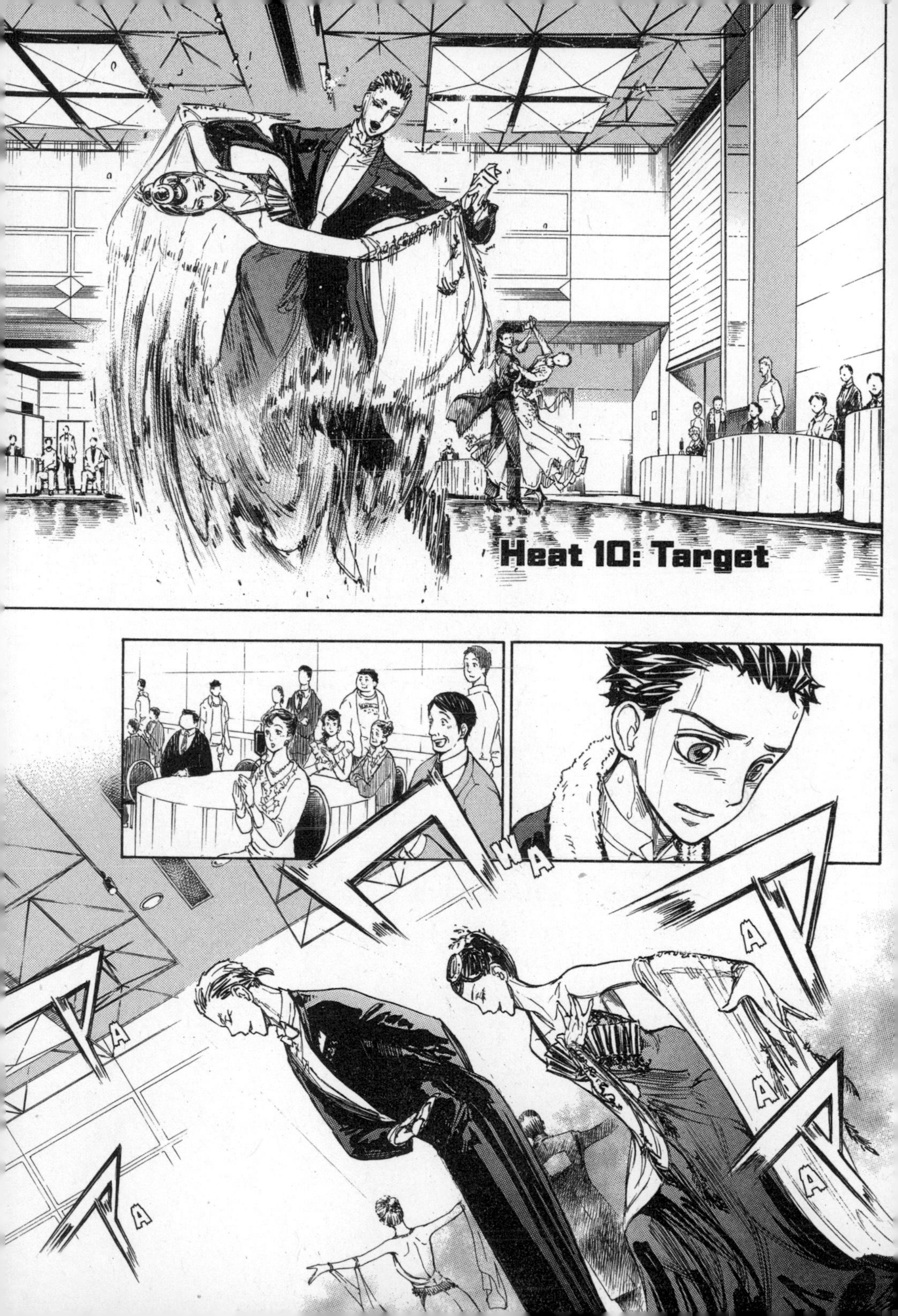
Heat 10: Target
WA
A
A
A
A
A
A

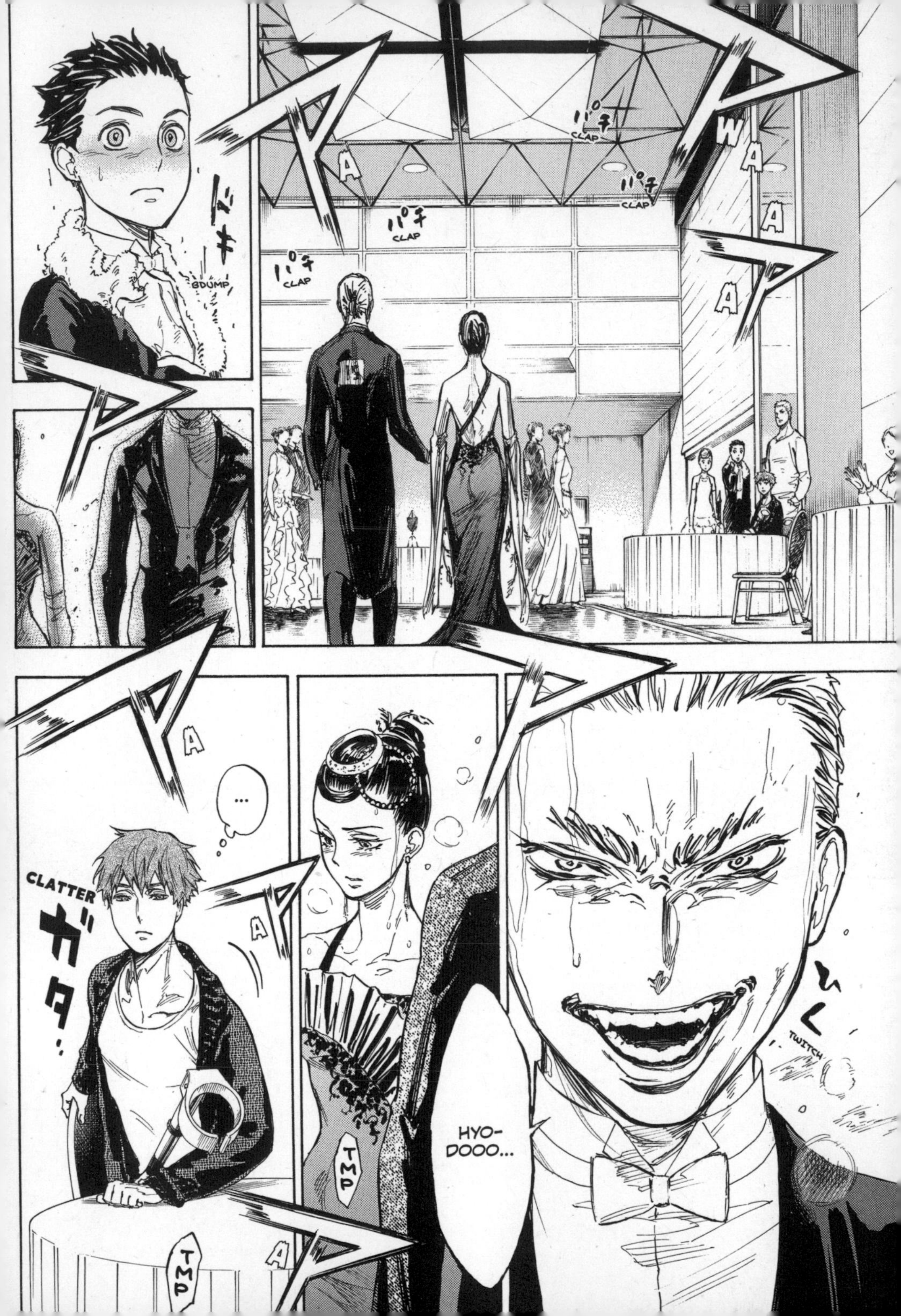
WA
A
A
A
パチ
CLAP
パチ
CLAP
パチ
CLAP
パチ
CLAP
A
ドキ
BDUMP
ひく
TWITCH
HYO-DOOO...
A
TMP
...
CLATTER
ガタ
TMP
A

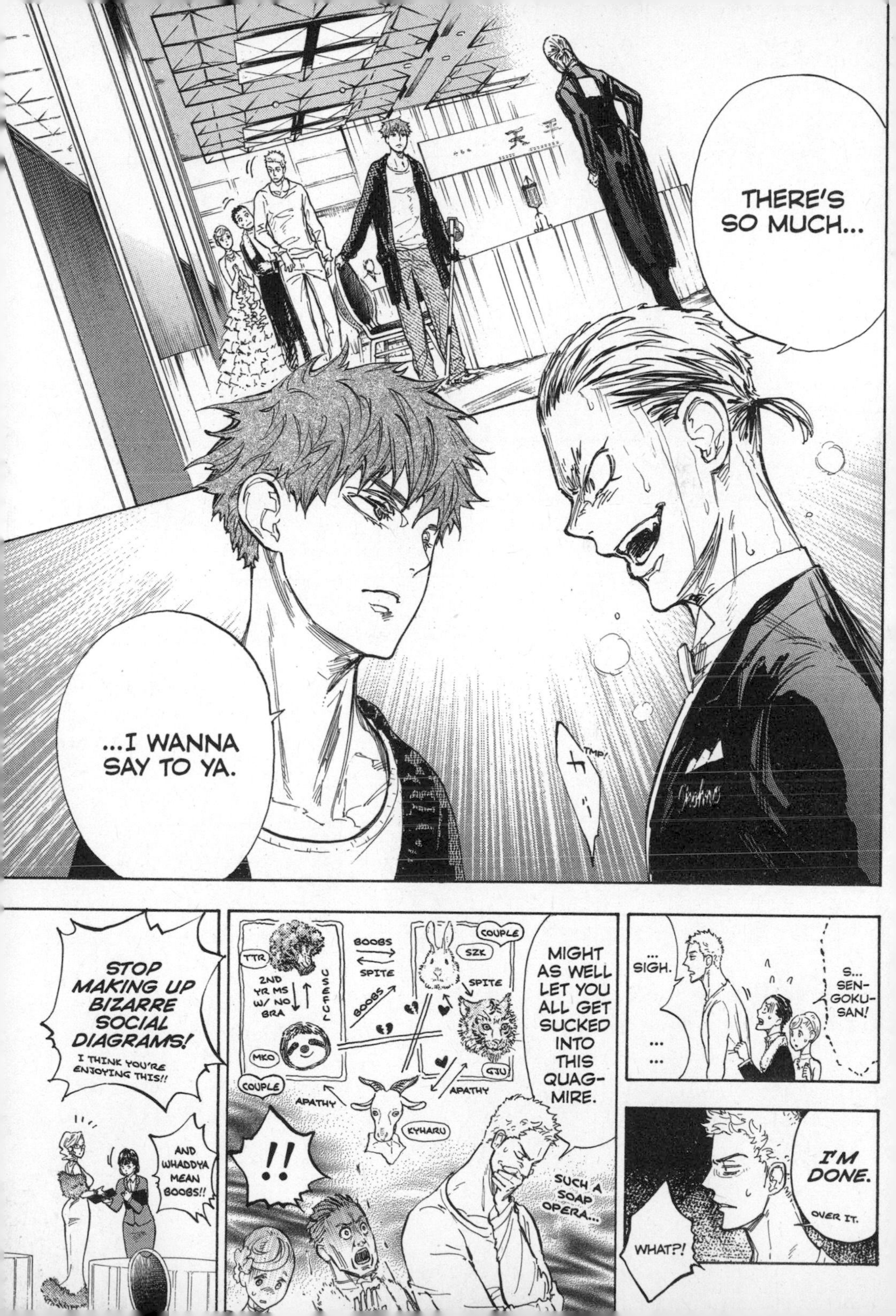
THERE'S SO MUCH...
...I WANNA SAY TO YA.
TMP!
S... SENGOKU-SAN!
... SIGH.
... ...
I'M DONE.
OVER IT.
WHAT?!
MIGHT AS WELL LET YOU ALL GET SUCKED INTO THIS QUAGMIRE.
COUPLE
SZK
BOOBS
SPITE
TTR
2ND YR MS W/ NO BRA
USEFUL
SPITE
BOOBS
MKO
GJU
COUPLE
APATHY
APATHY
KYHARU
SUCH A SOAP OPERA...
!!
STOP MAKING UP BIZARRE SOCIAL DIAGRAMS!
I THINK YOU'RE ENJOYING THIS!!
AND WHADDYA MEAN BOOBS!!

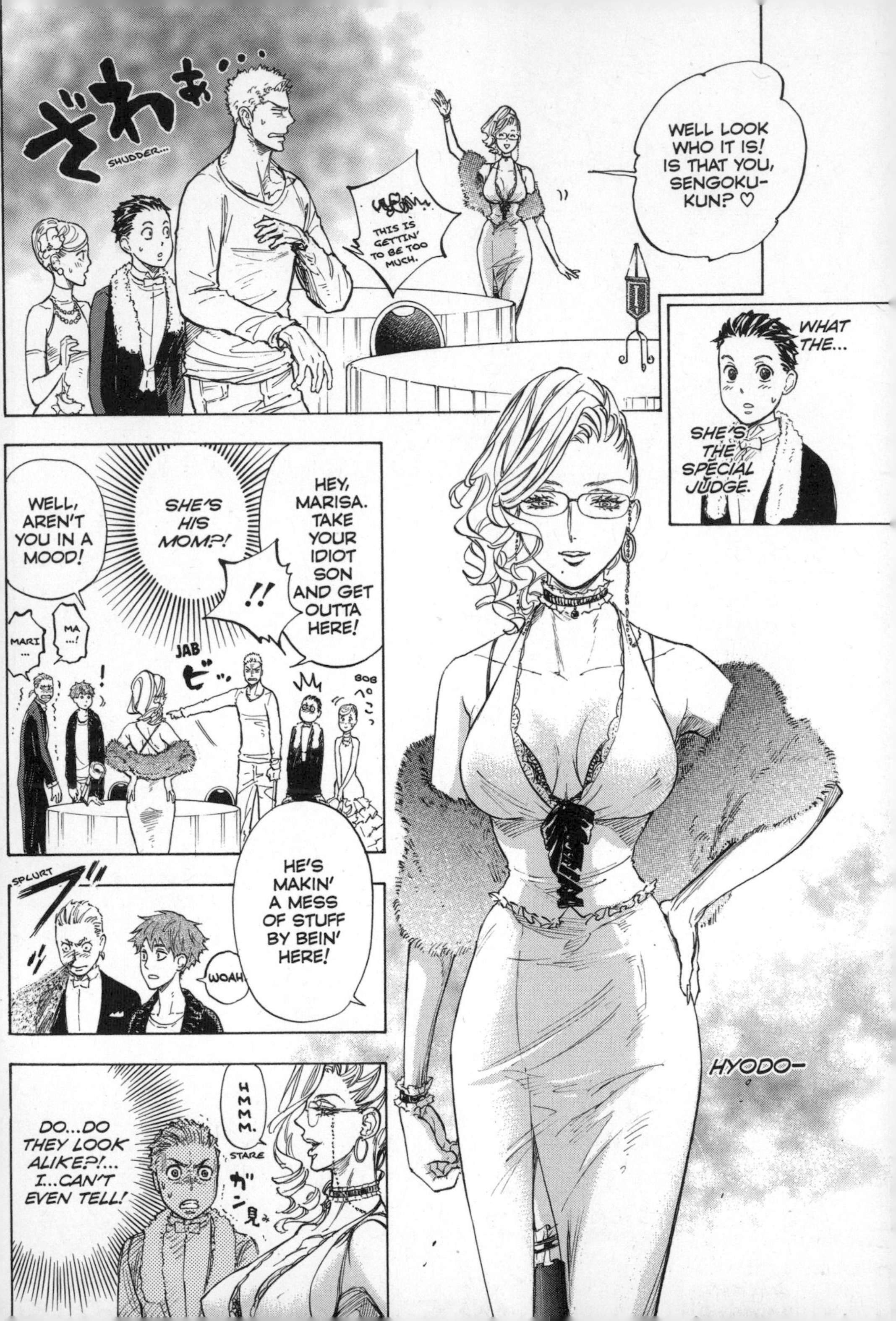
WELL LOOK WHO IT IS! IS THAT YOU, SENGOKU-KUN? ♡
THIS IS GETTIN' TO BE TOO MUCH.
SHUDDER...
WHAT THE...
SHE'S THE SPECIAL JUDGE.
HYODO-
HEY, MARISA. TAKE YOUR IDIOT SON AND GET OUTTA HERE!
!!
SHE'S HIS MOM?!
WELL, AREN'T YOU IN A MOOD!
BOB
JAB
MA...!
MARI...
HE'S MAKIN' A MESS OF STUFF BY BEIN' HERE!
WOAH
SPLURT
HMMM.
STARE
DO...DO THEY LOOK ALIKE?!... I...CAN'T EVEN TELL!

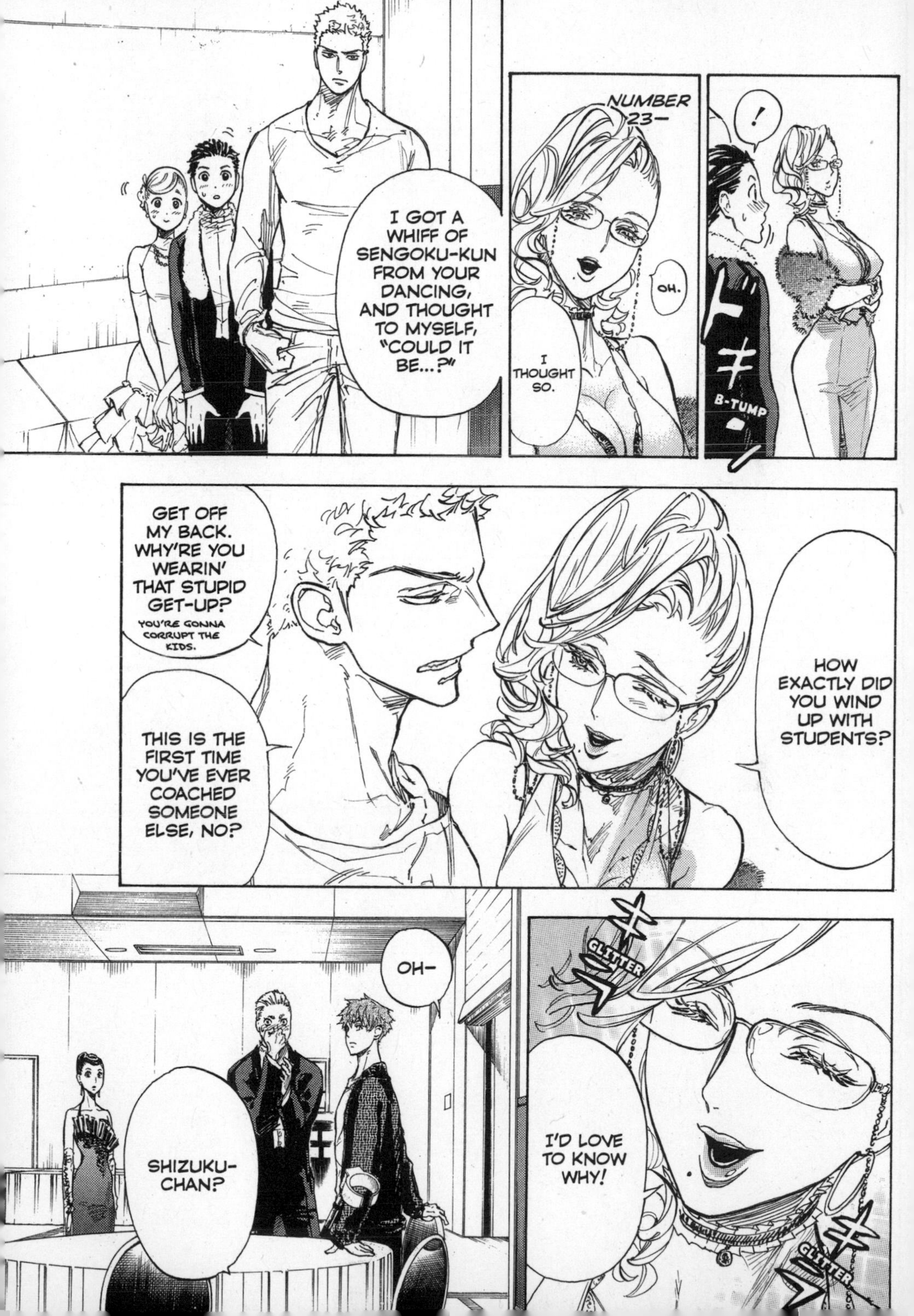
!
B-TUMP
NUMBER 23—
OH.
I THOUGHT SO.
I GOT A WHIFF OF SENGOKU-KUN FROM YOUR DANCING, AND THOUGHT TO MYSELF, "COULD IT BE...?"
HOW EXACTLY DID YOU WIND UP WITH STUDENTS?
GET OFF MY BACK. WHY'RE YOU WEARIN' THAT STUPID GET-UP?
YOU'RE GONNA CORRUPT THE KIDS.
THIS IS THE FIRST TIME YOU'VE EVER COACHED SOMEONE ELSE, NO?
GLITTER
I'D LOVE TO KNOW WHY!
GLITTER
OH-
SHIZUKU-CHAN?

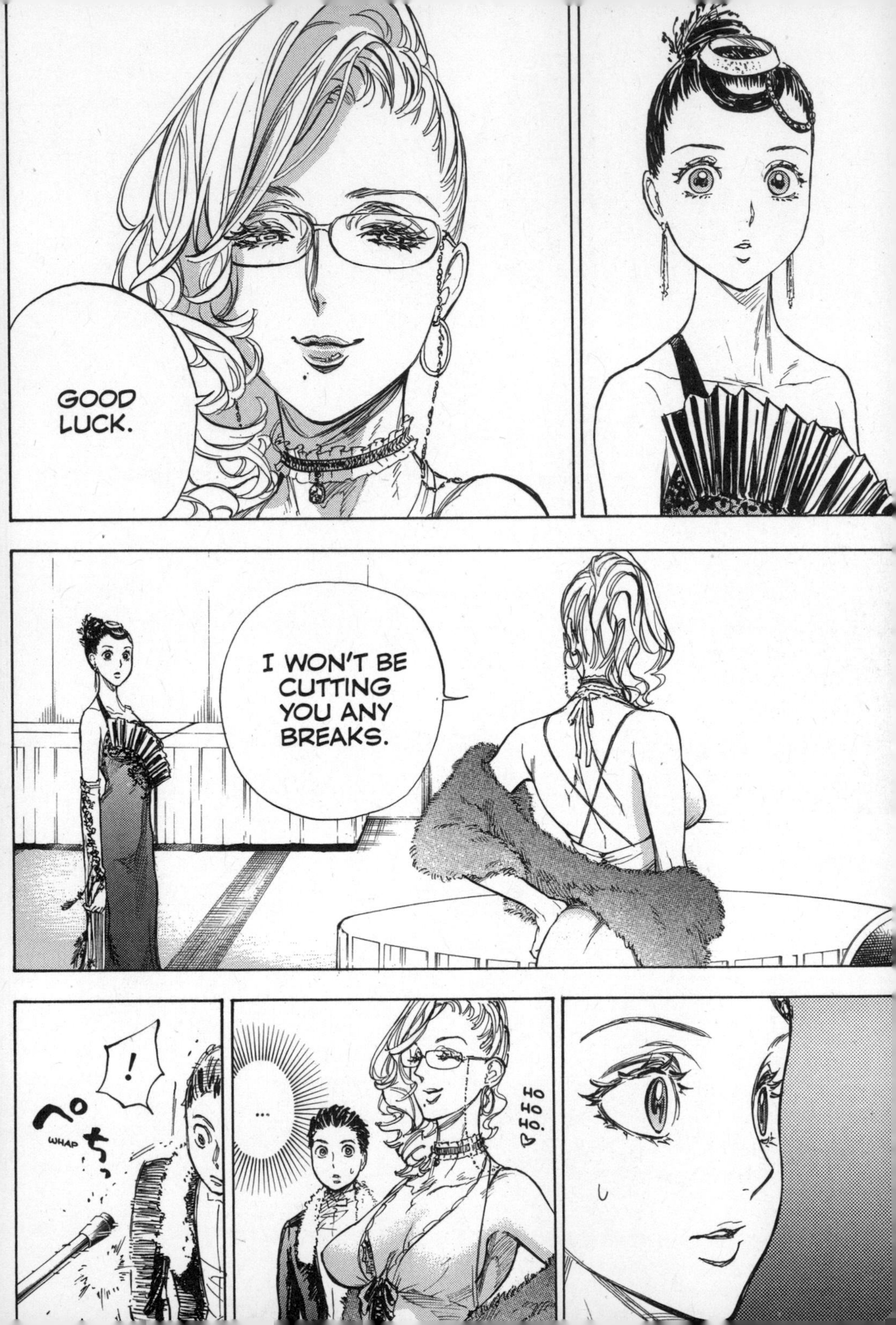
GOOD LUCK.
I WON'T BE CUTTING YOU ANY BREAKS.
HO HO HO.
...
!
ぺちっ
WHAP

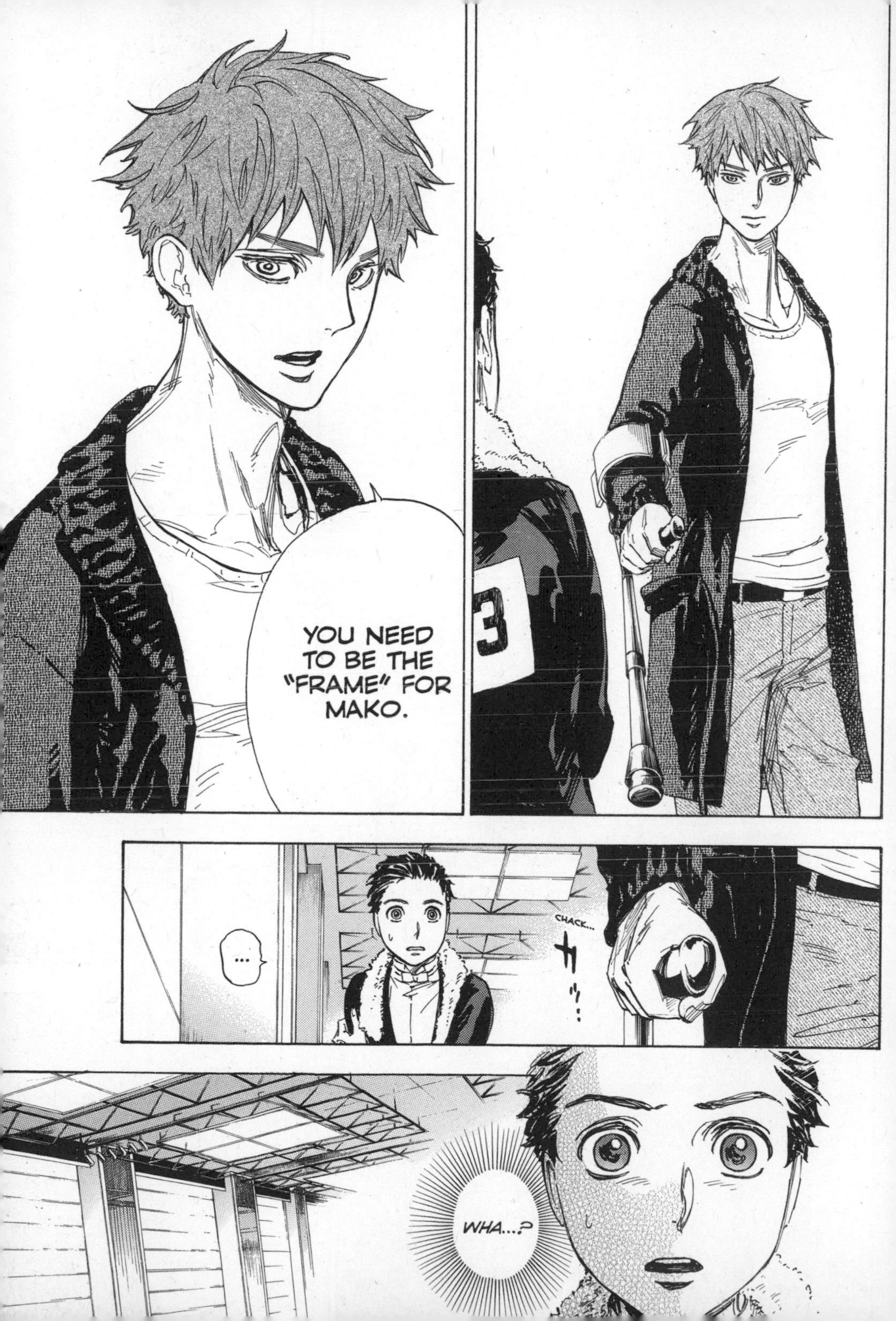
YOU NEED TO BE THE "FRAME" FOR MAKO.
CHACK...
...
WHA...?

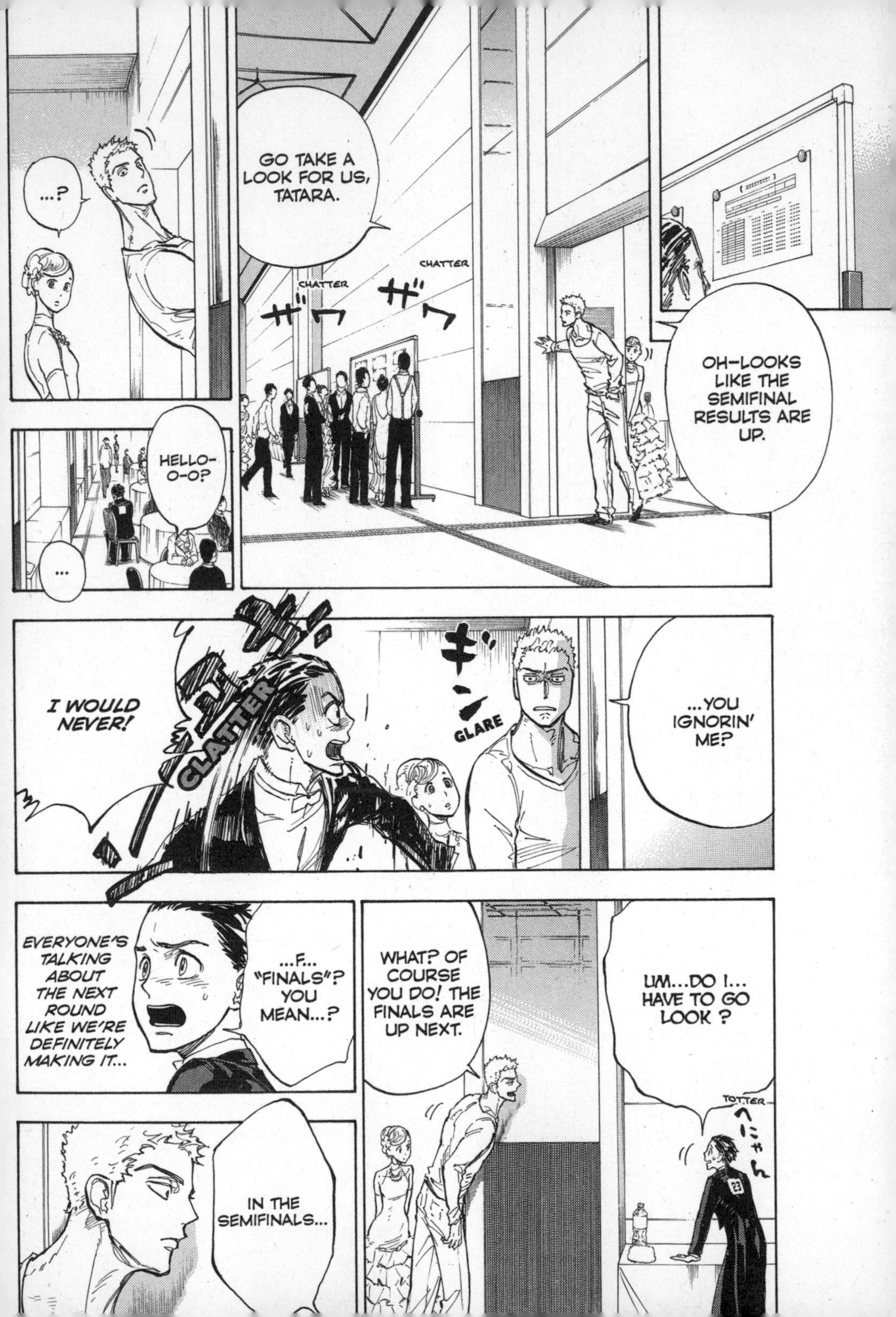
OH–LOOKS LIKE THE SEMIFINAL RESULTS ARE UP.
ザワ ザワ
CHATTER CHATTER
GO TAKE A LOOK FOR US, TATARA.
...?
HELLO-O-O?
...
...YOU IGNORIN' ME?
GLARE
CLATTER
I WOULD NEVER!
UM...DO I... HAVE TO GO LOOK ?
TOTTER
WHAT? OF COURSE YOU DO! THE FINALS ARE UP NEXT.
...F... "FINALS"? YOU MEAN...?
EVERYONE'S TALKING ABOUT THE NEXT ROUND LIKE WE'RE DEFINITELY MAKING IT...
IN THE SEMIFINALS...

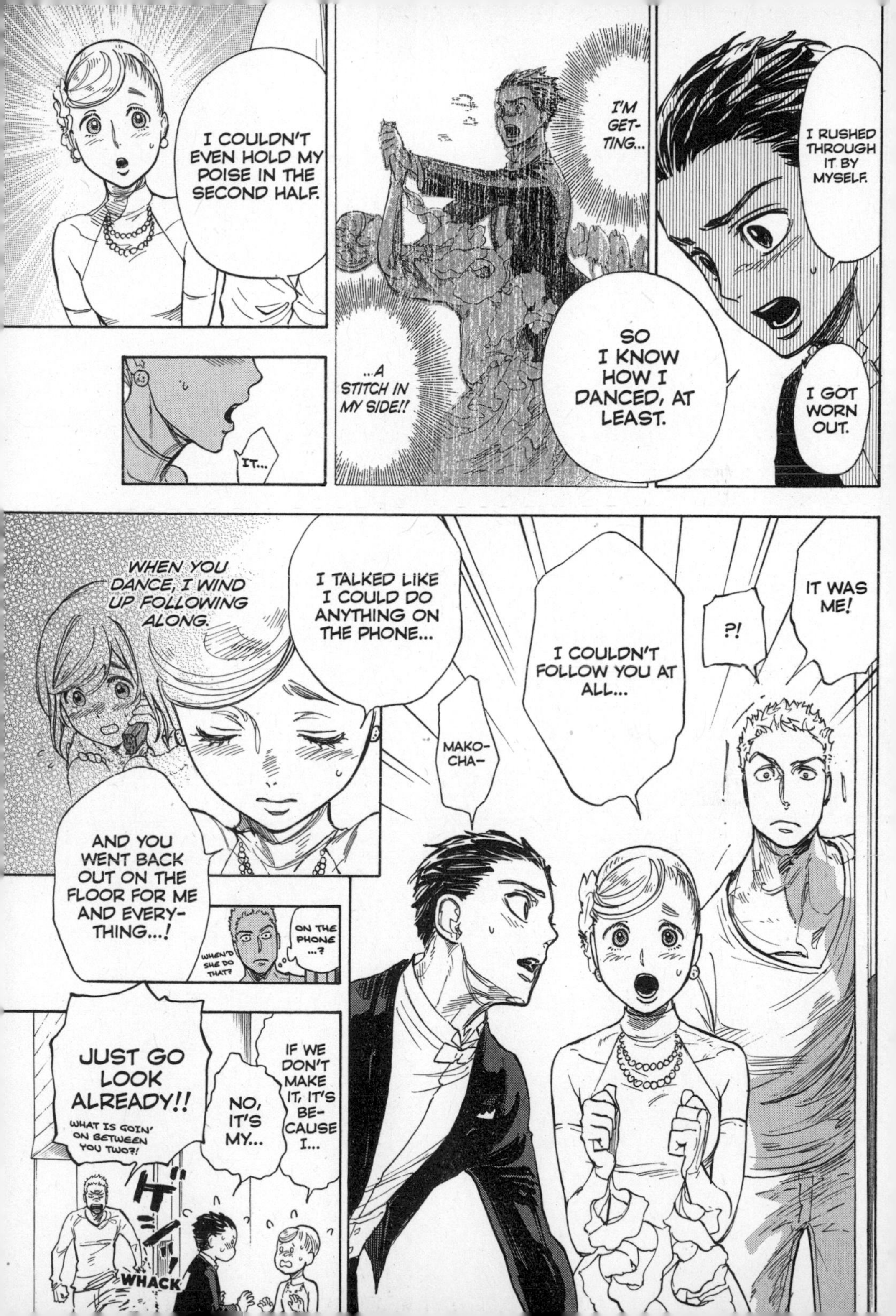
I RUSHED THROUGH IT BY MYSELF.
I GOT WORN OUT.
SO I KNOW HOW I DANCED, AT LEAST.
I'M GET-TING...
...A STITCH IN MY SIDE!!
I COULDN'T EVEN HOLD MY POISE IN THE SECOND HALF.
IT...
IT WAS ME!
?!
I COULDN'T FOLLOW YOU AT ALL...
MAKO-CHA-
I TALKED LIKE I COULD DO ANYTHING ON THE PHONE...
WHEN YOU DANCE, I WIND UP FOLLOWING ALONG.
AND YOU WENT BACK OUT ON THE FLOOR FOR ME AND EVERY-THING...!
ON THE PHONE ...?
WHEN'D SHE DO THAT?
IF WE DON'T MAKE IT, IT'S BE-CAUSE I...
NO, IT'S MY...
JUST GO LOOK ALREADY!!
WHAT IS GOIN' ON BETWEEN YOU TWO?!
WHACK

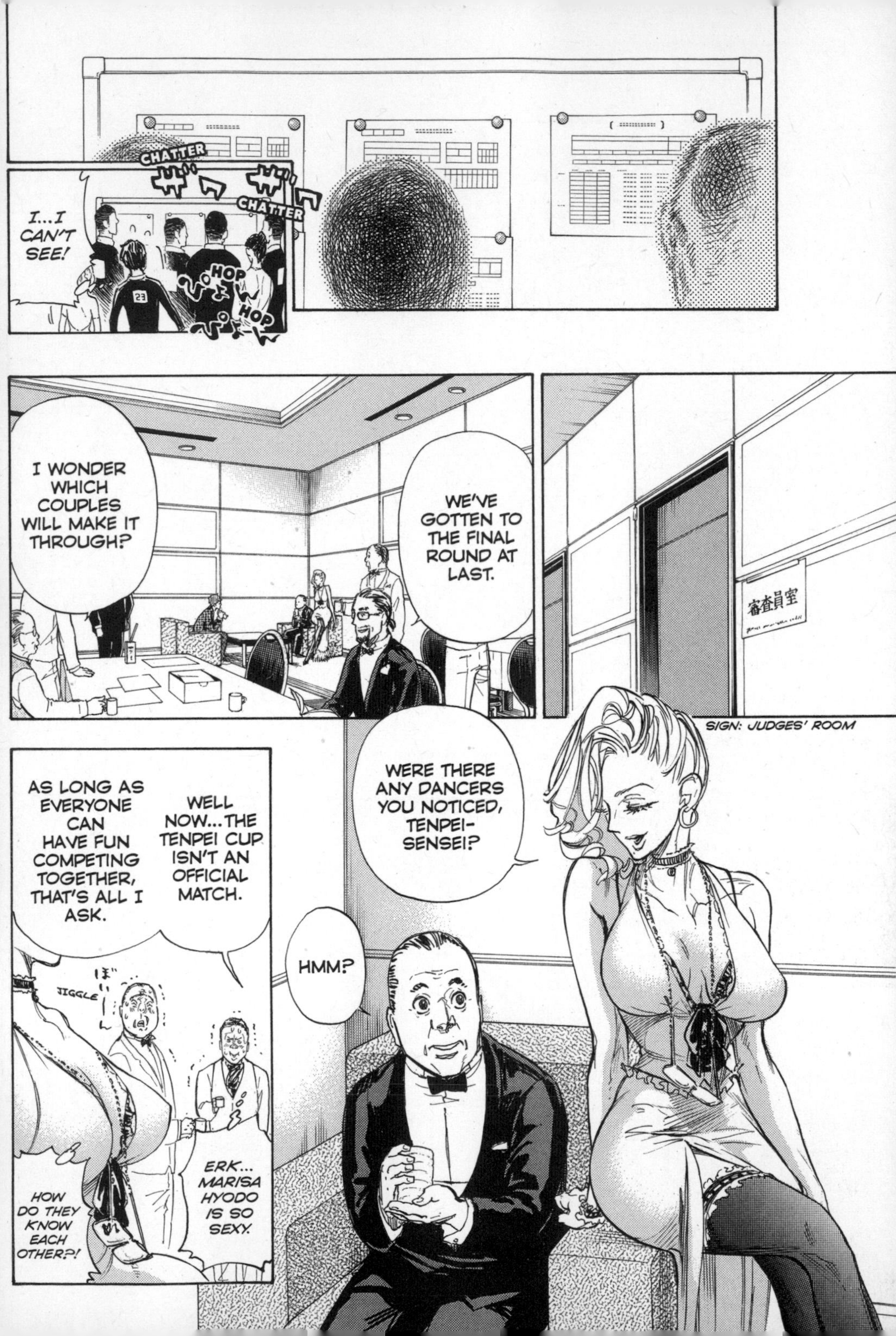
CHATTER
CHATTER
I...I CAN'T SEE!
HOP
HOP
審査員室
SIGN: JUDGES' ROOM
WE'VE GOTTEN TO THE FINAL ROUND AT LAST.
I WONDER WHICH COUPLES WILL MAKE IT THROUGH?
WERE THERE ANY DANCERS YOU NOTICED, TENPEI-SENSEI?
HMM?
WELL NOW... THE TENPEI CUP ISN'T AN OFFICIAL MATCH.
AS LONG AS EVERYONE CAN HAVE FUN COMPETING TOGETHER, THAT'S ALL I ASK.
JIGGLE
ERK... MARISA HYODO IS SO SEXY.
HOW DO THEY KNOW EACH OTHER?!

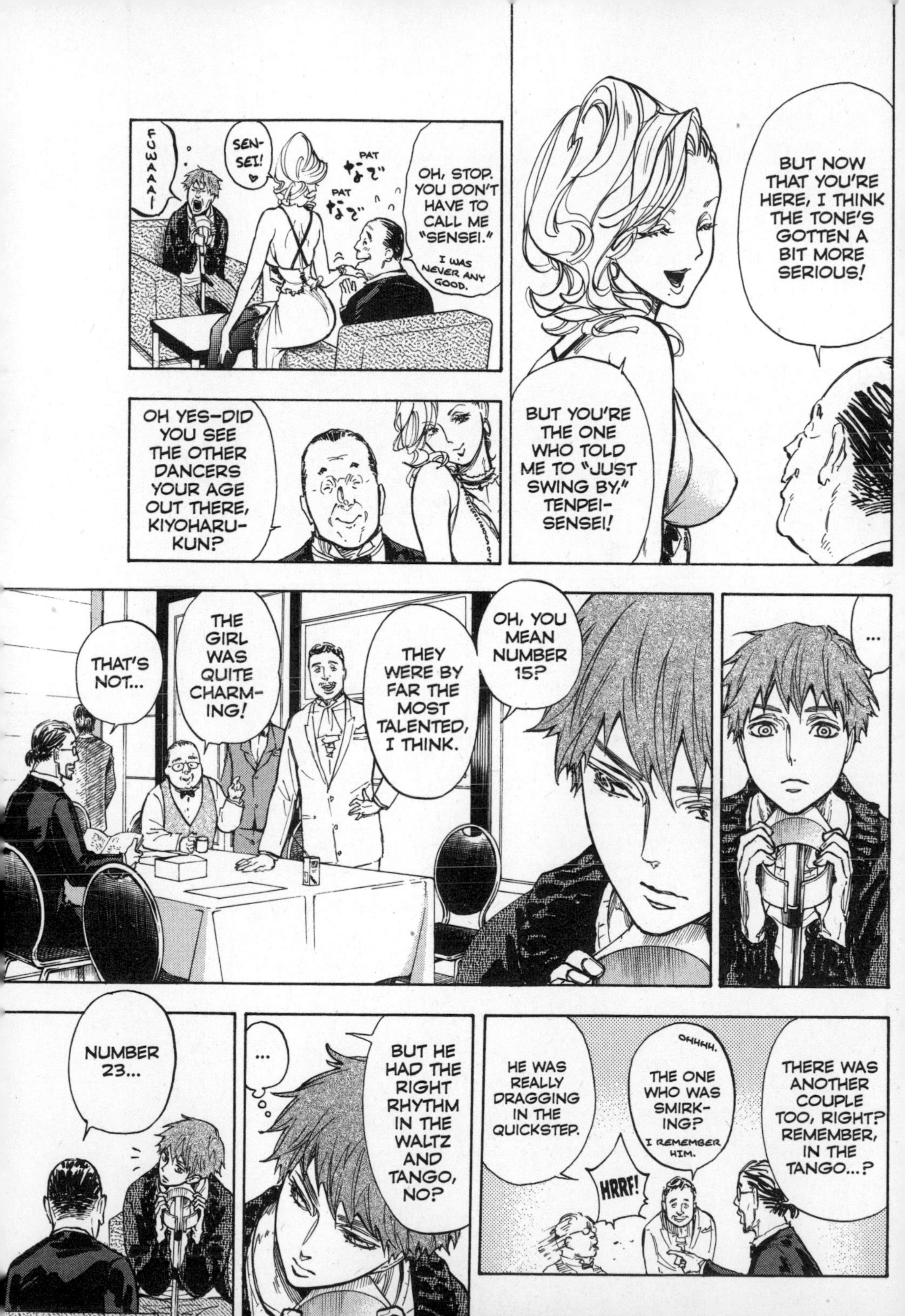
BUT NOW THAT YOU'RE HERE, I THINK THE TONE'S GOTTEN A BIT MORE SERIOUS!
BUT YOU'RE THE ONE WHO TOLD ME TO "JUST SWING BY," TENPEI-SENSEI!
OH, STOP. YOU DON'T HAVE TO CALL ME "SENSEI."
I WAS NEVER ANY GOOD.
PAT なで
PAT なで
SEN-SEI! ♥
FUWAAA!
OH YES—DID YOU SEE THE OTHER DANCERS YOUR AGE OUT THERE, KIYOHARU-KUN?
...
OH, YOU MEAN NUMBER 15?
THEY WERE BY FAR THE MOST TALENTED, I THINK.
THE GIRL WAS QUITE CHARMING!
THAT'S NOT...
THERE WAS ANOTHER COUPLE TOO, RIGHT? REMEMBER, IN THE TANGO...?
OHHHH.
THE ONE WHO WAS SMIRKING?
I REMEMBER HIM.
HE WAS REALLY DRAGGING IN THE QUICKSTEP.
HRRF!
BUT HE HAD THE RIGHT RHYTHM IN THE WALTZ AND TANGO, NO?
...
NUMBER 23...

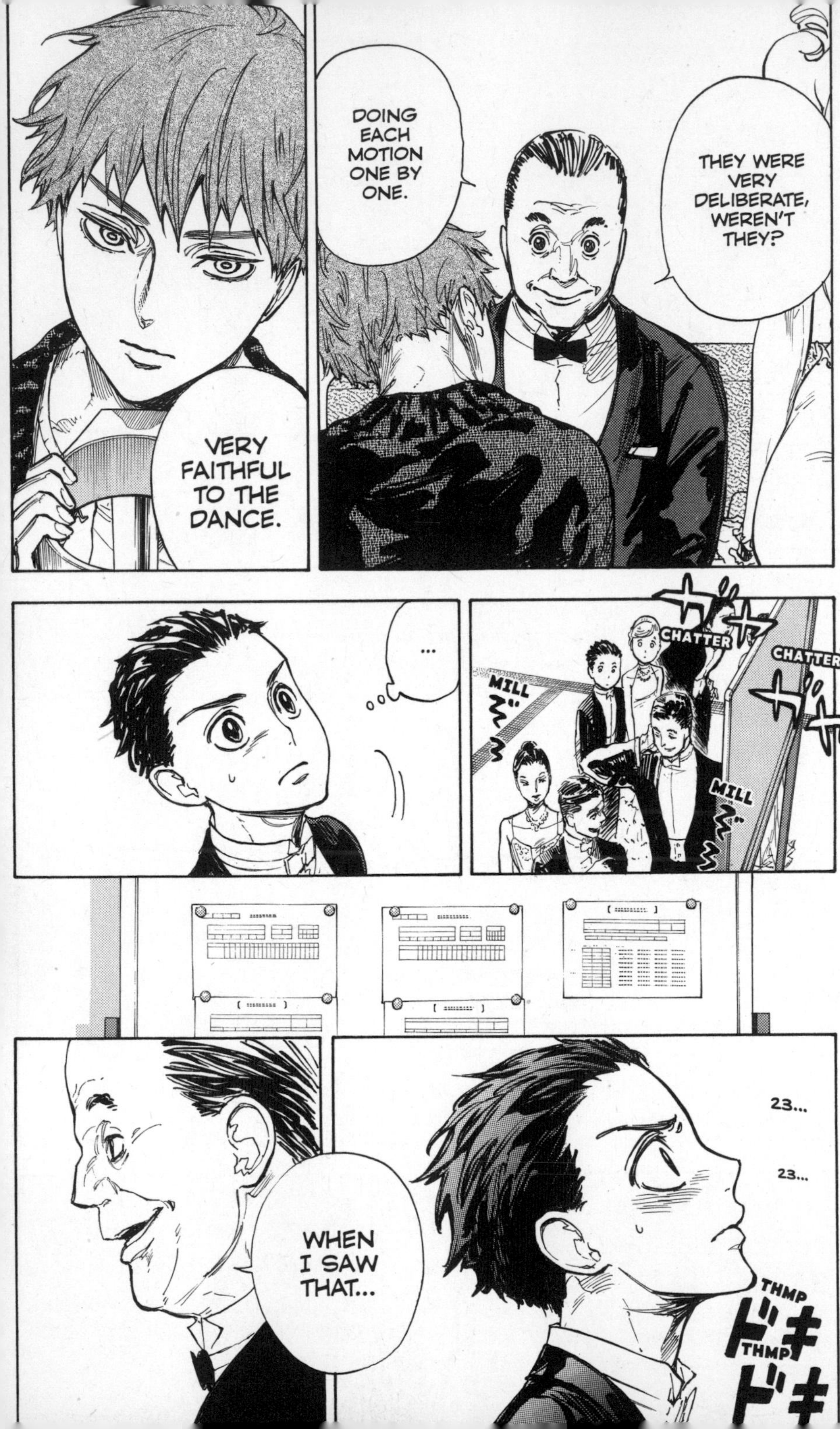
THEY WERE VERY DELIBERATE, WEREN'T THEY?
DOING EACH MOTION ONE BY ONE.
VERY FAITHFUL TO THE DANCE.
CHATTER
CHATTER
MILL
MILL
...
23...
23...
THMP
THMP
WHEN I SAW THAT...

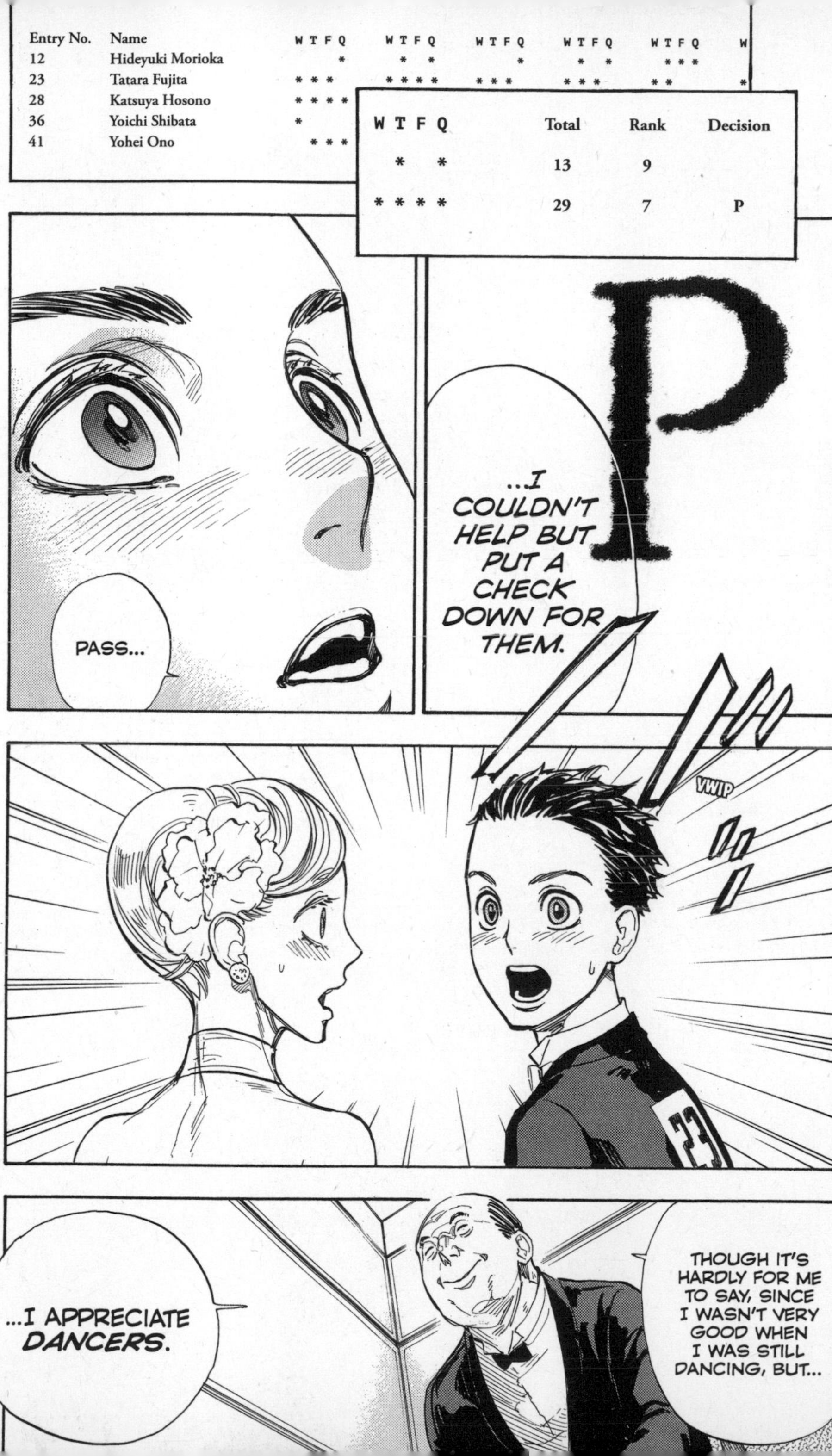
Entry No. Name W T F Q W T F Q W T F Q W T F Q W T F Q W
12 Hideyuki Morioka
23 Tatara Fujita
28 Katsuya Hosono
36 Yoichi Shibata
41 Yohei Ono
W T F Q Total Rank Decision
13 9
29 7 P
P
...I COULDN'T HELP BUT PUT A CHECK DOWN FOR THEM.
PASS...
VWIP
THOUGH IT'S HARDLY FOR ME TO SAY, SINCE I WASN'T VERY GOOD WHEN I WAS STILL DANCING, BUT...
...I APPRECIATE *DANCERS*.

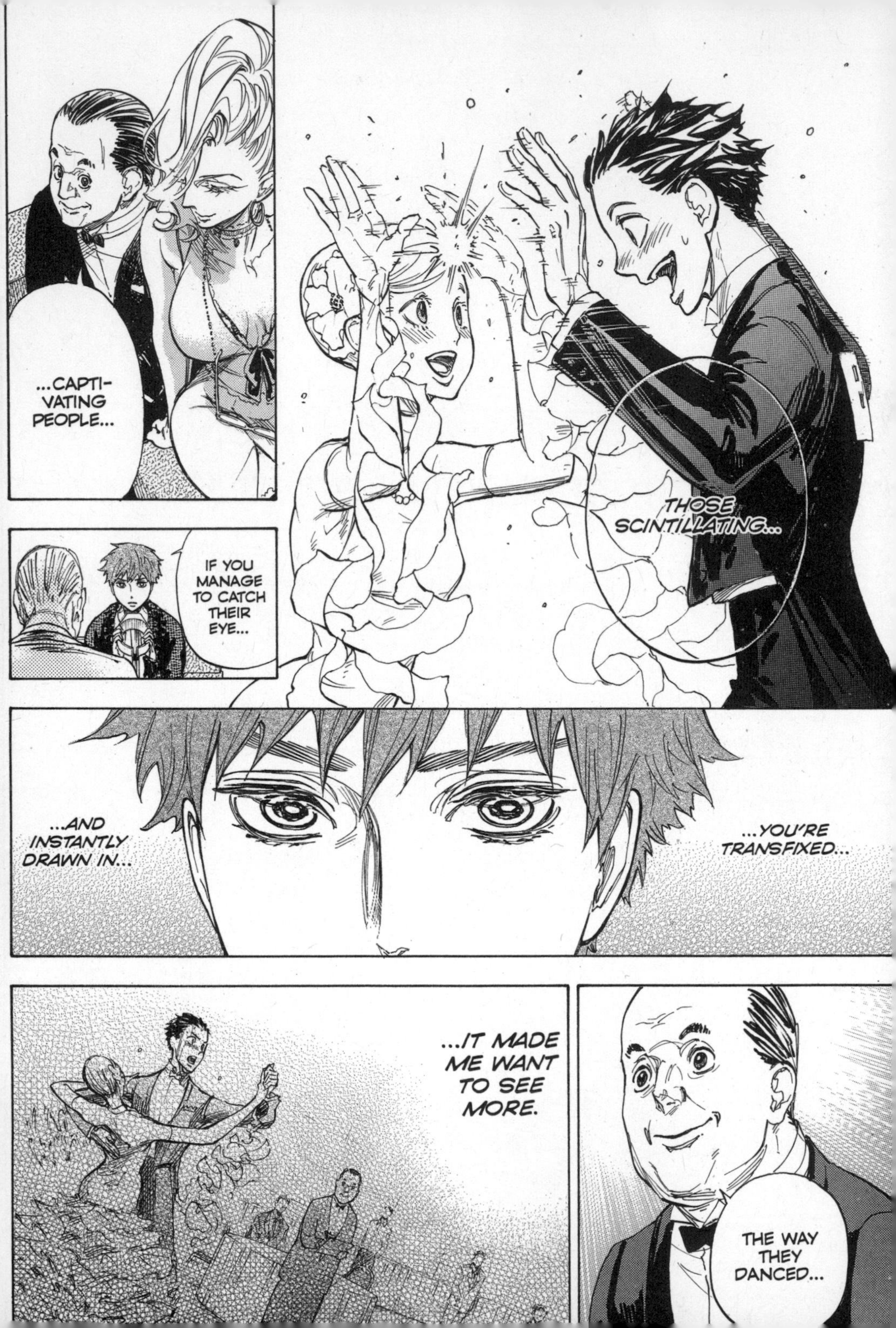
THOSE SCINTILLATING...
...CAPTI-VATING PEOPLE...
IF YOU MANAGE TO CATCH THEIR EYE...
...YOU'RE TRANSFIXED...
...AND INSTANTLY DRAWN IN...
THE WAY THEY DANCED...
...IT MADE ME WANT TO SEE MORE.

TENPEI CUP SEMIFINALS FIRST HEAT

														Hyodo				Hanageishi						
Entry No.	Name	W	T	F	Q	W	T	F	Q	W	T	F	Q	W	T	F	Q	W	T	F	Q	Total	Rank	Decision
12	Hideyuki Morioka				*		*		*				*		*		*		*	*	*	13	9	
23	Tatara Fujita	*	*	*		*	*	*	*	*	*	*		*	*	*		*	*	*	*	29	7	P
28	Katsuya Hosono	*	*	*	*	*	*	*	*	*	*		*		*	*	*	*	*					P
36	Yoichi Shibata	*								*														
41	Yohei Ono		*	*	*		*		*	*	*	*	*	*	*	*	*							

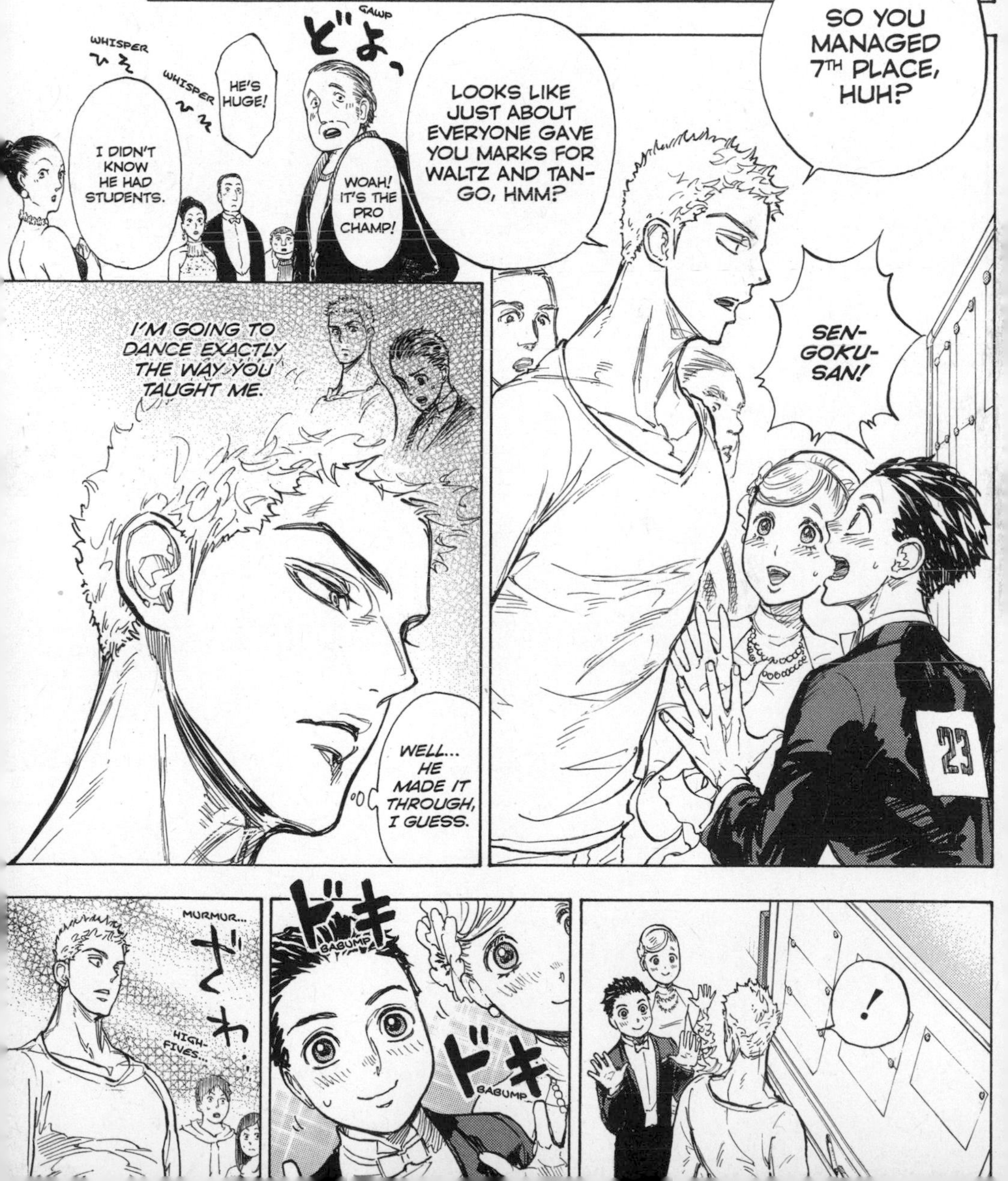
SO YOU MANAGED 7TH PLACE, HUH?
LOOKS LIKE JUST ABOUT EVERYONE GAVE YOU MARKS FOR WALTZ AND TAN-GO, HMM?
SEN-GOKU-SAN!
どよっ
GAWP
HE'S HUGE!
WHISPER
WHISPER
WOAH! IT'S THE PRO CHAMP!
I DIDN'T KNOW HE HAD STUDENTS.
I'M GOING TO DANCE EXACTLY THE WAY YOU TAUGHT ME.
WELL... HE MADE IT THROUGH, I GUESS.
!
ドキ
BABUMP
ドキ
BABUMP
MURMUR...
ざわ
HIGH-FIVES...

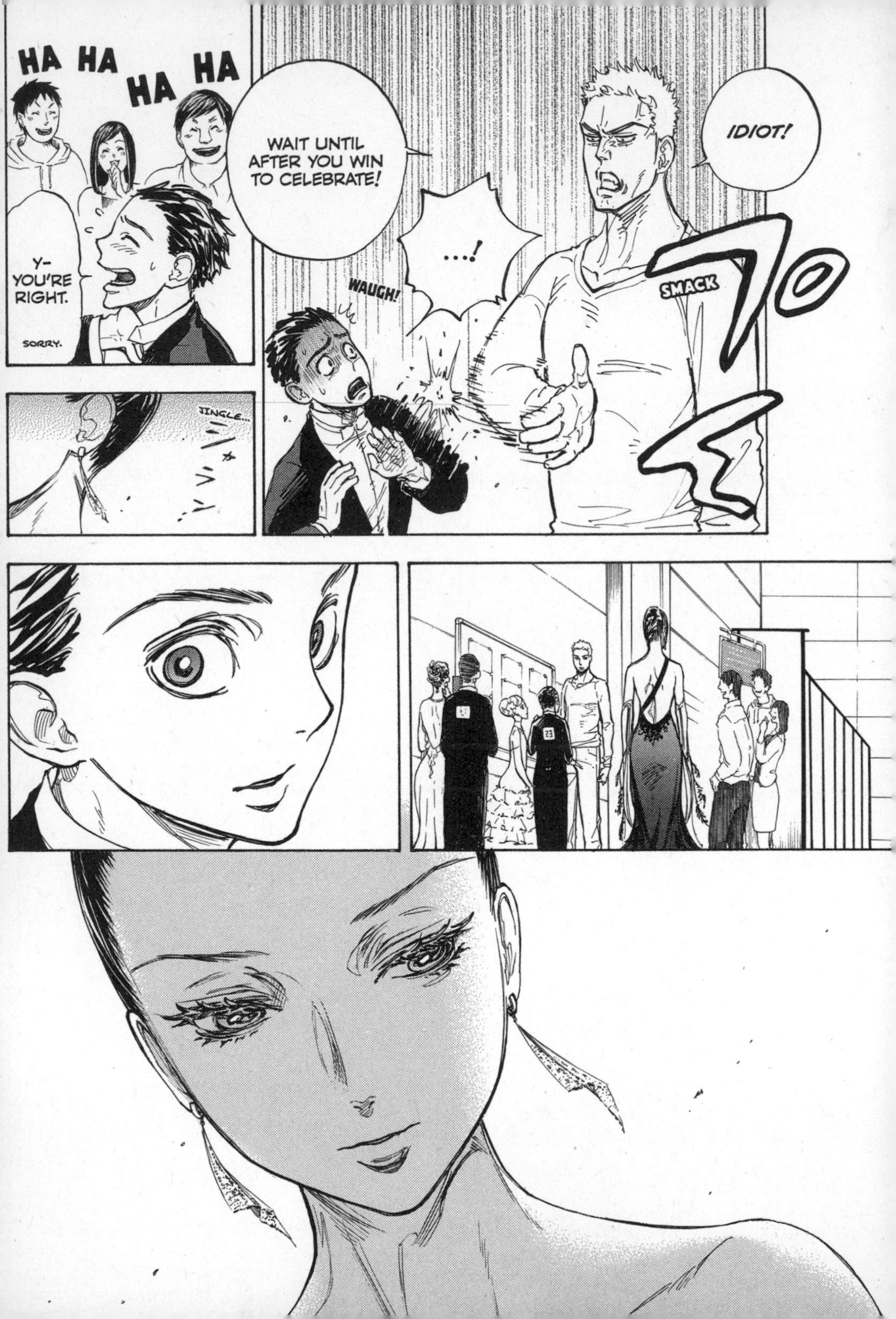
IDIOT!
WAIT UNTIL AFTER YOU WIN TO CELEBRATE!
...!
SMACK
WAUGH!
HA HA HA HA
Y- YOU'RE RIGHT.
SORRY.
JINGLE...

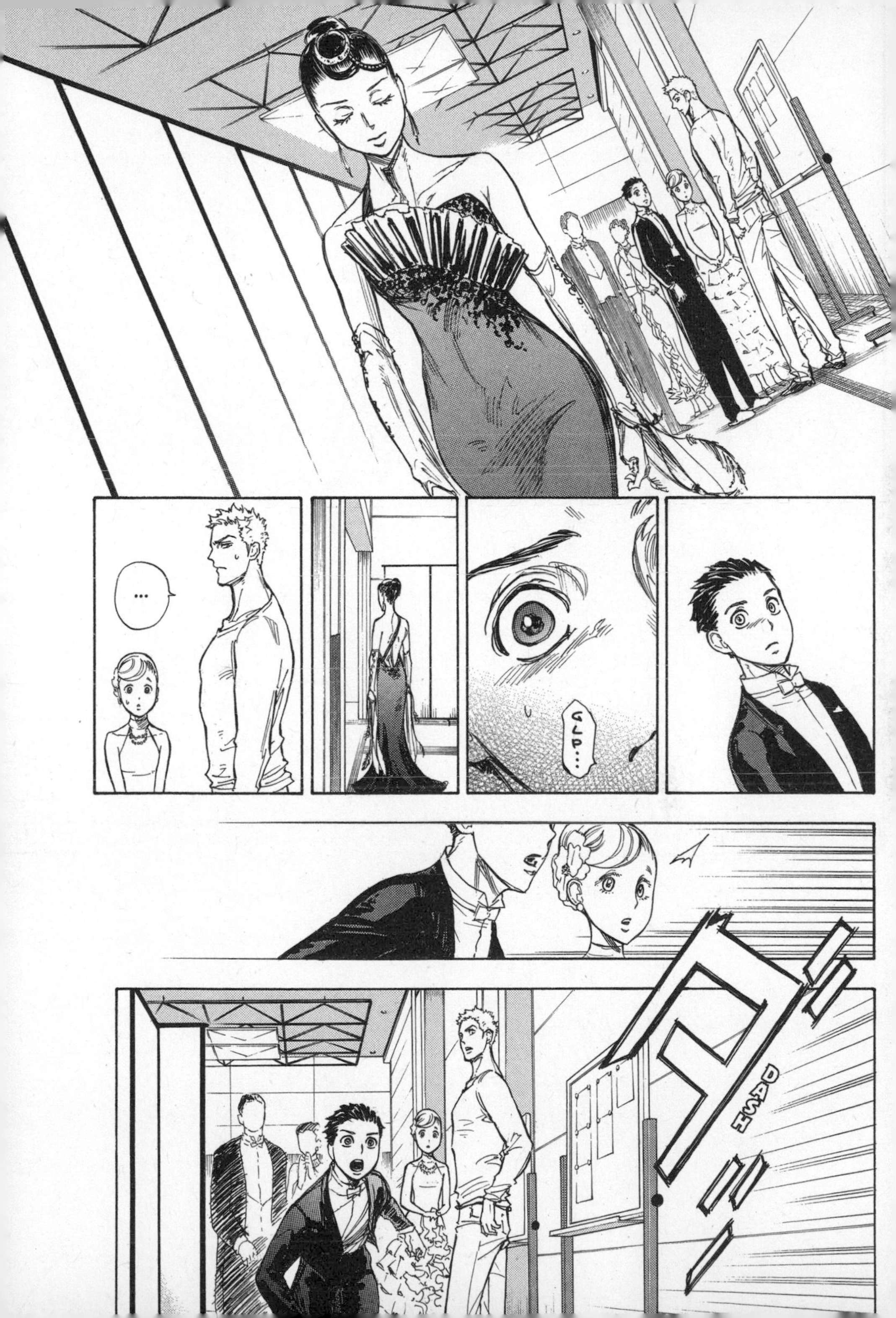
GLP...
...
DASH

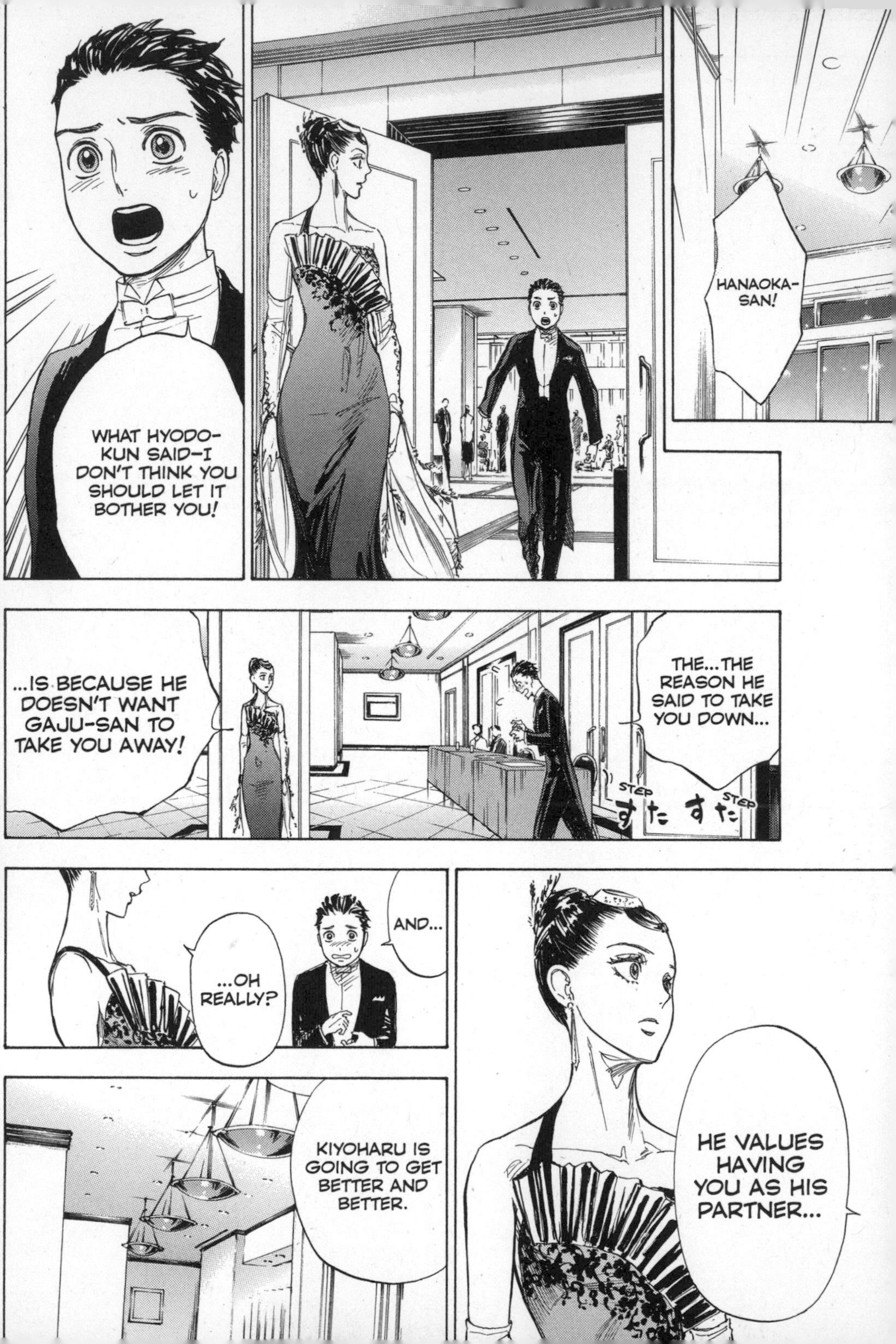
HANAOKA-SAN!
WHAT HYODO-KUN SAID—I DON'T THINK YOU SHOULD LET IT BOTHER YOU!
THE...THE REASON HE SAID TO TAKE YOU DOWN...
STEP すた すた STEP
...IS BECAUSE HE DOESN'T WANT GAJU-SAN TO TAKE YOU AWAY!
HE VALUES HAVING YOU AS HIS PARTNER...
AND...
...OH REALLY?
KIYOHARU IS GOING TO GET BETTER AND BETTER.

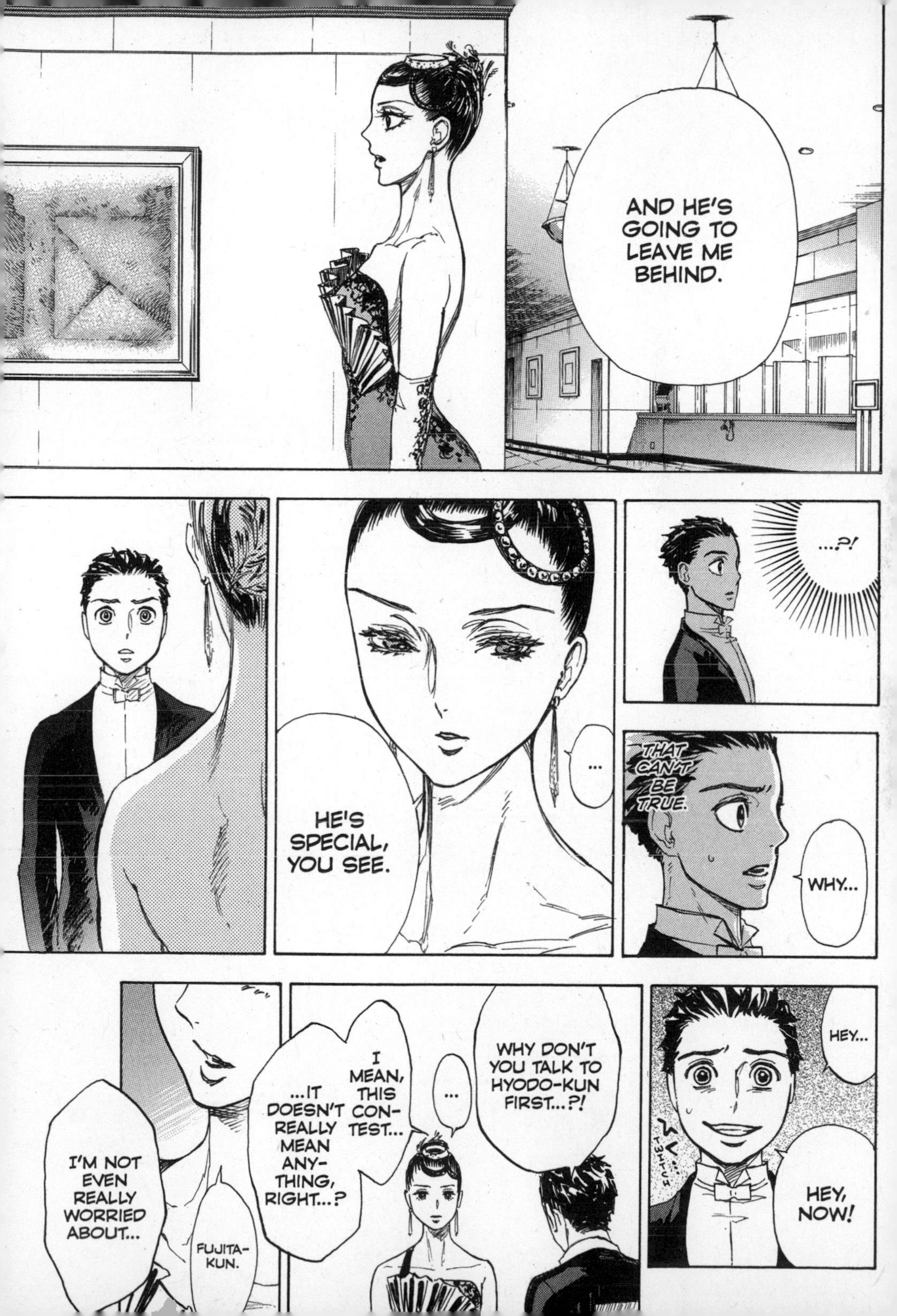
AND HE'S GOING TO LEAVE ME BEHIND.
...?!
THAT CAN'T BE TRUE.
WHY...
...
HE'S SPECIAL, YOU SEE.
HEY...
HEY, NOW!
WHY DON'T YOU TALK TO HYODO-KUN FIRST...?!
...
I MEAN, THIS CONTEST...
...IT DOESN'T REALLY MEAN ANYTHING, RIGHT...?
I'M NOT EVEN REALLY WORRIED ABOUT...
FUJITA-KUN.

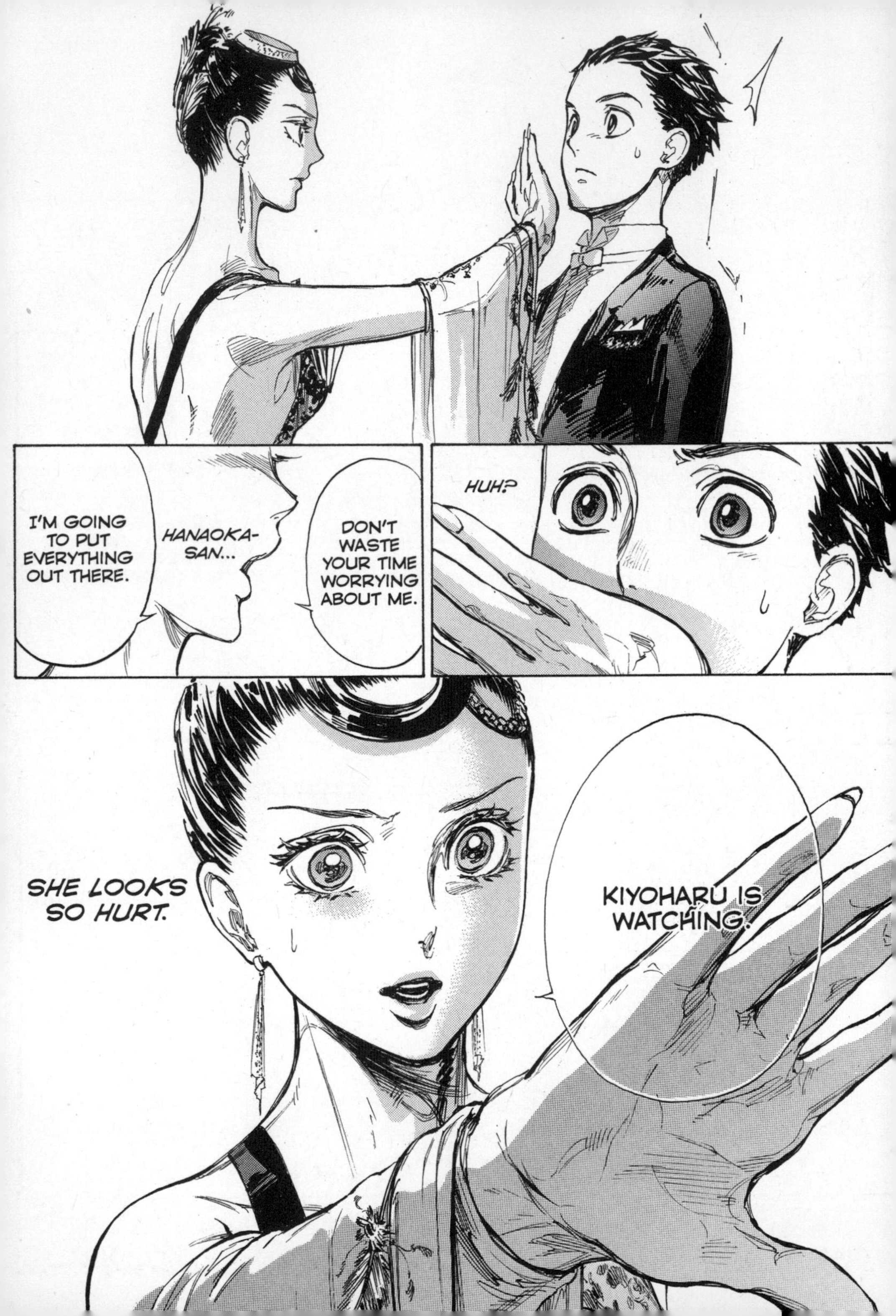
HUH?
DON'T WASTE YOUR TIME WORRYING ABOUT ME.
HANAOKA-SAN...
I'M GOING TO PUT EVERYTHING OUT THERE.
KIYOHARU IS WATCHING.
SHE LOOKS SO HURT.

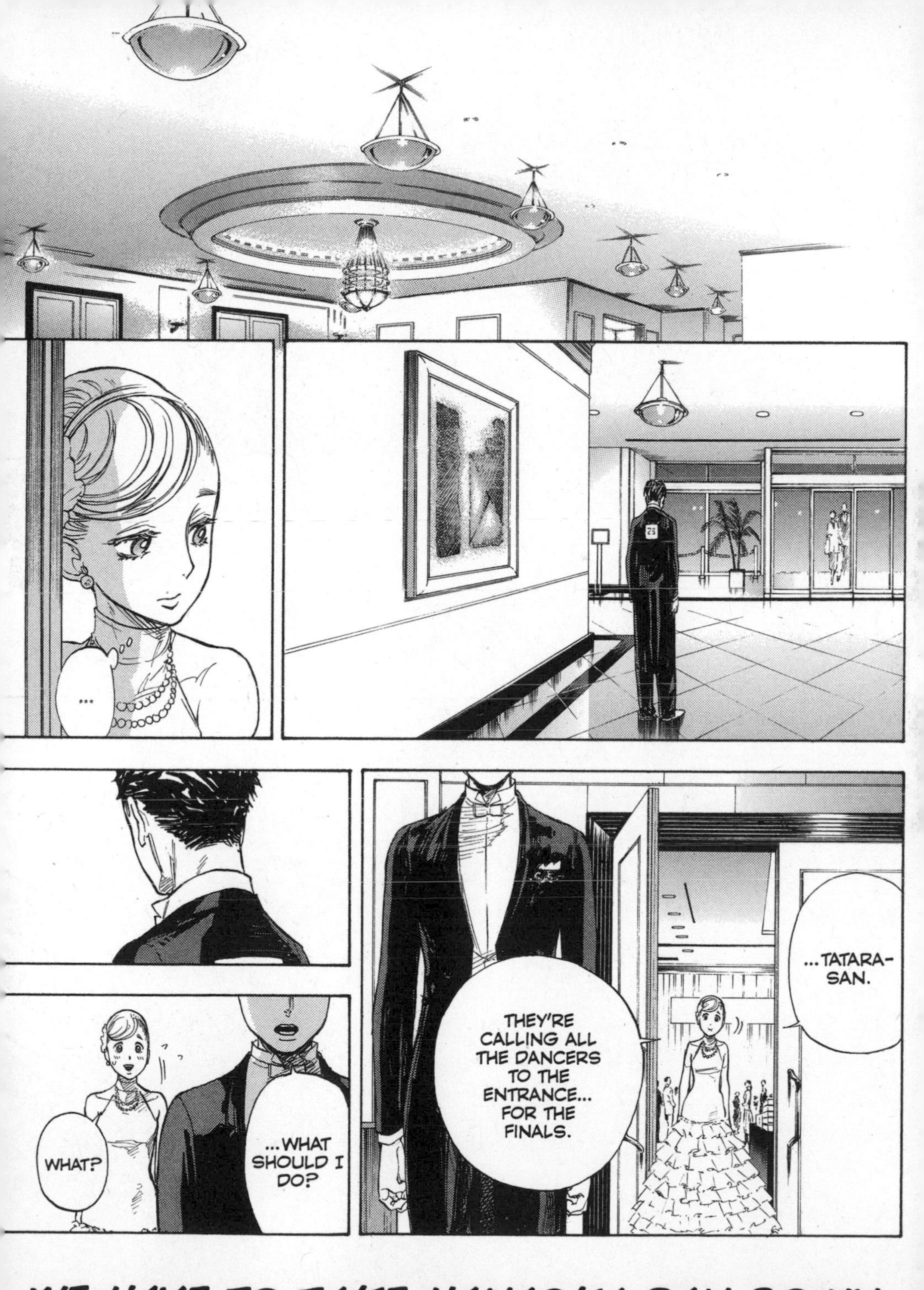
...
...TATARA-SAN.
THEY'RE CALLING ALL THE DANCERS TO THE ENTRANCE... FOR THE FINALS.
...WHAT SHOULD I DO?
WHAT?

WE HAVE TO TAKE HANAOKA-SAN DOWN...

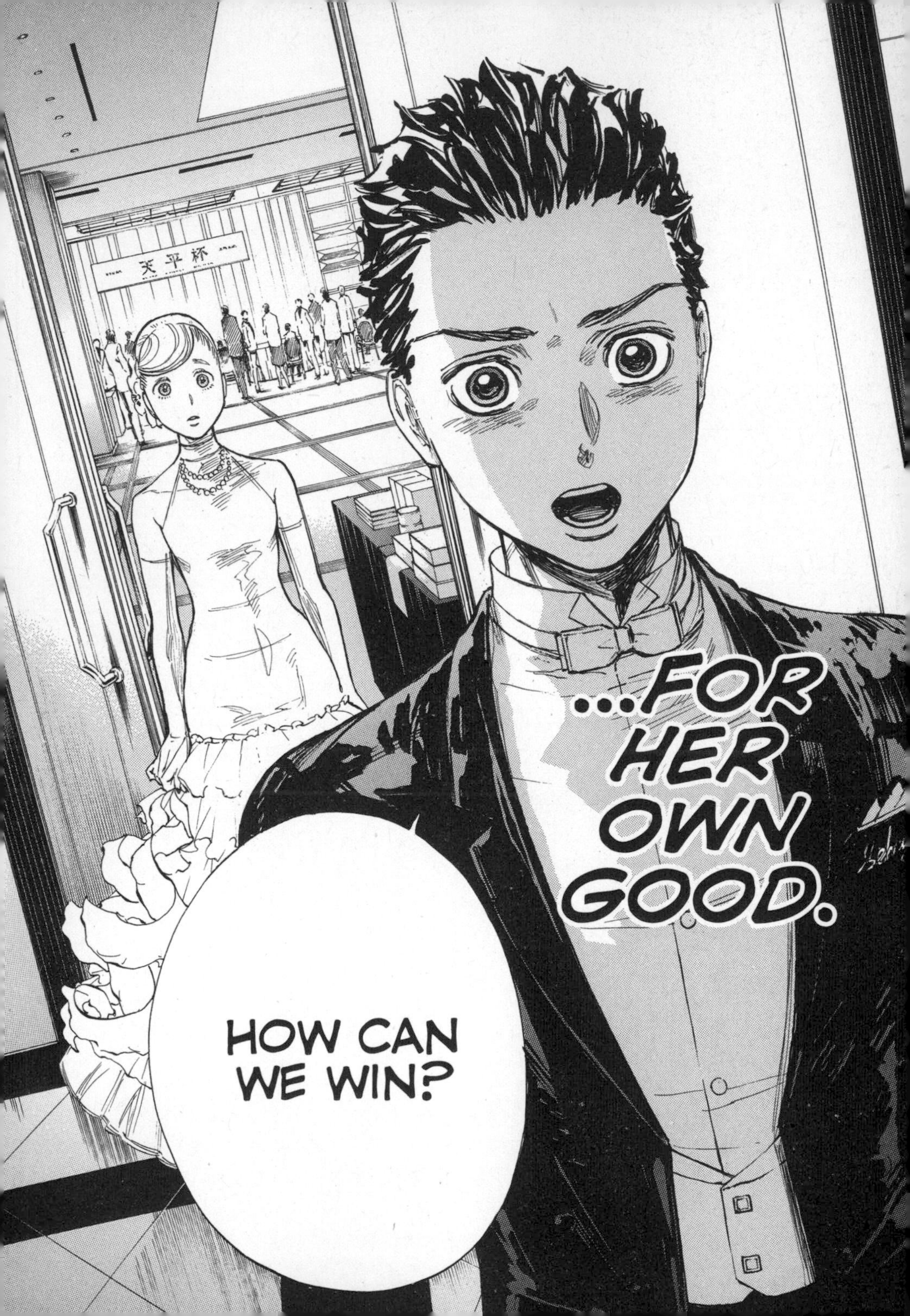
...FOR HER OWN GOOD.
天平杯
HOW CAN WE WIN?

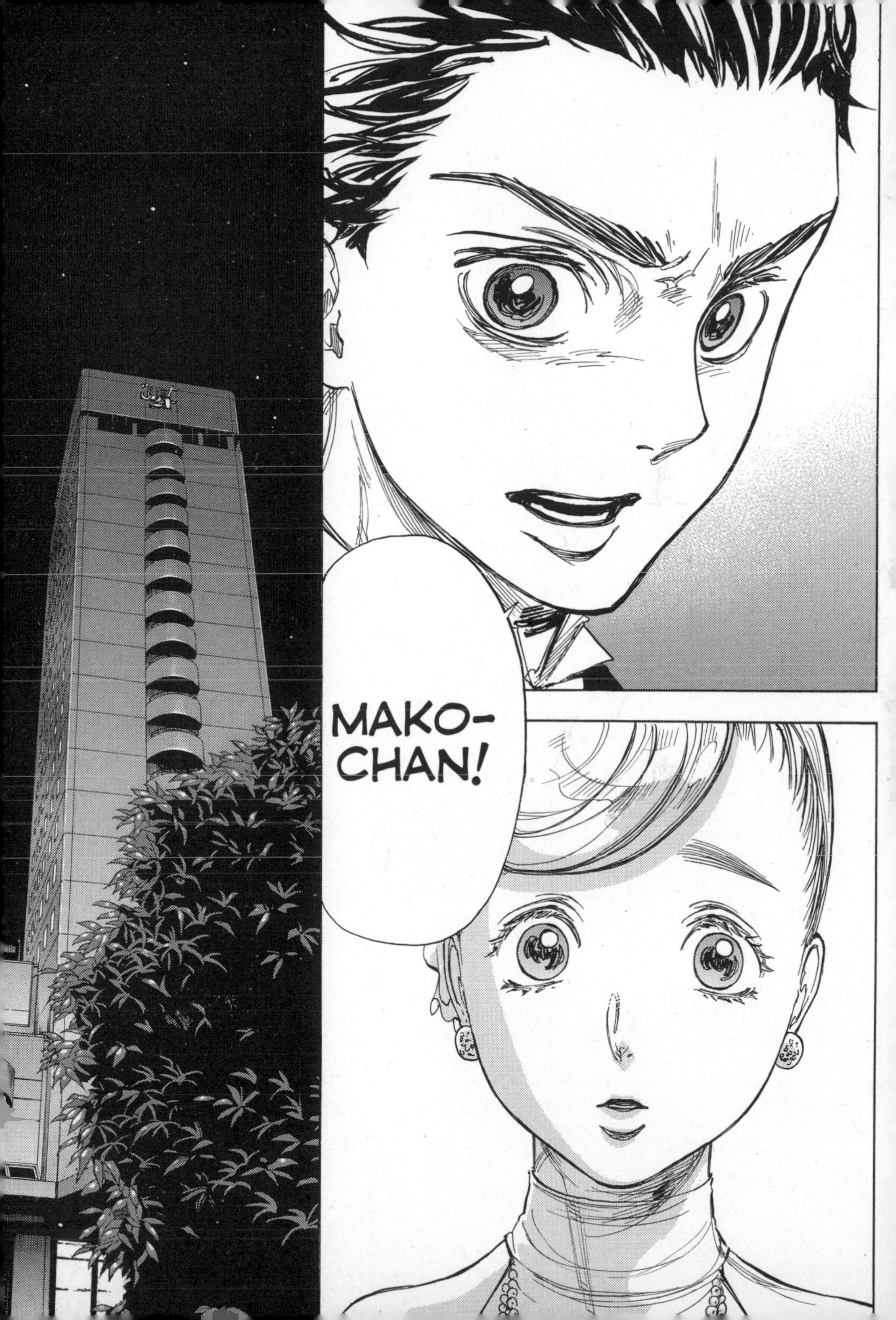
MAKO-CHAN!

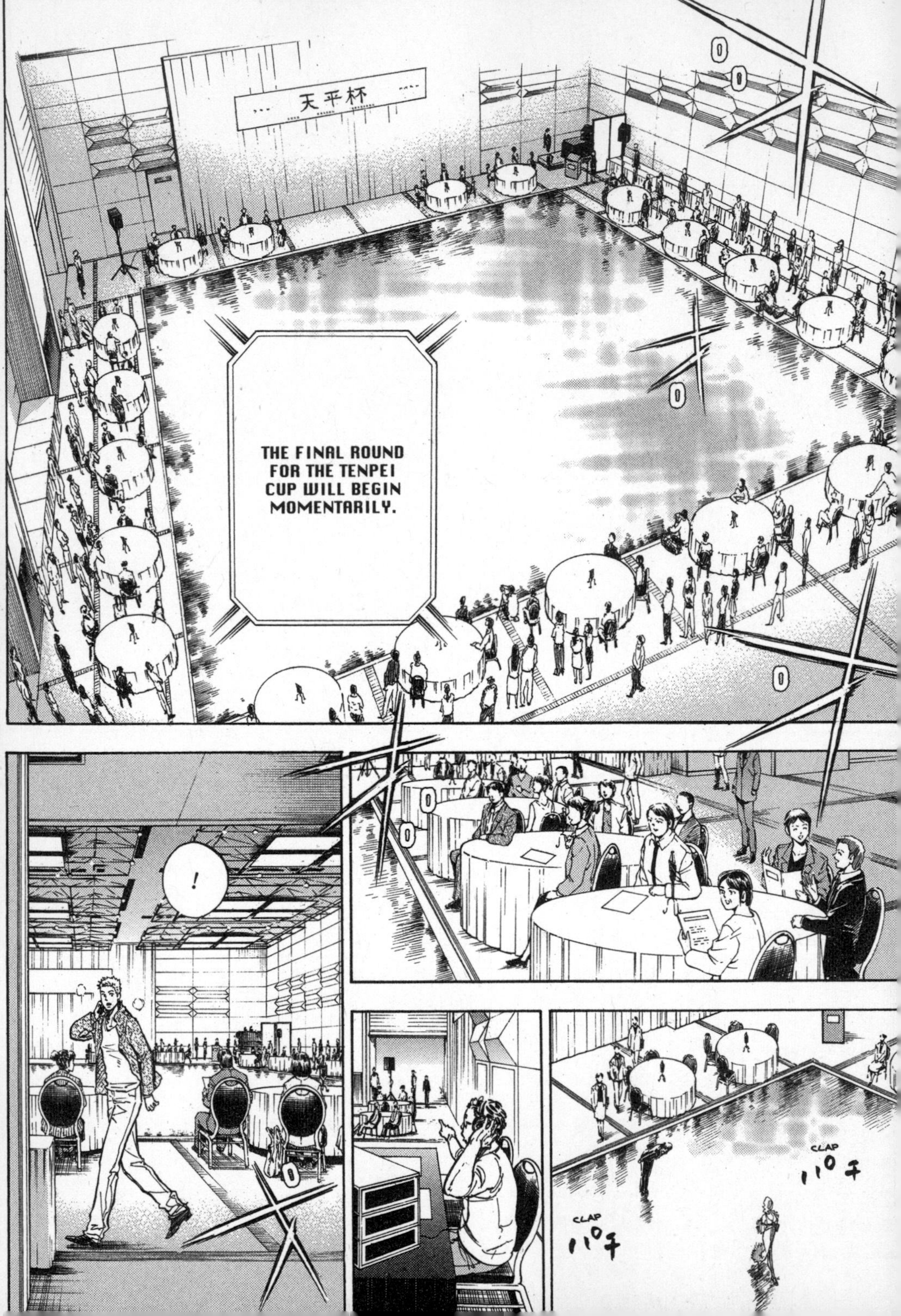
天平杯
THE FINAL ROUND FOR THE TENPEI CUP WILL BEGIN MOMENTARILY.
CLAP パチ
CLAP パチ
!

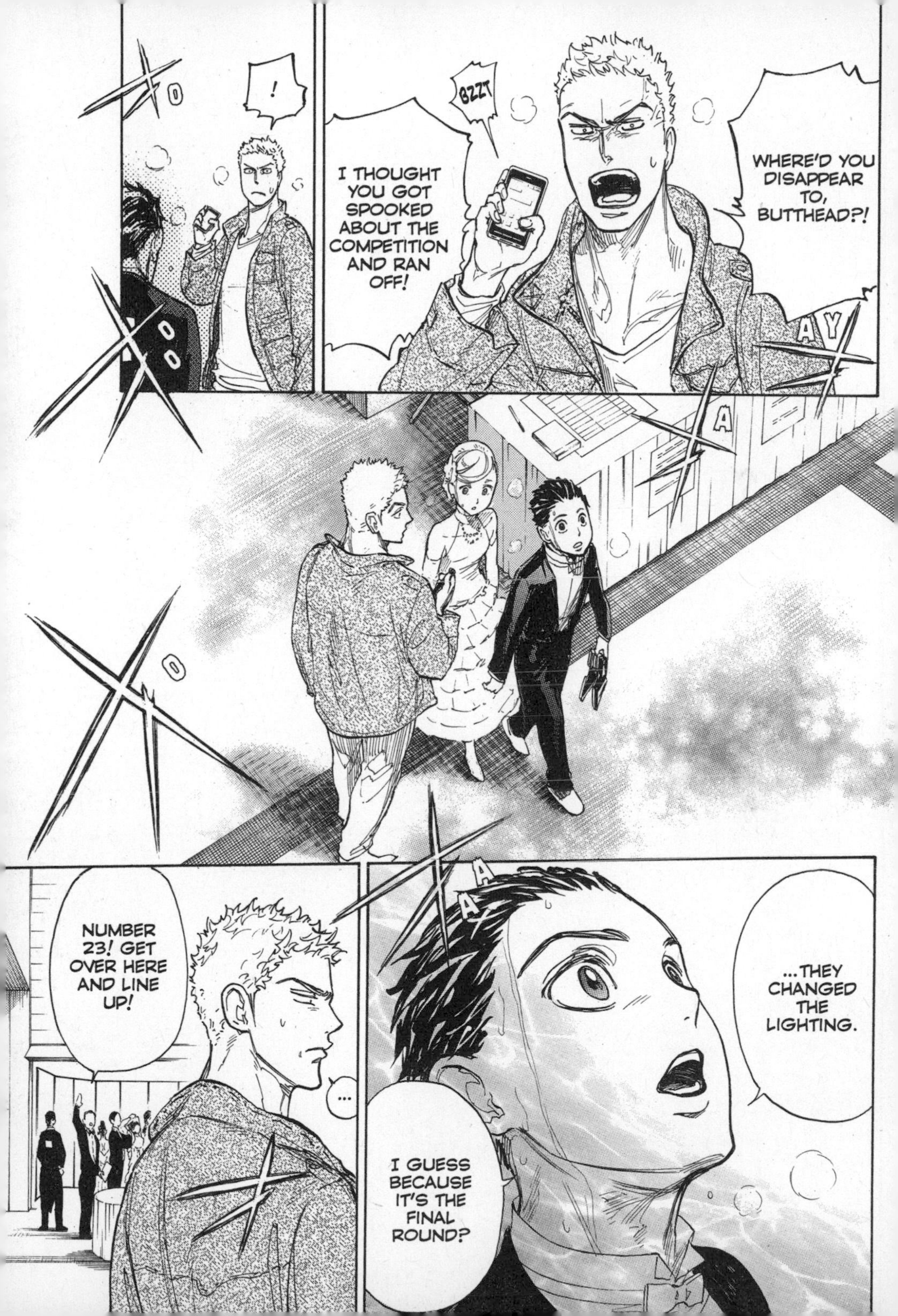
BZZT
WHERE'D YOU DISAPPEAR TO, BUTTHEAD?!
I THOUGHT YOU GOT SPOOKED ABOUT THE COMPETITION AND RAN OFF!
!
...THEY CHANGED THE LIGHTING.
I GUESS BECAUSE IT'S THE FINAL ROUND?
NUMBER 23! GET OVER HERE AND LINE UP!
...

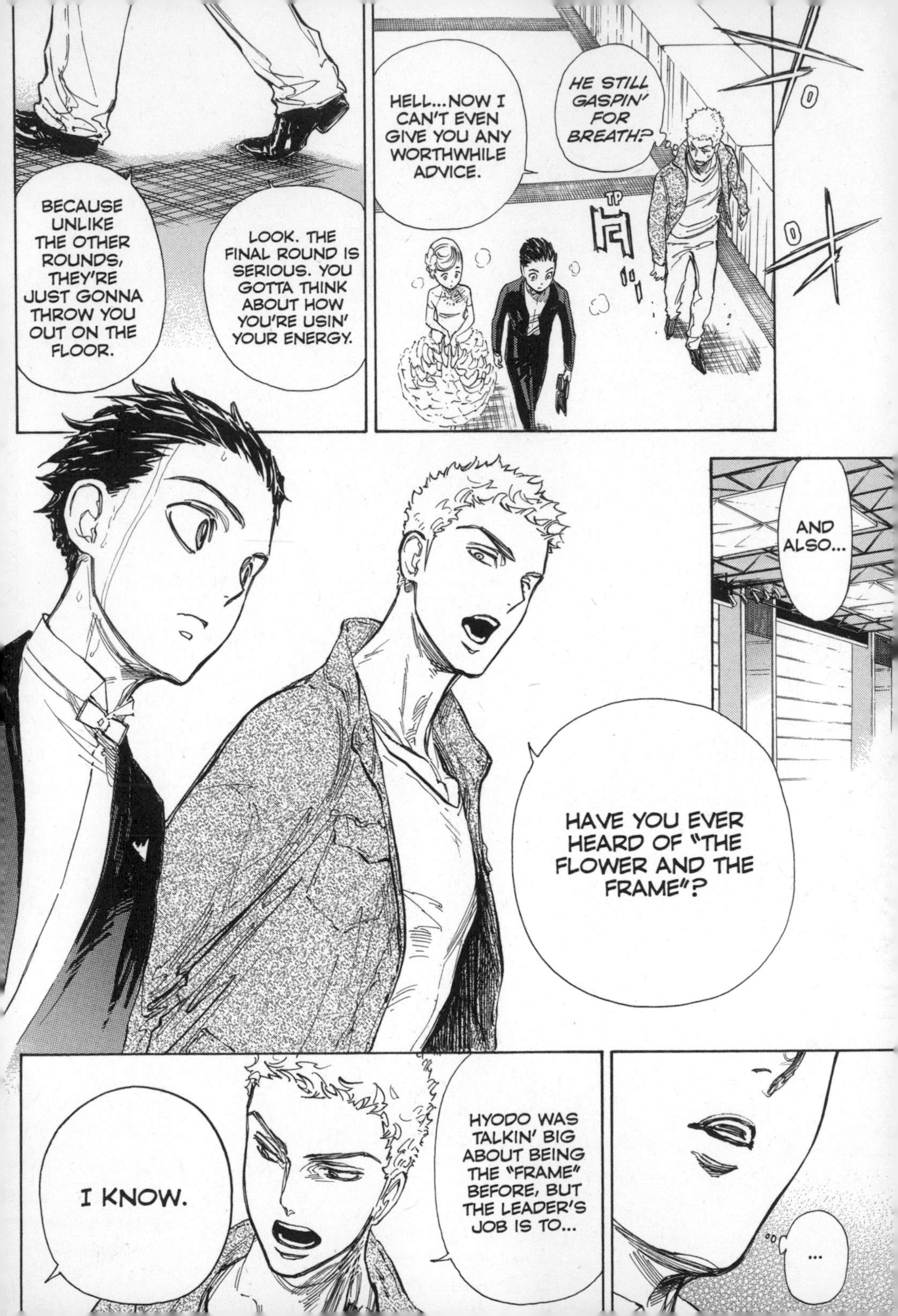
HE STILL GASPIN' FOR BREATH?
HELL...NOW I CAN'T EVEN GIVE YOU ANY WORTHWHILE ADVICE.
TP
LOOK. THE FINAL ROUND IS SERIOUS. YOU GOTTA THINK ABOUT HOW YOU'RE USIN' YOUR ENERGY.
BECAUSE UNLIKE THE OTHER ROUNDS, THEY'RE JUST GONNA THROW YOU OUT ON THE FLOOR.
AND ALSO...
HAVE YOU EVER HEARD OF "THE FLOWER AND THE FRAME"?
...
HYODO WAS TALKIN' BIG ABOUT BEING THE "FRAME" BEFORE, BUT THE LEADER'S JOB IS TO...
I KNOW.

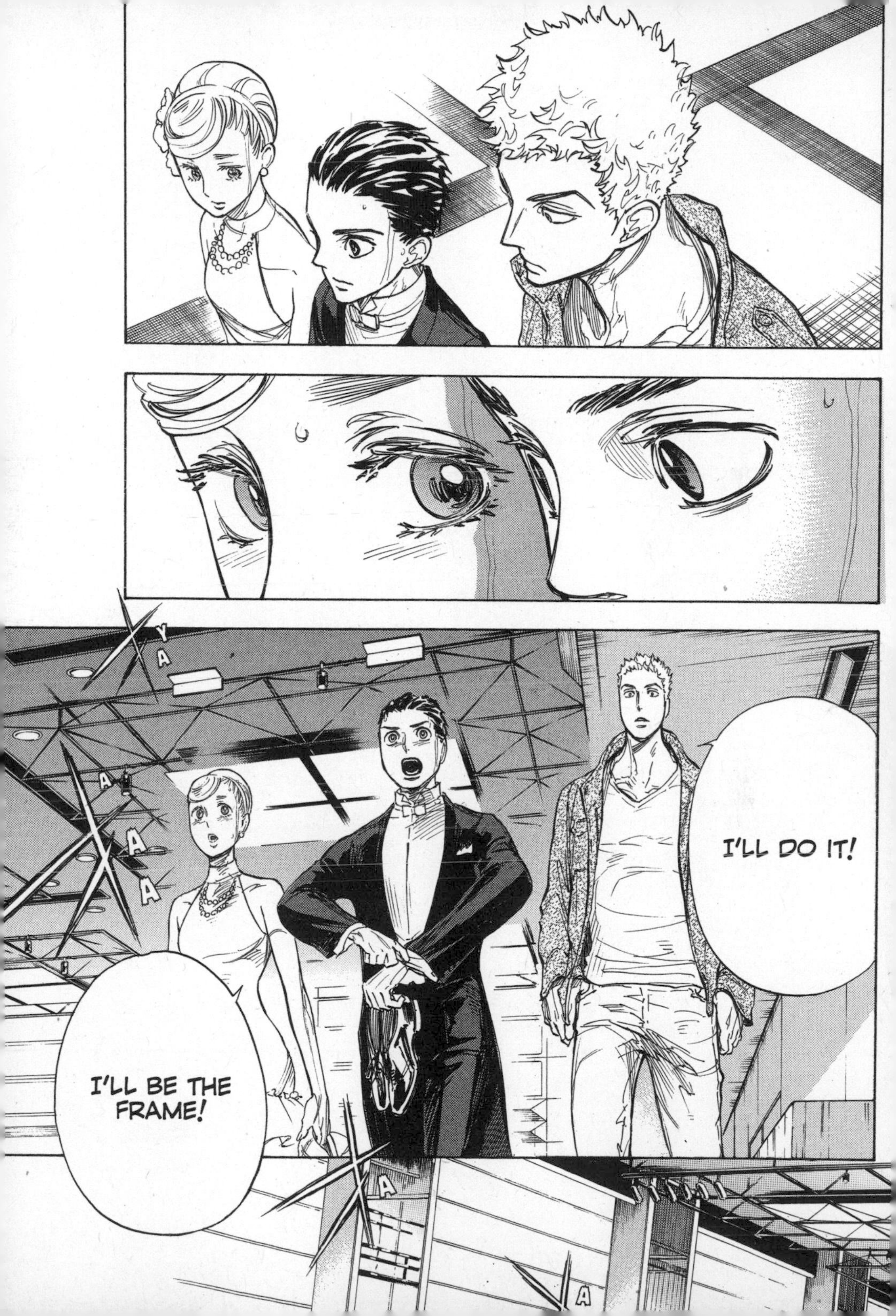
YAAAAAA
I'LL DO IT!
I'LL BE THE FRAME!

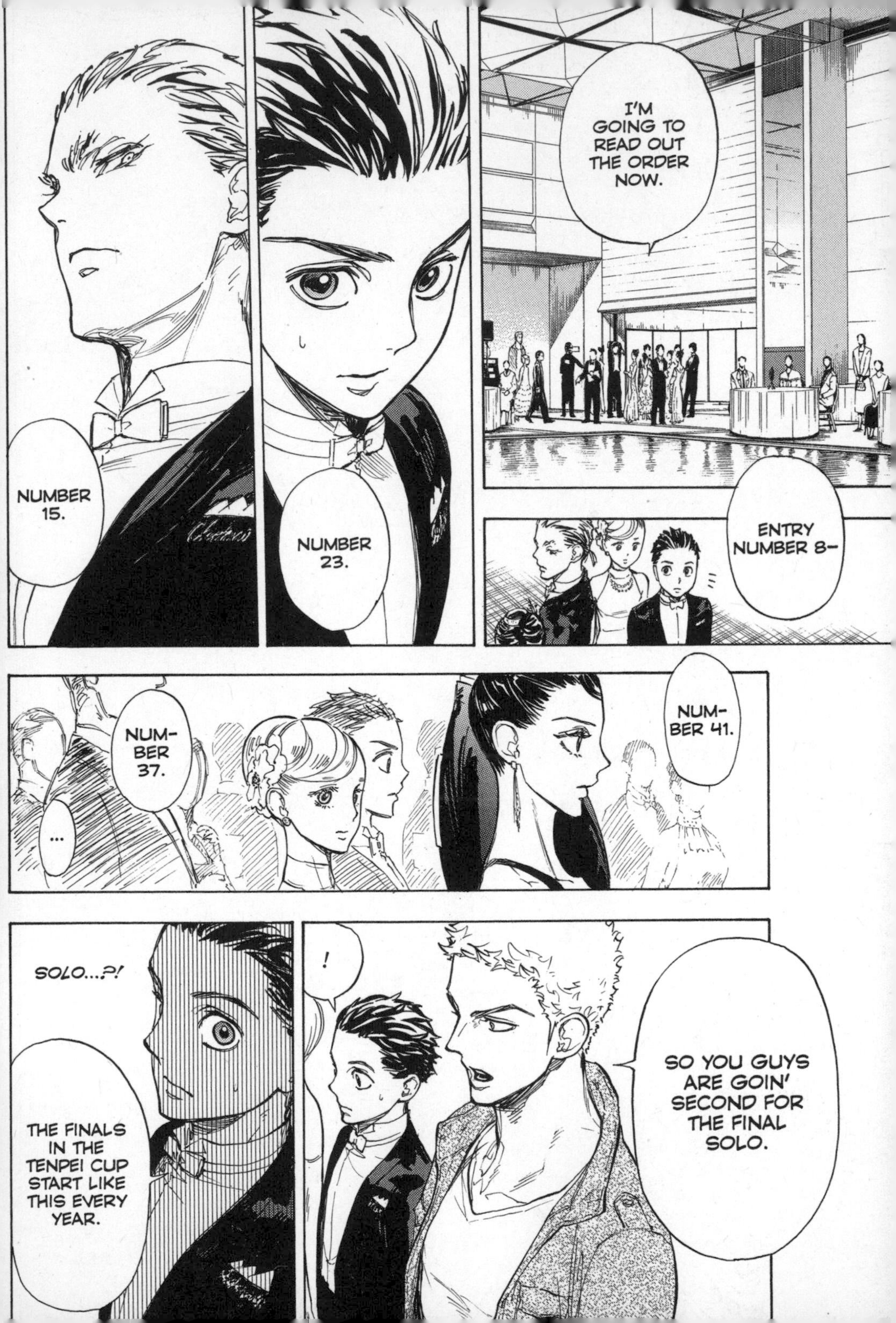
I'M GOING TO READ OUT THE ORDER NOW.
ENTRY NUMBER 8—
NUMBER 23.
NUMBER 15.
NUM-BER 41.
NUM-BER 37.
...
SO YOU GUYS ARE GOIN' SECOND FOR THE FINAL SOLO.
!
SOLO...?!
THE FINALS IN THE TENPEI CUP START LIKE THIS EVERY YEAR.

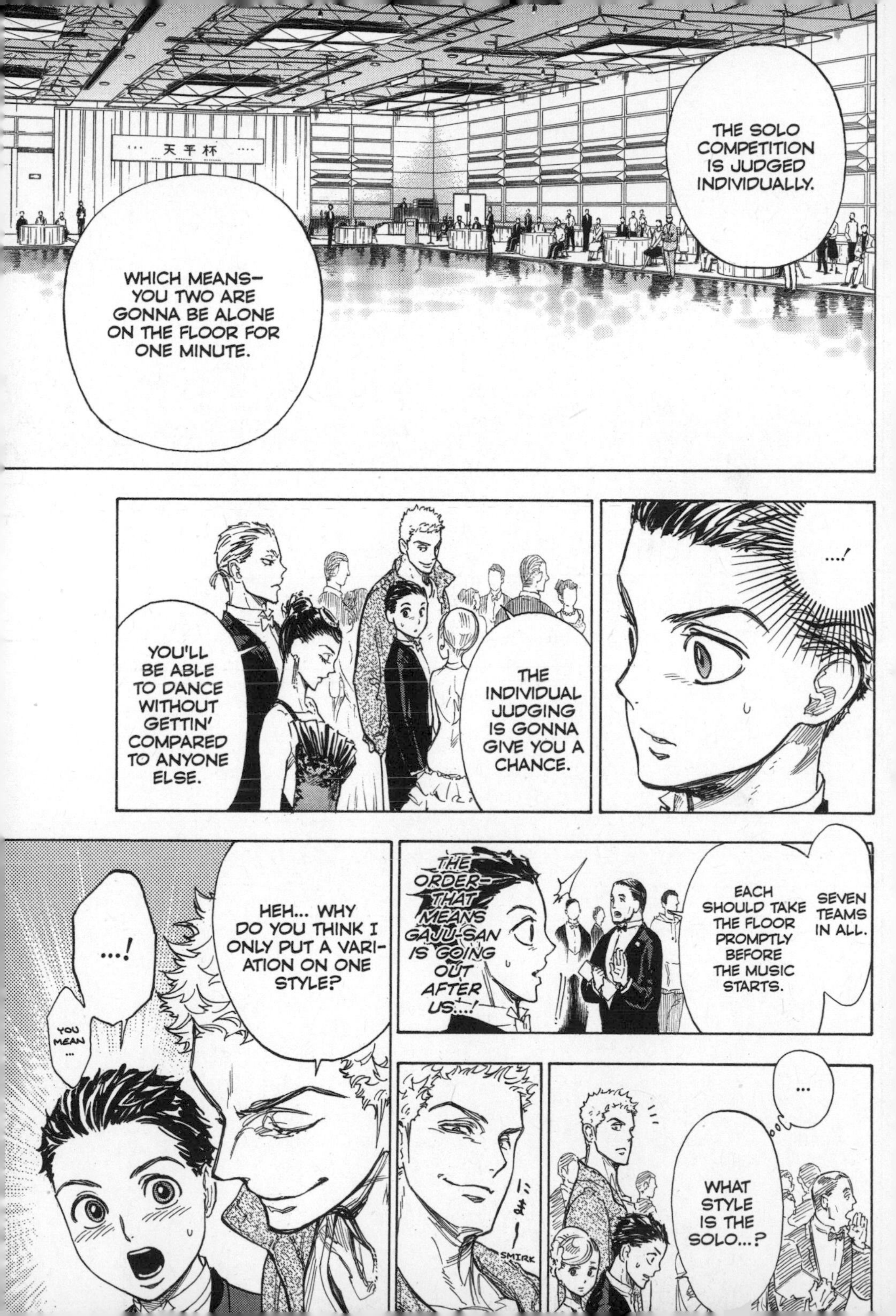
THE SOLO COMPETITION IS JUDGED INDIVIDUALLY.
天平杯
WHICH MEANS— YOU TWO ARE GONNA BE ALONE ON THE FLOOR FOR ONE MINUTE.
...!
THE INDIVIDUAL JUDGING IS GONNA GIVE YOU A CHANCE.
YOU'LL BE ABLE TO DANCE WITHOUT GETTIN' COMPARED TO ANYONE ELSE.
SEVEN TEAMS IN ALL.
EACH SHOULD TAKE THE FLOOR PROMPTLY BEFORE THE MUSIC STARTS.
THE ORDER— THAT MEANS GAJU-SAN IS GOING OUT AFTER US...!
...
WHAT STYLE IS THE SOLO...?
にまー
SMIRK
HEH... WHY DO YOU THINK I ONLY PUT A VARIATION ON ONE STYLE?
...!
YOU MEAN...

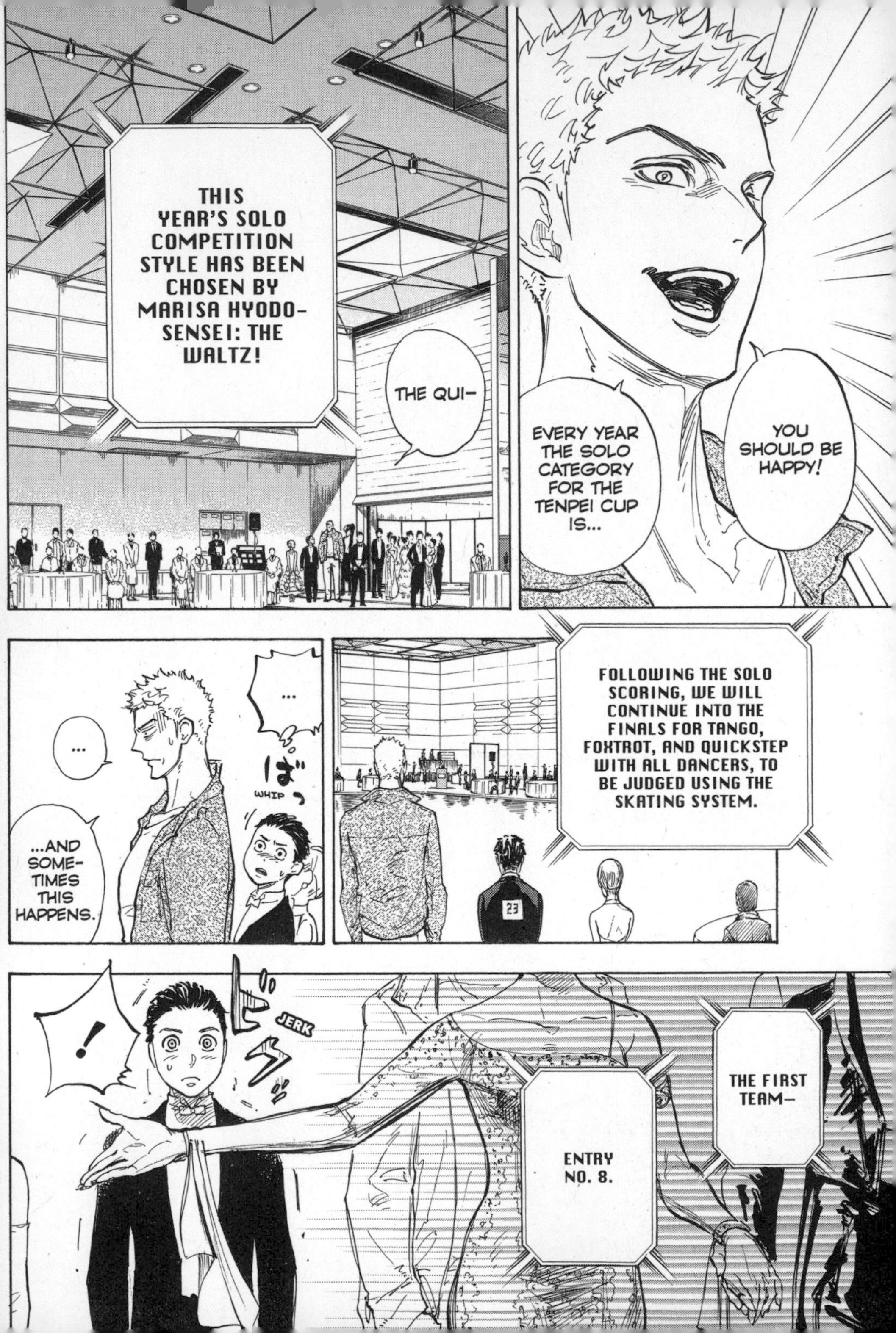
YOU SHOULD BE HAPPY!
EVERY YEAR THE SOLO CATEGORY FOR THE TENPEI CUP IS...
THE QUI–
THIS YEAR'S SOLO COMPETITION STYLE HAS BEEN CHOSEN BY MARISA HYODO-SENSEI: THE WALTZ!
FOLLOWING THE SOLO SCORING, WE WILL CONTINUE INTO THE FINALS FOR TANGO, FOXTROT, AND QUICKSTEP WITH ALL DANCERS, TO BE JUDGED USING THE SKATING SYSTEM.
...
...
ばっ
WHIP
...AND SOMETIMES THIS HAPPENS.
23
THE FIRST TEAM–
ENTRY NO. 8.
JERK
!

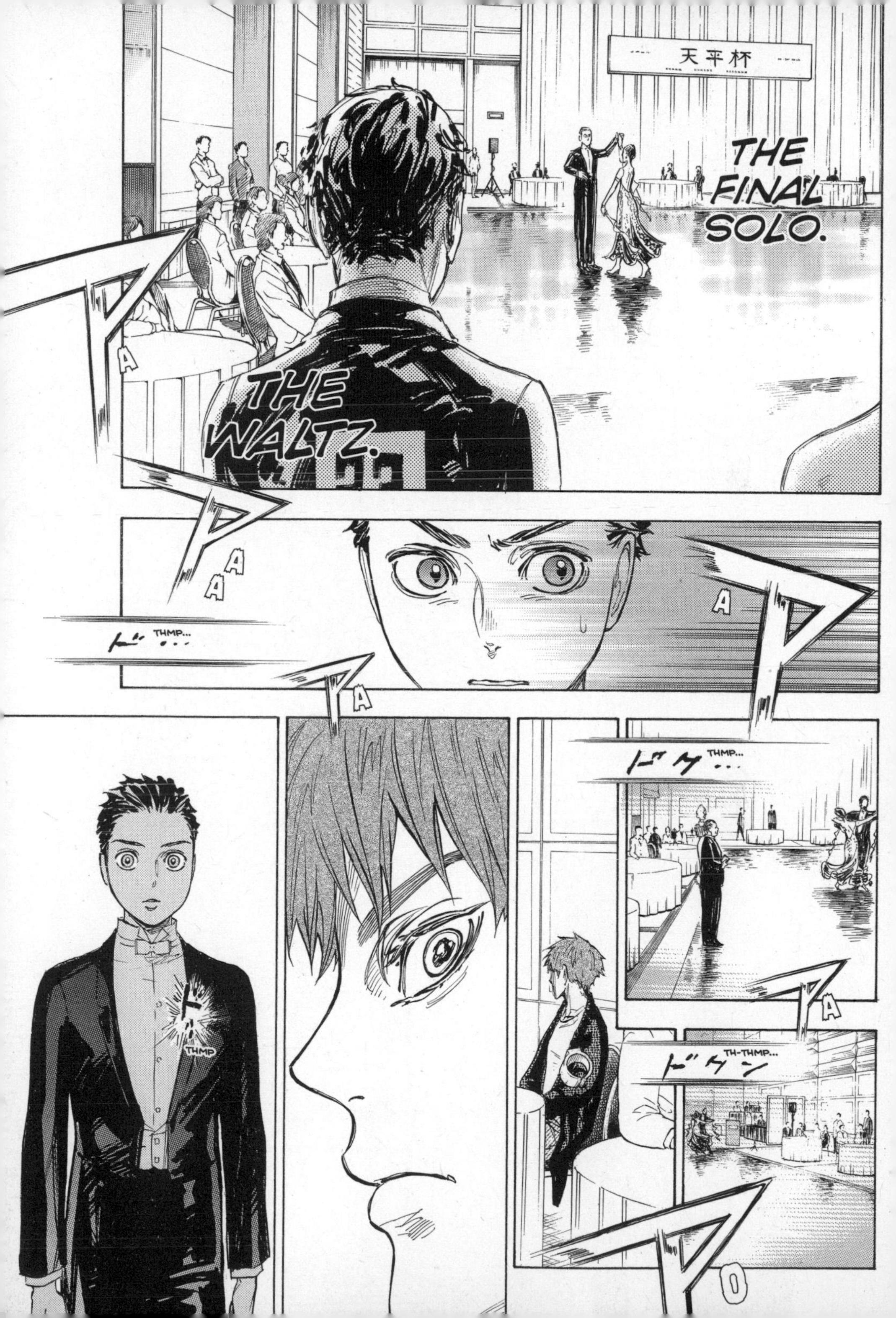
天平杯
THE FINAL SOLO.
THE WALTZ.
A
A
A
A
THMP...
A
THMP...
A
TH-THMP...
O
THMP

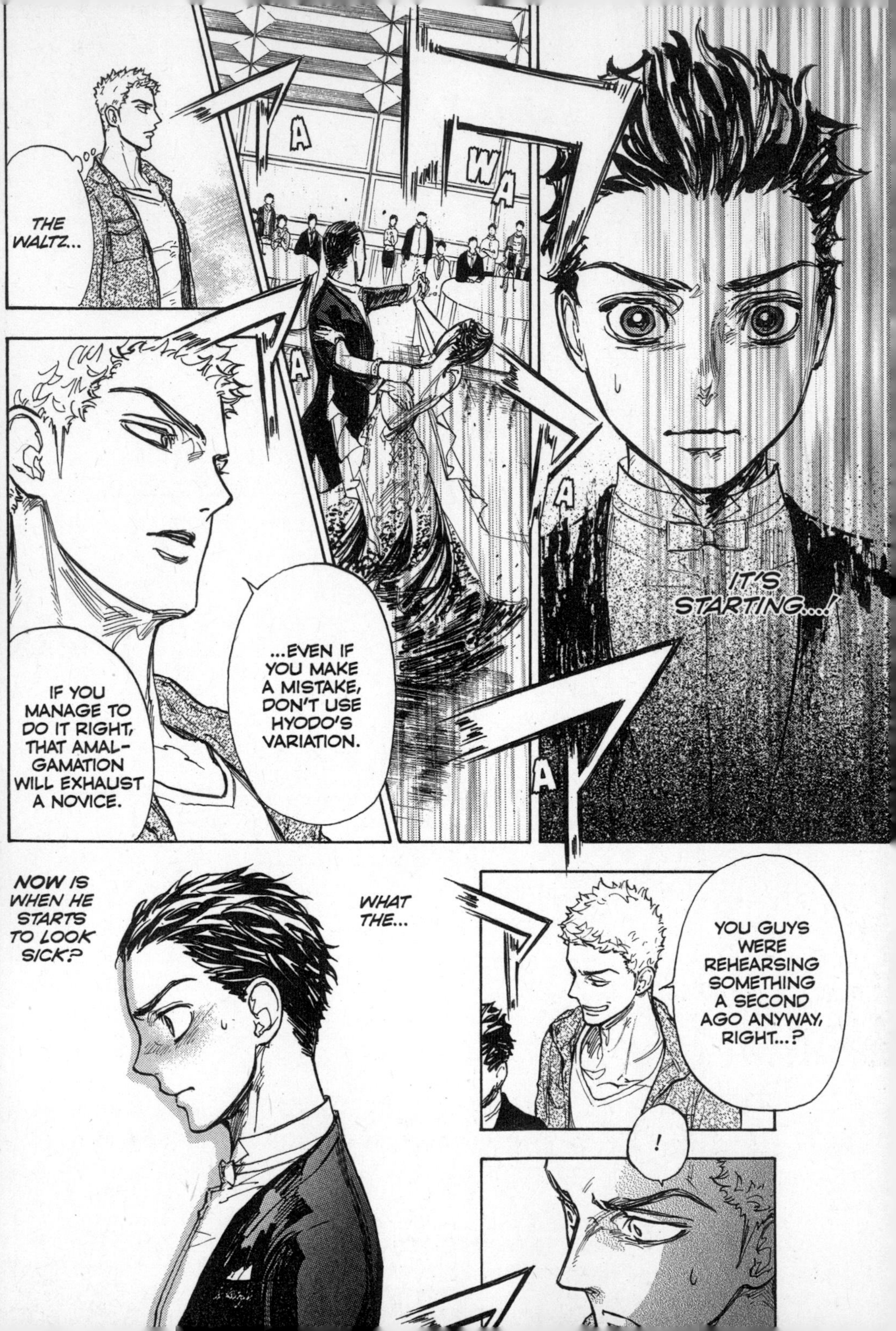
IT'S STARTING...!
A
WA
A
A
A
A
THE WALTZ...
...EVEN IF YOU MAKE A MISTAKE, DON'T USE HYODO'S VARIATION.
IF YOU MANAGE TO DO IT RIGHT, THAT AMAL-GAMATION WILL EXHAUST A NOVICE.
YOU GUYS WERE REHEARSING SOMETHING A SECOND AGO ANYWAY, RIGHT...?
!
WHAT THE...
NOW IS WHEN HE STARTS TO LOOK SICK?

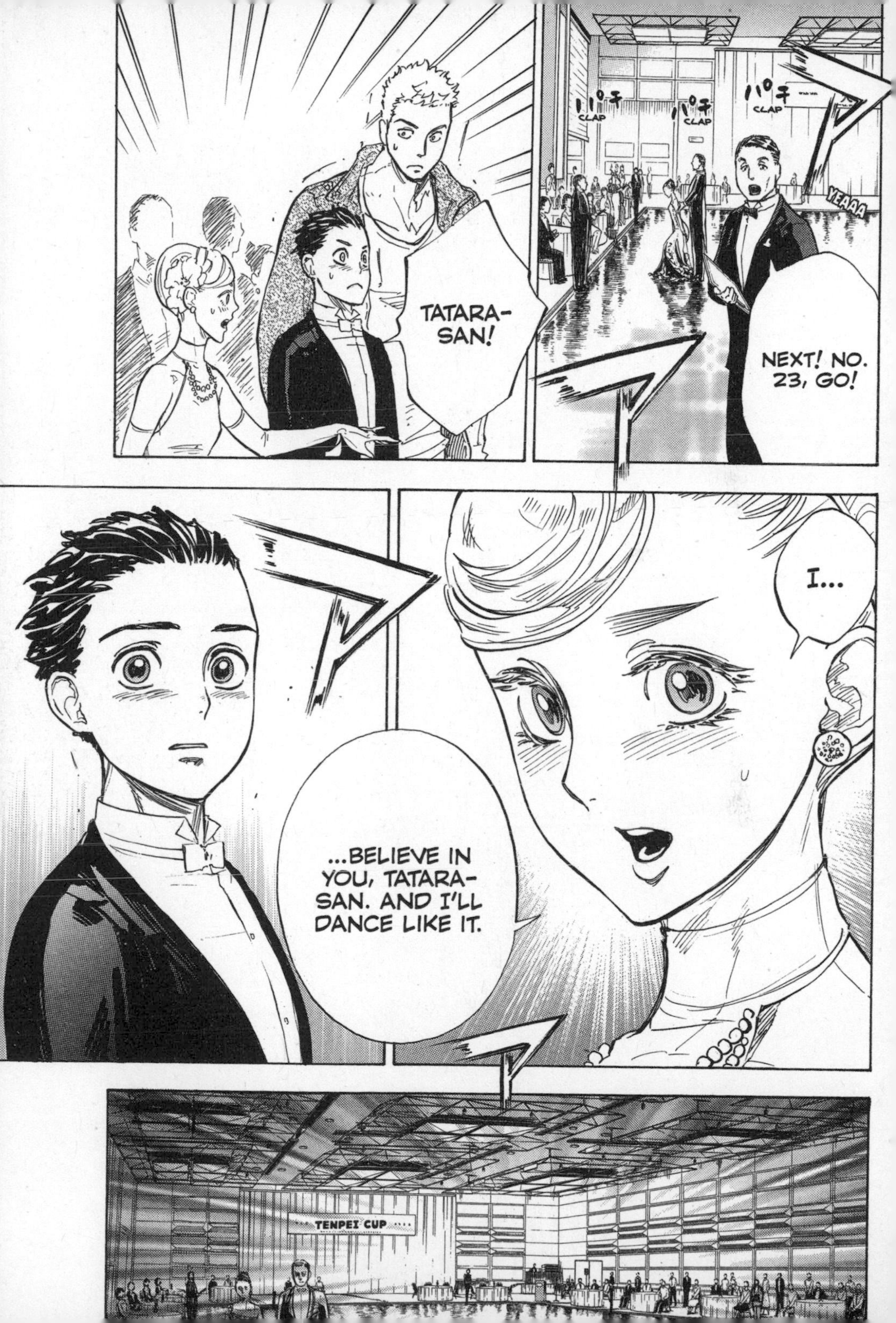
パチ
CLAP
パチ
CLAP
パチ
CLAP
YEAAA
NEXT! NO. 23, GO!
TATARA-SAN!
I...
...BELIEVE IN YOU, TATARA-SAN. AND I'LL DANCE LIKE IT.
TENPEI CUP

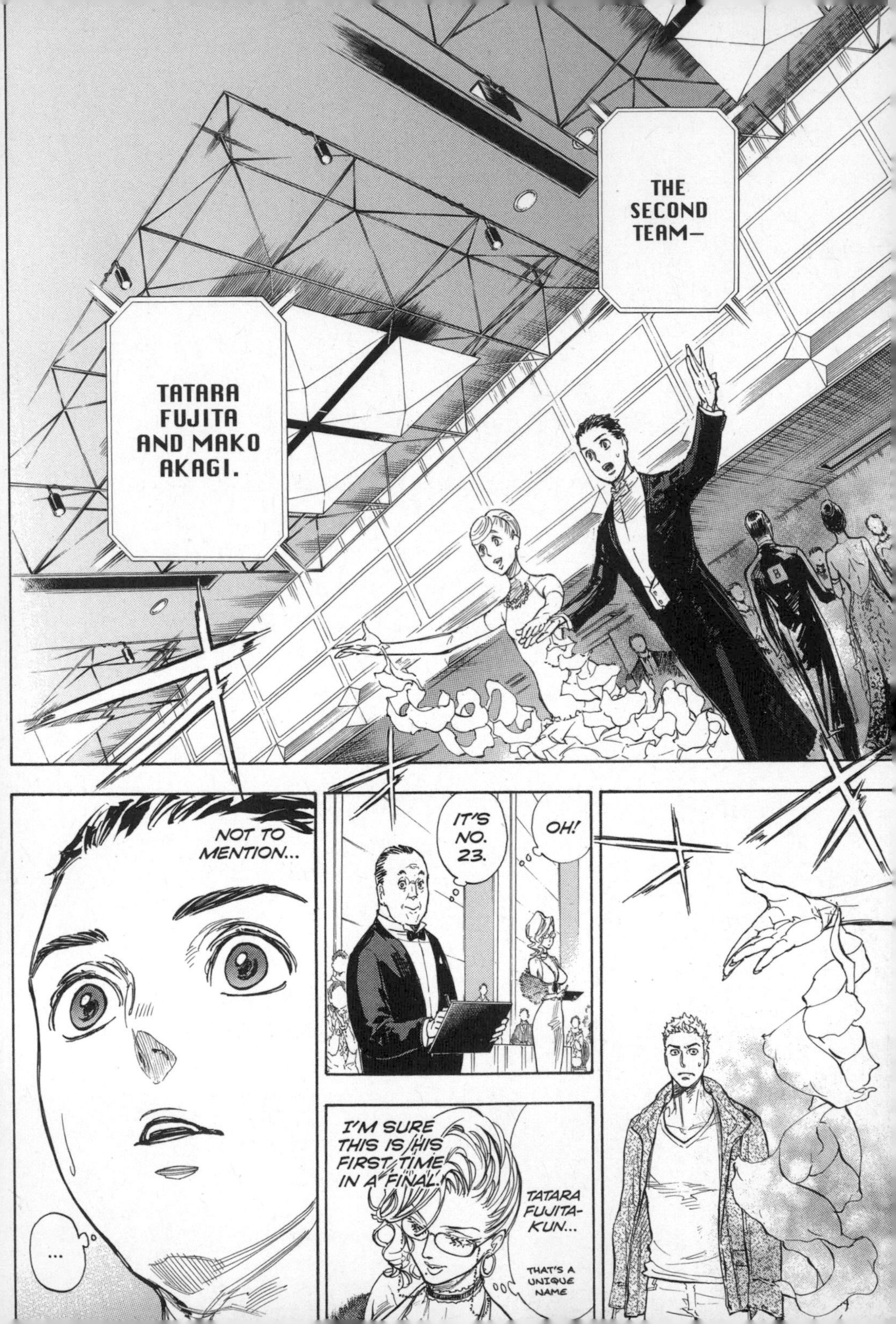
THE SECOND TEAM—
TATARA FUJITA AND MAKO AKAGI.
OH!
IT'S NO. 23.
NOT TO MENTION...
I'M SURE THIS IS HIS FIRST TIME IN A FINAL.
TATARA FUJITA-KUN...
THAT'S A UNIQUE NAME
...

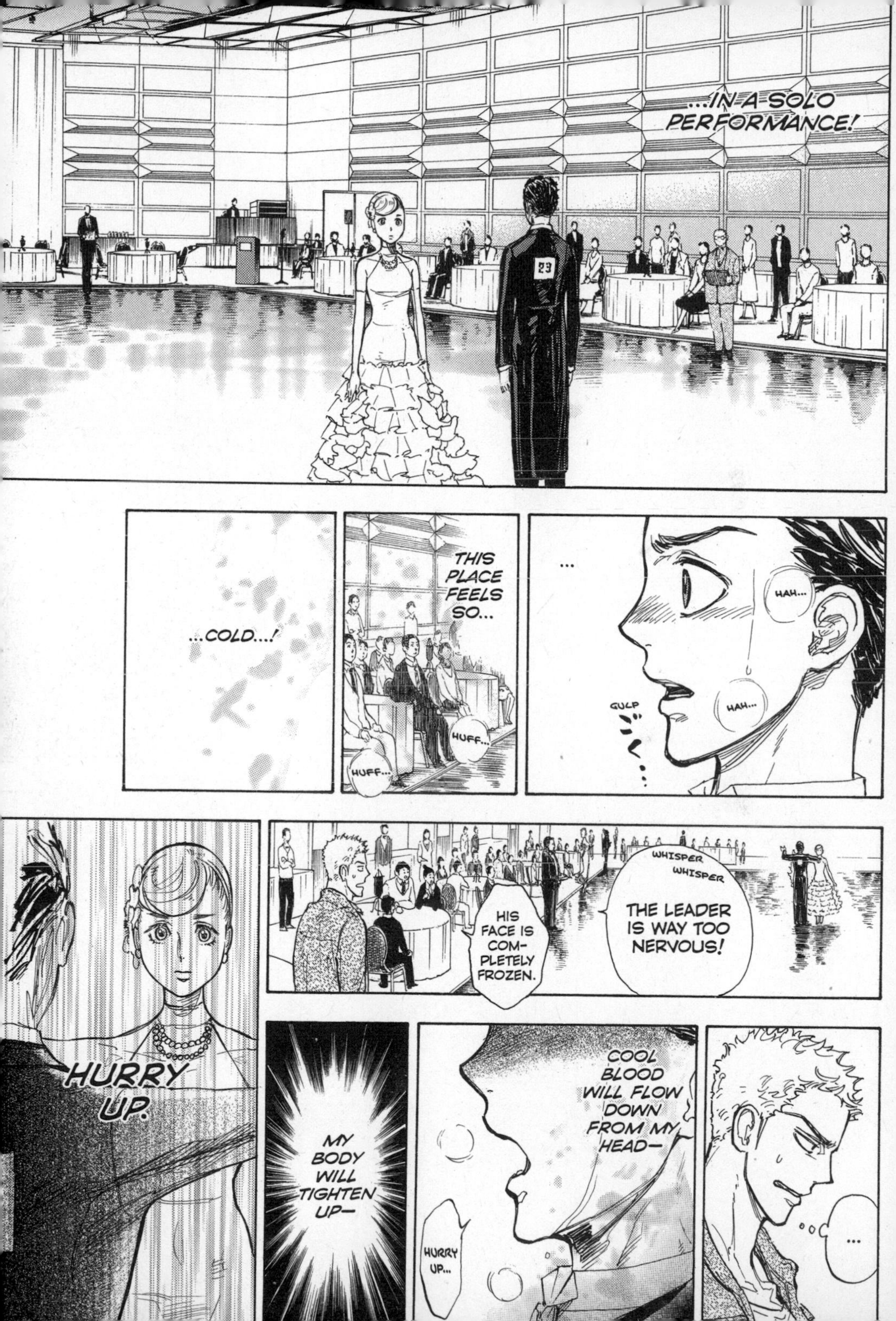
...IN A SOLO PERFORMANCE!
...
HAH...
HAH...
GULP
ごく...
THIS PLACE FEELS SO...
HUFF...
HUFF...
...COLD...!
WHISPER WHISPER
THE LEADER IS WAY TOO NERVOUS!
HIS FACE IS COMPLETELY FROZEN.
...
COOL BLOOD WILL FLOW DOWN FROM MY HEAD—
HURRY UP...
MY BODY WILL TIGHTEN UP—
HURRY UP.

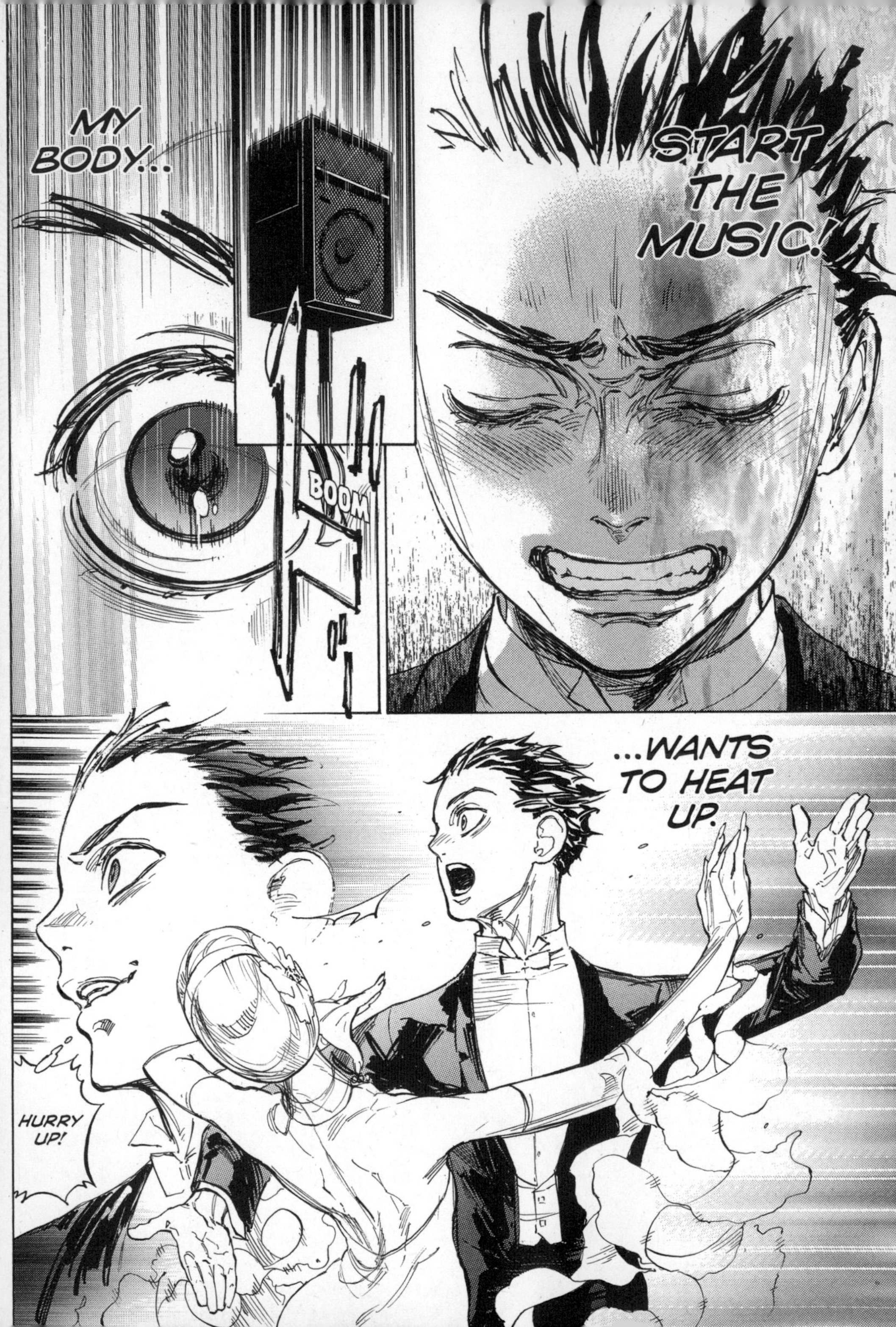
START THE MUSIC!
MY BODY...
BOOM
...WANTS TO HEAT UP.
HURRY UP!

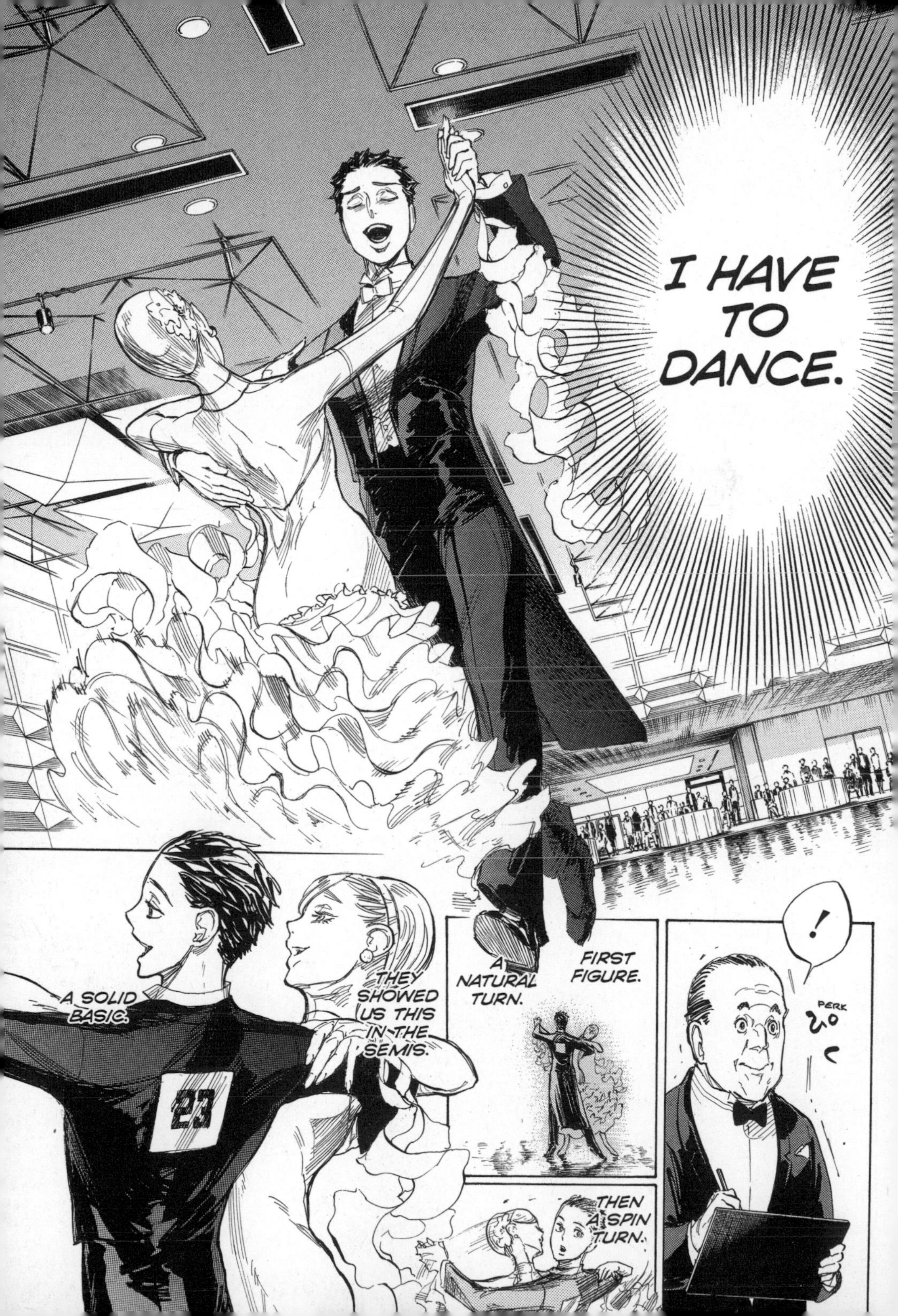
I HAVE TO DANCE.
!
PERK
ぴく
FIRST FIGURE.
A NATURAL TURN.
THEN A SPIN TURN.
THEY SHOWED US THIS IN THE SEMIS.
A SOLID BASIC.

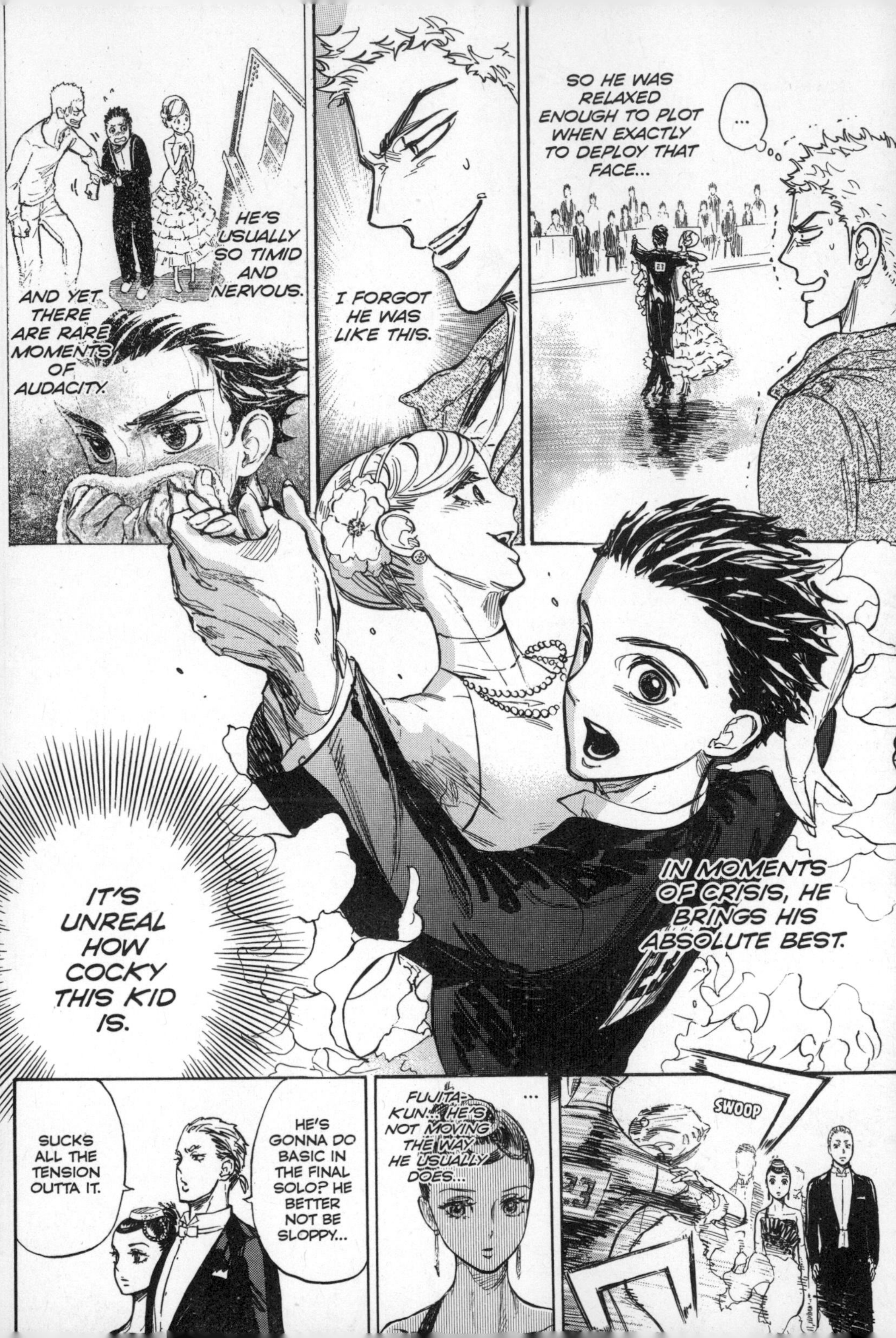
...
SO HE WAS RELAXED ENOUGH TO PLOT WHEN EXACTLY TO DEPLOY THAT FACE...
I FORGOT HE WAS LIKE THIS.
HE'S USUALLY SO TIMID AND NERVOUS.
AND YET THERE ARE RARE MOMENTS OF AUDACITY.
IN MOMENTS OF CRISIS, HE BRINGS HIS ABSOLUTE BEST.
IT'S UNREAL HOW COCKY THIS KID IS.
SWOOP
...
FUJITA-KUN... HE'S NOT MOVING THE WAY HE USUALLY DOES...
HE'S GONNA DO BASIC IN THE FINAL SOLO? HE BETTER NOT BE SLOPPY...
SUCKS ALL THE TENSION OUTTA IT.

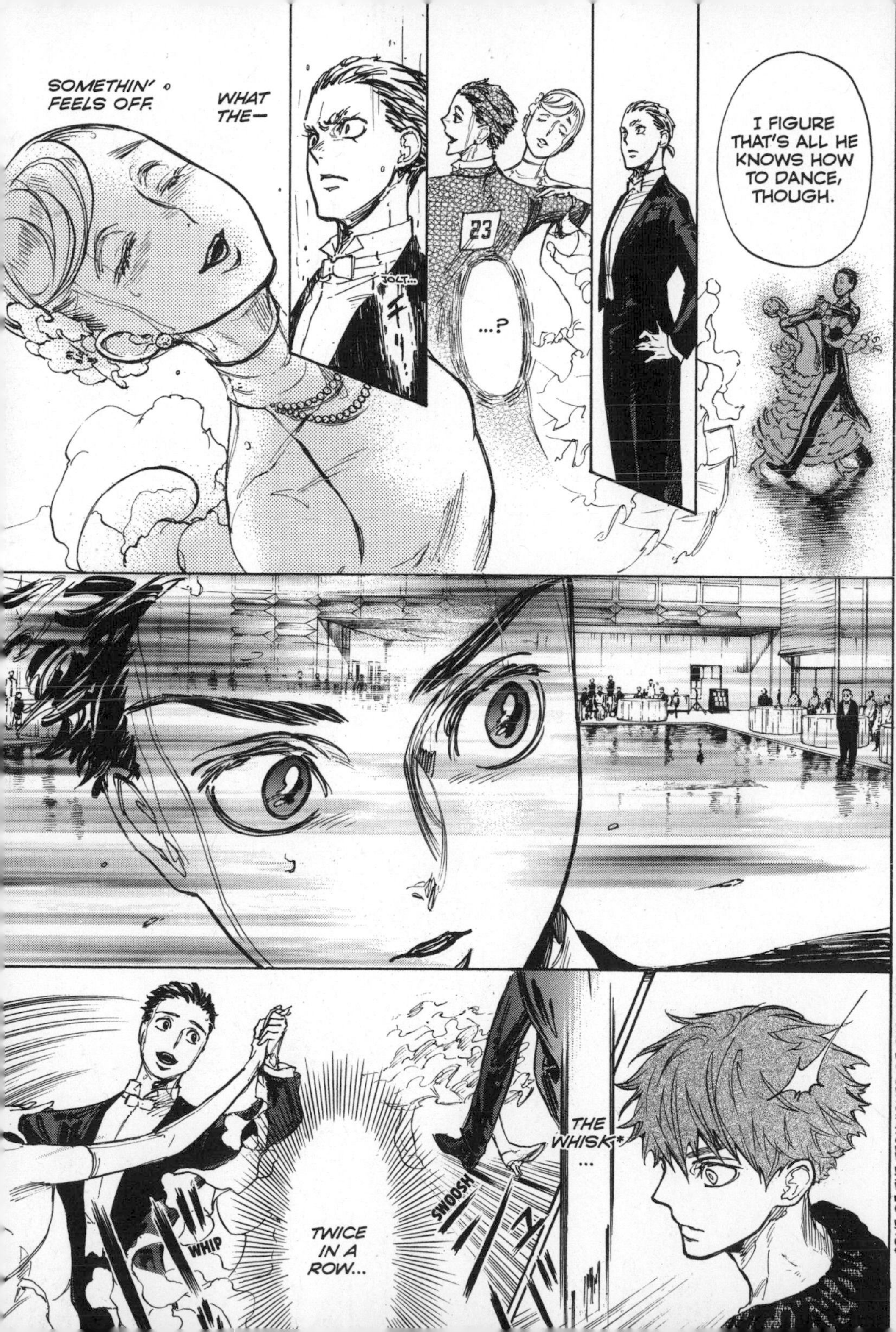
I FIGURE THAT'S ALL HE KNOWS HOW TO DANCE, THOUGH.
...?
WHAT THE—
JOLT...
SOMETHIN' FEELS OFF.
THE WHISK* ...
SHOOSH
TWICE IN A ROW...
WHIP

*ONE OF THE TECHNIQUES OF THE WALTZ

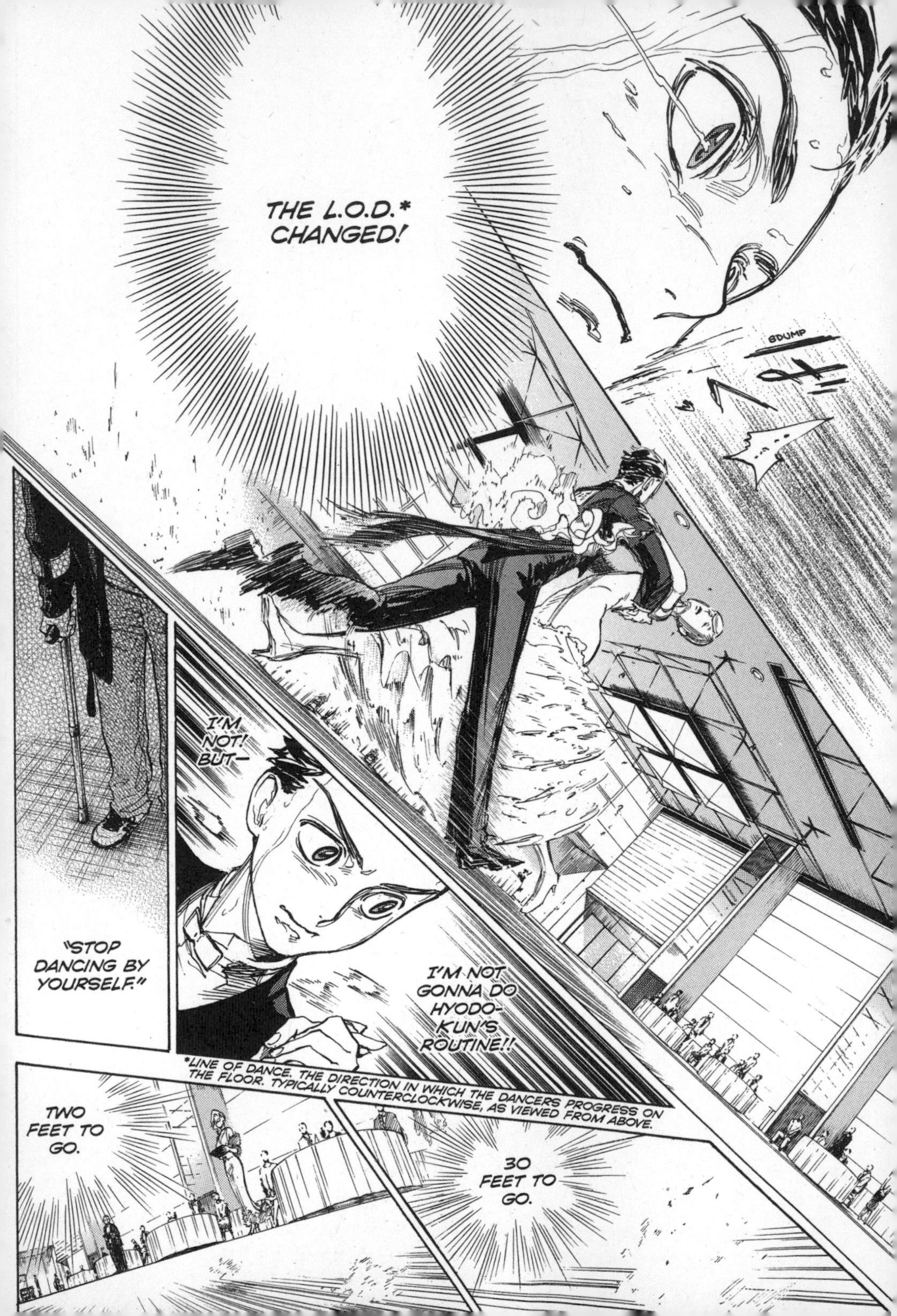
THE L.O.D.* CHANGED!
SDUMP
I'M NOT GONNA DO HYODO-KUN'S ROUTINE!!
I'M NOT! BUT—
"STOP DANCING BY YOURSELF."
*LINE OF DANCE. THE DIRECTION IN WHICH THE DANCERS PROGRESS ON THE FLOOR. TYPICALLY COUNTERCLOCKWISE, AS VIEWED FROM ABOVE.
30 FEET TO GO.
TWO FEET TO GO.

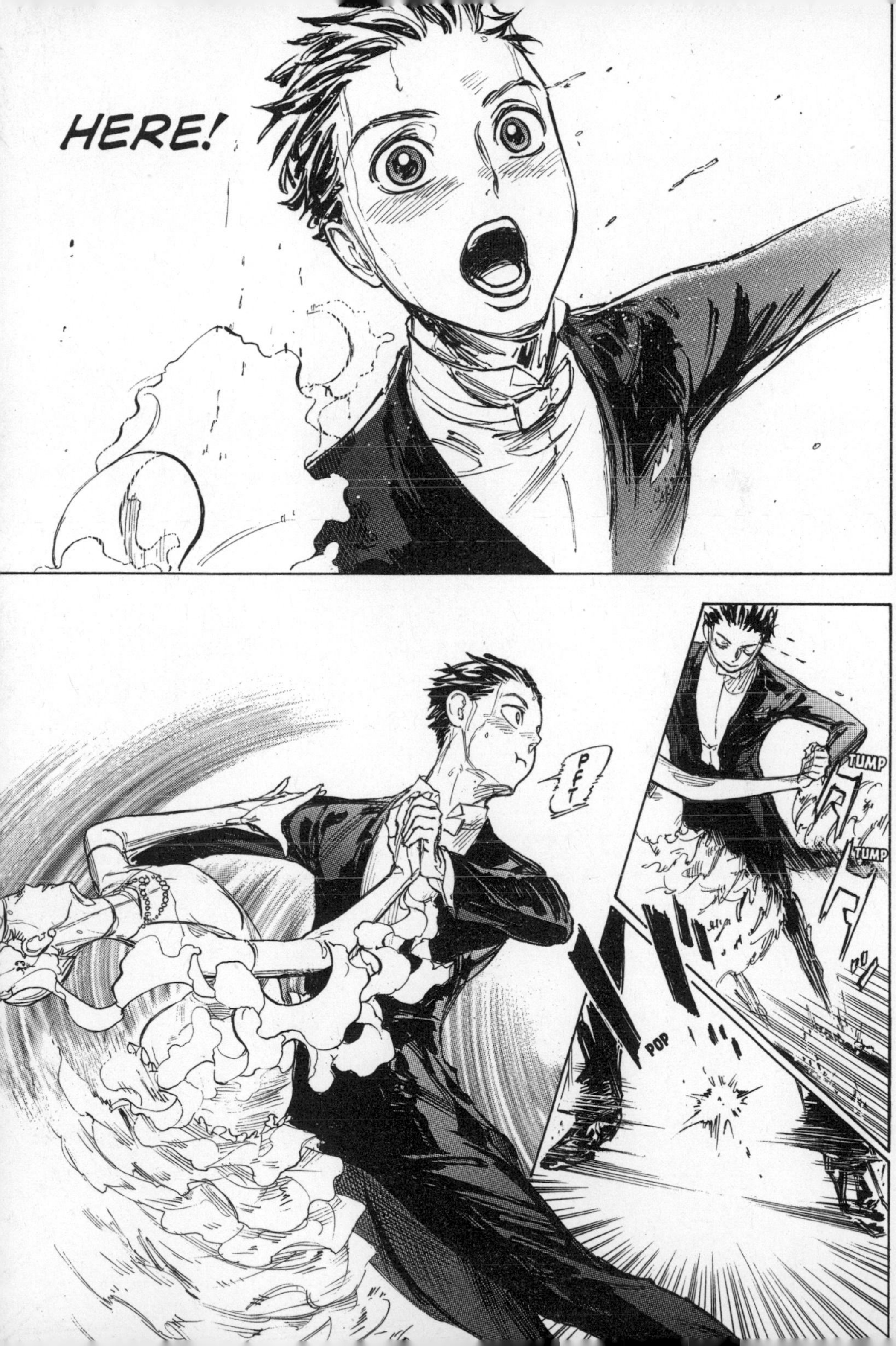
HERE!
TUMP
TUMP
PFT
POP

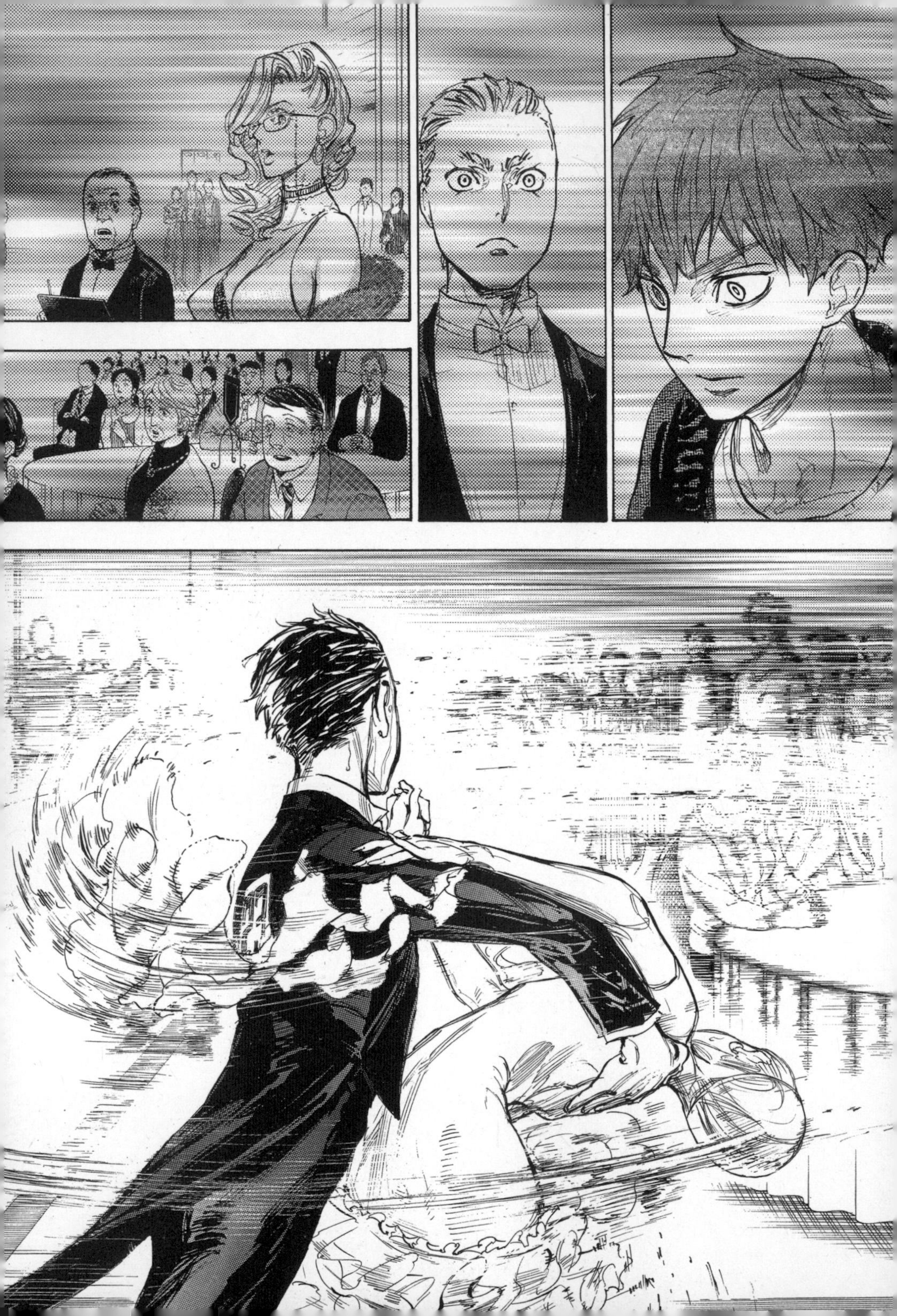

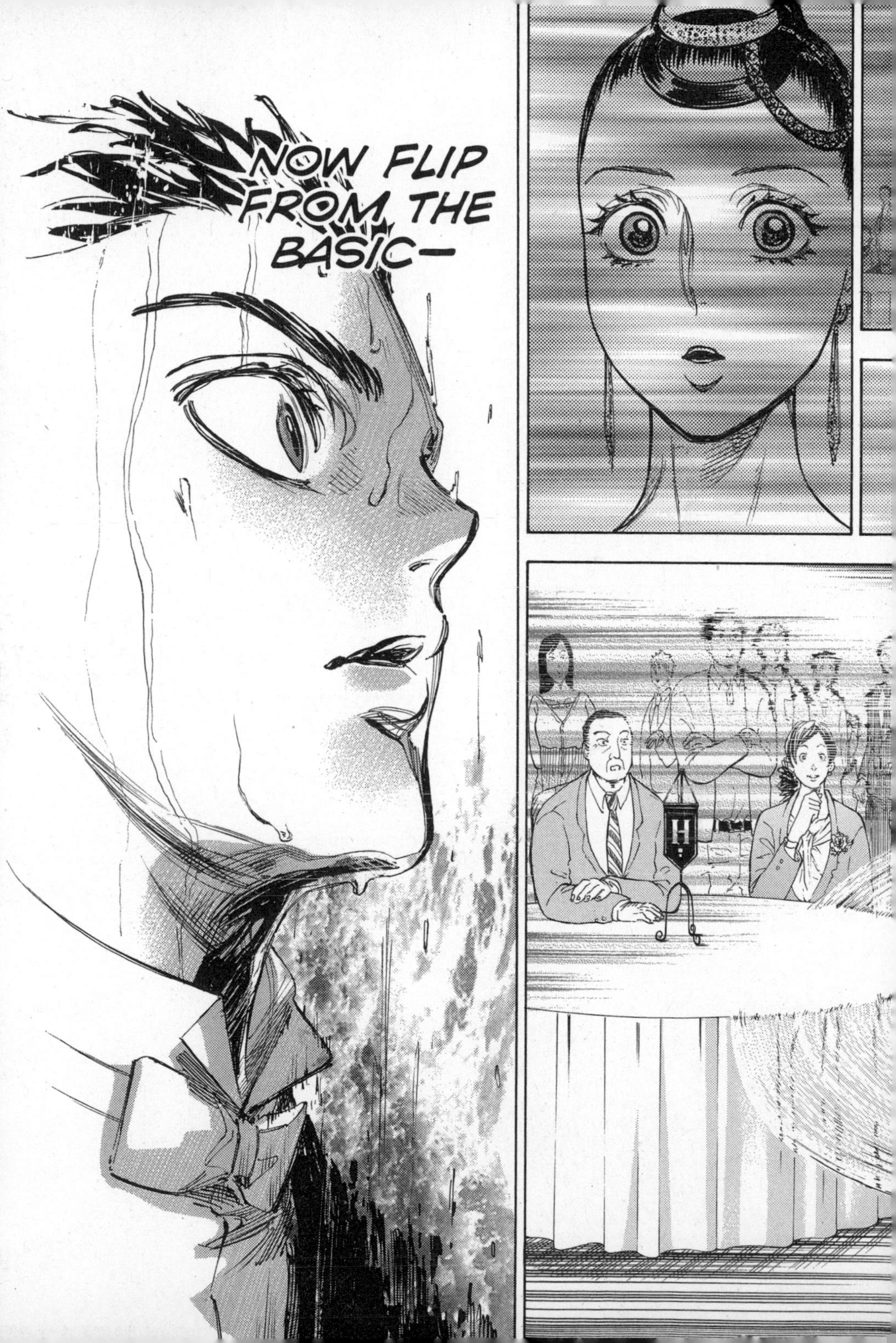
NOW FLIP FROM THE BASIC—

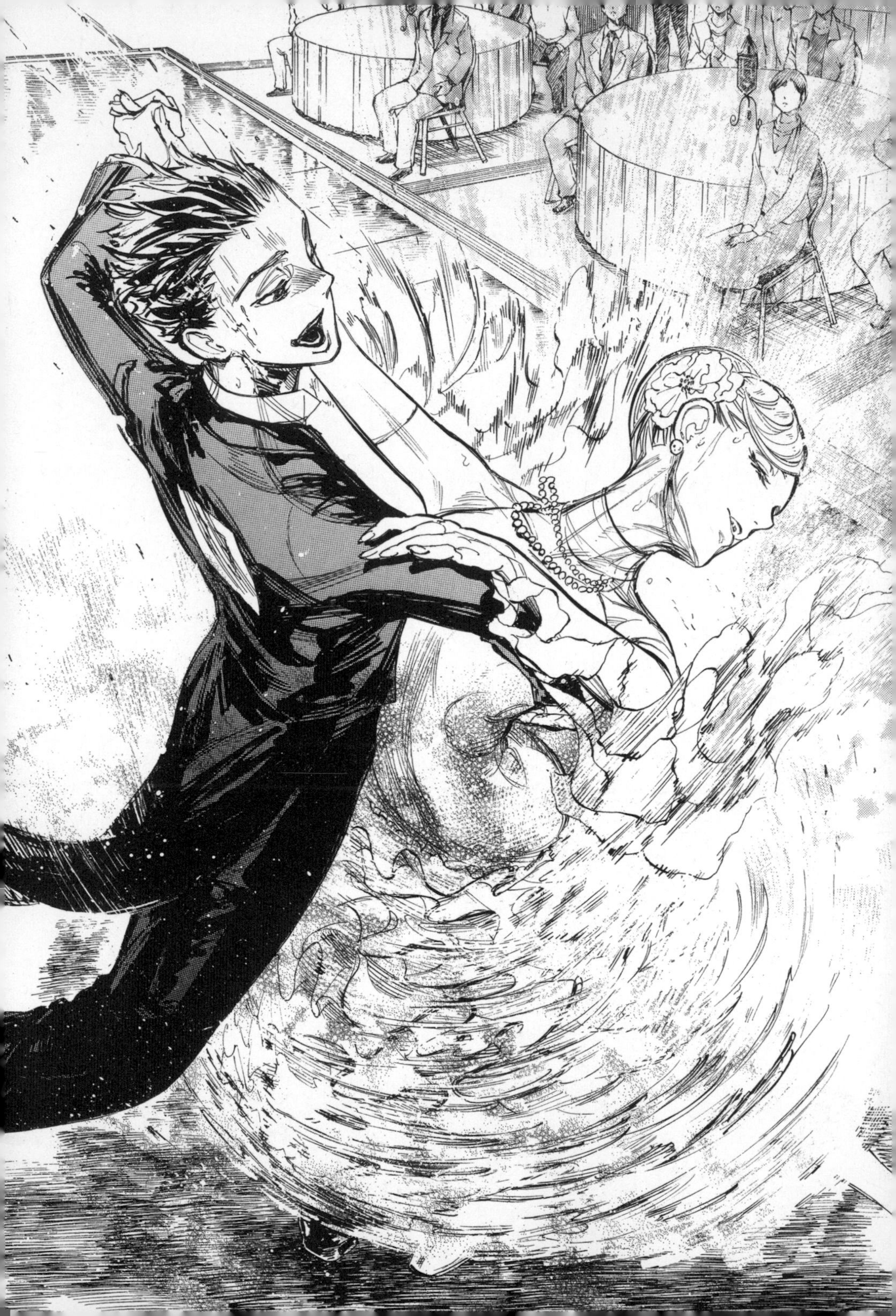

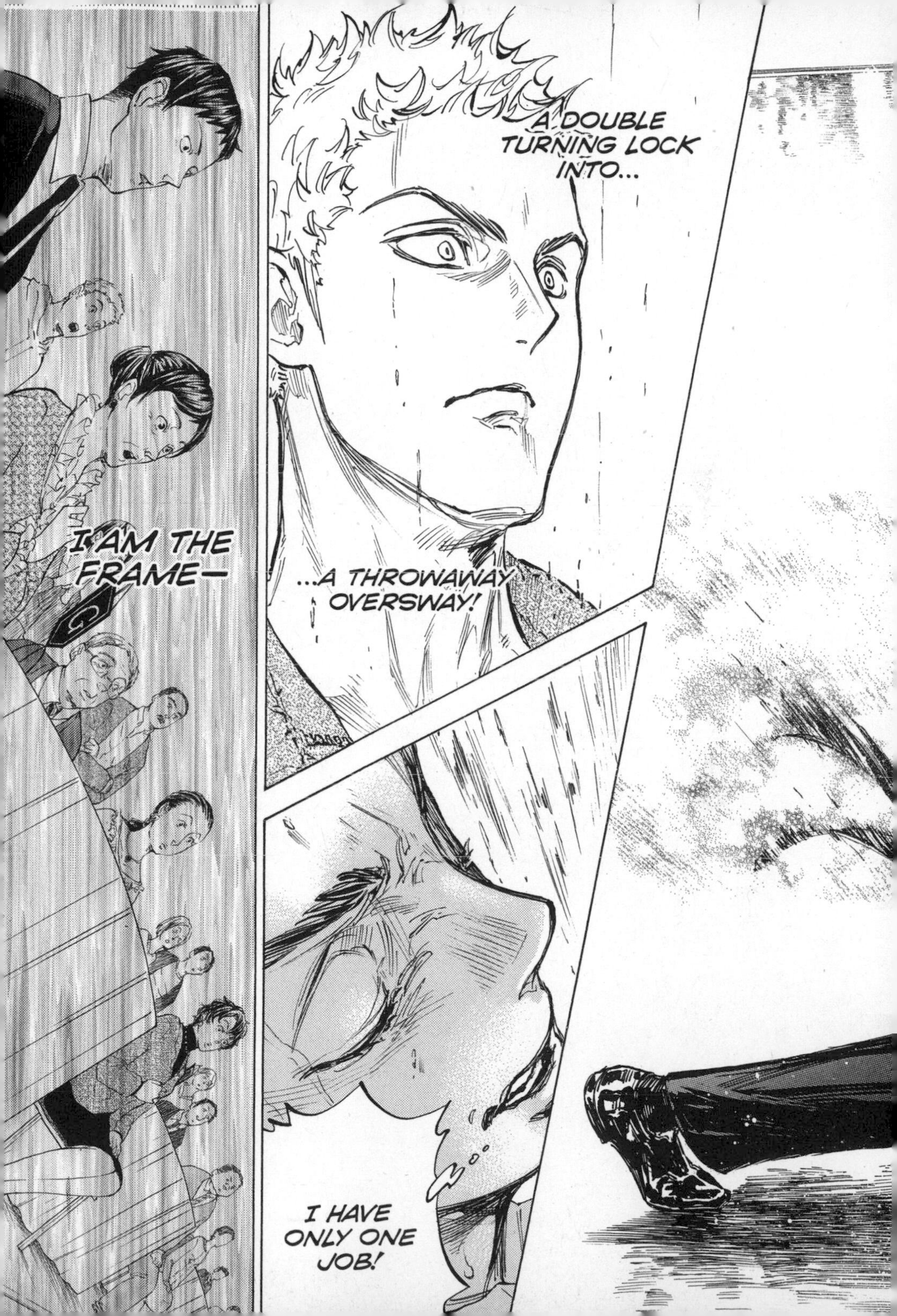
A DOUBLE TURNING LOCK INTO...
...A THROWAWAY OVERSWAY!
I HAVE ONLY ONE JOB!
I AM THE FRAME—

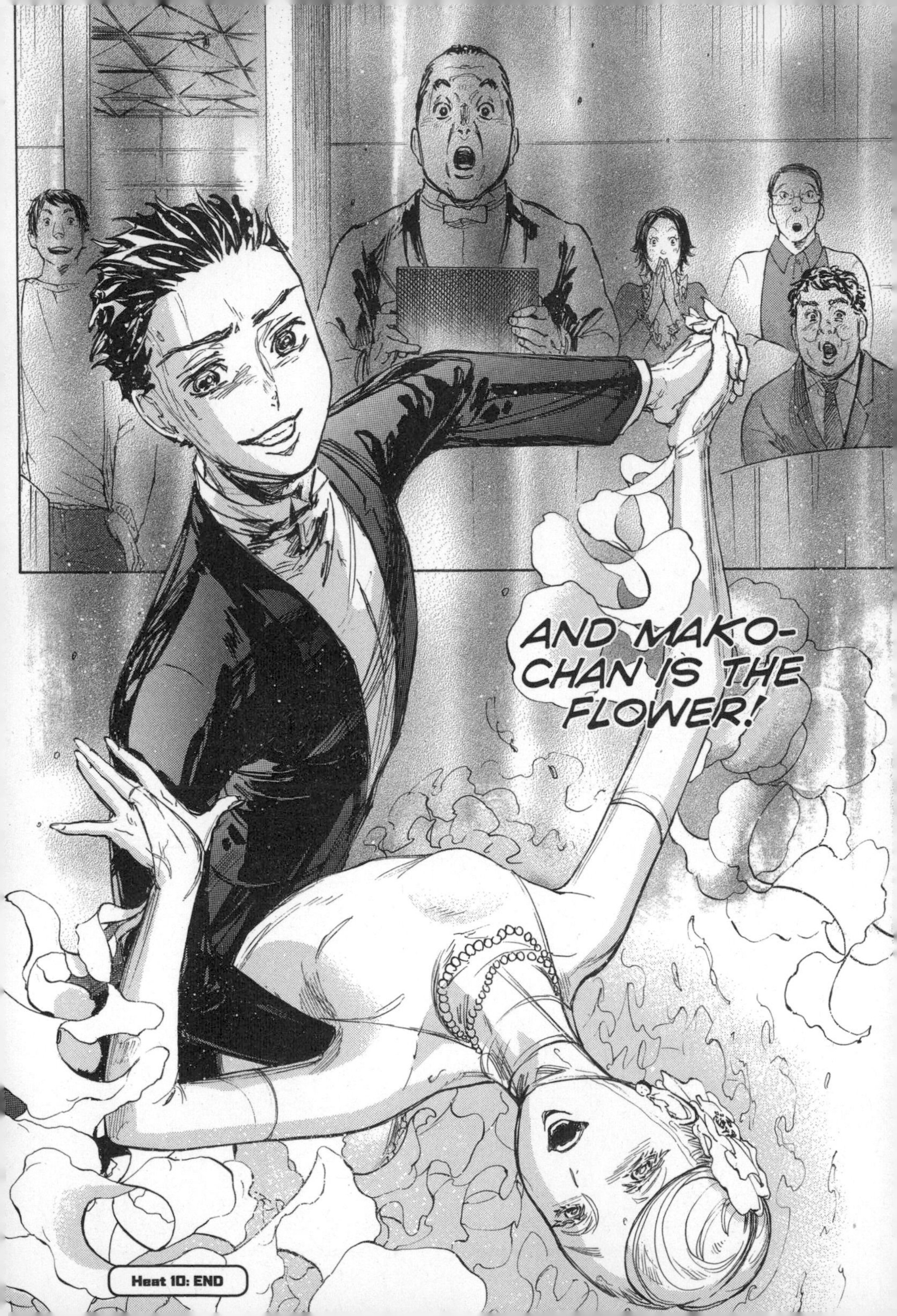
AND MAKO-CHAN IS THE FLOWER!
Heat 10: END

WELCOME TO THE BALLROOM

Special Thanks!

For help with waltz variations

Mr. Takahiro Akitani

Ms. Miho Tahara

Background assistance

Sakurada Dance School

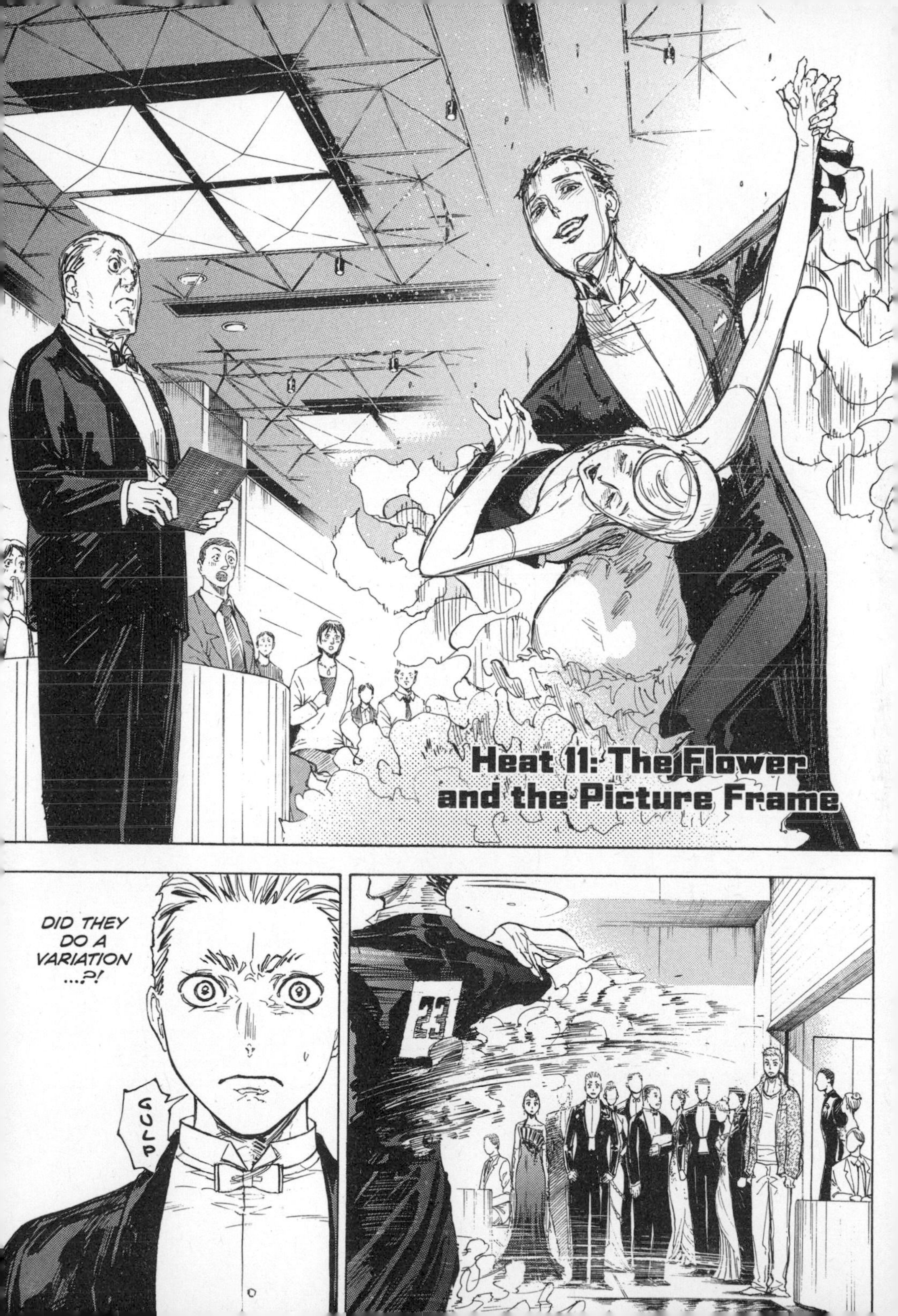
Heat 11: The Flower and the Picture Frame
23
DID THEY DO A VARIATION ...?!
GULP

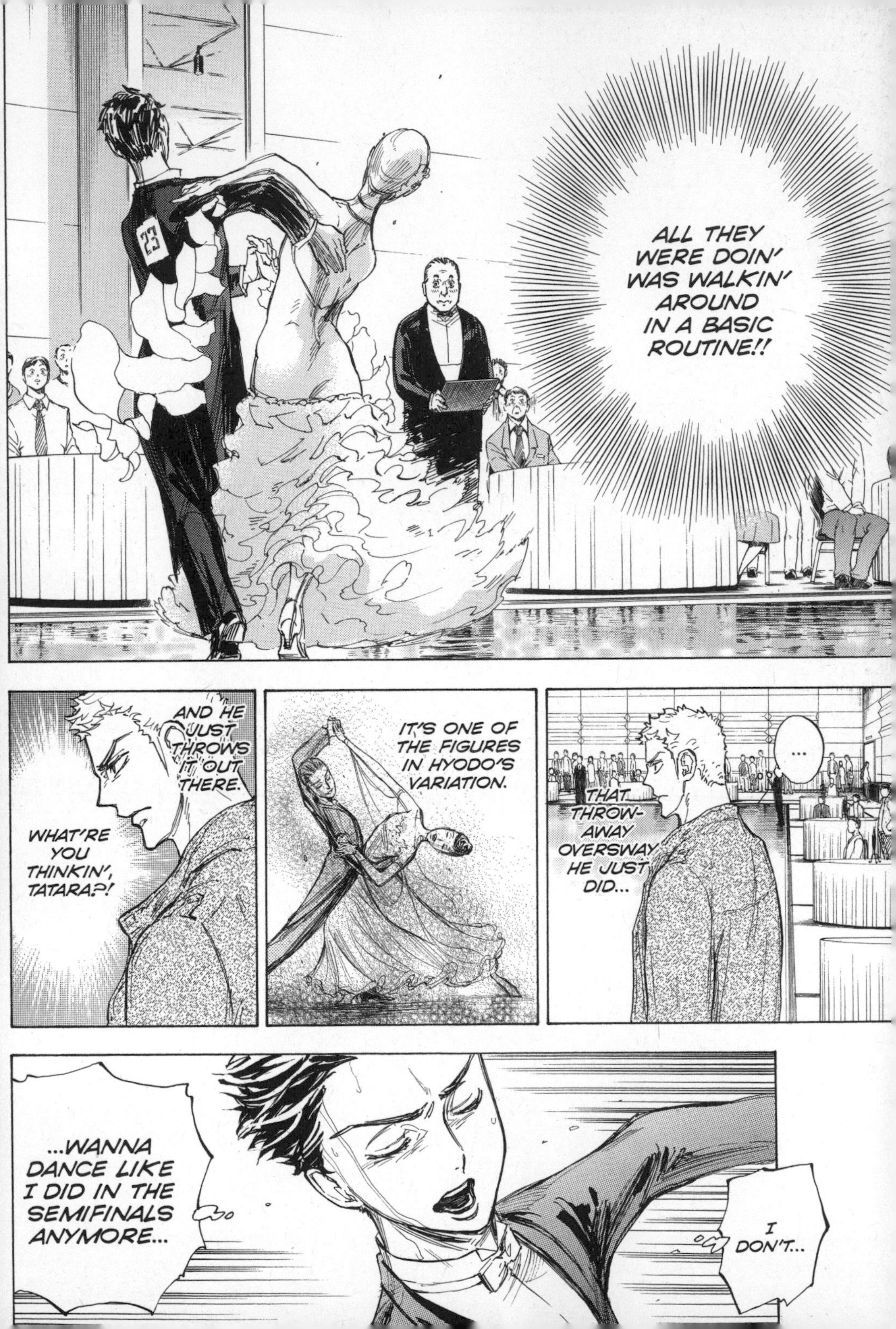
ALL THEY WERE DOIN' WAS WALKIN' AROUND IN A BASIC ROUTINE!!
...
THAT THROW-AWAY OVERSWAY HE JUST DID...
IT'S ONE OF THE FIGURES IN HYODO'S VARIATION.
AND HE JUST THROWS IT OUT THERE.
WHAT'RE YOU THINKIN', TATARA?!
I DON'T...
...WANNA DANCE LIKE I DID IN THE SEMIFINALS ANYMORE...

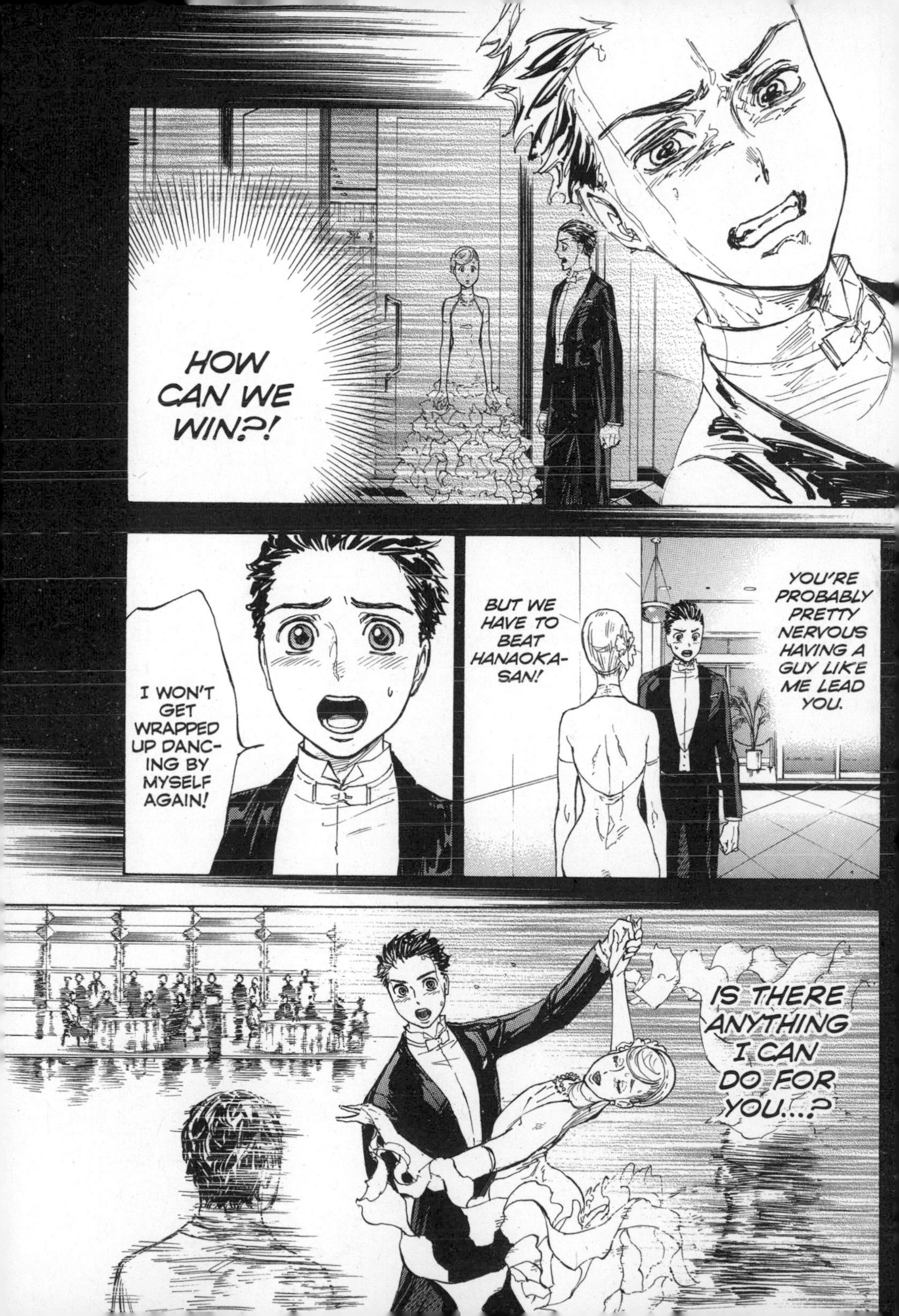
HOW CAN WE WIN?!
YOU'RE PROBABLY PRETTY NERVOUS HAVING A GUY LIKE ME LEAD YOU.
BUT WE HAVE TO BEAT HANAOKA-SAN!
I WON'T GET WRAPPED UP DANCING BY MYSELF AGAIN!
IS THERE ANYTHING I CAN DO FOR YOU...?

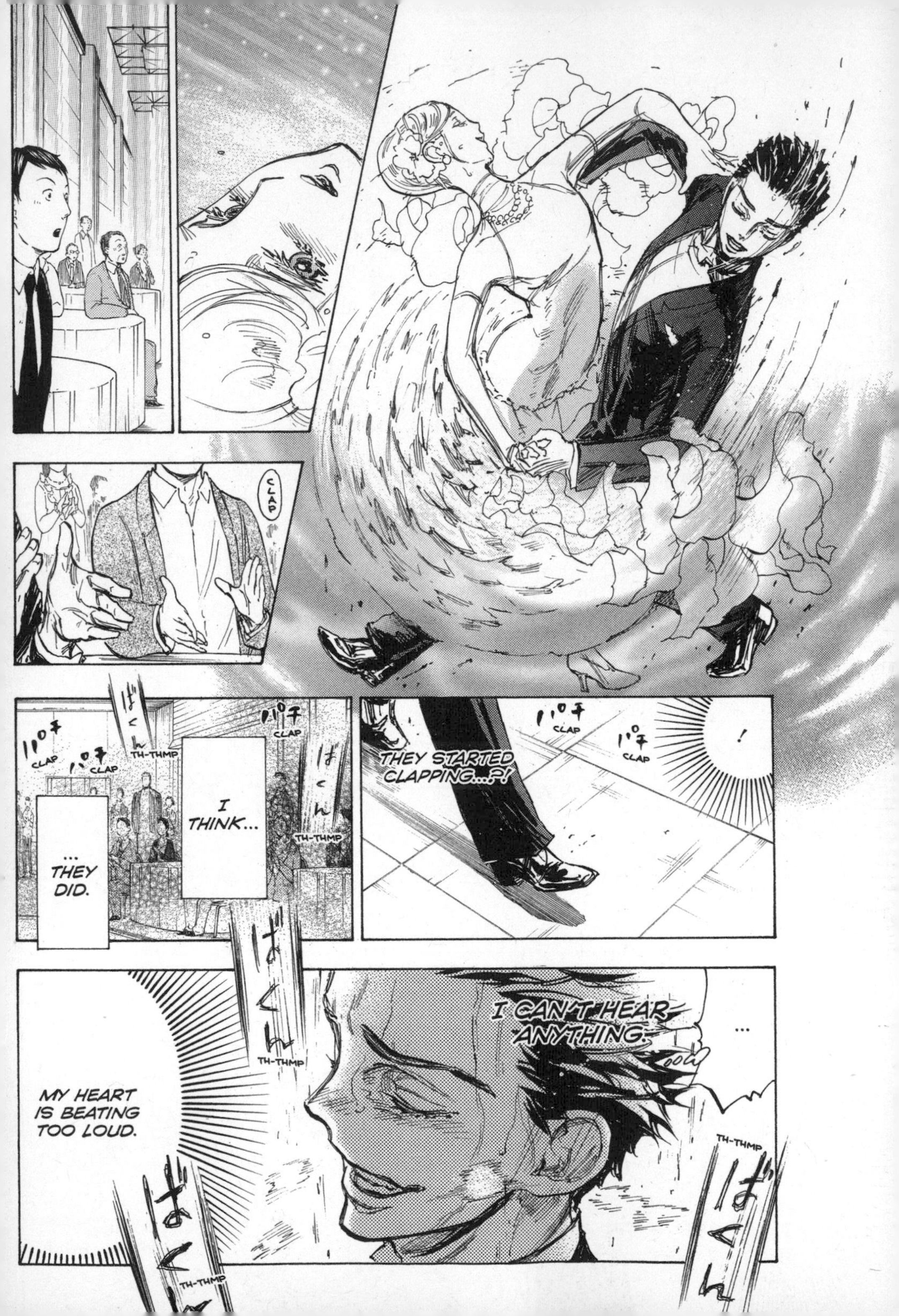

CLAP
CLAP
CLAP
THEY STARTED CLAPPING...?!
!
CLAP
CLAP
CLAP
TH-THMP
I THINK...
... THEY DID.
TH-THMP
I CAN'T HEAR ANYTHING.
...
TH-THMP
MY HEART IS BEATING TOO LOUD.
TH-THMP
TH-THMP

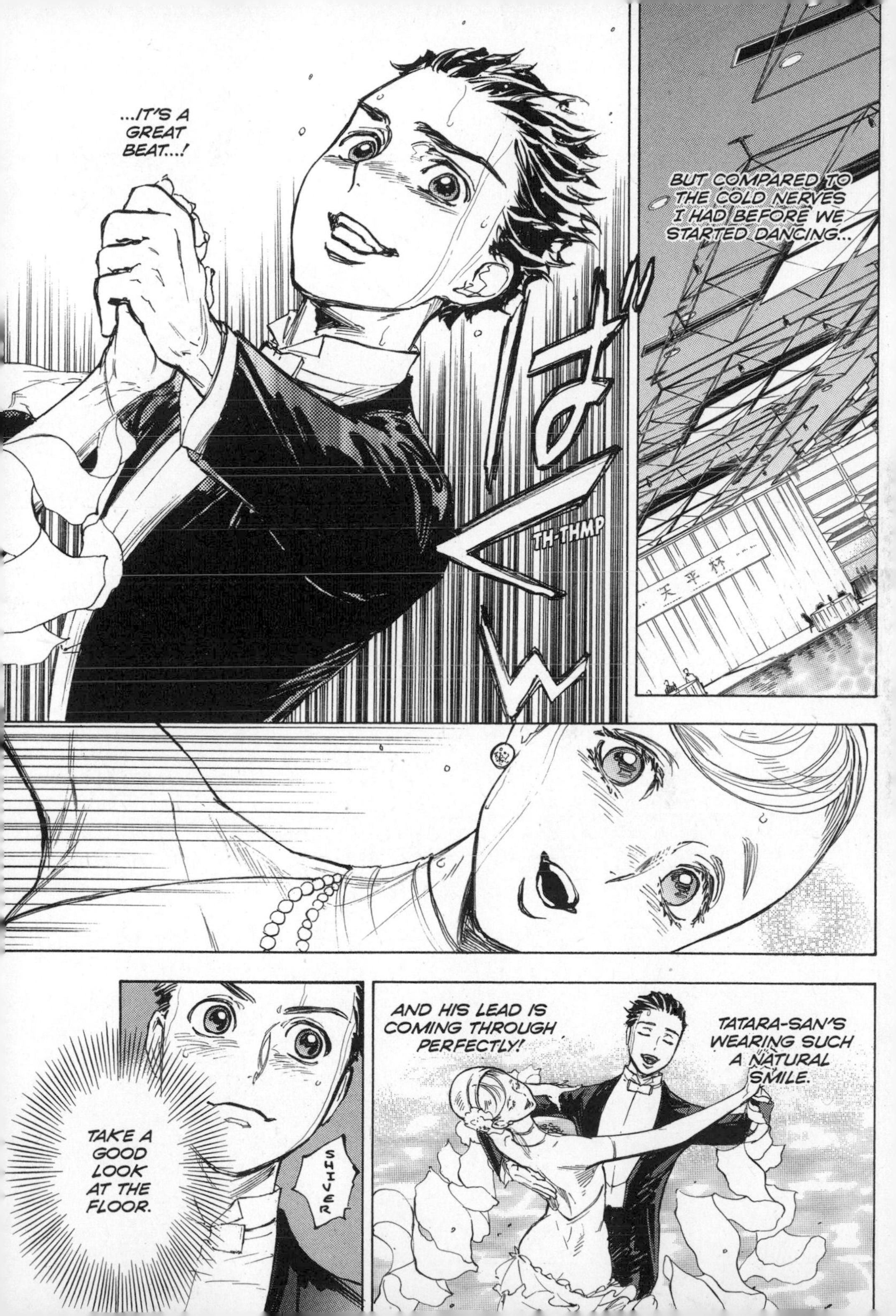
BUT COMPARED TO THE COLD NERVES I HAD BEFORE WE STARTED DANCING...
天平杯
...IT'S A GREAT BEAT...!
ばくん
TH-THMP
TATARA-SAN'S WEARING SUCH A NATURAL SMILE.
AND HIS LEAD IS COMING THROUGH PERFECTLY!
SHIVER
TAKE A GOOD LOOK AT THE FLOOR.

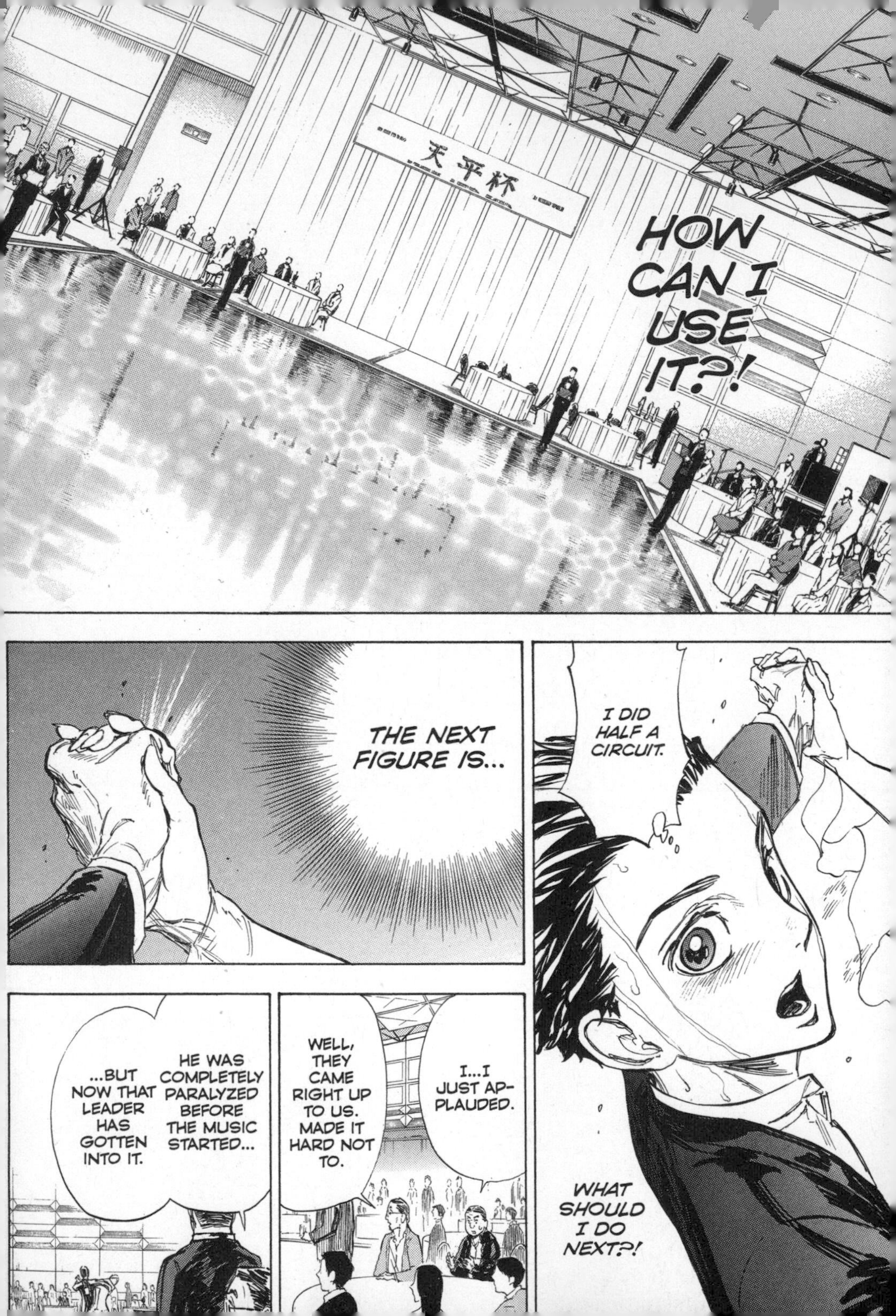
天平杯
HOW CAN I USE IT?!
I DID HALF A CIRCUIT.
WHAT SHOULD I DO NEXT?!
THE NEXT FIGURE IS...
I...I JUST AP-PLAUDED.
WELL, THEY CAME RIGHT UP TO US. MADE IT HARD NOT TO.
HE WAS COMPLETELY PARALYZED BEFORE THE MUSIC STARTED...
...BUT NOW THAT LEADER HAS GOTTEN INTO IT.

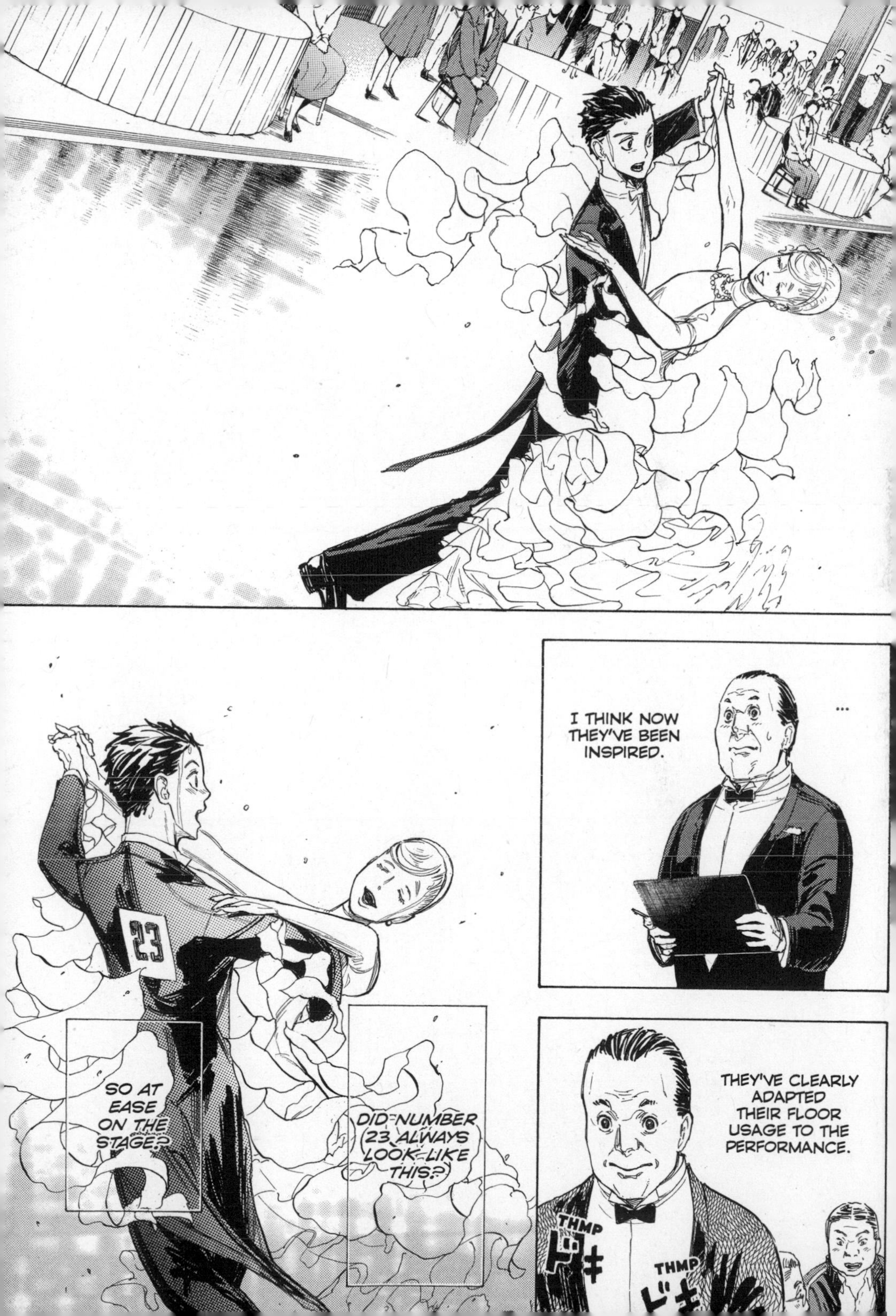
...
I THINK NOW THEY'VE BEEN INSPIRED.
THEY'VE CLEARLY ADAPTED THEIR FLOOR USAGE TO THE PERFORMANCE.
THMP ドキ
THMP ドキ
23
DID NUMBER 23 ALWAYS LOOK LIKE THIS?
SO AT EASE ON THE STAGE?

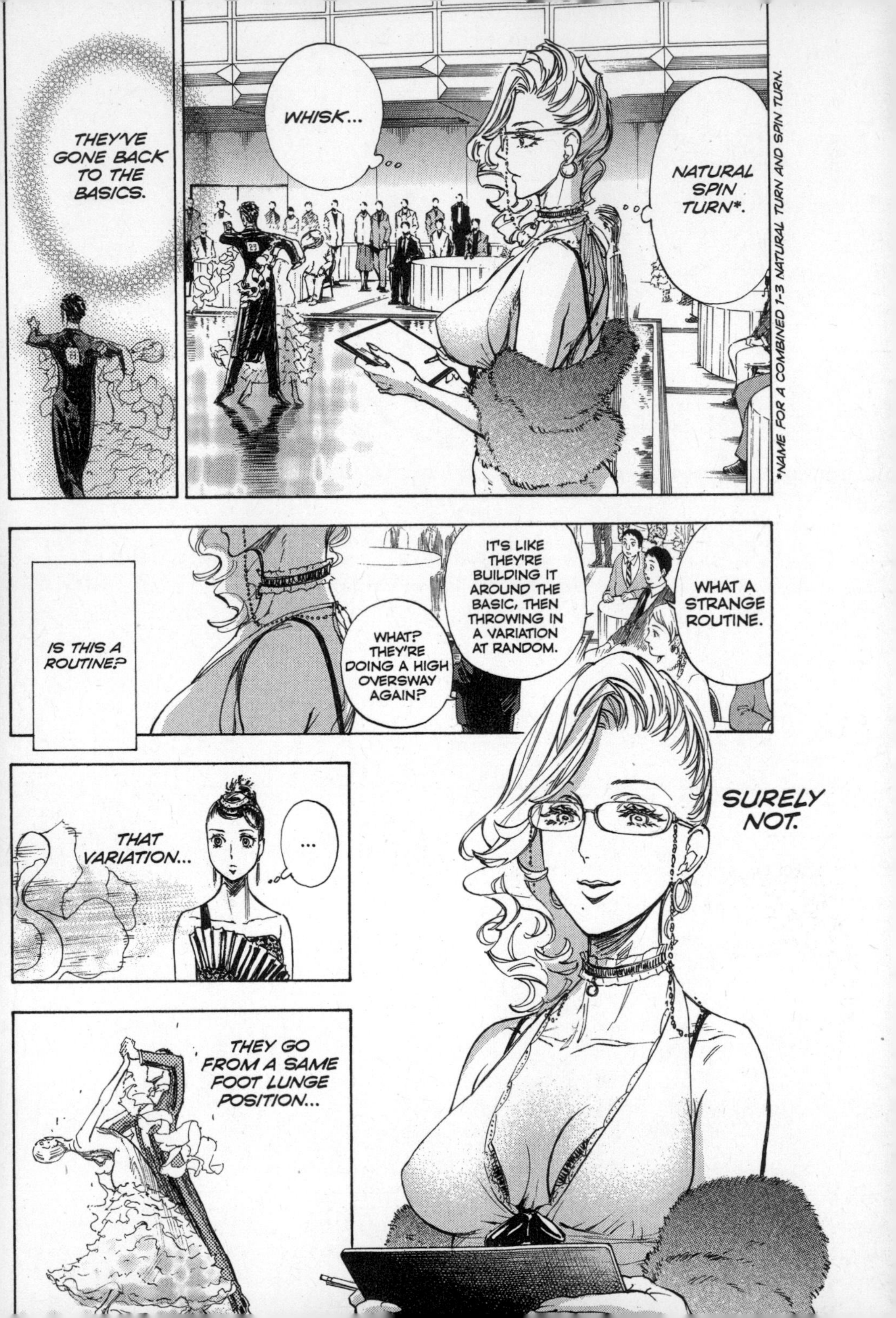
NATURAL SPIN TURN*.
WHISK...
THEY'VE GONE BACK TO THE BASICS.
WHAT A STRANGE ROUTINE.
IT'S LIKE THEY'RE BUILDING IT AROUND THE BASIC, THEN THROWING IN A VARIATION AT RANDOM.
WHAT? THEY'RE DOING A HIGH OVERSWAY AGAIN?
IS THIS A ROUTINE?
SURELY NOT.
...
THAT VARIATION...
THEY GO FROM A SAME FOOT LUNGE POSITION...

*NAME FOR A COMBINED 1-3 NATURAL TURN AND SPIN TURN.

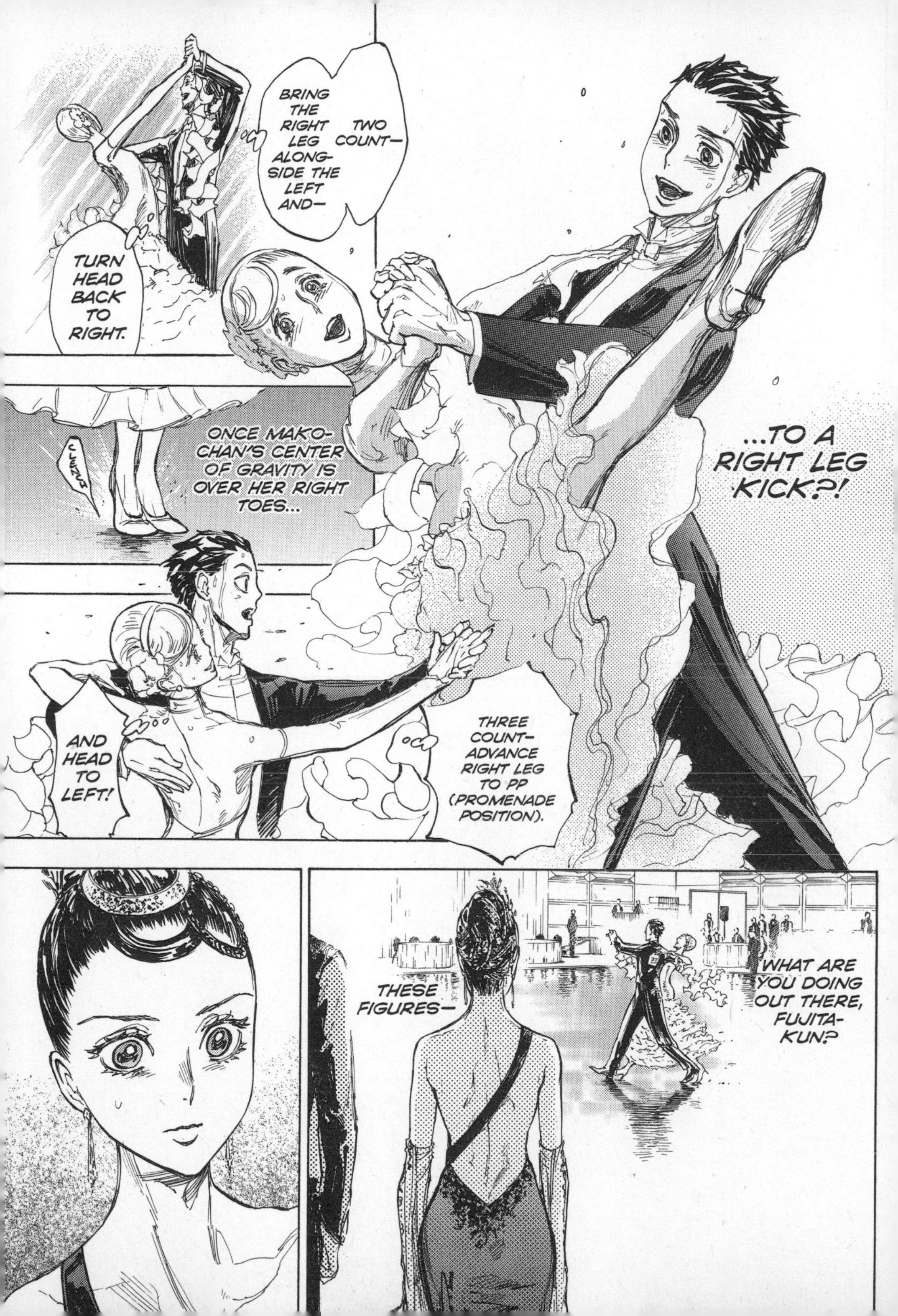

...TO A RIGHT LEG KICK?!
TWO COUNT— BRING THE RIGHT LEG ALONGSIDE THE LEFT AND—
TURN HEAD BACK TO RIGHT.
CLENCH
ONCE MAKO-CHAN'S CENTER OF GRAVITY IS OVER HER RIGHT TOES...
THREE COUNT- ADVANCE RIGHT LEG TO PP (PROMENADE POSITION).
AND HEAD TO LEFT!
WHAT ARE YOU DOING OUT THERE, FUJITA-KUN?
THESE FIGURES—

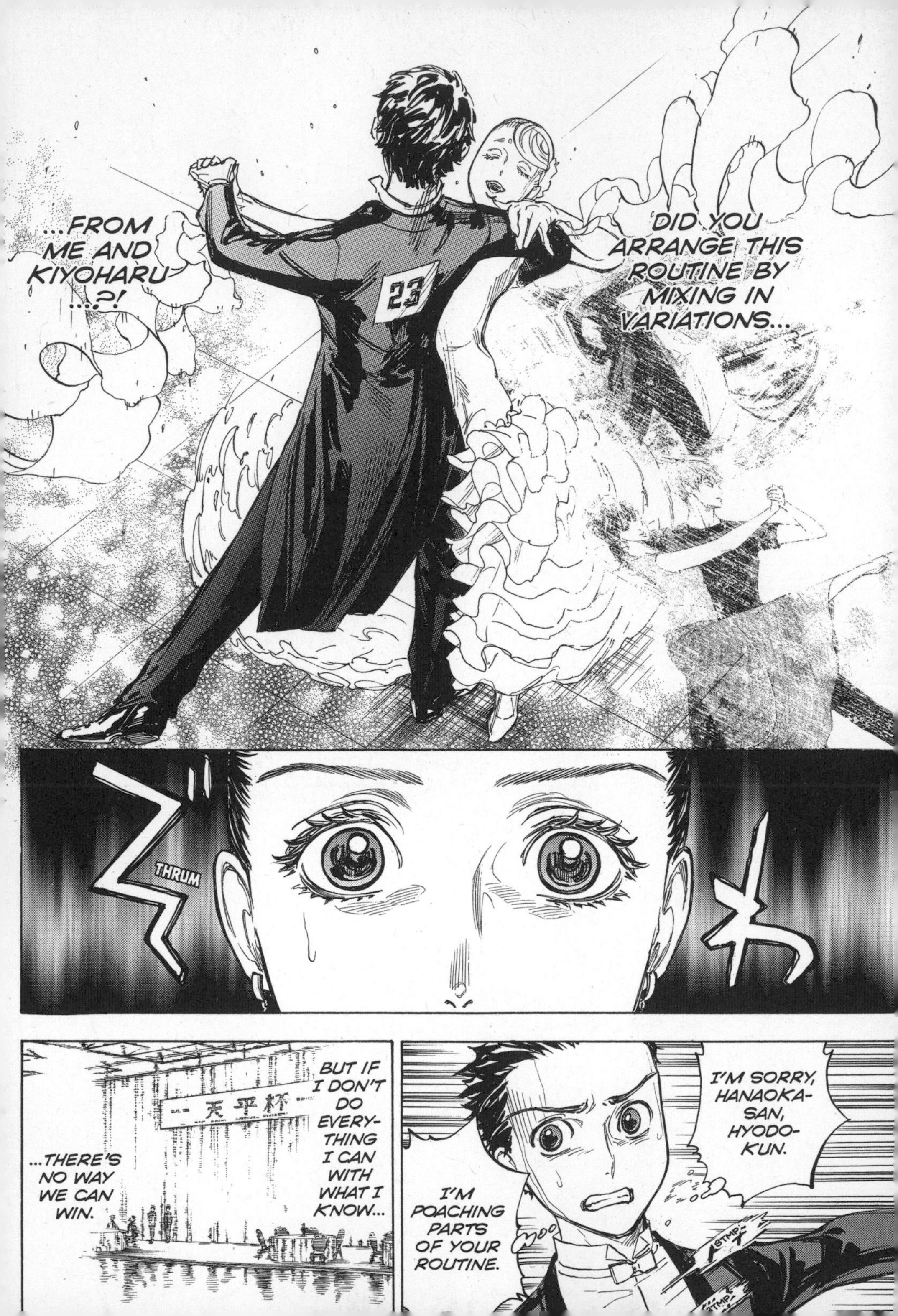
DID YOU ARRANGE THIS ROUTINE BY MIXING IN VARIATIONS...
...FROM ME AND KIYOHARU ...?!
THRUM
I'M SORRY, HANAOKA-SAN, HYODO-KUN.
I'M POACHING PARTS OF YOUR ROUTINE.
STMP
STMP
BUT IF I DON'T DO EVERYTHING I CAN WITH WHAT I KNOW...
...THERE'S NO WAY WE CAN WIN.
天平杯

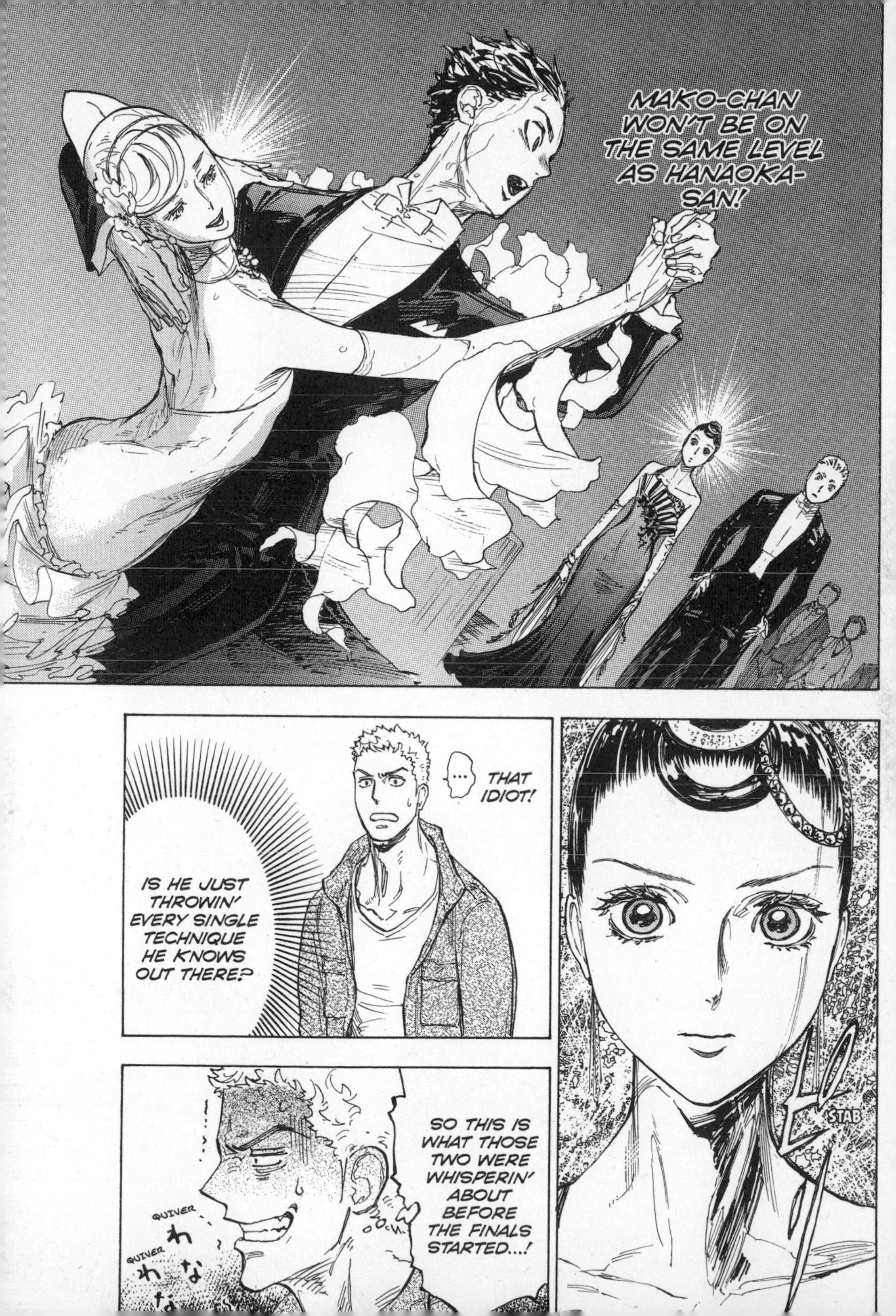
MAKO-CHAN WON'T BE ON THE SAME LEVEL AS HANAOKA-SAN!
STAB
...
THAT IDIOT!
IS HE JUST THROWIN' EVERY SINGLE TECHNIQUE HE KNOWS OUT THERE?
SO THIS IS WHAT THOSE TWO WERE WHISPERIN' ABOUT BEFORE THE FINALS STARTED...!
QUIVER
QUIVER

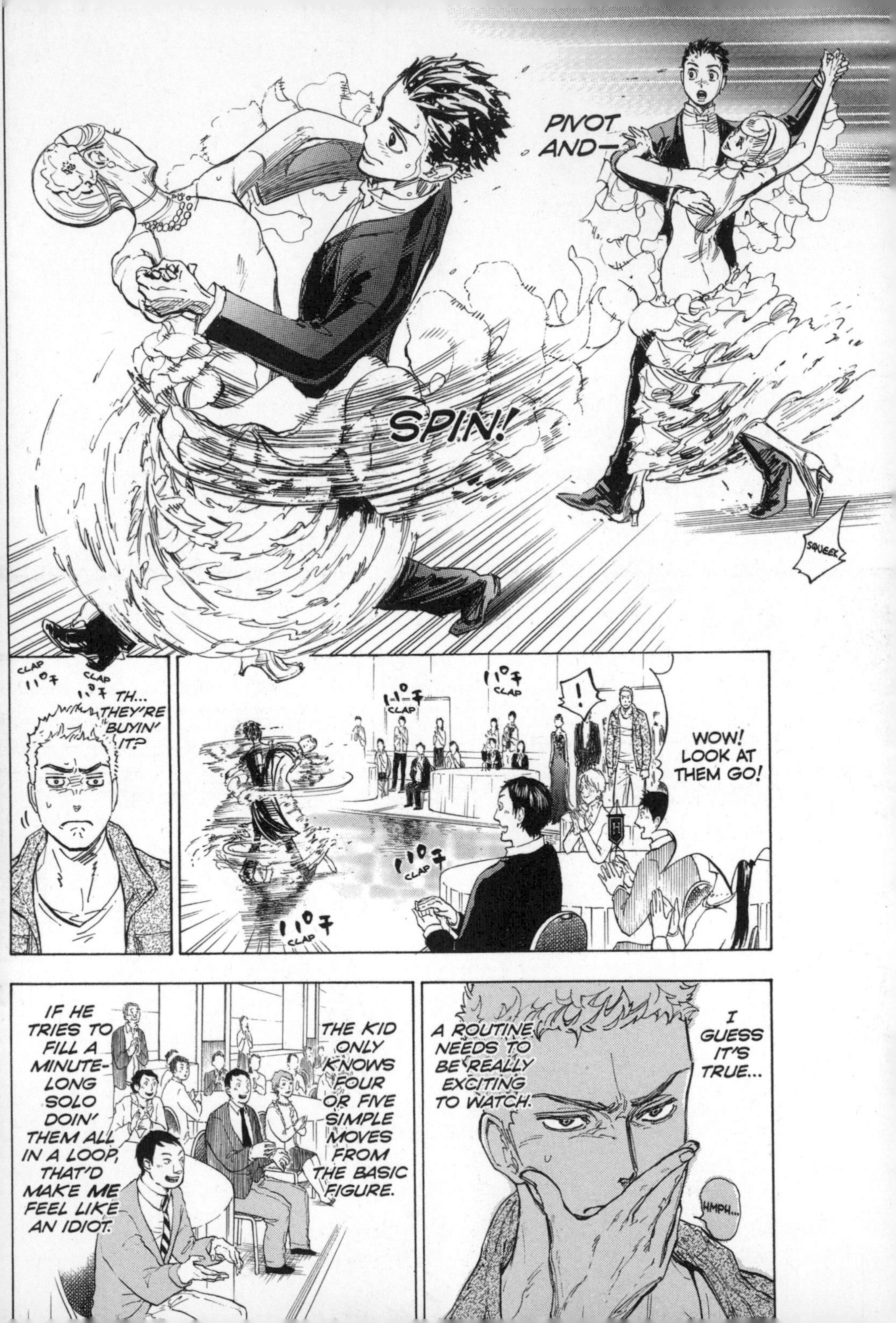
PIVOT AND—
SPIN!
SQUEEK
パチ CLAP
パチ CLAP
!
WOW! LOOK AT THEM GO!
パチ CLAP
パチ CLAP
CLAP パチ
CLAP パチ
TH... THEY'RE BUYIN' IT?
I GUESS IT'S TRUE...
A ROUTINE NEEDS TO BE REALLY EXCITING TO WATCH.
HMPH...
THE KID ONLY KNOWS FOUR OR FIVE SIMPLE MOVES FROM THE BASIC FIGURE.
IF HE TRIES TO FILL A MINUTE-LONG SOLO DOIN' THEM ALL IN A LOOP, THAT'D MAKE ME FEEL LIKE AN IDIOT.

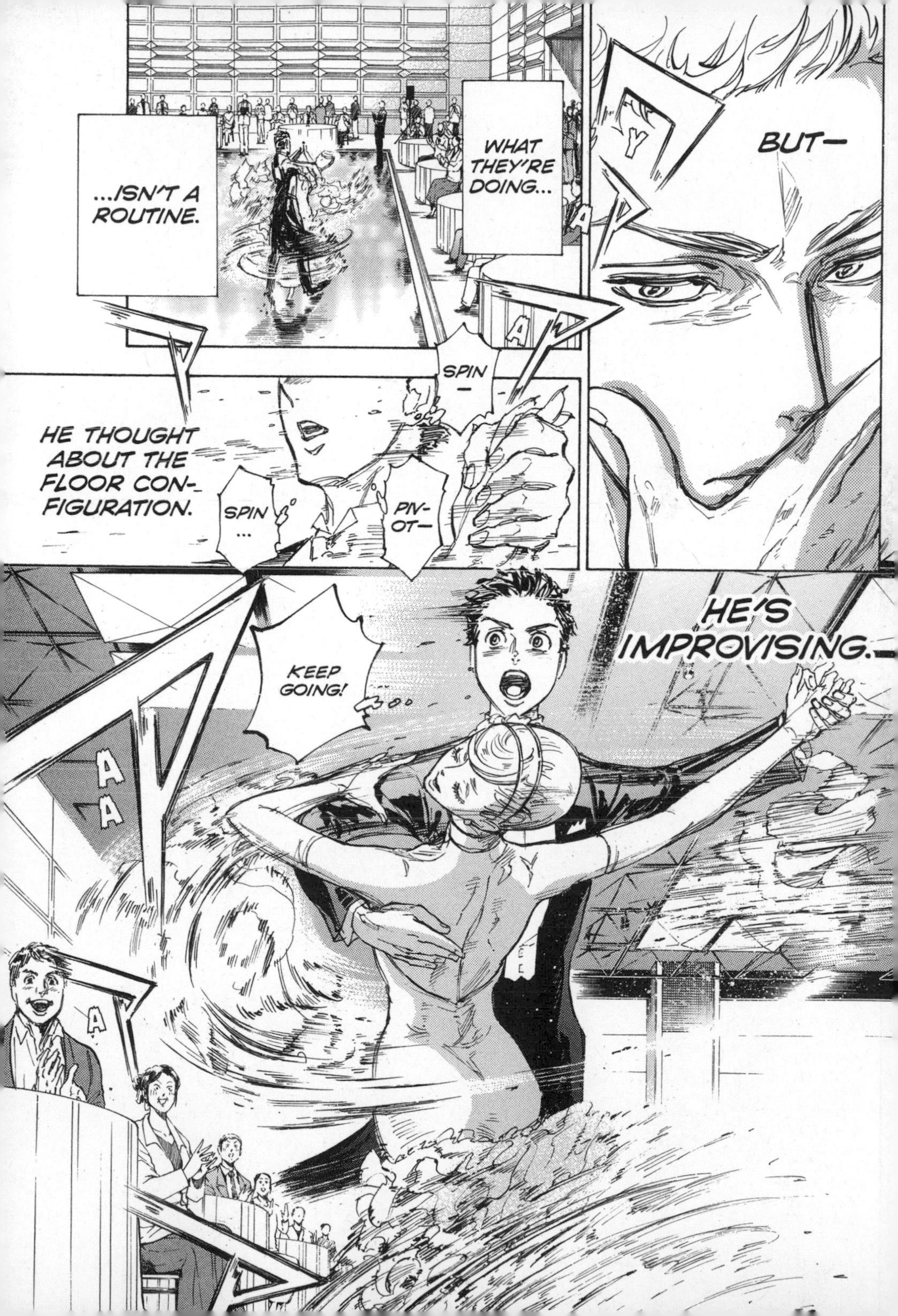

BUT—
Y
A
WHAT THEY'RE DOING...
...ISN'T A ROUTINE.
A
SPIN—
PIVOT—
SPIN...
HE THOUGHT ABOUT THE FLOOR CON-FIGURATION.
HE'S IMPROVISING.
KEEP GOING!
A
A
A

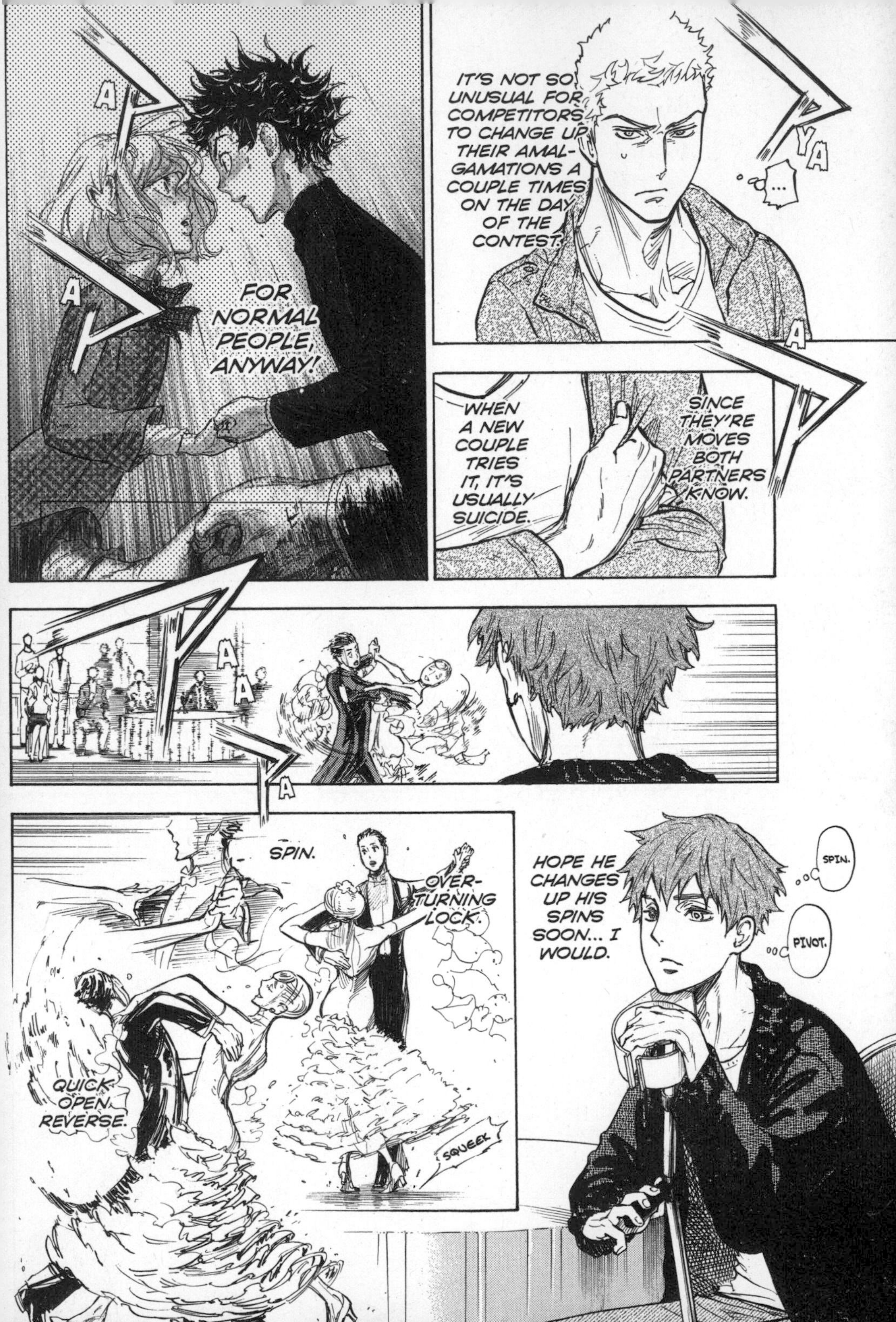
IT'S NOT SO UNUSUAL FOR COMPETITORS TO CHANGE UP THEIR AMALGAMATIONS A COUPLE TIMES ON THE DAY OF THE CONTEST.
YA
...
A
SINCE THEY'RE MOVES BOTH PARTNERS KNOW.
WHEN A NEW COUPLE TRIES IT, IT'S USUALLY SUICIDE.
A
A
FOR NORMAL PEOPLE, ANYWAY!
A
A
A
HOPE HE CHANGES UP HIS SPINS SOON... I WOULD.
SPIN.
PIVOT.
SPIN.
OVER-TURNING LOCK.
QUICK OPEN REVERSE.
SQUEEK

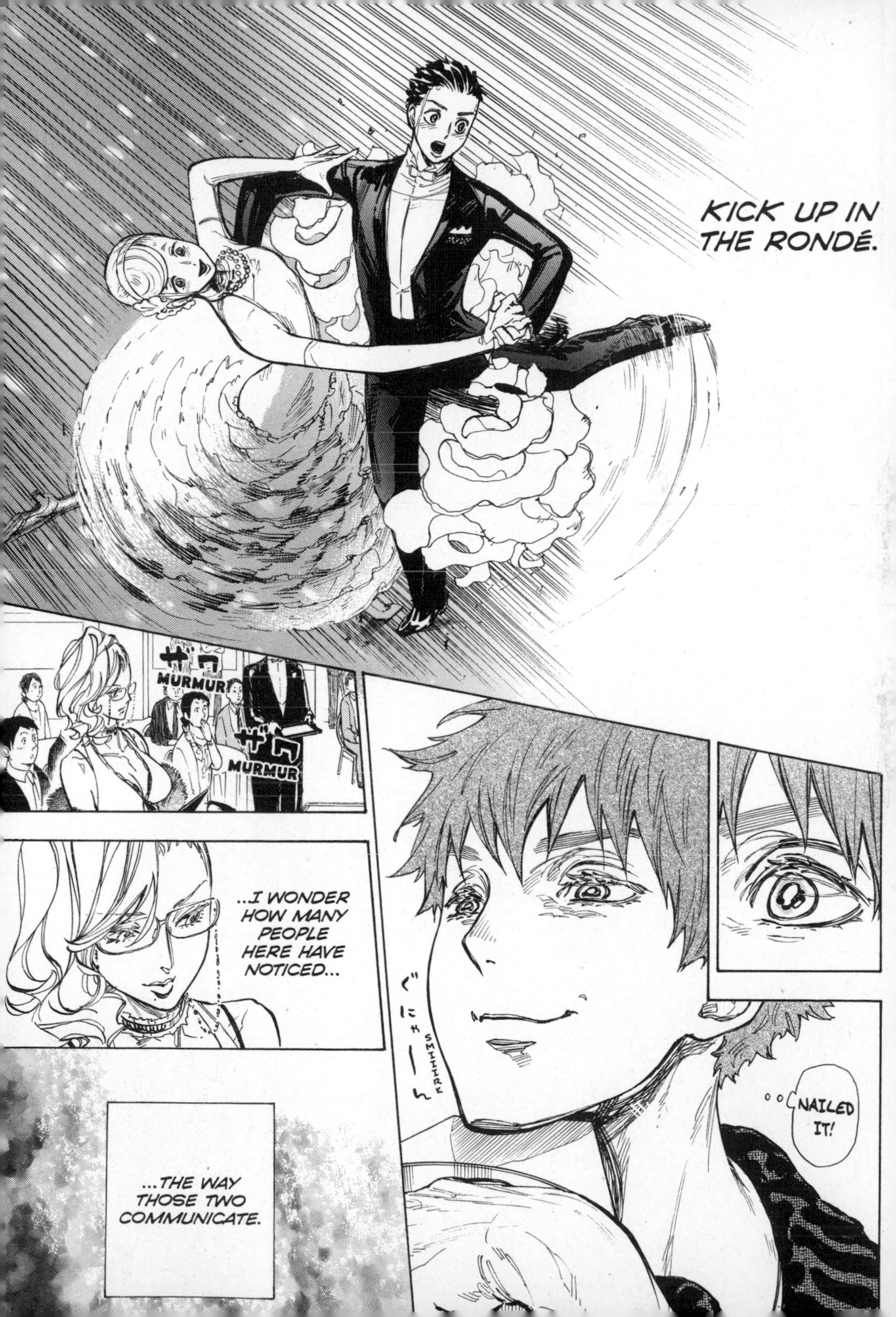
KICK UP IN THE RONDÉ.
ぐにゃーん
SMIIIIIRK
NAILED IT!
MURMUR
MURMUR
...I WONDER HOW MANY PEOPLE HERE HAVE NOTICED...
...THE WAY THOSE TWO COMMUNICATE.

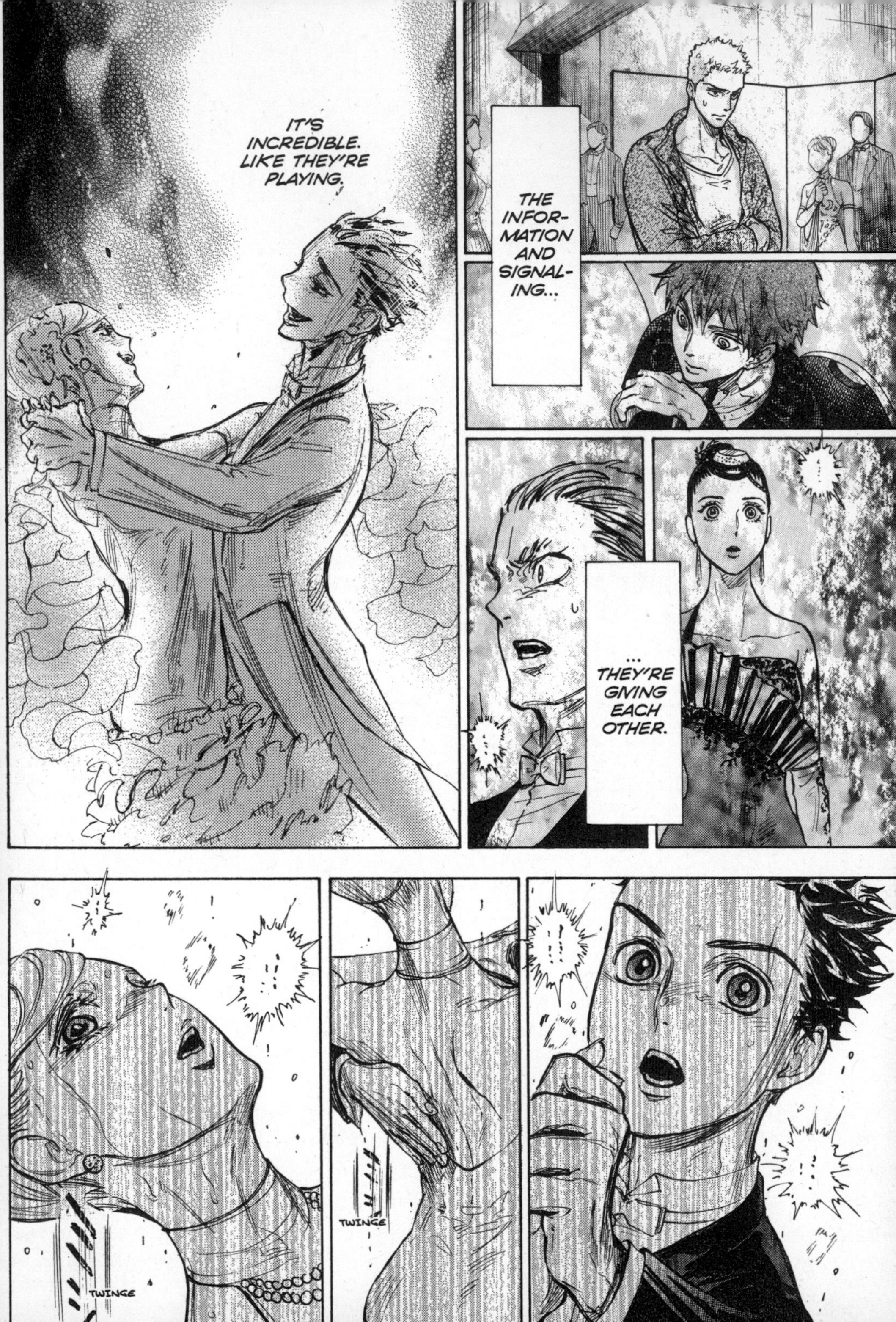
THE INFORMATION AND SIGNALING...
... THEY'RE GIVING EACH OTHER.
IT'S INCREDIBLE. LIKE THEY'RE PLAYING.
TWINGE
TWINGE

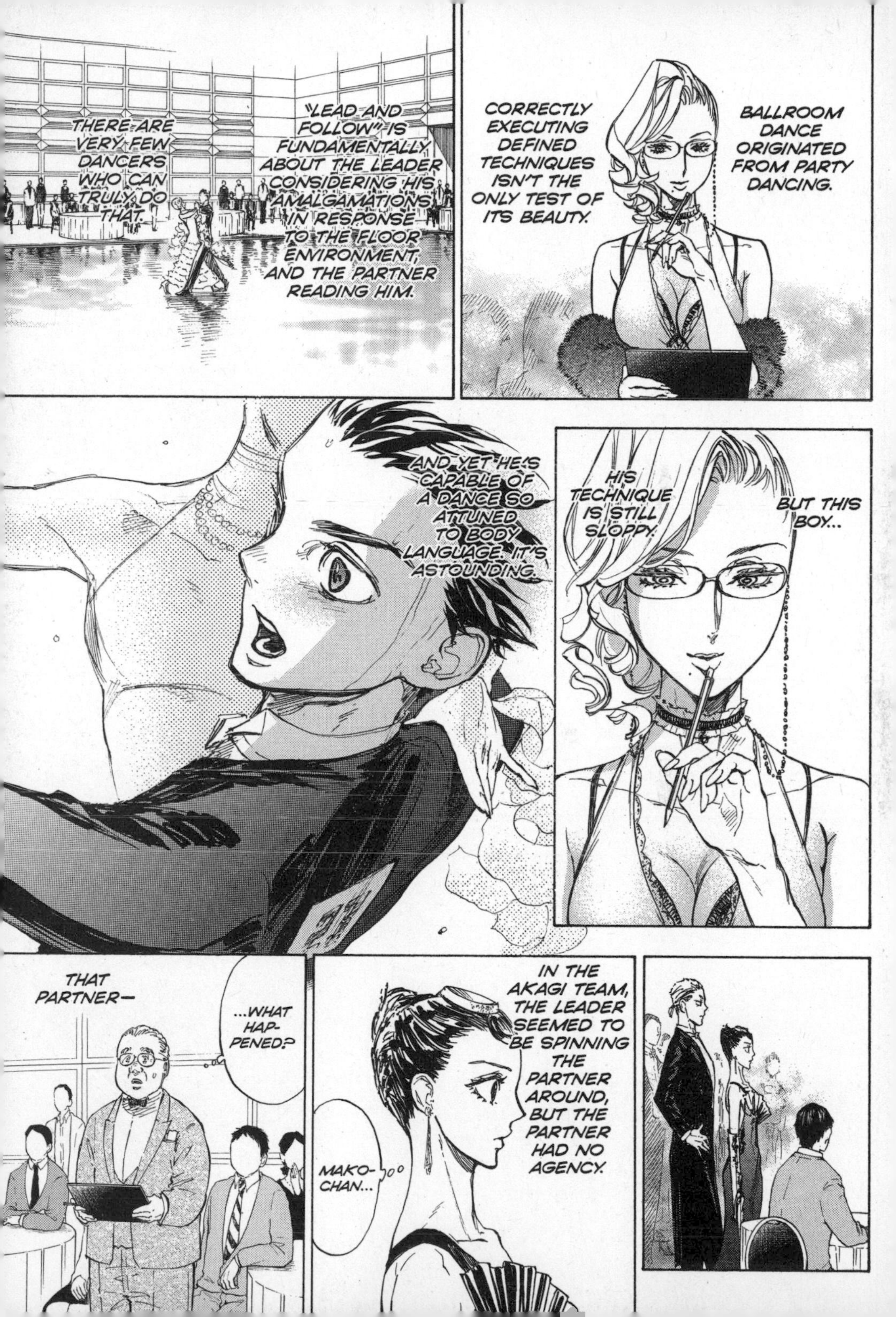
BALLROOM DANCE ORIGINATED FROM PARTY DANCING.
CORRECTLY EXECUTING DEFINED TECHNIQUES ISN'T THE ONLY TEST OF ITS BEAUTY.
"LEAD AND FOLLOW" IS FUNDAMENTALLY ABOUT THE LEADER CONSIDERING HIS AMALGAMATIONS IN RESPONSE TO THE FLOOR ENVIRONMENT, AND THE PARTNER READING HIM.
THERE ARE VERY FEW DANCERS WHO CAN TRULY DO THAT.
BUT THIS BOY...
HIS TECHNIQUE IS STILL SLOPPY.
AND YET HE'S CAPABLE OF A DANCE SO ATTUNED TO BODY LANGUAGE. IT'S ASTOUNDING.
IN THE AKAGI TEAM, THE LEADER SEEMED TO BE SPINNING THE PARTNER AROUND, BUT THE PARTNER HAD NO AGENCY.
MAKO-CHAN...
THAT PARTNER—
...WHAT HAP-PENED?

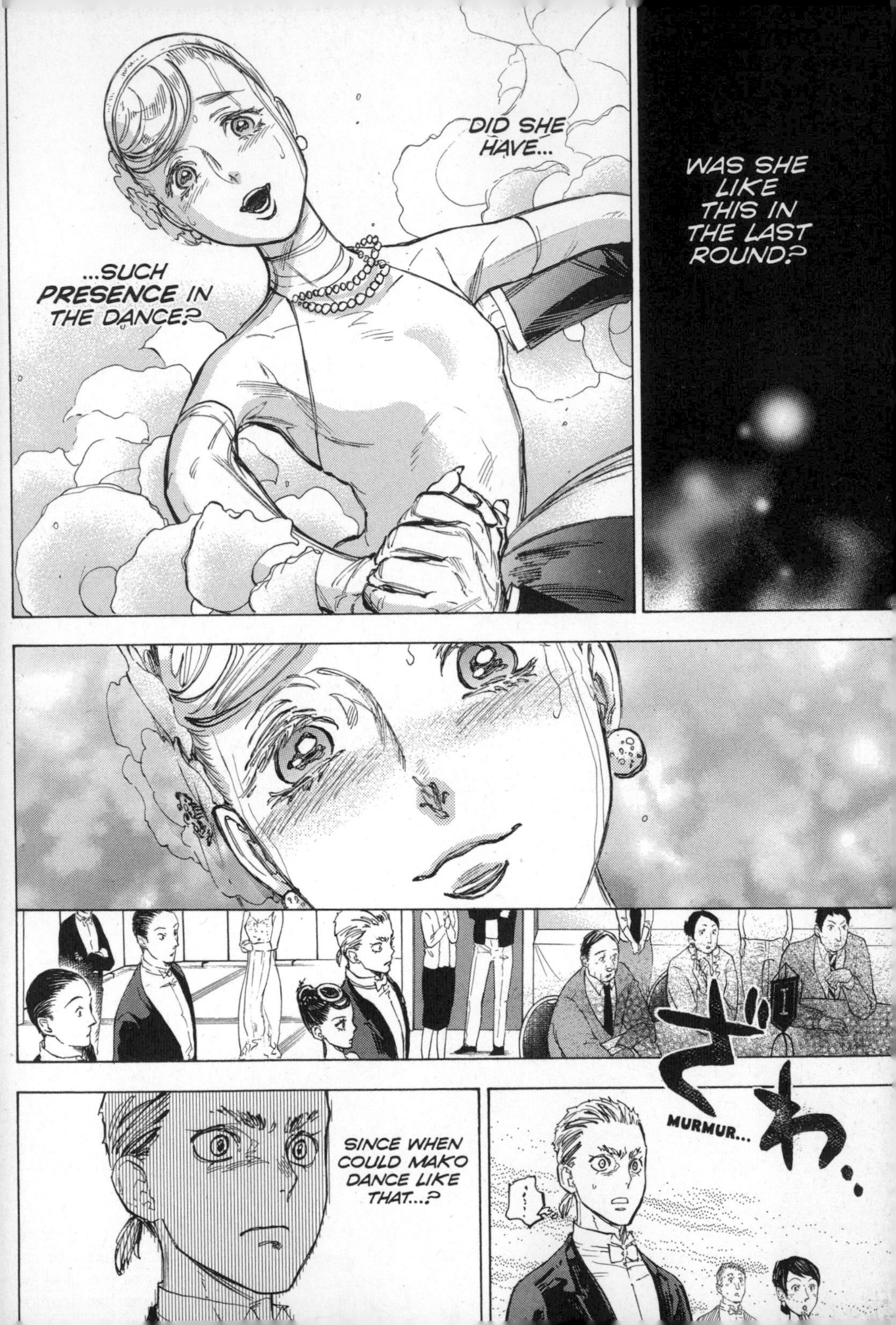
WAS SHE LIKE THIS IN THE LAST ROUND?
DID SHE HAVE...
...SUCH PRESENCE IN THE DANCE?
ざわ..
MURMUR...
SINCE WHEN COULD MAKO DANCE LIKE THAT...?

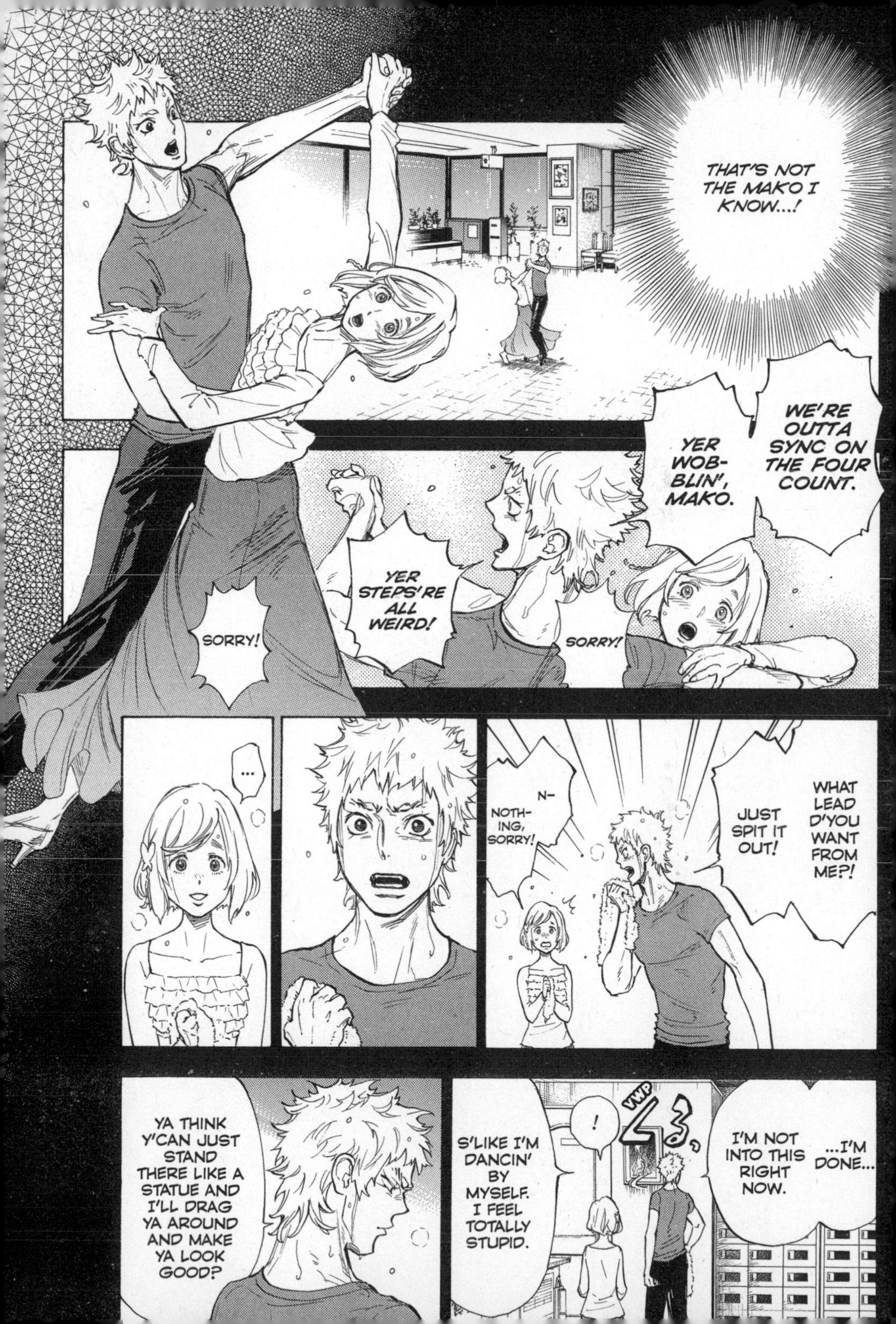
THAT'S NOT THE MAKO I KNOW...!
WE'RE OUTTA SYNC ON THE FOUR COUNT.
YER WOB-BLIN', MAKO.
YER STEPS'RE ALL WEIRD!
SORRY!
SORRY!
WHAT LEAD D'YOU WANT FROM ME?!
JUST SPIT IT OUT!
N-
NOTHING, SORRY!
...
...I'M DONE...
I'M NOT INTO THIS RIGHT NOW.
VWP
!
S'LIKE I'M DANCIN' BY MYSELF. I FEEL TOTALLY STUPID.
YA THINK Y'CAN JUST STAND THERE LIKE A STATUE AND I'LL DRAG YA AROUND AND MAKE YA LOOK GOOD?

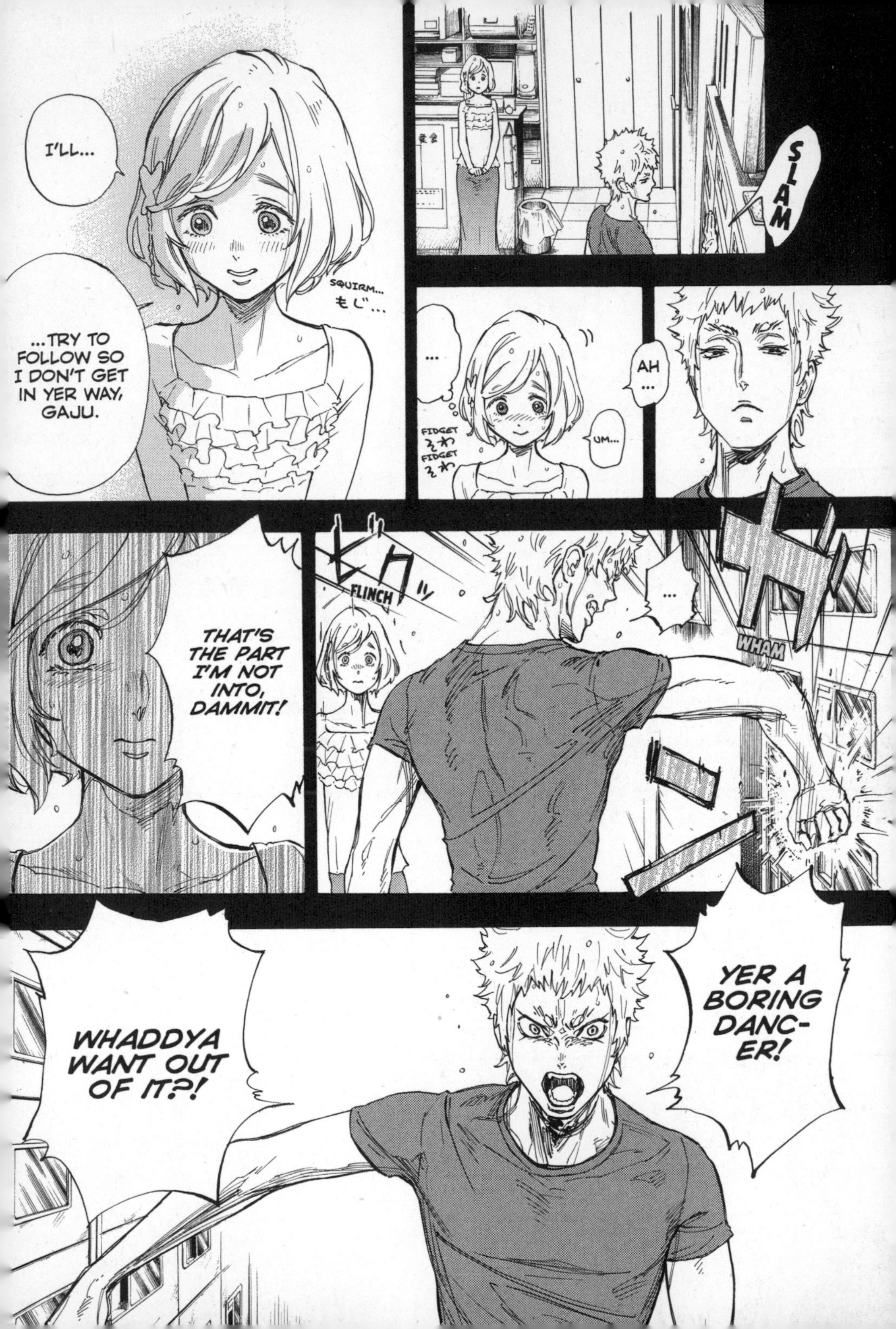
SLAM
AH ...
...
FIDGET
そわ
FIDGET
そわ
UM...
I'LL...
SQUIRM...
もじ...
...TRY TO FOLLOW SO I DON'T GET IN YER WAY, GAJU.
WHAM
...
FLINCH
THAT'S THE PART I'M NOT INTO, DAMMIT!
YER A BORING DANCER!
WHADDYA WANT OUT OF IT?!

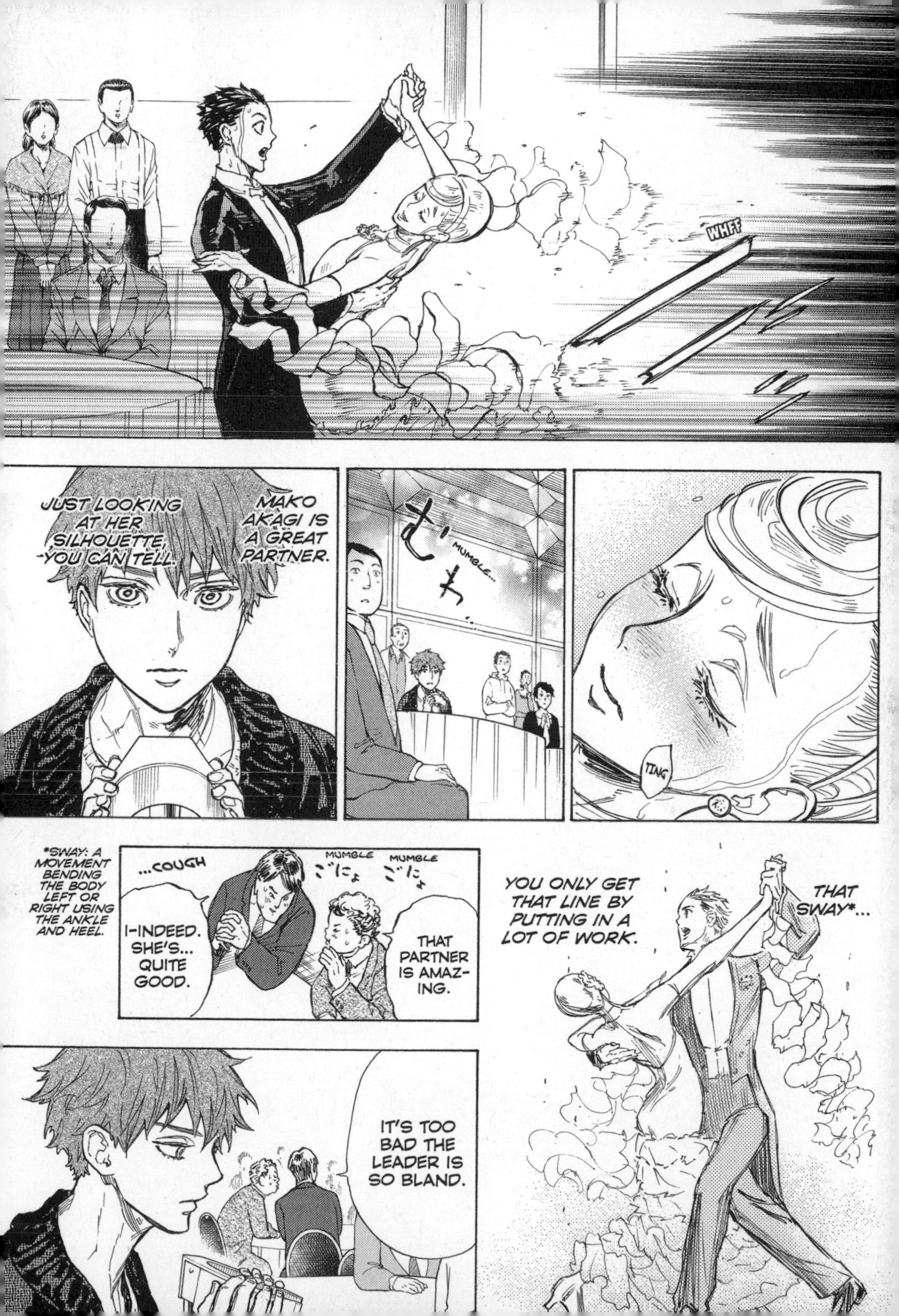
WHFF
TING
MUMBLE...
MAKO AKAGI IS A GREAT PARTNER.
JUST LOOKING AT HER SILHOUETTE, YOU CAN TELL.
THAT SWAY*...
YOU ONLY GET THAT LINE BY PUTTING IN A LOT OF WORK.
MUMBLE ごにょ
MUMBLE ごにょ
THAT PARTNER IS AMAZ-ING.
...COUGH
I-INDEED. SHE'S... QUITE GOOD.
*SWAY: A MOVEMENT BENDING THE BODY LEFT OR RIGHT USING THE ANKLE AND HEEL.
IT'S TOO BAD THE LEADER IS SO BLAND.

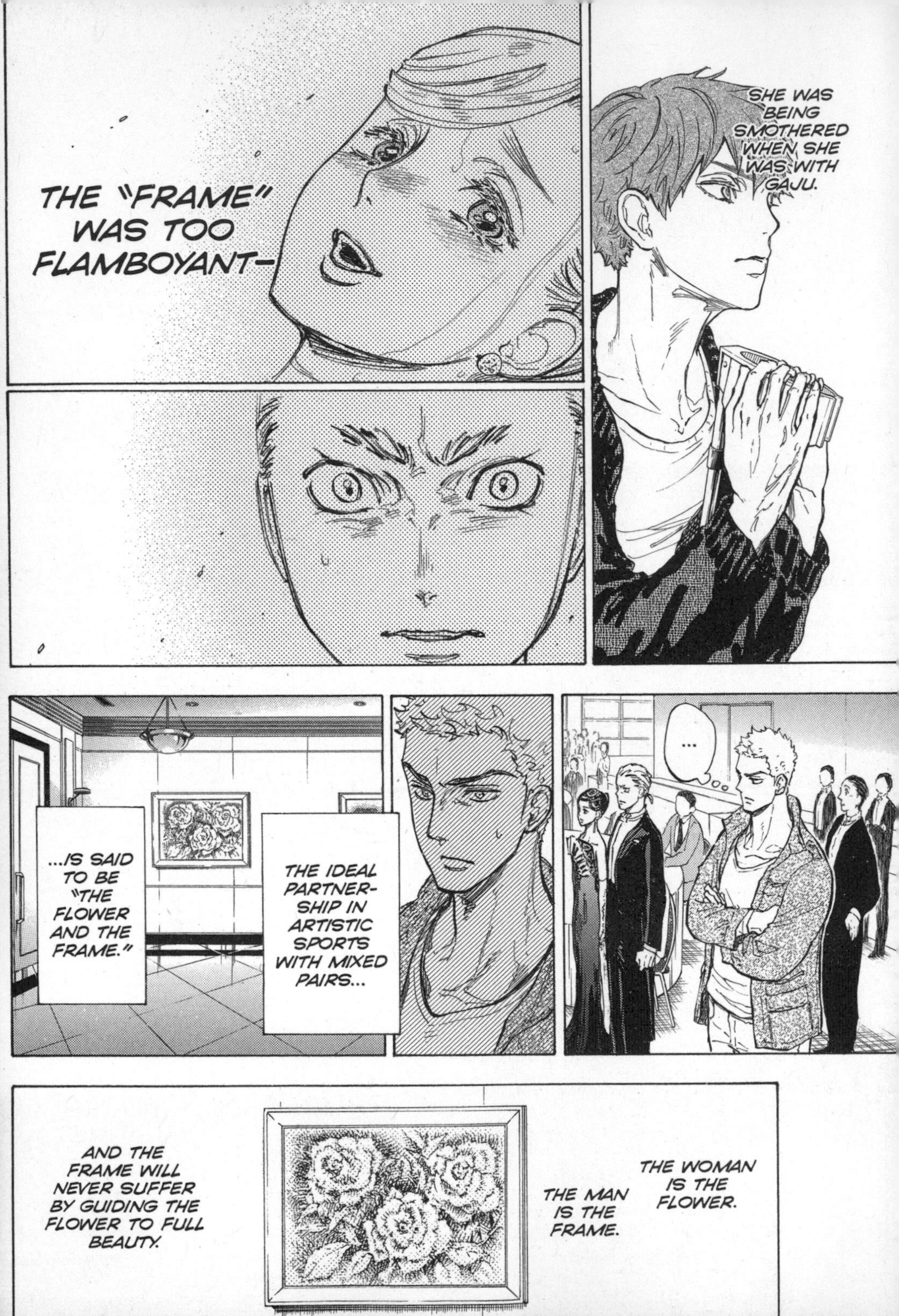
SHE WAS BEING SMOTHERED WHEN SHE WAS WITH GAJU.
THE "FRAME" WAS TOO FLAMBOYANT—
...
THE IDEAL PARTNER-SHIP IN ARTISTIC SPORTS WITH MIXED PAIRS...
...IS SAID TO BE "THE FLOWER AND THE FRAME."
THE WOMAN IS THE FLOWER.
THE MAN IS THE FRAME.
AND THE FRAME WILL NEVER SUFFER BY GUIDING THE FLOWER TO FULL BEAUTY.

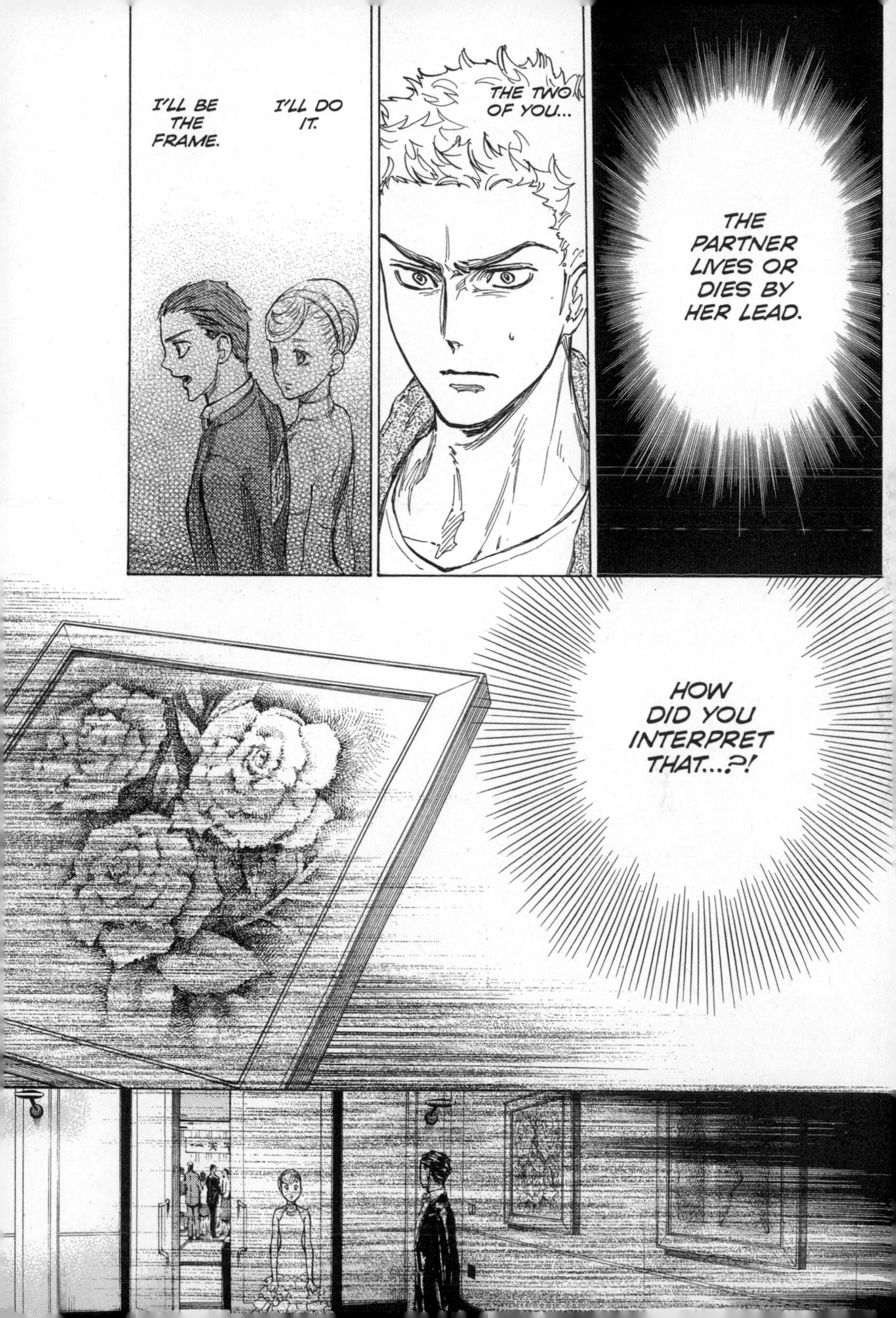
THE PARTNER LIVES OR DIES BY HER LEAD.
THE TWO OF YOU...
I'LL DO IT.
I'LL BE THE FRAME.
HOW DID YOU INTERPRET THAT...?!

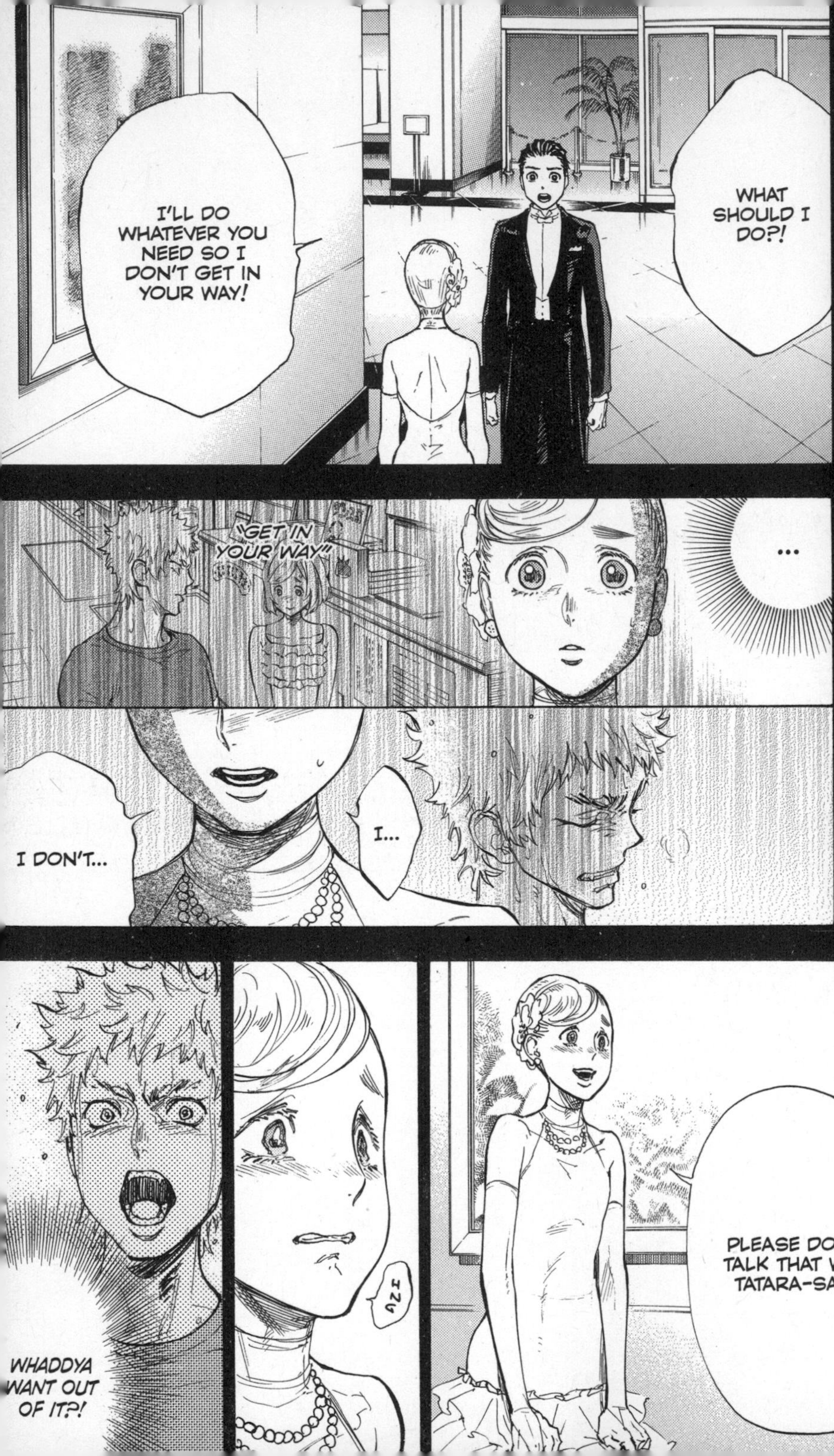
WHAT SHOULD I DO?!
I'LL DO WHATEVER YOU NEED SO I DON'T GET IN YOUR WAY!
...
"GET IN YOUR WAY"
I...
I DON'T...
PLEASE DON'T TALK THAT WAY, TATARA-SAN.
HNG
WHADDYA WANT OUT OF IT?!

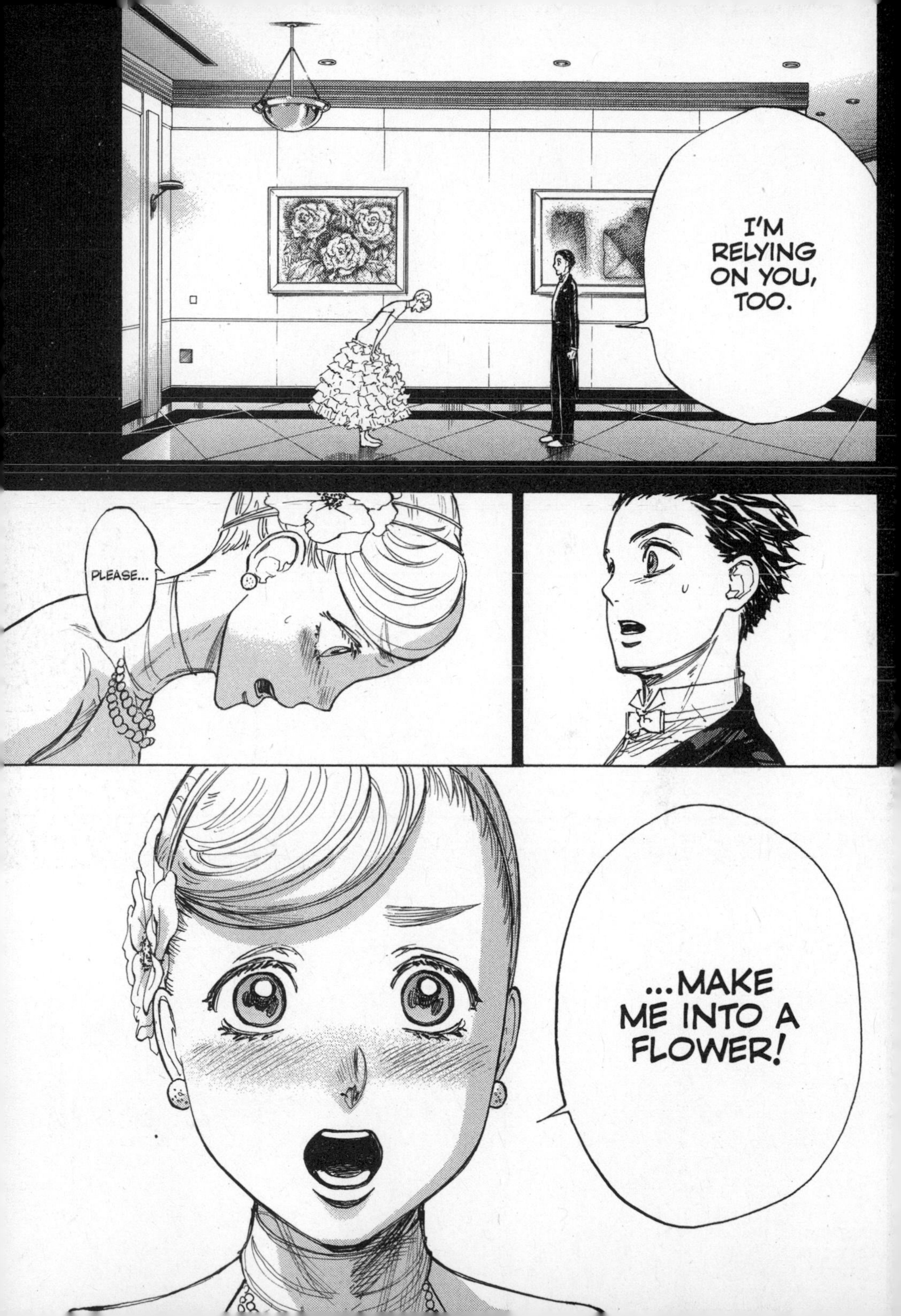
I'M RELYING ON YOU, TOO.
PLEASE...
...MAKE ME INTO A FLOWER!

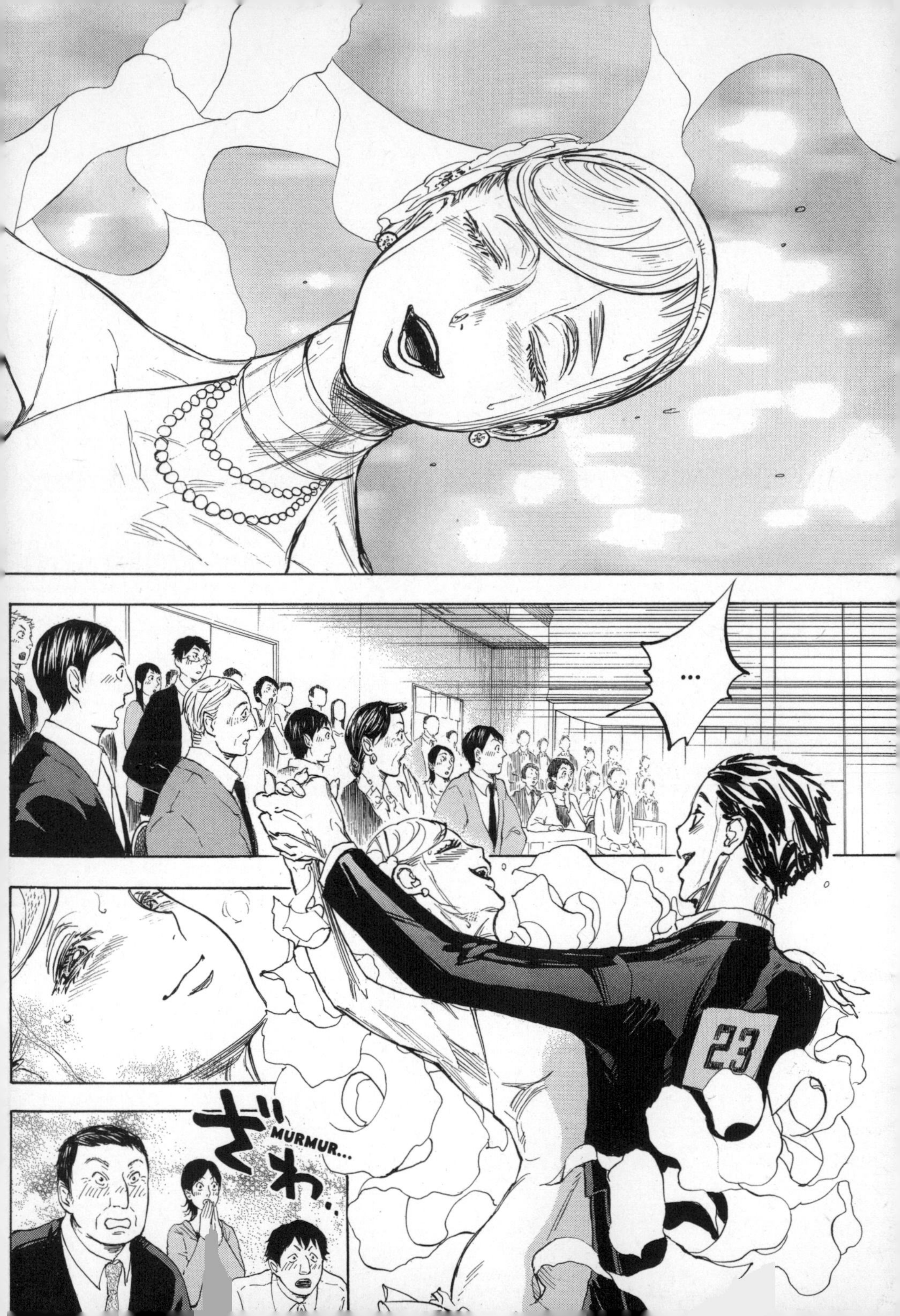
...
ざわ..
MURMUR...

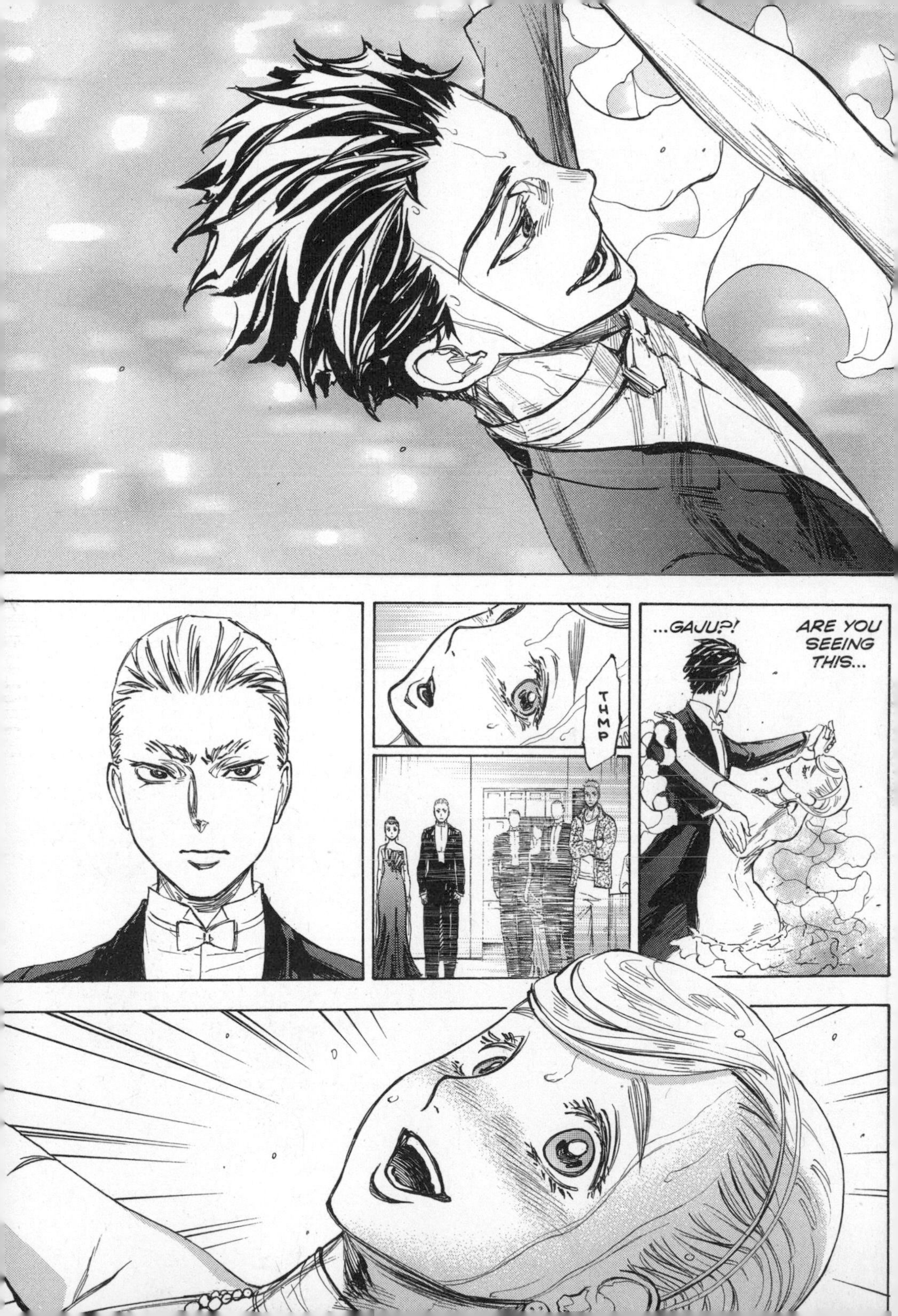
ARE YOU SEEING THIS...
...GAJU?!
THMP

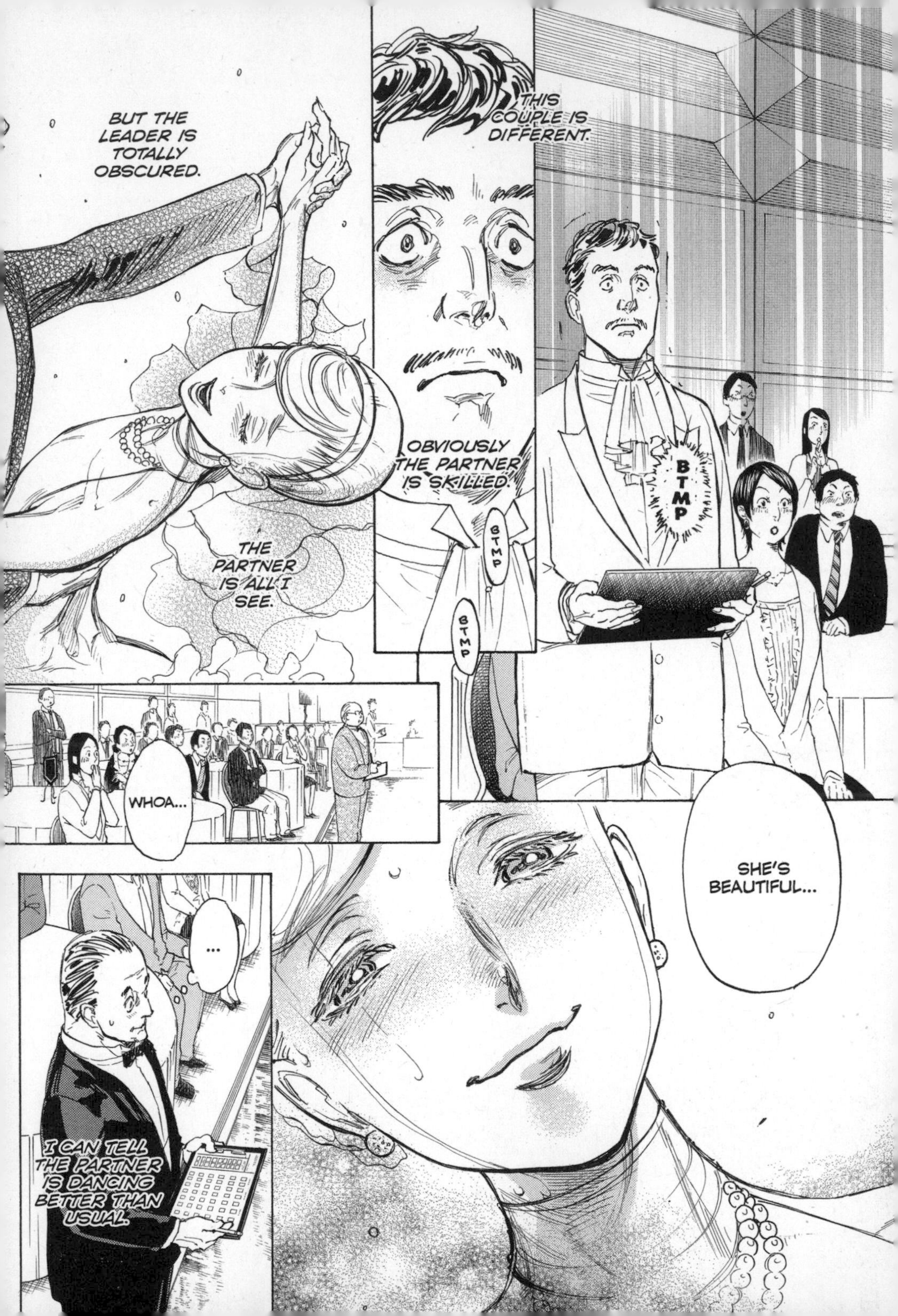
BTMP
THIS COUPLE IS DIFFERENT.
OBVIOUSLY THE PARTNER IS SKILLED.
BTMP
BTMP
BUT THE LEADER IS TOTALLY OBSCURED.
THE PARTNER IS ALL I SEE.
WHOA...
SHE'S BEAUTIFUL...
...
I CAN TELL THE PARTNER IS DANCING BETTER THAN USUAL.

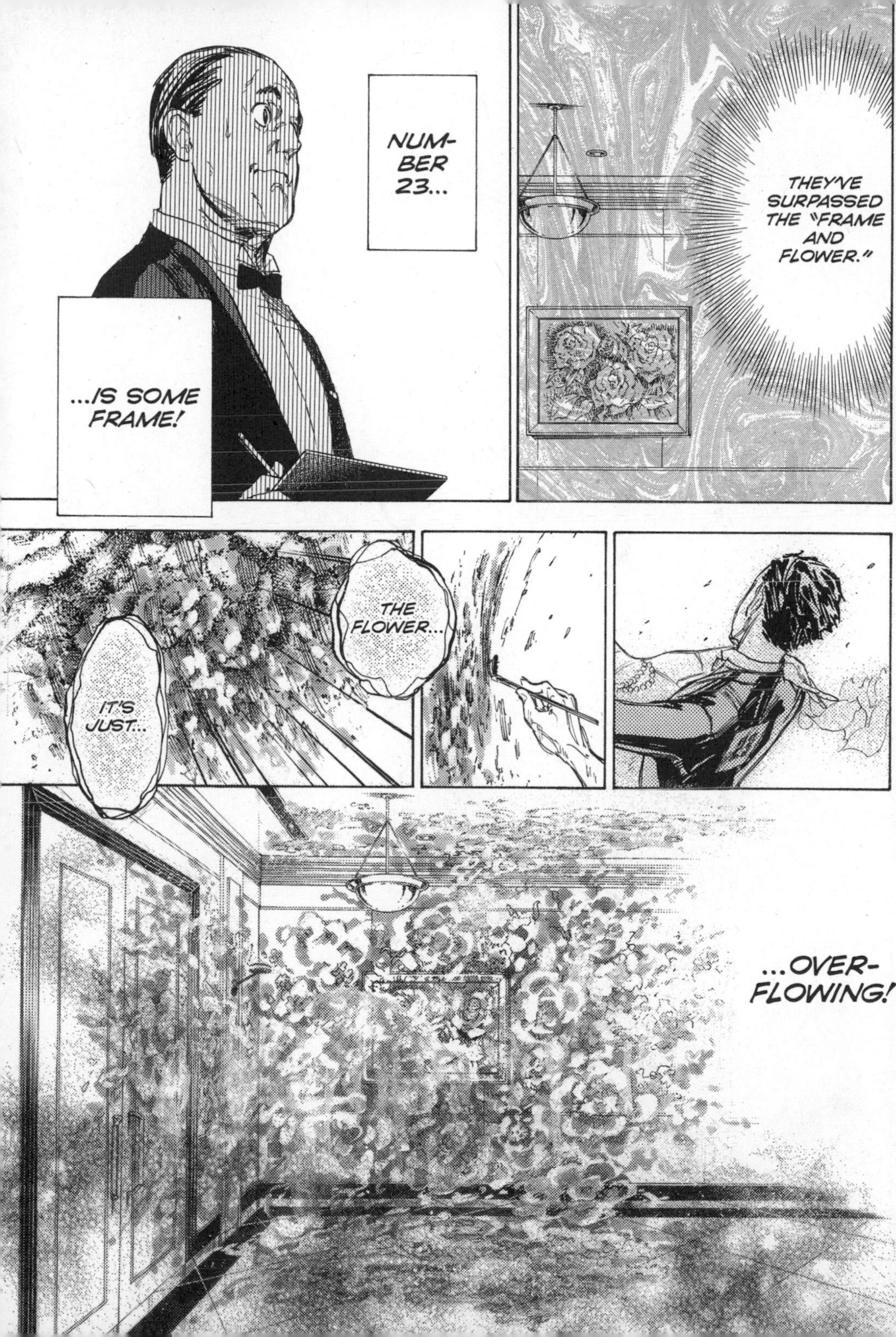
THEY'VE SURPASSED THE "FRAME AND FLOWER."
NUM-BER 23...
...IS SOME FRAME!
THE FLOWER...
IT'S JUST...
...OVER-FLOWING!

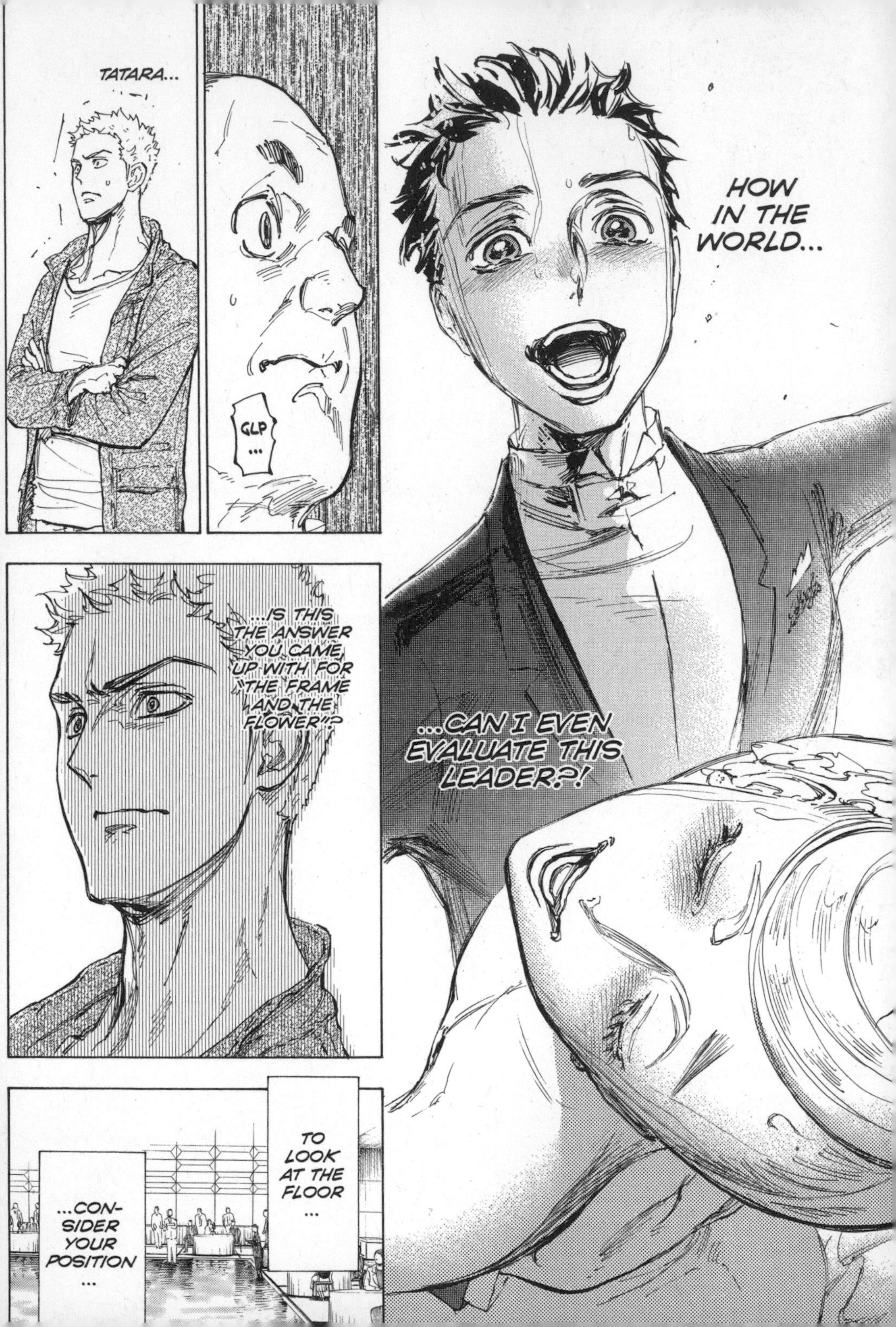
HOW IN THE WORLD...
...CAN I EVEN EVALUATE THIS LEADER?!
GLP ...
TATARA...
...IS THIS THE ANSWER YOU CAME UP WITH FOR "THE FRAME AND THE FLOWER"?
TO LOOK AT THE FLOOR ...
...CON-SIDER YOUR POSITION ...

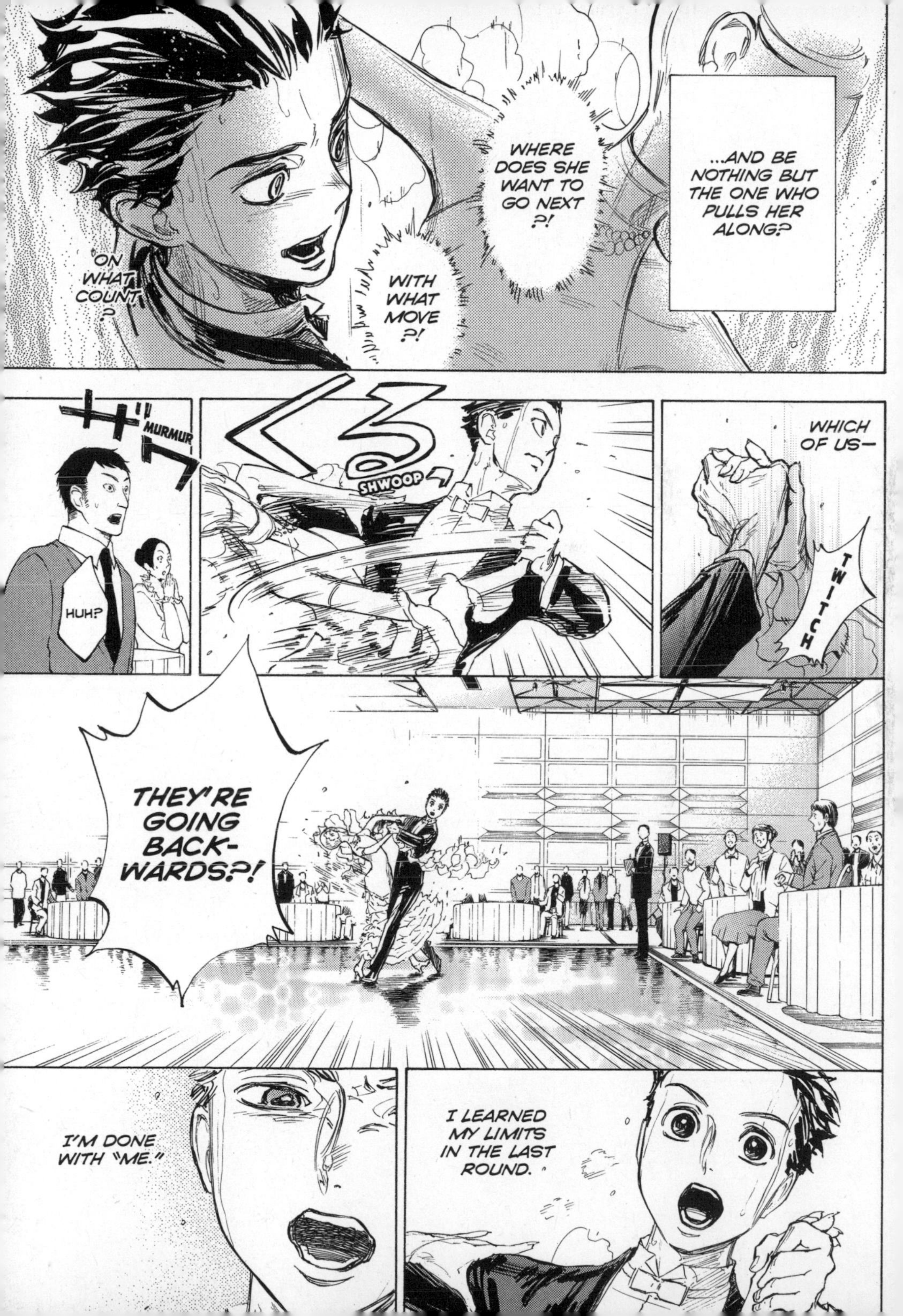
...AND BE NOTHING BUT THE ONE WHO PULLS HER ALONG?
WHERE DOES SHE WANT TO GO NEXT?!
WITH WHAT MOVE?!
ON WHAT COUNT?
WHICH OF US—
TWITCH
SHWOOP
MURMUR
HUH?
THEY'RE GOING BACK-WARDS?!
I LEARNED MY LIMITS IN THE LAST ROUND.
I'M DONE WITH "ME."

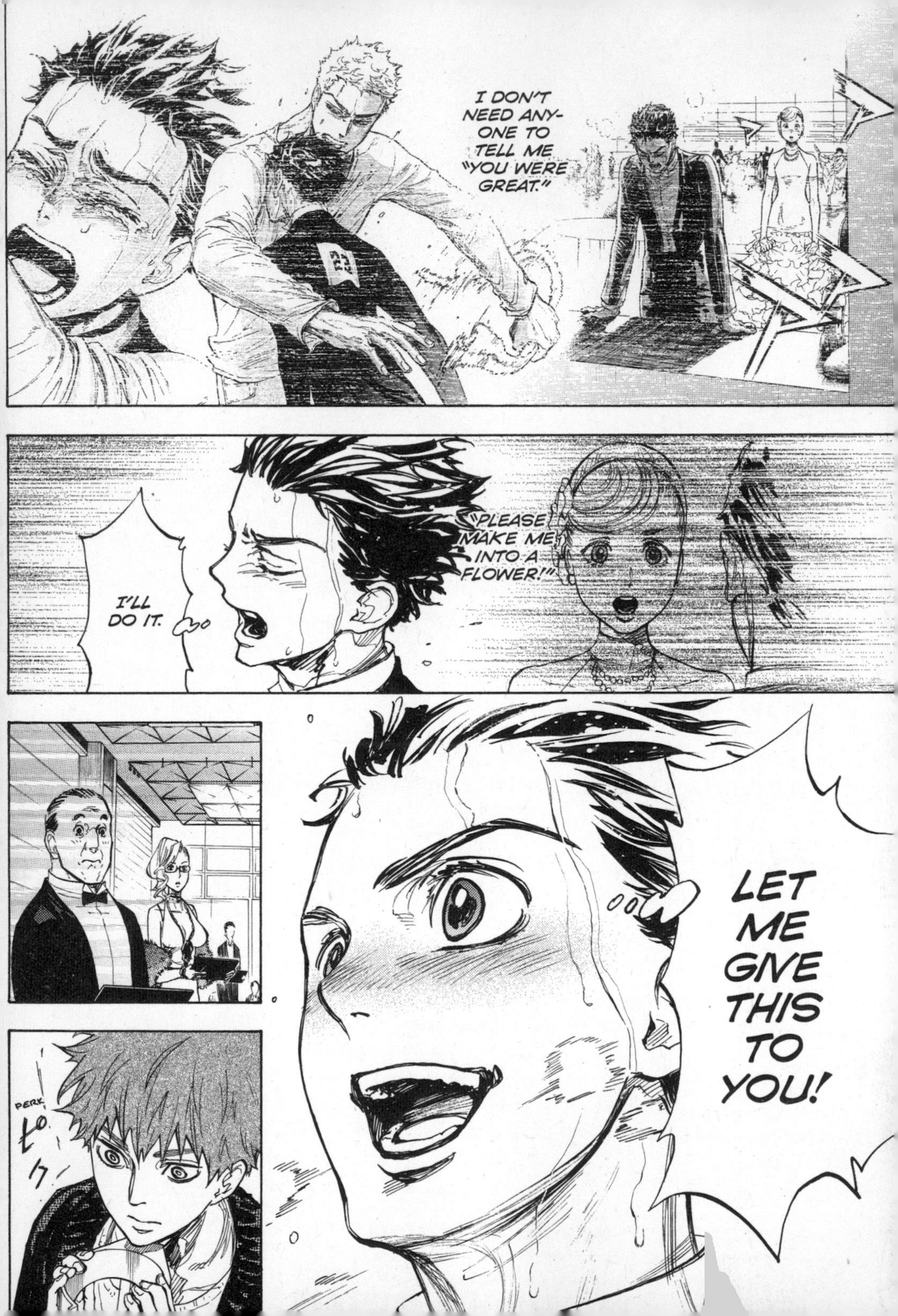
I DON'T NEED ANY-ONE TO TELL ME "YOU WERE GREAT."
"PLEASE MAKE ME INTO A FLOWER!"
I'LL DO IT.
LET ME GIVE THIS TO YOU!
PERK

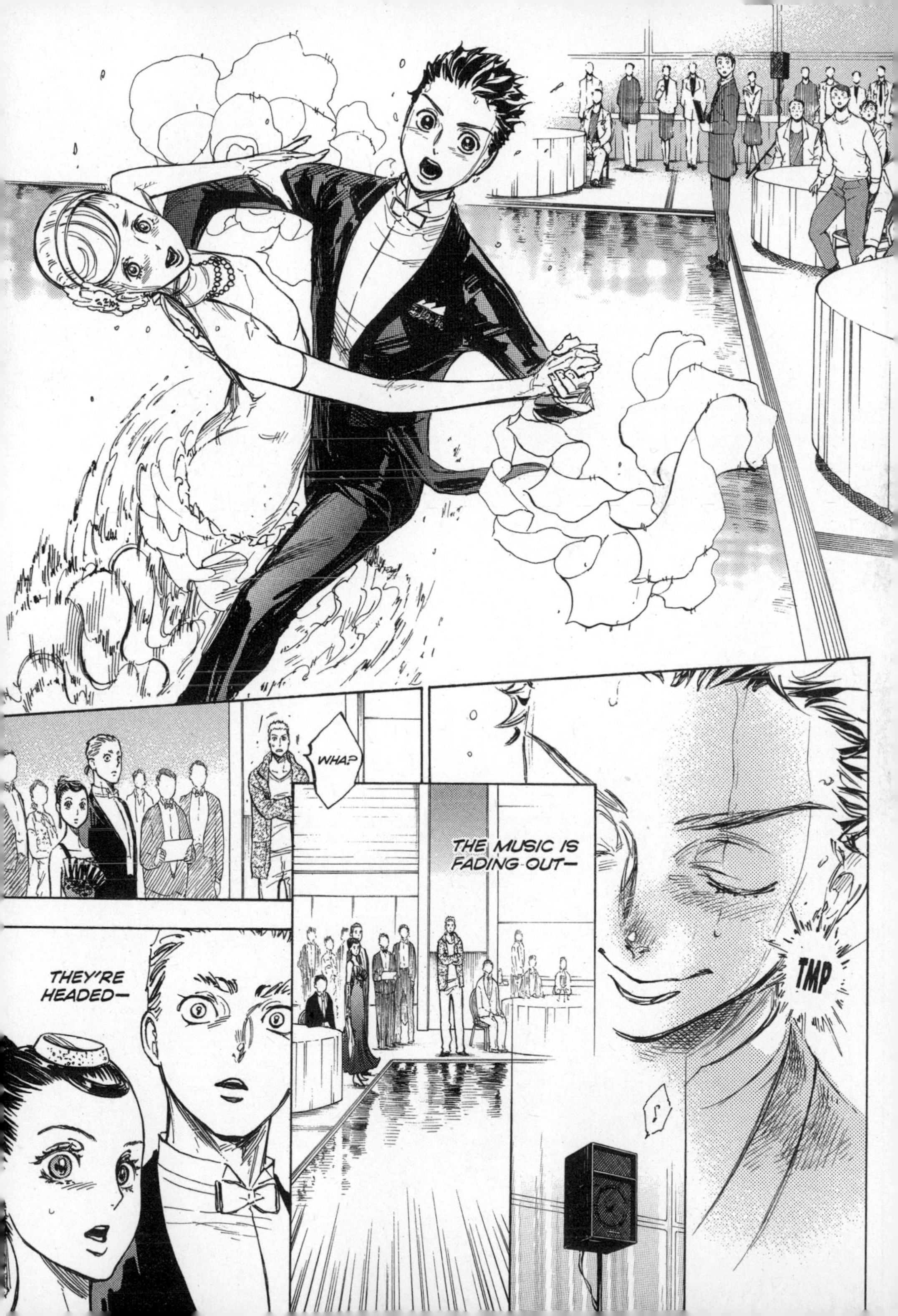
TMP
WHA?
THE MUSIC IS FADING-OUT—
THEY'RE HEADED—

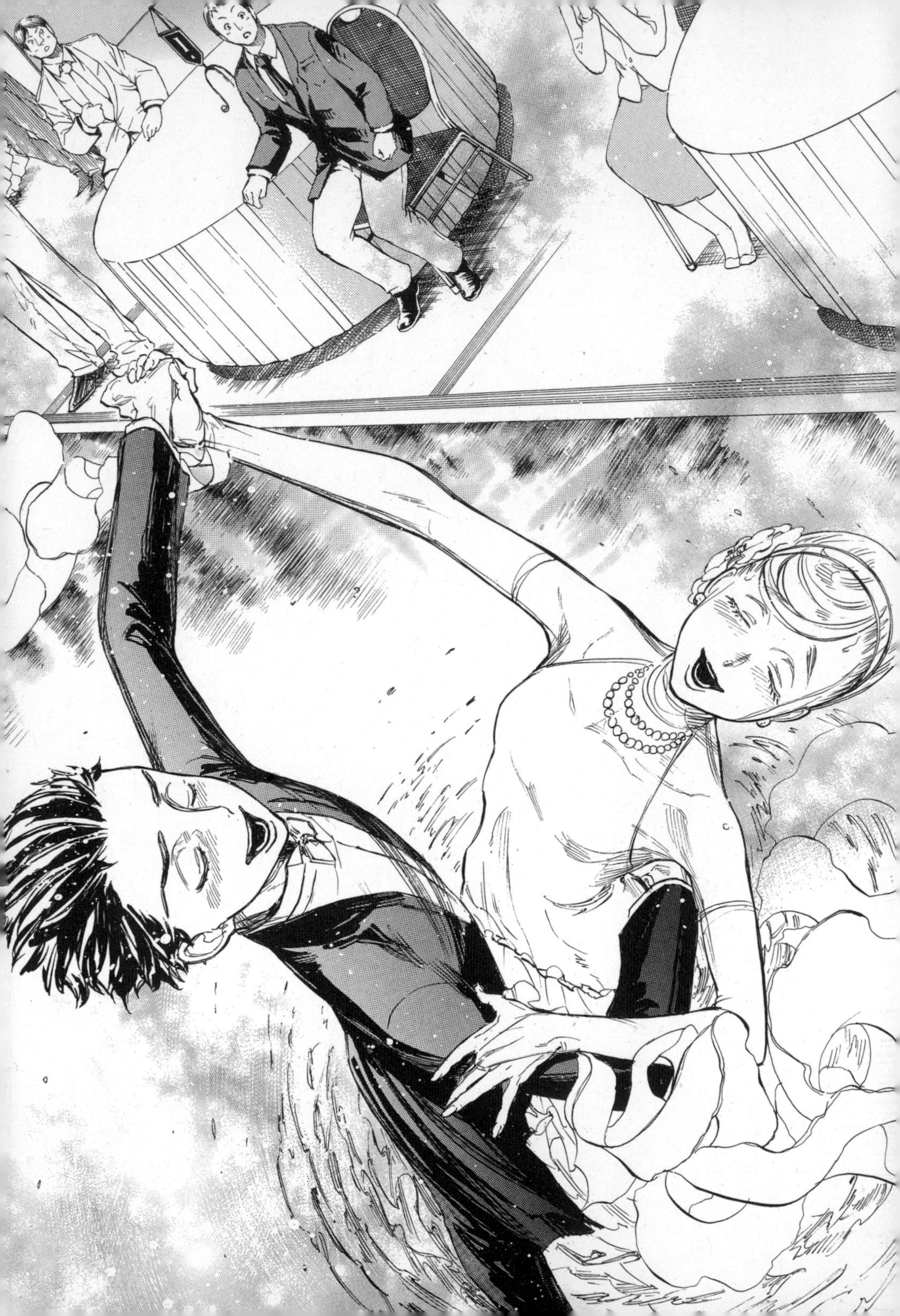

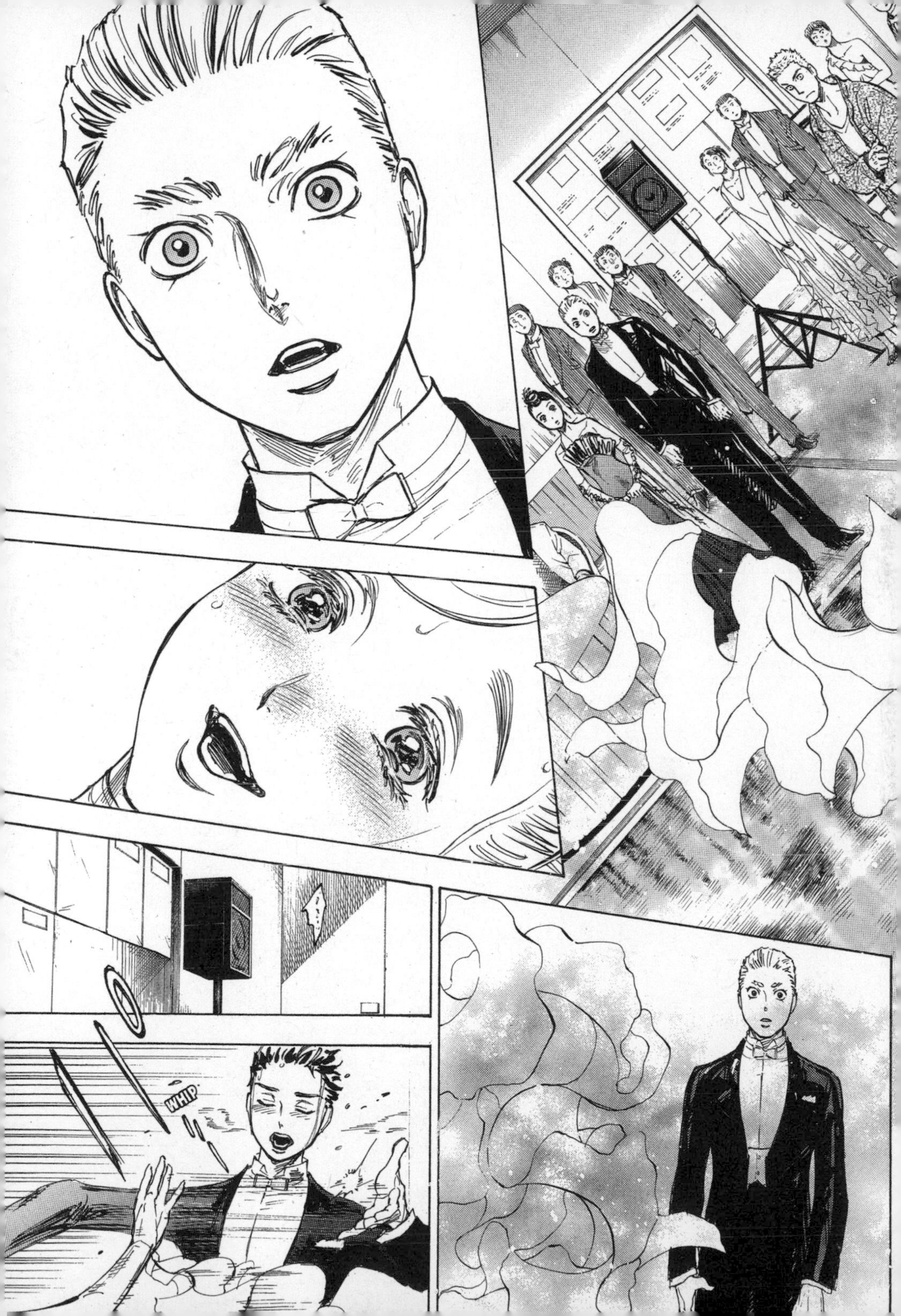
WHIP

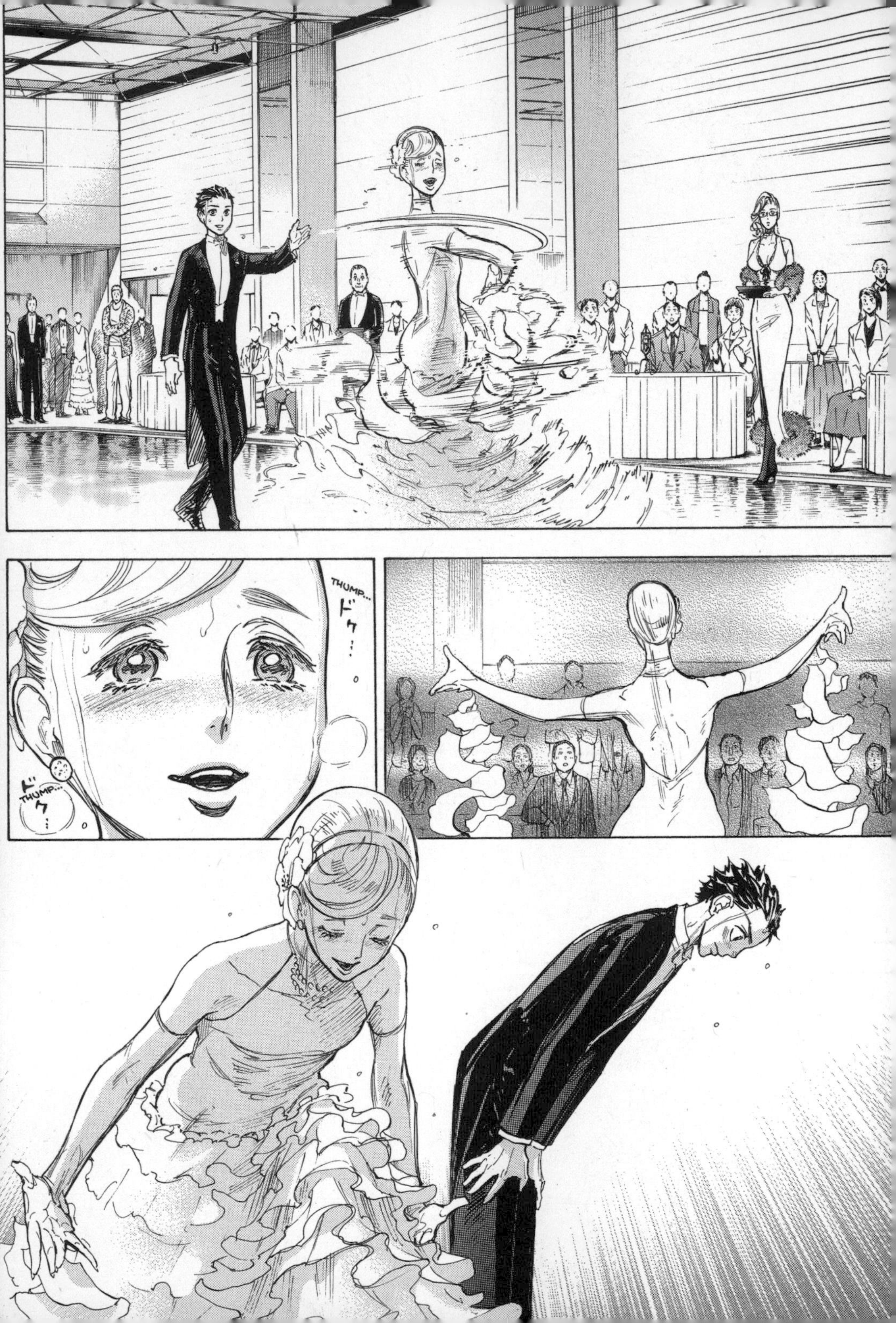
THUMP...
ドク…
THUMP...
ドク…

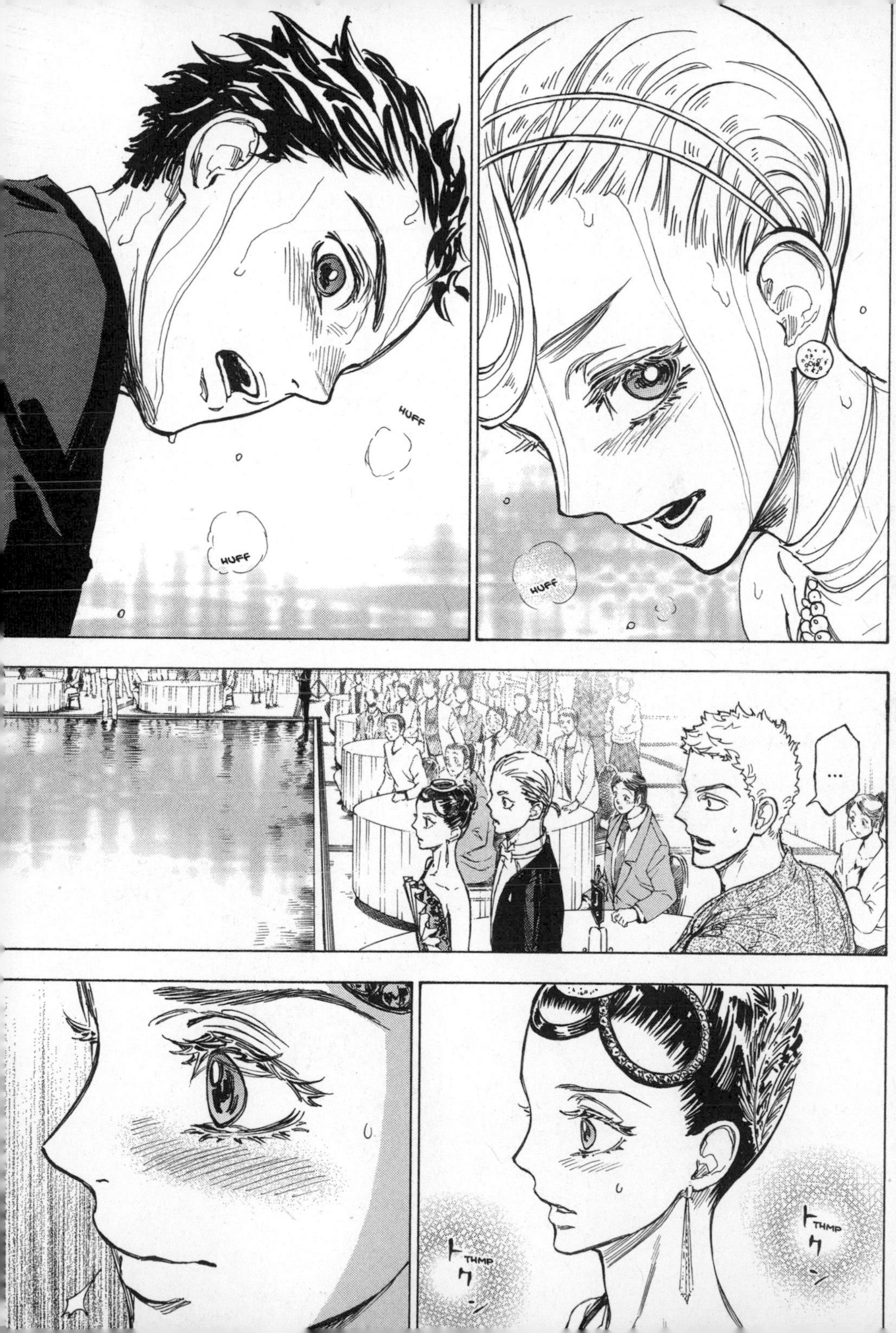
HUFF
HUFF
HUFF
...
THMP
THMP

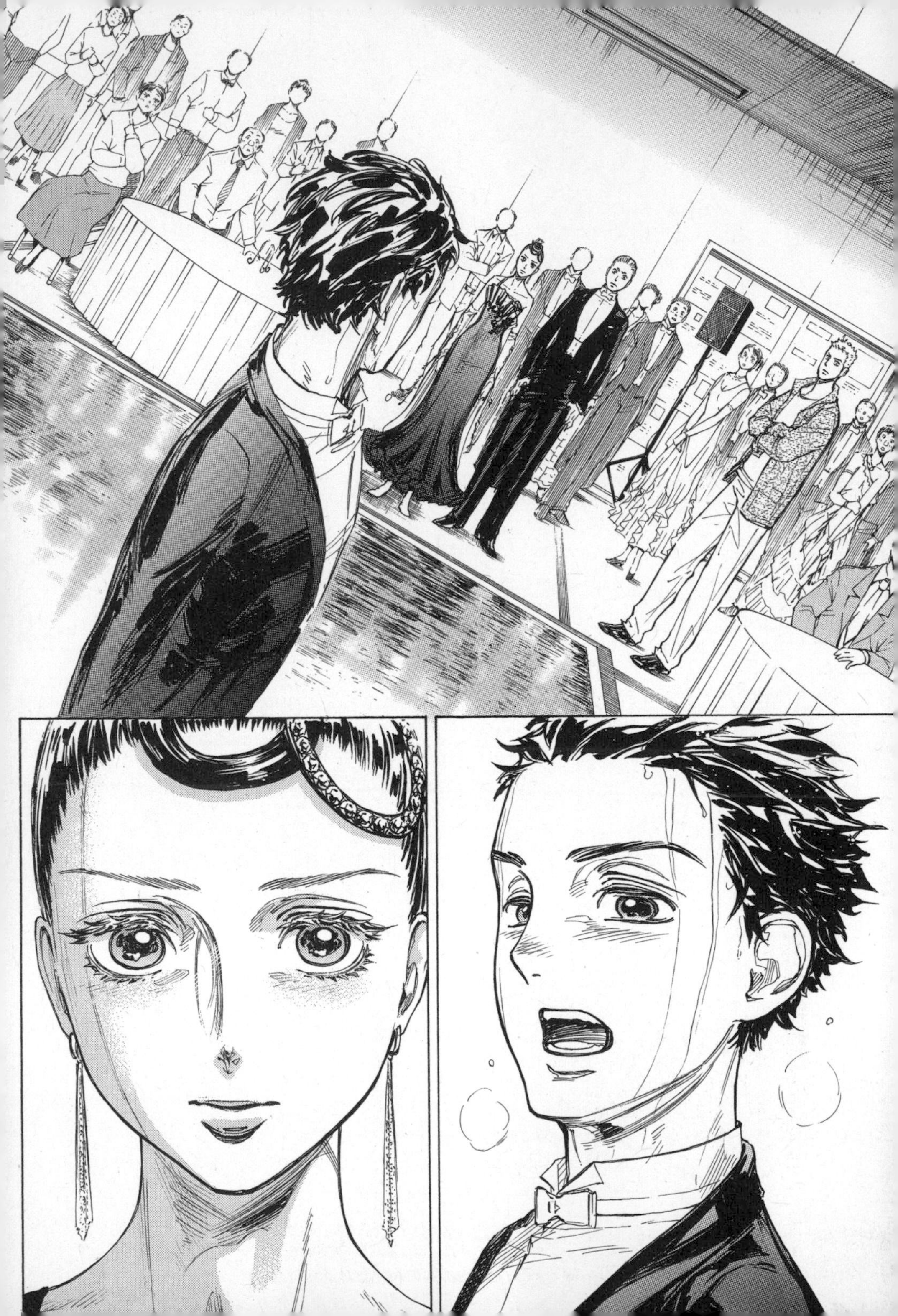

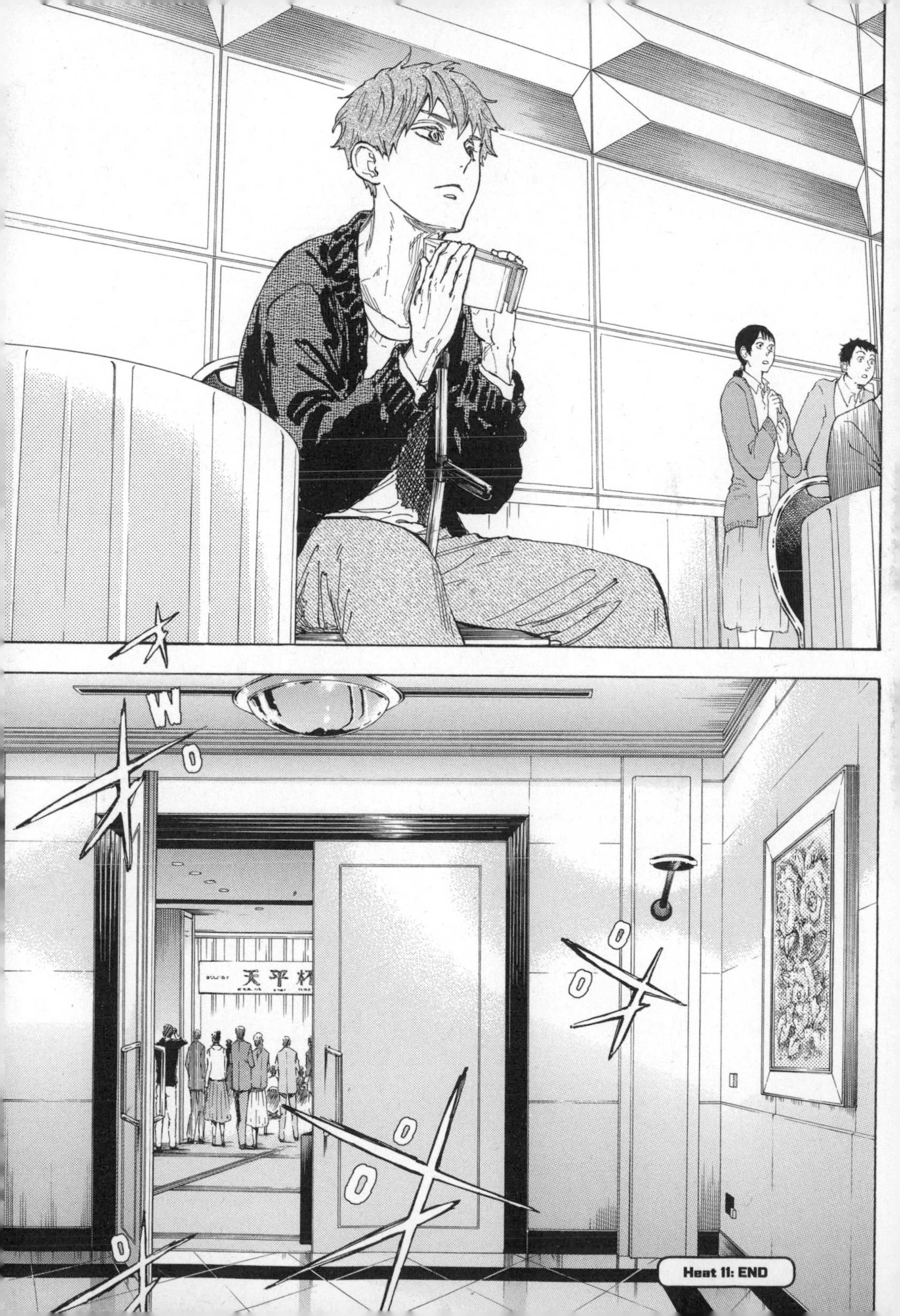
WOOOOOO
天平杯
Heat 11: END

Extra Heat

OGASAWARA DANCE STUDIO

GIRL TALK

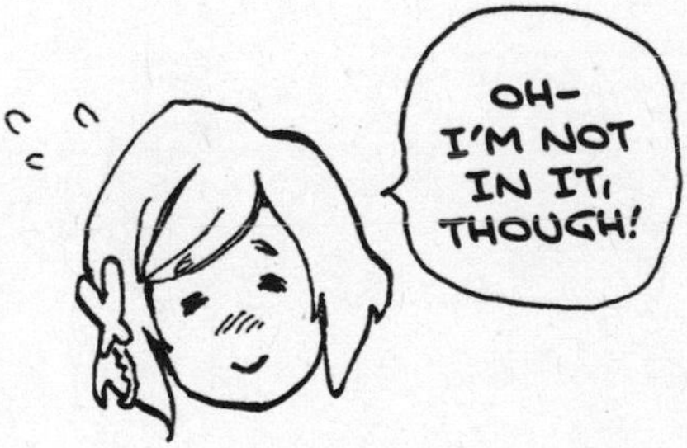
OH-
I'M NOT IN IT, THOUGH!

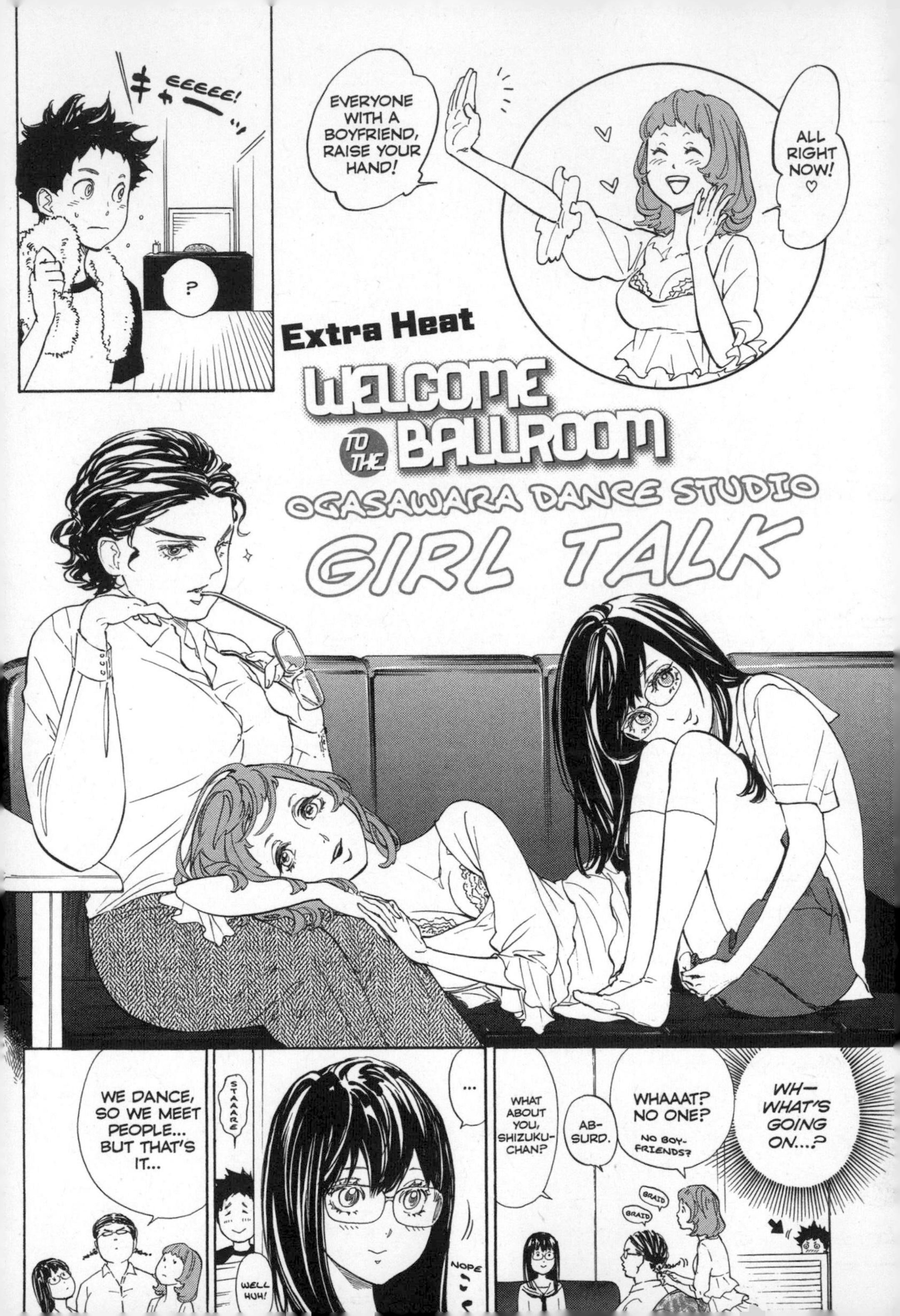
EVERYONE WITH A BOYFRIEND, RAISE YOUR HAND!
ALL RIGHT NOW! ♡
キャー EEEEEE!
?
Extra Heat
WELCOME TO THE BALLROOM
OGASAWARA DANCE STUDIO
GIRL TALK
WH— WHAT'S GOING ON...?
WHAAAT? NO ONE?
NO BOY-FRIENDS?
BRAID
BRAID
AB-SURD.
WHAT ABOUT YOU, SHIZUKU-CHAN?
...
NOPE
STAAARE
WE DANCE, SO WE MEET PEOPLE... BUT THAT'S IT...
WELL HUH!

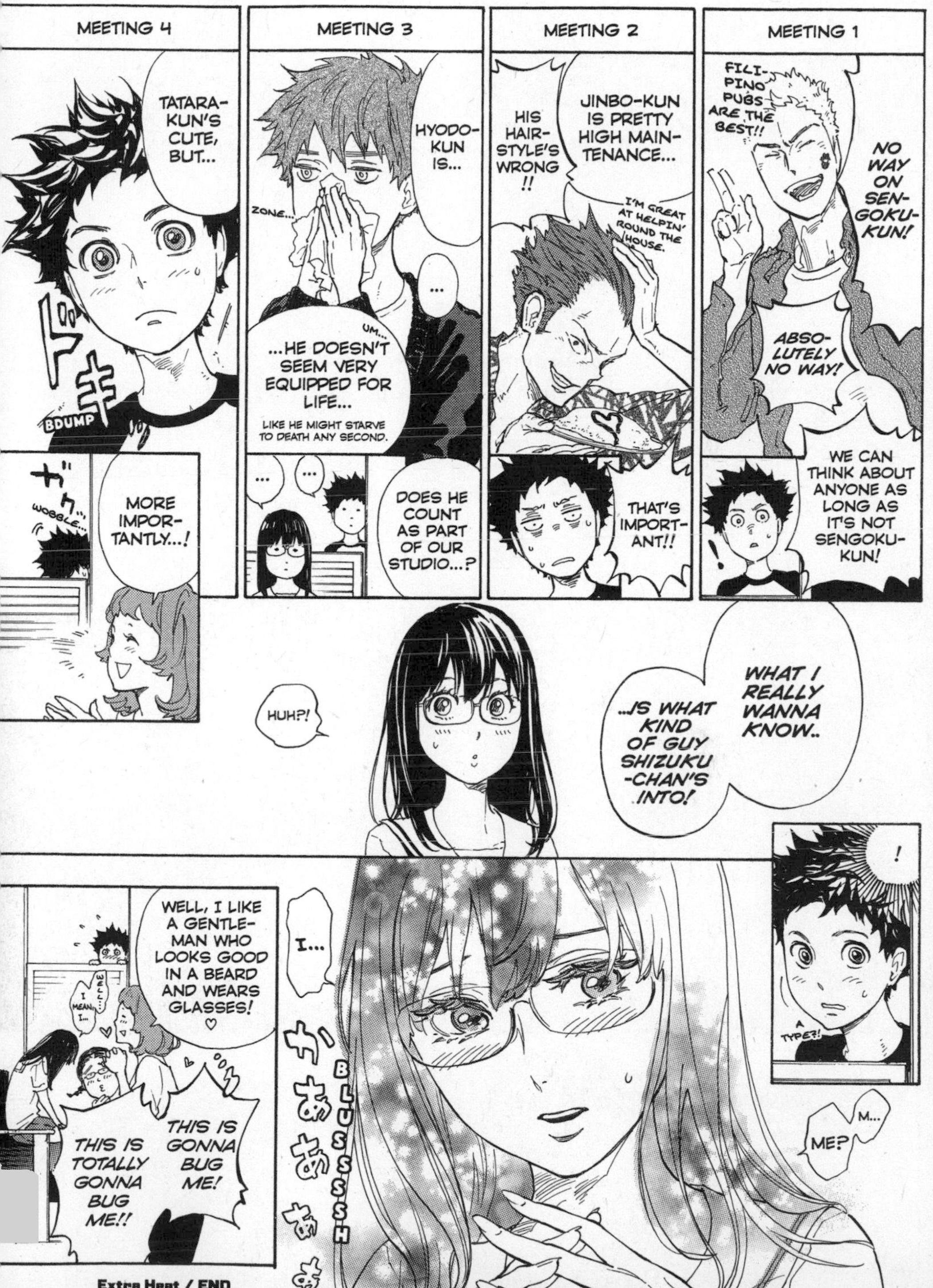
MEETING 1
FILI-PINO PUBS ARE THE BEST!!
NO WAY ON SEN-GOKU-KUN!
ABSO-LUTELY NO WAY!
MEETING 2
JINBO-KUN IS PRETTY HIGH MAIN-TENANCE...
HIS HAIR-STYLE'S WRONG!!
I'M GREAT AT HELPIN' ROUND THE HOUSE.
MEETING 3
HYODO-KUN IS...
ZONE...
...
UM...
...HE DOESN'T SEEM VERY EQUIPPED FOR LIFE...
LIKE HE MIGHT STARVE TO DEATH ANY SECOND.
MEETING 4
TATARA-KUN'S CUTE, BUT...
BDUMP
WE CAN THINK ABOUT ANYONE AS LONG AS IT'S NOT SENGOKU-KUN!
!
THAT'S IMPORT-ANT!!
DOES HE COUNT AS PART OF OUR STUDIO...?
...
...
MORE IMPOR-TANTLY...!
WOBBLE...
WHAT I REALLY WANNA KNOW..
...IS WHAT KIND OF GUY SHIZUKU-CHAN'S INTO!
HUH?!
!
A TYPE?!
I...
M... ME?
BLUSSSSH
WELL, I LIKE A GENTLE-MAN WHO LOOKS GOOD IN A BEARD AND WEARS GLASSES! ♡
WELL...
I MEAN, I...
THIS IS GONNA BUG ME!
THIS IS TOTALLY GONNA BUG ME!!

Extra Heat / END

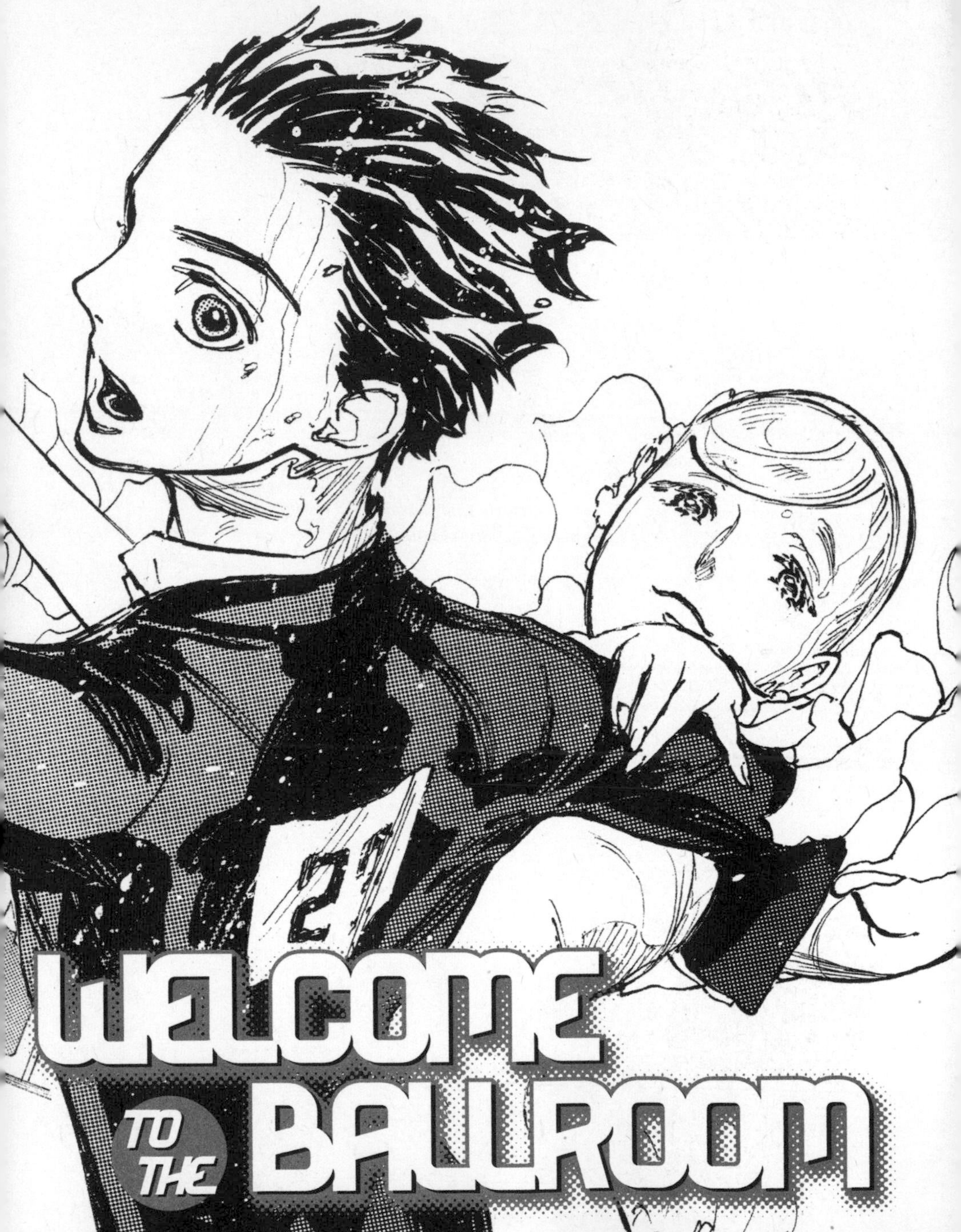
WELCOME TO THE BALLROOM

Volume 4 coming soon!

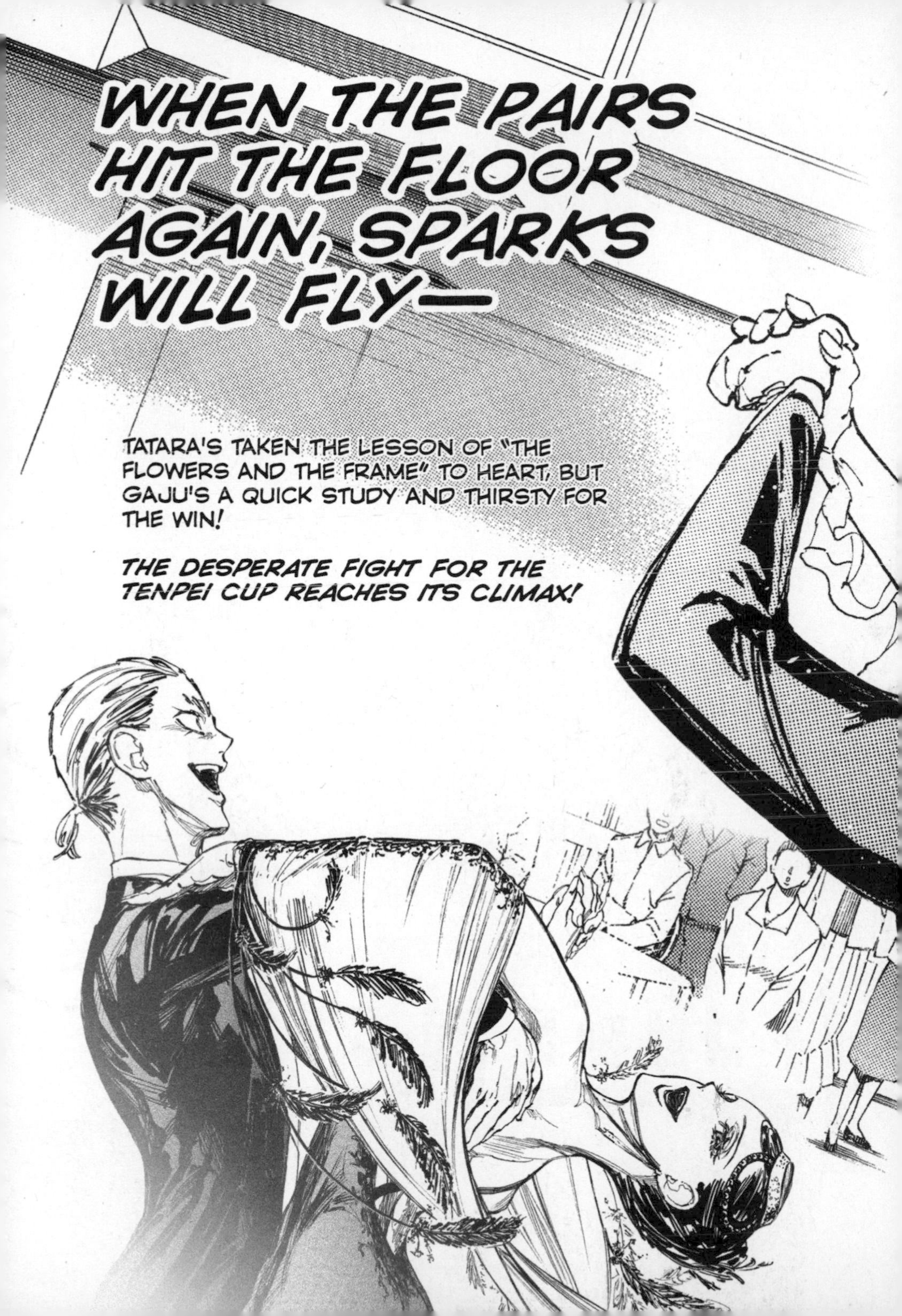
WHEN THE PAIRS HIT THE FLOOR AGAIN, SPARKS WILL FLY—
TATARA'S TAKEN THE LESSON OF "THE FLOWERS AND THE FRAME" TO HEART, BUT GAJU'S A QUICK STUDY AND THIRSTY FOR THE WIN!
THE DESPERATE FIGHT FOR THE TENPEI CUP REACHES ITS CLIMAX!

KC KODANSHA COMICS

Mei Tachibana has no friends — and says she doesn't need them!

But everything changes when she accidentally roundhouse kicks the most popular boy in school! However, Yamato Kurosawa isn't angry in the slightest—in fact, he thinks his ordinary life could use an unusual girl like Mei. But winning Mei's trust will be a tough task. How long will she refuse to say, "I love you"?

a Silent Voice

"The word heartwarming was made for manga like this." –Manga Bookshelf

"A harsh and biting social commentary... delivers in its depth of character and emotional strength." -Comics Bulletin

"A very powerful story about being different and the consequences of childhood bullying... Read it." –Anime News Network

Shoya is a bully. When Shoko, a girl who can't hear, enters his elementary school class, she becomes their favorite target, and Shoya and his friends goad each other into devising new tortures for her. But the children's cruelty goes too far. Shoko is forced to leave the school, and Shoya ends up shouldering all the blame. Six years later, the two meet again. Can Shoya make up for his past mistakes, or is it too late?

Available now in print and digitally!

Welcome to the Ballroom volume 3 is a wor
characters, places, and incidents are the products of the author's
imagination or are used fictitiously. Any resemblance to actual events,
locales, or persons, living or dead, is entirely coincidental.

A Kodansha Comics Trade Paperback Original.

Welcome to the Ballroom volume 3 copyright ©2012 Tomo Takeuchi,
English translation copyright ©2017 Tomo Takeuchi

All rights reserved.

Published in the United States by Kodansha Comics,
an imprint of Kodansha USA Publishing, LLC, New York.

Publication rights for this English edition arranged through Kodansha
Ltd., Tokyo.

First published in Japan in 2012 by Kodansha Ltd., Tokyo, as
Ballroom e Yōkoso volume 3.

ISBN 978-1-63236-405-0

Printed in the United States of America.

www.kodanshacomics.com

9 8 7 6 5 4 3 2 1

Translation: Karen McGillicuddy
Lettering: Brndn Blakeslee
Editing: Paul Starr

Kodansha Comics edition cover design: Phil Balsman